INDIAN HIGHER EDUCATION AND TRIBALS

Problems and Prospects

Contents

PART B

HIGHER EDUCATION AND HUMAN CAPITAL IN GLOBALISED ERA

PART D

POLICY IMPERATIVES FOR HIGHER EDUCATION

Acknowledgements

This book 'Indian Higher Education and Tribals: Problems and Prospects' is an outcome of the National Seminar, organized by Indian Economic Association and A.S. College Deoghar at Deoghar, Jharkhand. We are thankful to Prof. (Dr.) Victor Tigga, Vice-Chancellor, Professor Arvind Kumar, Pro-Vice-Chancellor, both from SKM University, Dumka for their valuable guidance and immense cooperation.

The success of the seminar was reflected in the lively debate among all the paper writers and discussants. The seminar attracted 34 papers, including the concern of economists on the sensitive topic, which is likely to have a major impact on the state as well as economy. We are also grateful to all the paper writers for incorporating the desired comments and revising their papers.

We extend our heartfelt thanks to our Colleagues, and all the teaching and administrative staff of the College for their active support in organising and making this seminar a success. Thanks to the Chairpersons and Discussants in different sessions for their valuable comments on the paper writers. We cannot forget the Members of Indian Economic Association who spent their valuable time and energy for organising the seminar and facilitating the publication of this book.

Our special appreciation is due to Dr. Dalip Kumar, Project Officer, National Council of Applied Economic Research, New Delhi and Dr. Anjani Kumar Jha, Chairman, Development of Indian Society and Culture (DISC), for a helping hand in bringing out this publication. We are indebted to many friends, colleagues, and teachers for their careful guidance and constant support.

We would like to acknowledge Mr. G.S. Bhatia and staff of M/s Deep and Deep Publications Pvt. Ltd., Delhi who deserve thanks for all the designing, typesetting and printing work to bring out this volume.

ANIL KUMAR THAKUR
NAGESHWAR SHARMA

List of Contributors

A.K. Singh, Lecturer in Sociology, Sabour College, TM.U., Bhagalpur.

Abhay Shankar, M.A. (LSW), Deoghar.

Amalesh Banerjee, (Rt.) Guest Professor, Jadavpur University, Former Vice-President, Indian Economic Association, 110B, N.S.C. Bose Road, Regent Park.

Anil Kumar Jain, Professor of Economics, Banaras Hindu University, Varanasi-221 005

Anil Kumar Thakur, College of Commerce, Patna.

Aniruddh Kumar, Lecturer in Geography, DAV PG College, Siwan, Bihar.

Ashwini Kant Jha, Professor and Head, P.G. Department of Economics, B.N.M. University (W.C), Saharsha (Bihar).

B. Appa Rao, Associate Professor, Lalitha College of Education, Hyderabad.

B. Satyanarayan, Former Head, Economics Department, Osmania University and Former chairman, Third State Finance Commission, Andhra Pradesh.

B.M. Jani, Professor of Economics, Saurashtra University, Rajkot-360 005.

B.N. Ghosh, 193, Goaltuly Road, Hooghly, W.B.

Baij Nath Singh, Lecturer Economics, G.B. College, Ramgarh (Kaimur).

Basabi Mukhopadhyay, Selection Grade Lecturer, Vivekananda College for Women, Barisha.

Basanti Das, Lecturer in Economics, Rayagada Women's College, Rayagada, Orissa.

Bhavna Jha, Lecturer in IRPM, MAM College, Naugachia, Bhagalpur (Bihar).

Bikrama Singh, D.Litt., Professor and Head, University Deptt. of Economics and Dean, Faculty of Social Sciences, Magadh University, Bodh-Gaya.

Dalip Kumar, Project Officer, National Council of Applied Economic Research, New Delhi.

Debasis Mukhopadhyay, Lecturer in Economics, Bejoy Narayan Mahavidyalaya, Itachuna, Hooghly.

Debes Mukhopadhyay, Guest Faculty, Presidency College, Kolkata, (Retired) Teacher-in-charge, St. Paul's C.M. College, Kolkata.

Dhurjati Prosad Bagchi, Reader in Economics, Bejoy Narayan Mahavidyalaya, Itachuna, Hooghly.

K. Hariharan, Plot No. 153, Kamraj Street, Ramakrishna Nagar, Chennai.

K.N. Mann, 199, Abhishek, Udyan-1, Eldeco Colony, Lucknow-226002.

Maheshwar Goit, Deptt. of Political Science, A.S. College, Deoghar, Jharkhand.

Mithilesh Kumar Sinha, Reader, Department of Economics, Nagaland University, Hqrs.-Lumami, Mokokchung-798601, Nagaland.

N.C. Jha, Meena Bazar, Bank Colony, Madhopur, Deoghar.

Nageshwar Sharma, Principal, A.S. College, Deogarh

P.K. Bose, 193, Goaltuly Road, Hooghly, W.B.

Praveen Sharma, Assistant Prof., Deptt. of EAFM, University of Rajasthan, Jaipur.

Premlata Kumari, (Research Scholar), Department of Economics, SKM University, Dumka, Jharkhand.

Pushpa Sinha, Lecturer in Economics, Patna Women College, Patna.

R.K. Singh, Lecturer in IRPM, MAM College, Naugachia, TMU.

R.U. Singh, Lecturer, P.G. Deptt. of Commerce and Co-ordinator, B.B.M. College of Commerce, Patna–20

Raj Kumar Sen, Formerly, Rabindra Bharati University, Kolkata.

Rajan Kumar Sahoo, Lecturer in Economics, U.N.S. Mahavidyalaya, Khairabad, Mugpal, Jajpur-755009, Orissa

Ratan Lal Basu, Reader in Economics, Bhairab Ganguly College, Kolkata.

Rewati Raman Jha, P.G. Department of Economics, M.S. College, Motihari, B.R.A. Bihar University, Muzaffarpur.

S.K.L. Das, Department of Eonomics, PKR Memorial College, Dhanbad.

Sandhya Rani, Deptt. of Economics, Maharaja College, Arah.

Sangeeta, Research Scholar, Magadh University.

Satyabrata Mishra, Deptt. of Economics, M.P.C.(A) College, Takhatpur, Baripada, Mayurbhang, Orissa.

Sharmishtha Priti, Lecturer in Economics, Dr. J.N. Mishra College, Muzaffarpur, Bihar.

Sheela Sharan Singh, Deptt. of Economics, S.M.D. College, Punpun, Patna.

Surendra Prasad Gain, H.O.D. of Economics, Mahatma Gandhi College, Sundarpur, Darbhanga-846004

Tarani Pd. Singh, P.G. Deptt. . of Economics, S.K.M. University, Dumka.

Tarashankar Prasad Singh, Former Principal, R.D.S. College, Muzaffarpur (Bihar).

V. Loganathan, New No. 16, 11th Street, TNHB Colony, Krahur, Chennai, T.N.

Yadwendra Singh, Lecturer in Economics, Gram Bharati College, Ramgarh, Kaimur, Bihar, V.K.S. University, Ara (India).

Yogendra Nath Mann, 195, Vindhyasini Nagar, Varanasi-221002.

Abbreviations

AICTE	: All India Centre for Technical Education
AIE	: Alternative and Innovative Education
CBTs	: Computer Based Tutorials
CEAB	: Central Education Advisory Board
CSIR	: Council for Scientific and Industrial Research
DAE	: Department of Atomic Energy
D. Phil.	: Doctors of Philosophy
D.Sc.	: Doctor of Science
DBT	: Department of Bio-technology
DPED	: District Primary Education Programme
DRDO	: Defense Research and Development Organization
DST	: Department of Science and Technology
EER	: Enrolment of Eligible Ratio
EGS	: Employment Guarantee Scheme
FOI	: Freedom of Information
GATE	: Graduate Aptitude Test in Engineering
GATS	: General Agreements of Trade and Services
GER	: Gross Enrolment Ratio
ICS	: Indian Civil Services
IITs	: Indian Institute of Technologies
IRAHE	: Independent Regulatory Authority for Higher Education
IRTT	: Institute of Road and Transport Technology
ISRO	: Indian Space Research Organisation
IT	: Information Technology
JTRC	: Joint Transport Research Centre
KGBV	: Kasturva Gandhi Balika Vidyalaya Scheme

LPG	: Liberalization, Privatization and Globalization
MOU	: Memorandum of Understanding
MSP	: Microsoft Student Partner
NAAC	: National Assessment and Accreditation Council
NAC	: National Advisory Council
NAFSA	: National Association of Foreign Student Advisers
NCERT	: National Council of Education Research and Training
NCF	: National Commission for Farmers
NCMO	: National Contract Management Association
NCMP	: National Common Minimum Programme
NEC	: North Eastern Council
NER	: Net Enrolment Ratio
NET	: National Eligibility Test
NKC	: National Knowledge Commission
NPE	: National Policy of Education
NPEGEL	: National Programme of Education for Girls at Elementary Level
NSFDC	: National SC&ST Finance and Development Corporation
NSSO	: National Sample Survey Organisation
NUEPA	: National University of Educational Planning and Administration
OECD	: Organisation for Economic Co-operation and Development
OIE	: Office of International Education
PC	: Population Council
PESA	: Provisions of Panchayats Extension to Scheduled Areas Act-1996
PG	: Post Graduate
Ph.D	: Doctor of Philosophy
PMS	: Post Metric Scholarship
PTGs	: Primitive Tribal Groups
PUC	: Pre-University Course
REC	: Regional Engineering College
RFRA	: Reorganization of Forest Rights Act-2006
SC	: Supreme Court

SCERTS	:	Social Communication, Emotional Regulation and Transactional Support
SES	:	Selected Education Statistics
SEZ	:	Special Economic Zones
SME	:	Small and Medium Enterprises
STs	:	Scheduled Tribes
STR	:	Scientific and Technical Revolution
UGC	:	University Grants Commission
UNESCO	:	United Nations Educational, Scientific and Cultural Organization
WTO	:	World Trade Organization

Introduction

Tribes are spread across the country mainly in forest and hilly regions. One concentration lives in a belt along the Himalayas stretching through Jammu and Kashmir, Himachal Pradesh, and Uttar Pradesh in the west, to Assam, Meghalaya, Tripura, Arunachal Pradesh, Mizoram, Manipur, and Nagaland in the north-east. In the north-eastern states of Arunachal Pradesh, Meghalaya, Mizoram, and Nagaland, upward 90 per cent of the population are tribals. Another concentration lives in the hilly areas of central India (Madhya Pradesh, Orissa, and, to a lesser extent, Andhra Pradesh); in this belt, which is bounded by the Narmada River to the north and the Godavari River to the south-east, tribal peoples occupy the slopes of the region's mountains. Other tribals, the Santhals, Munda, Orao, etc. live in Bihar and Jharkhand. There are smaller number of tribal people in Karnataka, Tamil Nadu, and Kerala, in western India in Gujarat and Rajasthan, and in the union territories of Lakshadweep and the Andaman and Nicobar Islands. The tribal population of the country, as per the 2001 Census, is 8.43 crore, constituting 8.2 per cent of the total population. The population of tribes has grown at the rate of 24.45 per cent during the period 1991-2001. The growth of ST population during the Census 1981, 1991 and 2001 was 7.83 per cent of total population, 8.08 per cent in 1991 and 8.2 per cent of total population in the Census 2001. More than half the Scheduled Tribe population is concentrated in the States of Madhya Pradesh, Chhattisgarh, Maharashtra, Orissa, Jharkhand and Gujarat. The total population of STs in newly created state of Jharkhand was 26.3 per cent of total population. Tribal communities live in about 15 per cent of the country's areas, in various ecological and geo-climatic regions ranging from plains and forests to hills and inaccessible areas. The State with pre-dominantly ST Population are Lakshadweep (94.5%).

Higher education includes teaching, research and social services activities of universities, and within the realm of teaching, it includes both the undergraduate level (sometimes referred to as tertiary education) and the graduate (or post-graduate) level (sometimes referred to as graduate school). Higher education specifically refers to post-secondary institutions that offer associate degrees, bachelor degrees, master's degrees or Ph.D. degrees or equivalents. Higher general education might be contrasted with higher vocational education, which concentrates on both practice and theory. A university is an institution of higher education and research, which grants academic degrees; including Bachelor's degrees, Master's degrees and Doctorate in a variety of subjects. However, most professional education is included within higher education, and many post-graduate qualifications are strongly vocationally or professionally oriented.

The book contains thirty-four papers elaborating on various aspects of Indian Higher Education and Tribals. For study points of view all papers are divided among four major heads, i.e. (A) Framework for Regulating Higher Education in India, (B) Higher Education and Human Capital in Globalised Era, (C) Regional Perspectives in Higher Education, and last (D) Policy Imperatives for Higher Education.

A. Framework for Regulating Higher Education in India

The paper "Inclusive Higher Education for SC/ST and Economic Growth" written by Amalesh Banerjee, expresses concern at increasing gap between literacy and illiteracy as well as between high level of scientific and technological knowledge attained by a small section and deprived vast populace who do not have an access to gain the benefits of knowledge revolution. The widening dualism in knowledge and economy is very much detrimental to tribal development. The author explains various aspects like education and knowledge structure and suggests for better access to higher education like learning by doing at farm and industry levels linkage of education policy with employment, etc. For inclusive higher education and economic growth there is need of dissemination of knowledge through several innovative researches.

Mithilesh Kumar Sinha highlights "Role of Universities in Tribals Higher Education" which plays vital role for socio-economic and socio-cultural development of a nation. With the helps of several tables containing demographic data and infrastructural facilities for ST's higher education the author finds glaring inequality which needs to be addressed to enable higher education as a tool for socio-equity in real sense of the term.

The chapter on "Higher Education and Tribals" written by K. Hariharan is an attempt to understand the various categories of aboriginals; and governmental policies and programmes for the development of Tribal Education after independence. The paper presents comparative pictures of Tribal literacy with other groups and finds various socio-economic and cultural constraints. The storm of modernity has terribly affected the homogeneity of the tribal society and it has created the feelings of isolation in the minds of tribal students. Finally, the author makes some suggestions to promote tribal education suitable to their culture so that their identity may be preserved.

"Present Status of Indian Higher Education" according to authors Yogendra Nath Mann and K.N. Mann is at he cross-road facing greater challenges in the twenty-first Century. There has been great change in employment pattern with declining trend in employment in government as well as non-governmental organization. Though there is need of participation of corporates but education should not be made costlier. There should be uniformity in the policy to give equal representation to all the institutions in the placement of pass outs.

In the chapter "Indian Higher Education and Tribals" authors B.N. Ghosh and P.K. Bose say that tribal people are the worst victims of development strategies after independence. Large dams, modern factories and mines have made large number of tribals refugees in their own homeland. It has created a state of confusion and a feeling of growing tribal discontents which are conspiracy-oriented, exploitation-oriented and development-oriented explanations. Language, planning, educational policy, and development strategies could not be geared so as to integrate tribals with the national mainstream. It has resulted into naxalite activities and separatist movements in tribal dominated regions. Hence, there is need to rethink and restructure the development strategy to promote inclusive growth and national integration.

Authors-duo R.U. Singh and Sangeeta paper on "Higher Education in India: An Analysis" analyse higher education in India and its various aspects including the impacts of globalization, WTO policy and Challenges faced by it. The higher education has been converted into merit good from public good and it has led to mushrooming of private institutions and commercialization depriving the socially and economically weaker sections of higher education. To make India a knowledge destination, the government must give priority to the higher education and research. It should not be left upon the market and it should ensure the accessibility, quality and equity in higher education.

The paper on "Tribal Women in Higher Education: Problems and Prospects", the author Baij Nath Singh accepts that tribal development is one of the main concerns of our constitution. Much has been done to promote education of tribal women. There has been some progress but still there are several problems like low enrolment rate, traditional social attitude, lack of quality education, lack of job-oriented education, economic backwardness and geographical constraints. Considering all these, there is need of special attention, change in the perceptions about tribal women and coordinated efforts by agencies working in the field of education with missionary zeal.

The chapter "Education: A Way Out for Tribal" is authored by Pushpa Sinha who thinks that the developmental process have brought in juxtaposition of two distinct value systems one based on tradition and ignorance and the other on technology and innovation. There is essential need of harmonious synchronization of these two systems. The paper throws some light on the causes of slow progress in literacy and gives some suggestions to make education a better way of progress and tribal folks.

In the chapter "Higher Education in India: A Path to Success", the author Yadwendra Singh says that education is the light of life. It considers the ancient Nalanda University as the classic example of ancient glory in the field of higher education. The chapter discusses the role of UGC, IGNOU, ICHR, Indian Council of Philosophical Research, Indian Institute of Advanced Study and Indian Council of Social Science Research. Both the Central and State governments are jointly accelerating various programmes in higher education but in the states of Bihar and Jharkhand the status of higher education is very pathetic wherein only 6% students in the age group of 17-23 are enrolled. There is earnest need of infrastructure development.

Surendra Prasad Gain in his chapter "Height of Higher Education in Developing India" explains the vital role of education in the process of modernization, building up of a democratic and pluralistic society and development of both the socio-economic resources and country as human resources to achieve social justice and equality. The author refers to enrolment rate, gender issues, and issues of equity, value orientation, academic issues and position of state-funding in higher education. He considers the importance of framing a system which should build-up excellence and maintain quality and relevance in the changing world. There is imperative need to free the system from unnecessary constraints and political interference so that it can provide the needed academic, administrative and financial freedom.

The chapter "Economics of Education and Reconstruction of Higher Education in India" is contributed jointly by Tarani Pd. Singh and Premlata Kumari. Being a catalyst in developmental efforts and economy with human resources, education is both as consumption goods and investments goods.

B. Higher Education and Human Capital in Globalised Era

The chapter "Globalization and its Challenges for

Higher Education" contributed by V. Loganathan attempts to pin point the challenges of globalization for higher education and its impact on inequality. He describes how commoditization, privatization and commercialization of higher education make things worse in a system characterized by inequality. The paper underlines the need for maintaining social sector expenditure by the state. Social justice should be the cornerstone of the state policy with regard to higher education and there is need of special attention on higher education among weaker sections like STs in states like Jharkhand.

The Chapter "Indian Higher Education in Globalized Era: Challenges and Opportunities" jointly written by Maheshwar Goit and Sheela Sharan Singh finds that the government is convinced of accepting education as one of the most effective means of stimulating economic growth. As such there is accelerated quantitative expansion of education creating a large force of educated unemployed youths. This is mainly due to lack of proper planning, declining, financial support to higher education, compromise with the quality and utter neglect of constitutionally defined socio-economic philosophy for disadvantaged groups.

The chapter "Impact of GATS on Indian Higher Education Services: Risks and Benefits" contributed by Rewati Raman Jha emphasizes the role of higher education in bringing desirable human capital formation. As India is a signatory to the WTO and GATS, the globalization and commercialization of higher education has become a reality. The paper elaborates the benefits and risks to Indian higher education from GATS. The paper pin points some options and offers the relevant prescriptions to make the higher education as an effective tool for human capital formation as well as socio-economic transformation in an age of rapid globalization in the 20th century.

The chapter "Educations Inequality and its Impact on Accessibility to Better Quality of Employment to Socially Marginalised Class" jointly contributed by Ashwini Kant Jha and Bhavna Jha traces the aim of higher education to the national development as visualized by the Education Commission of 1966. There is imperative need of equitable distribution of quality education in order to convert the vicious cycle of poverty into vicious cycle of prosperity. The paper explains the reality of disparity in access to higher education in context to social groups, regions and gender. Authors-duo renders ten suggestions for qualitative improvement and accessibility to higher education.

The paper on "Education, Skill Formation and India's Economic Development" written by Praveen Sharma expresses concern at discourse around higher education in the post- independence period which hardly includes its organic link with development. The disengagement between education and industrial development which has taken heavy toll has created a large number of illiterates, large number of literates but non-employable, large number of semi-literates but professionally untrained and it has created the situation in which industrial expansion is limited, employment generation is low and R&D is quite unsubstantial.

The chapter "Role of Elementary Education in Human Capital Formation: The Indian Experience" written by the author Anil Kumar Jain underlines the role of elementary education in human capital formation which its implications on health, hygiene demographic profile productivity and all that related to the quality of life. Peeping through the policy on education in India, especially expenditure and various programmes for elementary education, the author offers some pragmatic suggestions to achieve the goal of universalisation of primary education and its linkage with productivity.

The chapter "Tribal Access to the Higher Education in the New Millennium: Issues and Alternatives" written by Sharmishtha Priti and Tarashankar Prasad Singh finds that the present trend and changes in the structure, pattern contents, objectives and programmes in higher education is quite distinct from the Nehruvian vision. The declining budgetary allocation on higher education by the state has created space for Indian and foreign institutions leading to the privatization and commercialization. It has adverse impacts on economically and socially disadvantaged groups and hence the mission of social justice.

Referring to the role of higher education in developing full potential of an individual to achieve an equitable place, the chapter "Tribal Higher Education through E-learning in India: A Challenging Task" written by Sandhya Rani and Abhay Shankar expresses concern at the slow pace of growth of higher education of tribals. The present phase of higher education is fastly moving towards e-education which is likely to become hub of higher education. The success of e-learning will depend largely on availability of infrastructure, special softwares, broadband internet access and charges in the mind-set of students as well as teachers. The access of tribal's to e-learning can be possible only if government takes initiative to set-up the institutions for tribals as they are economically too weak to take advantage of changing scenario dominated by private institutions which are motivated more by commercial motive than the social one.

The chapter on "Quality Improvement in Higher Education in India: Voice and Vision for Hours" by Aniruddh Kumar calls the quality improvement in higher education as voice and vision of hours. It accepts that there has been tremendous achievement but by and large the present higher education is neither quite relevant nor effective to meet the challenges of 21st Century. The paper elaborates on scenario of higher education in India and makes some recommendation so that the education system may be able to face the emerging challenges in the globalising world.

In the chapter "Higher Education—A Paradigm Shift in Multicultural Society" written by authors-duo A.K. Singh and R.K. Singh considers higher education as a prime device to transmit the accumulated knowledge experiences and culture from one generation to another. The Indian education system reflects a huge gap between words and deeds, intentions and actions, inputs and outputs. This disparity is against the solemn principles of equality and justice.

C. Regional Perspectives in Higher Education

The chapter on "Tribals Accessibility to Higher Education: A Case Study of Santhal Pargana Division, Jharkhand", contributed by Nageshwar Sharma is an depth and analytical attempt to discuss the tribals' accessibility to higher education. It is based on a case study of Sanathal

Pargana in the state of Jharkhand. Based on a few tables with relevant data, the paper touches upon various aspects of higher education particularly among tribals, their accessibility, state allocation, the history and the present scenario of higher education in the pre-dominantly tribal region of Jharkhand.

The chapter "Higher Education and Tribals in India: With Special Reference to Jharkhand" by Dalip Kumar is a comprehensive elaboration of higher education of tribals in India with special reference to Jharkhand. It highlights various parameters of status of higher education including demographic trends, present educational status of STs, their literacy rate, gross enrolment ratio, pupil-teacher ratio, state-wise universities, gender-gap, number of Indian students in USA, etc. It discusses the strength and weaknesses of Indian higher education system, government initiatives and recommendations made by knowledge commission. It also summarizes some important findings and relevant suggestions.

The chapter "Tribal Education of Jharkhand: Concerns and Scrutiny" written by Basabi Mukhopadhyay and Debes Mukhopadhyay expresses concern at said state of affairs in the tribal education. The education must be made as a tool to empower the assetless, powerless and voiceless of masses. Although much has been done but still the elitist approach has not impacted the lives of socially and economically weaker sections. The state of Jharkhand must promote social inclusiveness so that the political gains achieved through years of struggle to create a separate tribal state start yielding desired economic benefits. The time has come when the voices of left-outs are heard in apt attention and their problems are acted upon.

In the chapter "Higher Education and Tribals: Problems and Prospects—A Case Study of Jharkhand", the author N.C. Jha touches upon the problems and prospects of higher education and tribals; economic compulsions and lack of proper counseling and guidance. Tribal students are interested more in getting jobs than pursuing higher education. They are attracted even by fourth grade jobs. Due to this reason, number of tribal students in post-graduate, research, fellowship programmes and in various competitive examinations is found to be very thin. The wastage in education is not only a loss to the institutions or to subsidizing agencies or the government but a great loss to the society and the nation.

The chapter on "Higher Education System in Jharkhand: Challenges and Opportunities" written by S.K.L. Das goes into history by referring to India's glorious achievements in education but expresses concern at present education system which is disoriented and disfunctional and which produces a large number of unemployed youths. The paper underlines the importance of Gandhian approach to education for the highest development of mind with emphasis on vocationalisation. It refers to various challenges faced by higher education in backward regions which leads neither to normal linear expansion nor pace and nature of improvement which can meet the needs of changing market. Need of the hour is increased government funding, encouragement to private sectors for establishing Institutions in backward regions and setting up of an agency for redressal of grievances of students and parents against private and public institutions.

"Economic Solvency and Academic Efficiency: A Case Study" is prepared jointly by Debasis Mukhopadhyay and Dhurjati Prasad Bagchi. The paper is based on case study in Itachuna village of Khanyan region which is predominantly inhabited by SCs, STs and OBCs. Authors suggest the restructuring of the reservation policy of giving adequate financial assistance to weaker sections rather than giving only seats and quota reservations in higher education and jobs.

The chapter on "Higher Education among Tribal People during Eighties of Twentieth Century in India with Special Reference to Orissa" is written by authors-duo Rajan Kumar Sahoo and Basanti Das. The chapter aims at studying the standard of higher education and point out the problems faced by tribal communities.

The chapter on "Higher Education among Tribals with Special Reference to Andhra Pradesh" jointly written by B. Satyanarayan and B. Appa Rao, is an attempt to evaluate the impact of constitutional safeguards, government policies and various development plans on the status of higher education of tribals in the state of Andhra Pradesh. Much has been said and done, yet more needs to be done to make the various development programmes and schemes more effective in order to achieve the desired goal of equity and social justice.

D. Policy Imperatives for Higher Education

Very scholarly presented chapter "Higher Education and Tribals in India: The Current Scenario and Future Policies" by Raj Kumar Sen gives comprehensive picture of Indian higher education system touching all its relevant aspects. It is lagging behind in terms of access and quality due to elitist character and the development strategies not taking proper care of weaker sections of society. The process of disparity has been further accelerated under the era of economic reforms and especially under the provision of the GATS and WTO. Analysing some aspects like current scenario about Indian tribals, higher education and tribals and efforts to utilize the potential of the tribals, the author concludes that the present development paradigm is inimical to the interest of tribals and alienated from their roots, traditional wisdom, skills and culture. There is an urgent need to change our outlook not only for the development of tribals but also for the overall development of the whole economy. Traditional skill and wisdom of tribal folks can be channelised towards the holistic management of the fragile forest and hill ecology.

"Mission of Higher Education in the Society of Tomorrow" is written by Bikrama Singh. This paper elaborates on the evolution of higher education, scientific and technological revolution in higher education, professionalization in higher education and linkage between higher education and social change. The author wants some change in the perceptions and prescription of higher education so that it can become a tool of social change and it can bring about the national and international unity.

The chapter on "Issue and Policy Options for Internationalizations of Higher Education in India" is contributed by B.M. Jani. It acknowledges the crucial role of internationalization of higher education in improving its quantity and quality in order to face the challenges of emerging market economy. The paper refers to the findings of several studies conducted in the past and discusses some emerging issues and prevailing practices in higher education. Concluding the chapter the author proposes a set of ten options for enabling the Indian higher education system to meet the changing needs in the rapidly globalizing world.

"Higher Education of Scheduled Tribes and Efficacy of Reservation Policy" is written by Ratan Lal Basu. Although the paper raised some issues of higher education of the STs with the help of a few tables containing some relevant data but, its main focus is on the efficiency of the reservation policy. Higher education especially the technical education is becoming costlier day-by-day for the empowerment of STs. There should be adequate financial assistance otherwise the policy of reservation would remain a political gimmick.

The chapter on "Indian Higher Education: Equity and Finance" is very carefully authored by Satyabrata Mishra to go deeper into the financial aspects of higher education in India. The chapter discusses some relevant issues like equity and finance, alternative sources of finance and equity and various challenges faced by higher education in India. The author suggests some measures to be adopted to make it effective, accessible and affordable to the masses in order to achieve the goal of inclusive growth and social justice.

In the age of knowledge revolution, education is the engine of growth. But higher education is passing through the phase of transition. The public expenditure on higher education is still too low to compete with developed countries in the globalised world. In the context recommendations of National Knowledge Commission (NKC) will certainly help in steering the engine of growth. Mushrooming of private institutions and coming of international universities are welcome but these should not be above the governmental scrutiny and control. Tribal communities are living in object poverty. They can not afford the costly education imparted by private and foreign institutions. Need of the hour is to consider the socio-economic and cultural aspects of diverse groups especially the marginalized tribal group otherwise the system will widen the already prevailing disparities. In this book, paper contributors have tried to see the problems and prospects of higher education through different angles. Certainly, these will help the policy-makers, planners and legislators to shape the Indian higher education in order to promote inclusive growth.

ANIL KUMAR THAKUR
NAGESHWAR SHARMA

Inclusive Higher Education for SC/ ST and Economic Growth

AMALESH BANERJEE

I. INTRODUCTION

In the education field, India has reached a stage of take-off phase. It is now the task of reducing the double/ gaps: the gap between the literacy and illiteracy and backwardness on the one hand and knowledge gap between the high level of scientific and technological knowledge attained by a small section of population and the vast section of populace, who do not have access to that store of knowledge. Dualism in knowledge and dualism in the economy both are widening to the detriment of tribal population. Exploration of knowledge and the application of those innovations at the production level are the important structural adaptations which the administration has to ensure in the interest of high growth and employment. Extensive cost-effective education programme will make it possible to diffuse the knowledge to the grass-root level and benefit the people from the revolutionary changes in knowledge. This paper first makes a brief reference to the knowledge innovation and economic progress at the macrolevel in the section II. India's education and population structure are discussed in section III. The mechanism of diffusion of high knowledge are treated in the section IV. The prospects of application of knowledge in agriculture and industry and the potentiality of employment expansion are also assessed in the section V. Education policy and employment are treated in the section VI. Conclusions are in the section VII.

II. KNOWLEDGE INNOVATION AND GROWTH

Modern economic growth has two important base level conditions. First is the knowledge-based innovation and technological diffusion at firm level resulting in augmenting growth. The second source of growth is the development of human resources through improvement of social sector activities including education and health. While higher education including latest technological innovation can go for adaptation and diffusion at the firm level the human development in general raises the productivity of labour and the quality of products. Both the level of education are complementary to each other. Technical education produces innovation. In the endogenous model this knowledge spills over to other firms and hence, as Schumpeter thought, a cluster of innovation come into being. Hence higher education in science and technology generate the extensive possibility of development. A Corolary of this process is the learning-by-doing process in which knowledge finally rolls over to number of firms and helping higher and higher production in the trails.

But it is possible with larger investment. There must be extensive investment, private or public, to encourage this dynamic process of knowledge spill over and higher production. The knowledge expansion therefore implies technical progress and the larger the technical progress the larger is the potentiality of growth. Under the present state of globalization the growth strategy is couched in terms of high technical expansion, export promotion and growth. This strategy has worked considerable in our economy without significant expansion of employment. In the Eleventh Plan draft an alternative inclusive growth strategy has been accepted. Under this strategy the emphasis on small mechanical enterprises (SME) on the one hand and the extension of micro-finance, a La Mohammad Yunus have become the prime mover of growth and employment generation as well as poverty alleviation.

This strategy has a great potentiality of generation of higher technology are successfully adoption to the SME. If we consider higher education and technology knowledge as the social pool of knowledge of the industrial art and the rate of technical progress as the rate at which this stock of knowledge is increasing then two things become important. First, is the task to enhance the pool of high-technical knowledge and second is the art transmission of that knowledge to the different level of production activities. Hicks and Kaldor have made important classification of technology utilization. Technology is often capital and labour-saving. This is for further research which will adopt the technology at the production level. India has attained a high pool of technical knowledge which have become a remarkable achievements. Now it is the task of endogenizing the technical knowledge (progress) by successive application at production level and to attain the productivity growth. To understand this process and to recommend the process for that we are to know first, in the next section, the knowledge (education structure) in India and its limitation and then to examine in the Section IV the state of diffusion of technical knowledge in different sectors and to the tribals.

III. EDUCATION AND KNOWLEDGE STRUCTURE

India as has made impressive record in the field of higher education. It is reported that between 1997-98 to 2003-04 student enrolment in higher education has increased significantly. Against this the 55th Round NSS also recorded that there were inequalities in enrolment across various groups and castes particularly among the SC/ST.

If we analyse the system of acquiring knowledge in our country it appears that only a handful of our young generation receive that rate opportunity. On average around thirty per cent of our population is illiterate and another ten/ fifteen per cent leave the school at quite an early age. This implies that not more than ten per cent of student force has access to higher education. Besides cost, caste, infrastructure and poverty, there are many of reasons which impede the access of limited students to the even limited citadel of higher education institutions. A vast section of SC/ST population virtually remain outside this relm of high knowledge.

Higher technical and scientific institutions are beyond the reach of poorer segment of population. IITs, IIMs Research Laboratories and other specialized scientific institutions are only for well-off section of population. The reasons are that students of poorer section of population particularly SC/ST or do not possess requisite quality of their teaching background. As such those communities who live on those backward regions do not get enrolment in those high-tech enterprises. Most of the high-cost scientific research and teaching institutions are situated in metropolitan centres.

The entire rural education system of our country is dismal. Apart from the critical primary education, the school and college level educational institutions are awafully inadequate, inefficient and insufficient. Hence knowledge creation process in laboratories and technical institutions in most of the rural education set-up of the country is far from satisfactory. Under this condition of knowledge infrastructure the development of knowledge society and human resource development will be hardly satisfactory. Our status in this respect in the world is insignificant. Although about fifty per cent of our population is women, about fifty per cent of women are in darkness of illiteracy. Majority of SC/ST population who are 24.4 per cent of total population of the country are poor and uneducated. Throughout the world, women literacy above 15 years of age is 73 per cent, in our country this rate is only 44.4 per cent. Even Sri Lanka has much better record, 94.5 per cent. It is recorded that there are still about 45 districts in the country where women literacy is less than 30 per cent.

Against this perspective the Central Government has formed a National Knowledge Commission in order to hasten the emergence of knowledge society. The Commission has envisaged a number of recommendations for continuous implementation. The knowledge society includes both farmers and non-farmers. Knowledge is not only the adoption of a machine designed or borrowed/imported from abroad. It is a composition of ideas for creativity which develops from habitual acquaintance with traditional and non-traditional skill. In this knowledge process both rural and urban education system have to develop an array of activities which spurts ideas and creativity and which generates ideas for upgradation of existing knowledge. National Knowledge Commission (NKC) as well as the National Commission on Farmers (NCF) both ultimately hinge on this education system for generation of knowledge stage by stage resulting in higher level of human and physical capital formation and growth.

IV. RECOMMENDATIONS FOR ACCESS TO HIGHER EDUCATION

(a) The first essential task of the knowledge society is to ensure facilities of basic education for all, with special care for all the girl child and SC/ST population who are traditionally neglected.

(b) Cluster of institutions have to be built for learning at the Panchayat level. Committees have to be formed for proper implementation of universal literacy programme.

(c) Panchayat level committees have to be formed for proper implementation of universal literacy programme and ensure the access to higher education for SC/ST.

(d) Special camps have to be organized for imparting for vocation training of groups of turn in computer and various other operational implements.

(e) Formation of Self-help groups in dissemination of

knowledge and setting up knowledge-based activities necessary institutional financial support have to be implemented throughout the country, particularly among the backward communities.
Once the base level education become stronger the higher knowledge-based education has to be evenly spread. We have a tendency to concentrate universities at the big cities. But the backward regions should have greater necessity because universities have the responsibilities in imparting technical knowledge.

(f) The present tendency of privatization of education is detrimental to the rapid growth of knowledge society. This is because the tendency of globalization has the result of inroad of multinationals in higher education which is by nature 'exclusive and leave out the poor people and poor regions. Because cost is a deterrent.

(g) Research and development are the key functions of higher education. At present we have a very low allocation for R & D which is much lower than many advanced countries. Extensive research can develop innovation which result clustered development of industries. This process of industrial growth can fit well with endogenous growth process initiated by solow and other celebrated economists who contributed to the emergence of New. Growth Theory.

(h) Modern information technological knowledge is location non-specific in character and can be imparted throughout rural and urban set-up with the support of limited infrastructural facilities. It has brought about a revolutionary changes in different fields. Our higher education system can thus be made accessible to the remote corner of the country and to the marginalized section of the community as well without much effort. Universal tele-education delivery system can virtually convert the wide region in a class room. The

Distant Education Programme can thus be, if properly worked out in a net-work, an effective means of reaching out to the end line of social and economic bounds, to the backward regions and backward class.

(i) Massive expenditure on R & D is a major step to make access to the world of knowledge for the distant people. Both the government and MNCs are making extensive investment in research and development sector. But this is still not sufficient compared to other advanced countries. Indian advance in modern information industry is remarkable but access to those by the weaker segment of students is hardly possible. A complete overhauling of our education curriculum and the infrastructure of the institutions are urgent for these modern knowledge to be disseminated to the larger segment of students. India has world famous science and technology institutions. With 400 state-run labs, 380 universities and 2900 research centres, India provide a strong infrastructure for advancement of science and technology. She produces 2 lakh engineers and 3 lakh graduates and PG students annually. To transmit the benefits of these research down to the grass-root level for augmenting production at farm and factories it requires a special structure of learning by doing programme. Let us now see how their learning by doing mechanism makes possible access to knowledge for the under privileged regions and casts in agriculture and industry. Special network of institutions of higher education has to be set-up for SC/ST, not for crème layer alone.

V. LEARNING BY DOING—AT FARM LEVEL

Access to scientific knowledge particularly in farming technology has made progress in different parts of the country. Farm level training of the peasants and the extensive experiment in the demonstration farming has widely benefited the large segments of farmers in our country. The green revolution has brought to the farmer a lot but the second green revolution requires learning in an extensive way to raise productivity and to diversify the farm output. Extensive training and work at different stages will raise productivity. Farm research in genetically modified seeds in an important advance. Extension of scientific education to the SC/ST will intensify this process. Inclusive higher education will strengthen the higher rate of economic growth.

Learning by Doing—At Industry Level

Learning by doing is vastly practiced in the IT sector. IT sector has made extensive progress in our country and ordinary IT firms and manufacturing units may score as the training spot for the unlettered workers. CSIR with its network of 38 laboratories and collaboration with 35 countries provide a tremendous support to the young entrepreneurs.

One important channel for dissemination of IT technology at the production level is the setting up of a cluster of small manufacturing enterprises. Small scale industries serve as the learning stage for the enterprising youths. Modern technology has to be fitted even at the small production units. This will not only serve as the learning stage but will also open the employment opportunity. IT innovation and the cluster net-work in Bangalore and Hyderabad provide a good example of learning and development. The innovation cluster in a series of laboratories doing IT, Bio-technology, electronics and aeronautics work in Bangalore and Hyderabad are strong pull of knowledge spill over. Practically these industrial research centres have become attraction for new industrialization in Asian and European Countries.

VI. EDUCATION POLICY AND EMPLOYMENT

For economic progress education policy has to be oriented with industrial advance. Investment in education and research has to be oriented with production and job requirements. A large segment of our un-employmented people are in the rural sector. Hence educational advance must equip the rural unemployed and should help reorient rural production base so that unemployed are absorbed in upgraded traditional activities as well as in new lines of manufacturing at non-farm level. The policy has to be designed to include the SC/ST people particularly.

We have at present two pieces of documents pertaining to education before us. The Approach Paper of the Eleventh Plan and the Model Right to Education Bill of 2006. The Approach paper envisages steps towards 'Faster and More Inclusive Growth'. It calls for a more market-oriented system which only the richer and corporate entities will avail of.

The Model Bill, 2006 should mould the higher education and endozenising the trend. At present a host of our talented students are going abroad. In the USA at present of the foreign students as major segment is Indian. The country is being deprived of the services of those talents.

Our present Approach paper on education makes provision for special treatment of giving education by setting up. National Programme for Education of Girls at Elementary Level (NPEGEL). It also envisages subsidized private schools that will earn profit. Thus the Approach Paper hinges at commercialization of higher level education which will be beyond the reach of poor people.

The Education Policy must also address the Indian knowledge capital play. At the present stage China has become the leading high-tech manufactured country and India has become a leading IT services export hub. Since major US firms spent huge amount on R & D and make trade on knowledge generation and export, third world countries are spending only poultry among on R & D. Many of our IT firms are foreign origin and many products of these firms are expatriated in foreign countries for trade. This type of high-tech employment generation is neither for growth of domestic output nor for sustained employment propagation. Higher education policy of the Governmentt must address this problem of facile growth and elitist education expansion.

VII. CONCLUSION

Entire education system in our country is in a mismatch. While around forty per cent of population is virtually illiterate, the top level limited education centres are beyond the reach of common men and SC/ST. Most of our high level education centres and universities are ill-equipped and inefficient. Hence the products of those institutions are not sufficiently capable of technical employment.

Education system has to be not only inclusive for all section of learners irrespective of caste, creed and gender, it must also be job-oriented. Modern endogenous economic growth theory is based on human resource development and knowledge generation.

Dissemination of higher education to the farms, factories and un-reached tribal is possible by extensive research for adaptation. Green revolution and manufacturing revolution which is now in the offing require setting up of extensive training at different levels so that knowledge can be widely applied at the production level. Our educational policy must aim at extensive investment in R & D so that generation of innovation and application of those at the farm and industry level is possible. Public and private collaboration is necessary in this area.

India has become the hub of IT services export while China has become the hub of high-tech manufacturing exports. Our education policy must aim at controlling the higher education such that our intellectual property rights (IPR) are not exploited by foreign firms for the benefit of multinational corporations. Education policy must walk on two legs. On the one hand the policy should be for inclusion of all children in the knowledge process even at the elementary level, on the other hand, the higher education should be cost-effective and accessible. to all. Cluster of education institutions should be set-up in all concerns of the country for all sections of communities. Along with that higher education must generate output and employment at different levels. The process of learning by doing at farm and factories is relevant. Small manufacturing enterprises are effective mechanism for knowledge transmission, output and employment generation.

TABLE 1

Percentage of SC/ST Population to Total Population and Marginal Working on 2001

State	ST (Descending order)	SC	Total SC/ST
India	8.2	16.2	24.4
Mizoram	94.5	Neg	94.5
Lakhadeep	94.5	Neg	94.5
Nagaland	89.1	Neg	89.1
Meghalaya	85.9	0.5	86.4
Arunachal Pradesh	64.2	0.6	64.8
D. Nagar Haveli	62.2	1.9	64.1
Manipur	34.2	2.8	37.0
Chhattisgarh	31.8	17.5	49.3
Tripura	31.1	17.4	48.5
Jharkhand	26.3	11.8	38.1
Orissa	22.1	16.5	38.6
Sikkim	20.1	5.0	25.1
Madhya Pradesh	20.3	15.2	35.5
Gujarat	14.8	7.1	21.9
Rajasthan	12.6	17.2	31.8
Assam	12.4	6.9	19.3
J & K	10.4	7.6	18.5
Maharashtra	8.9	10.2	19.1
Daman and Diu	8.8	3.1	11.9
Andaman N.	8.3	NSE	8.3
Andhra Pradesh	6.6	16.2	22.8
Karnataka	6.6	16.2	22.8
West Bengal	5.5	23.0	28.5
H.P.	4.0	24.7	28.7
Uttaranchal	3.0	17.9	20.9
Kerala	1.1	9.8	10.9
Tamil Nadu	1.0	19.0	20.0
Bihar	0.9	15.7	16.6
U.P.	0.1	21.1	21.2
Goa	Negligible	1.8	1.8
Punjab	NST	28.9	28.9
Chandigarh	NST	17.5	17.5
Delhi	NST	16.9	16.9
Pondicherry	NST	16.2	16.2

Neg. = Negligible
Census-2001.

TABLE 2

Combined Expenditure of the Centre and States on Social Sector

Item	*2004-05*	*2005-06 (BE)*	*2005-06 (BE)*	*2006-07 (BE)*
1	2	3	4	5
Expenditure social sector*	2,30,956	2,66,630	2,86,259	3,09,444
Of which social services	1,77,013	2,05,351	2,22,172	2,42,722
Education	85,792	99,238	1,03,194	1,35,416
Medical and Public Health	25,764	32,528	33,874	39,251
Per cent to GDP				
Exp. on social sector*	7.4	7.7	8.1	7.8
Of which social services	5.7	5.9	6.3	6.1
Of which				
Education	2.7	2.9	2.9	3.4
Medical and Public Health	0.8	0.9	1.0	1.0
Per cent to Total Expenditure				
Exp. on social sector*	26.6	27.2	28.4	28.0
Of which social services	20.4	21.0	22.0	22.0
Of which				
Education	9.9	10.1	10.2	12.3
Medical and Public Health	3.0	3.3	3.4	3.6

* Expenditure on social sector includes expenditure on social services, rural development and food subsidies.

REFERENCES

Government of India (2006), *Economic Survey*, 2005-06.

Reserve Bank of India (2006), *Annual Report*, 2006, Bombay.

Romer, David (1996), Advanced Macro-economics, McGrow-Hill Companies, Singapore.

Yojana, (2006), Parameters of Knowledge Society, February (Summery of President Dr. Abdul Kalam's Convocation address at Maulana Azad National Urdu University, Hyderabad).

Foray, Dominique (2000), The Economics of Knowledge, MIT Press, Cambridge, MA.

2

Role of Universities in Tribals' Higher Education

MITHILESH KUMAR SINHA

PROLOGUE

The central purpose of education is the attainment of the 'good life', or the enrichment of the quality of life (Aristotle). Education is the knowledge and knowledge is the source of power. It is the key to empowering unprivileged groups in order to overcome poverty and to ensure equitable development. It is a tool for community empowerment and liberation.

Higher education plays a vital role for socio-cultural and economic development of a nation. The role of higher education is to impart training and skill for the empowerment of socially disadvantaged groups. Higher education is generally regarded as an effective instrument of upward socially mobility. Abraham Lincoln of the United States, who creditably performed the journey from 'the Log Cabin to the White House', is a shining example of social mobility. In our own country, Shri Lal Bahadur Shastri, the son of poor parents, by dint of education and hard work, rose to become the Prime Minister of India. Lincoln and Shastri are inexhaustible source of inspiration for the daydreamers of the disadvantaged socio-economic sections of the country.

In today's world the 'Knowledge Society', the 'Knowledge Economy' have become household terminologies. Knowledge has become a way of survival and competition. The experience of various countries in last four decades has indicated that mere physical and capital resources alone are not sufficient input for developing a nation. Improvement in the quality of people is necessary condition for achieving sustainable and accelerated development (Rao: 2002). Way back in 1961 Halsey, Floud and Anderson suggested that the economies of advanced industrial societies are dependent to an unprecedented extent on the result of scientific research, on the supply of skilled and responsible manpower, and consequently on the efficiency of education system.

Japan is one of the small countries, which have no sufficient land to cultivate, and natural resources for industries. Moreover, it was reduced to ashes by dropping two nuclear bombs just two years before our independence. Its efforts for human resource development yielded desired results to become a developed nation. India is dreaming to be a developed nation. However, our huge population is considered biggest hurdle. Since, education has tremendous potential to transfer the population into national asset; it could play a crucial role in realizing our dream.

Students in India although learn in the same class but everybody does not come from the same class or caste. Our society is hierarchically structured into castes. As a result, the socially disadvantaged groups, particularly Scheduled Tribes (STs) faced with an intense discrimination and inequalities associated with caste system and untouchability. These were/ are subjected to social, economical, and cultural exploitation. This marginalized group constitutes a very large section of India's population. The progress of Japan suggested that keeping such large population of ST socially and economically backward, goes against the interest of the country. Our dream to be developed nation could not be realized without empowering the tribal people. Education is the machinery, which can generate the power from human capital, to be used for the development of the nation.

I

POPULATION DISTRIBUTION ACCORDING TO GEOGRAPHY AND CASTE GROUPS

According to 2001 Census, 72 per cent of India's population was rural and 28 per cent urban. Of the overall population, the Census classified 80.5 per cent of the population as being Hindus and 19.5 per cent as being from other religions. In rural India, 82.3 per cent of the population were Hindus and 17.7 per cent from other religions whereas in urban India, the proportions whereas in Urban India, the population were 75.6 and 24.4 respectively, obviously suggesting that people of other religious persuasions are, on the average, relatively more urban than the average Hindu.

NSSO's last large sample survey (55th Round) was conducted in 1999-2000 and collected data by social groups. It classified the population as belonging to scheduled tribes, scheduled castes, other backward castes and others. The category 'others' includes Upper Caste Hindus (UCHs) and all non-Hindu religious denominations.

TABLE 1

Population Distribution According to Social Groups, 1999-2000

(in %)

	ST	*SC*	*OBC*	*Others*
Rural	10.5	20.4	37.6	31.4
Urban	3.4	14.3	30.4	51.7

Source: Statement 5, NSS Report 472: Differences in Level of Consumption among Socio-Economic Groups, 1999-2000

The sample survey result of the population break-up according to social groups is given in Table 1.

Given that estimates of both a large sample survey and a Census are subject to errors, albeit of different kinds, we should treat them as being reasonably representative of the overall population, rather than being definitive. It is therefore reassuring to note that the NSSO's large sample survey population estimates and those of Census 2001 are broadly in consonance with each other.

For example, according to Table 1, in 1999-2000, STs and SCs accounted for 10.5 and 20.4 per cent of the rural population respectively. According to the 2001 Census these proportions were 10.4 and 17.9 per cent respectively. Similarly, for urban India, NSS sample survey data would suggest that STs and SCs constitute 3.4 and 14.3 per cent of the population. According to the Census, these proportions were 2.4 and 11.8 per cent respectively.

As a reasonable approximation, we use Census 2001 estimates for other religions to disaggregate NSS. Others into UCHs and "Other Religions" and the results are reported in Table 2.

TABLE 2

Population Distribution According to Social Groups: Including UCH*, 1999-2000

	ST	*SC*	*OBC*	*UCH*	*Other religions*
Rural (72 per cent)	10.5	20.4	37.6	23.7	17.7
Urban (28 per cent)	3.4	14.3	30.4	27.3	24.4

Notes: UCH stands for upper caste Hindus. Figures in parentheses refers to shares in total population.

What immediately obvious from Table 2 is that UCH and "Other Religious" denominations are relatively more urban, whereas ST, SC and OBC populations are relatively more rural. Indeed, STs are the most under-represented in what is already a very small urban population.

II

PERSPECTIVE OF HIGHER EDUCATION IN TRIBALS

Education was historically confined to certain section of society and excluded large section of population making it highly undemocratic in access (Thorat: 2004). Although, concerns for disadvantaged have been shown since long by many, Dr. Ambedkar and Phule remained at the forefront to liberate them from the sufferings due to lack of education. After Independence, the state made efforts to eliminate the educational disparities. Our constitution enshrined democratizations as one of the main objectives of education and anticipated the democratic expansion of education would serve social and economic mobility. Provisions made for social and educational development could be seen in the Articles such as 15(2), 15(4), 17, 46, 335, etc. of the constitution. Different commissions and policies on education in Independent India explicitly stated the commitment mandated by the constitution (India 1950, 1966, 1986).

The spread of education among the ST/SC has been slow compared to non-tribal communities. Only small fraction not more than 2.4 per cent of the SC/ST students which entered in school manages to go to higher education. The picture is likely to be worse in case of ST. This results into lower presentation in education compared to their proportionate representation in the population. In higher education the percentage of SC students is around 7.5 and that of ST is around 2.5 (Rao: 2002). If we consider the enrolment of SC at various levels of the higher education, only 10 per cent and 0.25 per cent to post-graduate and Ph.D./D.Sc./D.Phil. respectively from undergraduate level (India, 1993). Apart from access, to a great extent, there is no equity, equality or relevance in the education system for SC/ST students. The entire education system has been oriented to meet the requirement of one-third of the population, ignoring the interest of the rest (Naik, 1974, Ahmad, 1979).

According to the latest report of the National Sample Survey Organization (NSSO), the educational achievements of different social groups differ widely across the country.

Predictably, the other group—the tribal class—has far less record of academic achievements compared to general class and other backward classes. The divergence among the social classes rises with the rise in educational level. The proportion of persons reporting their educational level as higher secondary was less in tribal category than among any other social groups. Only 29 persons in ST in every 1000 persons passed higher secondary examination while 90 in others group.

The divergence was even sharper among the social groups in the educational level of graduate and above. Against 111 in the others category only 19 persons in ST were reported to have educational qualifications of graduate and above.

The divergence was very sharp among social groups in the technical/specialisation level of education. Against 18 in the others category only 5 persons in ST were reported to have diploma/certificate.

The poor academic position of the Scheduled categories was equally visible across the states. In Kerala, which has the highest literacy rate, for example, only 29 persons in ST households were found graduate and above among each 1000 samples against 101 in others group.

Among the major states only Bihar, Punjab and Uttaranchal have more than 50 graduates and above among every 1000 ST samples (Table 3)

III

UGC's ROLE IN EMPOWERMENT OF STs THROUGH HIGHER EDUCATION

UGC is an apex statutory body for coordination, determination, and maintenance of standards of University education. It has always been responsive to the need and constrains of disadvantaged social groups particularly SC/ST. It has been contributing towards social equity and Socio-economic mobility and in turn empowerment of SC/ST through the special schemes. These special schemes are likely to retain SC/ST students in education system and help them to enhance their academic performance.

TABLE 3

Per 1000 Distribution of Persons (15 years and above) by Level of General Education

State/UT	ST (Rural + Urban)			SC (Rural + Urban)			OBC (Rural + Urban)			Others (Rural + Urban)		
	Higher Secondary	Dip./ Cert.	Graduate and Above	Higher Secondary	Dip./ Cert.	Graduate and Above	Higher Secondary	Dip./ Cert.	Graduate and Above	Higher Secondary	Dip./ Cert.	Graduate and Above
1	2	3	4	5	6	7	8	9	10	11	12	13
A.P.	43	3	31	32	15	28	36	12	35	68	17	84
Aru P	60	3	28	115	40	53	80	0	2	70	15	85
Assam	37	2	11	13	0	20	50	3	29	61	2	39
Bihar	31	0	59	21	1	11	33	2	25	91	2	88
Chhatti	27	2	19	48	4	34	60	5	32	163	37	184
Delhi	152	24	210	83	2	36	100	14	82	147	23	290
Goa	0	135	0	41	2	16	61	37	34	101	87	116
Gujarat	42	16	27	48	13	33	39	10	25	99	23	119
Haryana	149	36	19	34	9	18	65	6	31	107	24	122
Hima P	58	9	28	54	10	28	86	29	34	97	29	75
J & K	30	0	25	41	4	8	42	4	31	68	10	51
Jharkh	21	2	21	24	1	9	45	6	29	82	20	151
Karna	19	4	12	42	6	15	44	9	33	89	19	107
Kerala	23	29	29	50	31	21	59	52	46	81	83	101
M.P.	14	2	4	26	4	14	43	6	28	129	17	165
Maharas	34	10	13	61	24	50	61	36	46	84	29	111

(Contd.)

TABLE 3 *(Contd.)*

1	2	3	4	5	6	7	8	9	10	11	12	13
Manipur	42	4	28	53	6	49	113	13	111	55	1	36
Meghala	35	3	32	70	0	3	29	2	11	73	52	148
Mizoram	59	4	44	93	0	244	15	0	0	62	0	84
Nagaland	136	9	91	0	0	0	22	0	13	150	14	65
Orissa	14	1	8	21	2	21	40	5	41	59	13	99
Punjab	79	25	57	52	10	15	79	25	34	116	24	114
Rajasth	22	1	29	21	4	22	41	4	29	93	13	106
Sikkim	52	1	32	7	0	18	50	4	30	62	2	67
T.N.	74	13	27	47	11	27	70	19	62	141	46	322
Tripura	27	1	11	19	1	22	35	0	35	68	5	76
Uttrakh	68	18	52	37	5	32	48	3	28	117	7	132
W.B.	25	1	15	26	2	19	45	5	48	60	4	60
A & N Is	519	0	0	0	0	0	-	-	-	84	16	74
Chandigarh	492	0	0	175	29	75	131	3	1	177	36	322
Dad & N H	9	25	20	0	116	348	29	90	0	159	38	285
Da & Diu	13	7	12	147	23	21	138	20	44	146	34	154
Lakshdwe	21	31	30	0	-	-	0	21	0	85	141	239
Pondicherr	-	-	-	47	8	32	71	41	69	138	11	357
All India	29	5	19	36	7	23	49	12	37	90	18	111

Source: Employment and Unemployment Situation among social groups in India, 2004-05—NSSO (Report No. 516—61st Round)

Note: A.P.—Andhra Pradesh, Aru. P.—Arunachal Pradesh, J&K—Jammu and Kashmir, Jharkh-Jharkhand, Hima. P.—Himachal Pradesh, Karna-Karnatak, Chhattti—Chhattisgarh, M.P.—Madhya Pradesh, Maharas—Maharashtra, T.N.—Tamil Nadu, Uttrakh—Uttarakhand, A.& N. Is—Andman and Nagar Islands Dad. and N.H.—Dadar and Nagar Haveli Lakshdwe—Lakshadweep.

SC/ST Cells in Universities

University Grants Commission introduced the scheme of Establishment of SC/ST Cells in Universities in the year 1983. UGC provides the financial assistance to make the cell functionally effective. In non-recurring, 50,000 are given for computer and printer. In Recurring, the Commission provides assistance for salary of staff as per actual expenditure (Table 4). Apart from staff salary, UGC provides Rs one lakh per annum as contingencies to be used for TA/DA for field work, data collection and its analysis and evaluation.

TABLE 4

Assistance for the Staff Position in SC/ST Cell

Positions	*No. of Positions*
Coordinators	One
Administrative Assistant	One
Research-*cum*-Statistical Officer	One
Steno-Typist/Data Entry Operator	One
Peon	One

UGC established 88 SC/ST Cells till the end of 8th Five Year Plan. Expectedly, the Commission stopped providing any assistance/staff salary to these SC/ST Cells particularly in State Universities as respective State Government/ Management had given an assurance to take over the financial liabilities with effect from April 1997. Therefore, these cells were supposed to be maintained by the respective University/State Governments after the end of the 8th Five Year Plan.

During 9th Plan period UGC established/approved 21 SC/ST Cells in Universities (Table 5).

In financial year 2004-05, the Standing Committee on SC/ST considered fresh proposals as well as few proposals from the Universities which had earlier been given/approved SC/ST Cells but could not start functioning. The Committee approved the proposals of 13 Universities to establish the SC/ST Cells. As a result by the end of 2004-05, the UGC was

TABLE 5

SC/ST Cells in Universities Approved during 9th Plan Period

Year	*No. of SC/ST Cells*
1997-98	-
1998-99	7
1999-00	8
2000-01	3
2001-02	3
Total	21

Note: Number of SC/ST Cell at the end 8th Plan was 88.
Source: UGC Annual Report, 2001-02.

able to approve/establish SC/ST Cells in 120 Universities of the country. The year-wise working SC/ST Cells in different Universities is shown in Table 6.

TABLE 6

Year-wise Working SC/ST Cells in Different Universities

Year	*No. of SC/ST Cells*
1996-97	88
1997-98	-
1998-99	103
1999-00	-
2000-01	107
2001-02	109
2003-04	113
2004-05	120

Source: Compiled from the University Grants Commission.

It may be mentioned that there are around 300 Universities in the country. It means more than 50 per cent of these Universities were/are without SC/ST Cells. It might be interesting to see how these Universities implement Reservation Policy and other welfare schemes, and protect the interests of SC/ST without the Cells. Therefore, the efforts are need to be made to increase the SC/ST cells in the Universities. It took 22 years to establish 120 SC/ST Cells in the Universities. We have to accelerate the work to cover more Universities under this scheme. Moving with the old same speed would be detrimental.

It was quite disturbing that SC/ST Cells established during 9th Plan did not start functioning due to non-commitment of the State Government to take over liability of recurring expenditure on posts in the SC/ST Cells after the end of 10th Plan period, as the responsibility of UGC of providing grant for the recurring expenditure ceased after the end of plan period.

Meeting/Workshops of Sub-Committee of UGC Standing Committee on SC/ST have started from September, 2005 in different regions of the country to review the work. In such meetings/workshop, it came to notice that many Universities were keen to continue or want to establish a SC/ST Cell and approached the respective State Government for its concurrence. However, they failed to get the same. It appears some State Governments do not like to take over SC/ST Cells after five years. These States perhaps think that SC/ST Cell is unnecessary financial liability/burden for them. This approach of State Government kills such important Programme of UGC at the bud itself.

An availability/supply of fund is essential for smooth running of the any project and achieving its objectives. The year-wise release of grants for SC/ST Cells functioning in different Universities is shown in Table 7. These figures in the table indicate clear trends. Unexpectedly, the grant released for SC/ST Cells was almost continuously decreased. In year 2003-04, the rent was not released at all, as the revised guidelines to establish SC/ST Cells in 10th Plan were not finalized by UGC. It may be mentioned that the 10th Plan period guidelines for establishment of special Cells for SC/ST was published and released only in September 2004. In anticipation, UGC should have taken some interim measures for this period to avoid the non-release of grants for such important scheme. The continuous decrease in grants and non-release of grants in 2003-04 might have adversely affected the smooth functioning of many SC/ST Cells.

TABLE 7

Year-wise Release of Grants for SC/ST Cells in Universities

Year	*Grants Released (in Rs)*
1997-98	193,59000
1998-99	50,66000
1999-00	65,65000
2000-01	37,86000
2001-02	42,56000
2002-03	29,58000
2003-04	Not Released
2004-05	13,18703
Total	433,15703

Source: Compiled from the UGC Report, 2001-02 and Reports/Information.

Remedial Coaching Scheme for SC/ST

The SC/ST students mainly come from a rural background where opportunities for quality education are so limited that weakness in academic performance is inevitable. The weaknesses have to be removed by remedial education and in turn help them to do well in Studies (Kale: 2005). Therefore, the Commission introduced in 1994 one such special scheme namely "remedial Coaching at the Undergraduate (UG) and Postgraduate (PG) level for students belonging to the weaker sections of the society, particularly the SCs/STs."

The main objectives of the scheme are:

(i) To improve the academic skills and linguistic proficiency of the students in various subjects.
(ii) To raise the level of comprehension of basic subjects to provide a stronger foundation for further academic work.
(iii) To strengthen their knowledge, skills and attitudes in such subjects, where quantitative techniques and laboratory work are involved, so that necessary guidance and training provided under the programme may enable the students to come-

up to the level necessary for pursuing higher studies efficiently.

(iv) To improve overall performance of these students in the examinations.

The tenure of assistance to implement the scheme in Universities and colleges is five years but initially assistance is provided for three years, called first phase. The nature of financial assistance available for scheme of remedial coaching for SC/ST is given in Table 8. The period of assistance is linked with performance. The work of Centre can be reviewed at the end of third year with the help of Standing Committee on SC/ST and if found satisfactory, further extension of two years would be granted to College/ University. Each University/College is expected to cover a minimum 100 students per year and place the coaching centre under one of the senior faculty members as coordinator of this scheme.

The year-wise position of the proposals approved by UGC during 1997-98 to 2004-05 is given in Table 9. As such academic institute is expected to cover, on average, 100 students the total number of beneficiaries per annum could be at least 10,000 students. It is important that the appraisal reports (For example of year 2000-01) confirm the scheme as a beneficial to SC/ST students. The remarkable improvement in academic performance (UGC Annual Report, 2001-02) suggested to make all efforts to encourage more and more Universities and Colleges to establish Remedial Coaching Centres for the benefit of SC/ST students.

However, on the other hand, when 202 institutes selected for financial assistance during 1996-97 were reviewed for their work, UGC Committee recommended extension only for 24 institutes for another period of two years (UGC Annual Report, 2000-01). Similarly, the commission also reviewed the work of those colleges, which were selected in the year 1999. The committee could recommend 18 institutes for further assistance in second phase, i.e. for two years duration (UGC Annual Report, 2002-03).

During 2003-04, proposals were invited as per the Ninth Plan guidelines of the scheme. Five and 113 proposals

TABLE 8

Nature of Financial Assistance Available for Remedial Coaching and Coaching Scheme for Entry in Services for SC/ST Students

		Coaching for SC/ST (Rs in lakhs)	*Entry in Services for SC/ST (Rs in lakhs)*
	Universities		
	Non-Recurring		
1.	Audio-Visual Aids/Computer (One)	1.25	1.25
2.	Photocopier	1.25	1.25
3.	Books and Journals	1.25	1.25
4.	Invertor/Generator	0.25	0.25
	Total	4.00	4.00
	Recurring (p.a)		
1.	Honorarium to Coordinator	0.12	0.12
2.	Remuneration to Teachers/Scholars	1.50	1.50
3.	Part-time LDC with Computer Knowledge	0.18	0.18
4.	Contingency	0.20	0.20
	Total	2.00	2.00
	Colleges		
	Non-Reccuring		
1.	Audio-Visual Aids/Computer (One)	1.00	1.00
2.	Photocopier	0.50	0.50
3.	Books and Journals	1.00	1.00
	Total	2.50	2.50
	Recurring (p.a.)		
1.	Honorarium to Coordinator	0.10	0.10
2.	Remuneration to Teachers/Scholars	1.10	1.10
3.	Part-time LDC with Computer Knowledge	0.18	0.18
4.	Contingency	0.10	0.10
	Total	1.48	1.48

Source: University Grants Commission.

TABLE 9

Year-wise Position of Proposals Approved for Remedial Coaching

Year	*Number of proposals approved*
1997-98	94
1998-99	90
1999-00	70
2000-01	48
2001-02	92
2002-03	44
2003-04	106
2004-05	74

Source: Compiled from the UGC Reports.

of Universities and Colleges respectively were selected to establish Remedial Coaching to SC/ST students. However, the UGC did not convey its approval/sanction of grant to these Universities and Colleges as the guidelines of the schemes for the 10th Plan were at the finalization stage (UGC Annual Report, 2003-04). During the same year (2003-04), progress of the coaching centres approved during 2000-01 was reviewed after completion of the three years. The committee recommended extension of 13 coaching centres for further period of two years (UGC Annual Report, 2003-04).

The above monotonous details, deliberately given here, appear like mere rituals, lacking an academic component to great extent. It could be seen that the large number of proposals are approved and reviewed but the few are recommended for extension. At the same time, as mentioned above the scheme is beneficial and found a remarkable improvement in performance of SC/ST students. In this light, the scheme has to be examined and modified suitably to make it more popular among the Universities and Colleges and in turn more beneficial to SC/ST students.

Table 10 shows the year-wise release of grants for the remedial coaching scheme. This is one of the scheme for SC/

ST which relatively gets maximum grant. Expectedly, the UGC has recognized importance of coaching and supported the scheme liberally. However, considering the extend of need of SC/ST students; the grant is quite small in volume. Moreover, the grant for remedial coaching remained of the tune of around 300 lakh from the year 1997-98 onward till date. Since, the social returns from the remedial coaching are expected to be least three times more than what it was in year 1997-98.

TABLE 10

Year-wise Release of Grants under the Remedial Coaching

Year	*Grants Released (Rs in lakh)*
1996-97	227.25
1997-98	275.00
1998-99	354.00
1999-00	277.00
2000-01	343.00
2001-02	372.00
2002-03	284.23
2004-05	367.73

Source: Compiled from UGC Reports.

Apart from above, the UGC also faces problem in implementing the different special schemes including remedial coaching. Universities/Colleges do not submit Utilization Certificate, Statement of Expenditure, Appraisal Report, etc. against grant released which causes delay in releasing the next instalment. Non-compliance of UGC orders/procedures leads to discontinuation of the scheme.

Scheme of Coaching for SC/ST Candidates to Prepare for NET

In order to provide an adequate number of qualified SC/ST candidates for recruitment as lecturers in Universities and Colleges, the Commission has decided to introduce a scheme of conducting Coaching Classes to prepare them for appearing in the National Eligibility Test (NET) which an essential qualification for becoming a lecturer in Universities or Colleges. Therefore, the main objective of the scheme is to prepare SC/ST candidates for appearing in the National Eligibility Test (NET) so that sufficient number of candidates become available for selection of Lecturer in the University System.

Selected Universities for which grant on 100 per cent basis is made available could organize the coaching classes. UGC is making efforts to allocate at least one centre in each State. The details of grant provided under the scheme during 10th Plan are given in Table 11. There is no provision for appointing of staff on a permanent basis in the coaching centre.

TABLE 11

Grant for the Scheme of Coaching to Prepare for NET

A.	**Non-Recurring**	**Rs 3.25 lakh** (To be paid in 1st year)
1.	Computer with printer— (One Set) and Audio-visual aids	Rs 1.25 lakhs
2.	Photocopier machine (One)	Rs 1.25 lakhs
3.	Inverter/Generator (One)	Rs 0.25 lakhs
4.	Teaching learning-aid material	Rs 0.25 lakhs
B.	**Recurring**	**Rs 5.42 lakh p.a.**
1.	Honorarium (to coordinator)	Rs 12000/- p.a.
2.	Honorarium (to faculty members for paper I, II, III)	Rs 4,50,000/- p.a.
3.	Part-time LDC having computer knowledge	Rs 18,000/- p.a.
	Part-time peon/attendant	Rs 12,000/- p.a.
	Contingency	Rs 50,000/- p.a.

During 2004-05, the first year of introduction of the scheme, 32 Universities have been selected to implement the scheme, for which the Commission released a grant of Rs. 12,800,000 during the year. Each university is expected to cover a minimum 100 candidates for each examination to be held in June and December every year. UGC conducts NET examination in 76 subjects, which cover Arts, Humanities (including languages), Social Sciences, Computer Application, and Electronic Sciences. In Science subjects, CSIR conducts NET examination on behalf of UGC. The scheme is for plan period and assistance will be available to the University up to the end of 10th Plan. The University is to continue the scheme after commission's assistance ceases.

Since the methods of instruction/coaching include class work, tutorials, and work assignments followed by discussion and face-to-face interactions as well as formation of study group to help each other, the candidates are likely to benefit immensely and expected to strive for higher level of attainment.

Coaching Scheme for Entry in Services for SC/ST Candidates

During 10th Plan period the Coaching Scheme for Entry in services for students belong to SC/ST community is being implemented through selected Universities and Colleges to gain useful employment in group A, B and C including Indian Services. The scheme of Coaching Classes for Entry in Services for SC/ST Students has been introduced by UGC during 2004-05. The coaching scheme is operates at two levels: (i) coaching for group B and C level posts and (ii) All India Services, State/Provincial services (Xth Plan guidelines, 2004).

There is no provision for appointing of staff on a permanent basis in the Coaching Centre. Table 10 gives the details of financial assistance available for this scheme.

During 2004-05, the UGC selected 11 Universities and 28 colleges to introduce this scheme first time. An amount of Rs 8,673,000 has been released by the Commission for the same. Usefulness of this scheme as an instrument of empowerment SC/ST could be seen after appraisal and reviews.

Teacher Fellowships for SC/ST Candidates

The commission had a scheme for "Direct Award of Teacher Fellowship" for SC/ST College teachers by the UGC to do research work leading to the award of M.Phil./Ph.D.

degree. Last selections under the scheme were made during 1997-98. Sixty-three teachers were selected for the award of teacher fellowship. The tenure of the fellowship had already expired in June, 2001. The scheme has been discontinued thereafter (UGC Annual Report, 2001-02). The year-wise released grants to these teachers during the Ninth Plan period could be seen Table 12.

TABLE 12

Year-wise Positions of Release of Grants to SC/ST Teachers during Ninth Plan Period

Year	*Grants Released (Rs in lakh)*
1997-98	13.13
1998-99	16.31
1999-00	17.43
2000-01	32.56
2001-02	13.11
Total	[illegible].54

Many SC/ST teachers were benefited from this scheme. If UGC conducts the study even today it would get pleasant surprises. Large number of teachers from the lot of awardees has contributed to education in both teaching and research. Some have excelled in academics. Few of them are serving the nations in different capacities. This was also one of the schemes whose social returns were quite high. The UGC should have reviewed the scheme carefully before its discontinuation. It is not known what the constraints of UGC were. It appeared that UGC was not serious. It was amazing that no selections were made for the "Direct Award to Teacher" by UGC during 1996-97 due to paucity of funds. Was it so difficult for UGC to reallocate/arrange the funds for this scheme? Or was UGC so poor at that time, it even could not financially support the welfare scheme specially introduced for the depressed and oppressed sections of the Indian Society. There was also scheme on Research

Associateship for SC/ST candidates. It met the same fate as that of Direct Award of Teacher Fellowship.

Standing/Monitoring Committee on SC/ST

To oversee the effective implementation of reservation policy in Universities, a Standing Committee on SC/ST was constituted by the UGC in 1997. UGC has reconstituted the Standing Committee in 2003. The Committee reviews time to time functioning of SC/ST cells and implementation of various special schemes and programme for SC/ST introduced by UGC.

The Commission has also constituted a Monitoring Committee to discuss the problems in implementing the reservation policy for SC/ST in central and Deemed to be Universities. The meeting of Monitoring Committee is organized once in a year.

The Commission has been organizing region-wise (North, East, West and South) meeting/workshop of Universities having SC/ST Cells to discuss matters related to effective implementation of reservation policy and to interact and share experiences of each other.

The meetings/workshops of Sub-Committee of Standing Committee on SC/ST have already started from September 2005. Such meetings/workshops were found to be very effective and useful for UGC to implement its welfare schemes. Apart from above, the Committee has been giving several suggestions and asking UGC to take various measures for the empowerment of SC/ST. For example, recently, the Committee suggested UGC to re-introduce Research Associateship Scheme for SC/ST students and provide Scholarship to SC/ST students to undertake Post-Graduate studies in professional courses. The Standing Committee has also recommended UGC to hold National Convention to discuss and debate the role of higher education in empowerment of SC/ST. Thus, UGC keeps watch and control on SC/ST for effective implementation of reservations. In addition, UGC also seeks guidance from the same committee(s) on matters related to welfare of SC/ST.

IV

FINDINGS AND CONCLUSION

- Scheduled Tribes are still far behind in higher education.
- Only those STs, who have better economic conditions, came first in the field of education and got benefit from the public funds. The poor with miserable economic conditions inhabiting the remote areas have been out of touch with the welfare schemes.
- The inequalities lie at the base of higher education in India. Socio-economic factors mould the policy of higher education- where the urban rich in general are favoured than the rural poor. Nearly four-fifths of the beneficiaries are drawn from the top 30 per cent income group of urban areas.
- The inequalities also exist between the institutions of higher education. There has been a cry for excellence by the elite in society, who successfully lobby in fattening some institutions with modern amenities and resources for education.

Social disparities are still prevalent. Since, higher education is tool for social and economic equity, UGC has been addressing the national concern of access and equity by promoting several schemes for the disadvantaged groups particularly SC/ST, that help in eliminating social disparities. SC/ST cells are functioning in Universities to ensure effective implementation of the reservation policy in admissions, recruitments, provision of residential facilities, etc. Remedial Coaching are being run for SC/ST students for qualifying the NET for lectureship and for Entering in Services. At present there are 120 SC/ST Cells, 136 Remedial Coaching, 39 for Entering in services coaching and 32 NET Coaching Centres functioning in various Universities (Table 13). From some of the appraisals reports and interaction with University representatives in Regional meetings/workshops, these schemes were found to be beneficial to the SC/ST students.

Effectiveness of SC/ST cells in implementing reservations was evident from the increased percentage in enrolment and recruitments particularly in Central Universities. The facts are suggestive of potential of these special schemes to attract and retain SC/ST students in higher education system as well as help them to enhance their academic performance and success in examinations related to services. However, administrative handling and not following UGC procedure/ guidelines often affect the implementation of special schemes, some time leading to their discontinuation. In Review Committee Meetings emphasis should be given more on academic/benefits/outcome of the schemes rather than the administrative procedures. If necessary, the administrative procedures may be modified providing more freedom to the Universities which are implementing the special schemes. In vision for 21st century it is stated, "UGC is pursuing a forward looking strategy for development of a human resource which will not only meet the demand for skilled human power but also safeguard the interest of country". Therefore, it would be appropriate to undertake a systematic studies to find out to what extent the implementation of strategies/special schemes have been translated into social returns. It is possible that the outcome of such exercises might make UGC proud, for contributing to empowerment of SC/ST through higher education.

TABLE 13

Number of Schemes for SC/ST in Universities/Colleges in Year 2004-05

Scheme	*Number of College/ Universities*
SC/ST Cell	120
Remedial Coaching	136
Entry in Services Coaching	39
NET Coaching	32

Source: Compiled from the UGC Reports.

REFERENCE

Ahmad, Karuna (1979): "Towards a Study of Education and Social Change", *Economic and Political Weekly*, Vol. 4, January 27, pp. 158-64.

India, Government of (1950): "Report of the University Education Commission", December 1948-August 1949, Ministry of Education, New Delhi.

India, Government of (1996): "Report of the Education Commission" (1964-66), Ministry of Education, New Delhi.

India, Government of (1986): "National Policy on Education".

India, MoHRD (1993). Selected Education Statistics: 1991-92, New Delhi.

Kale, R.K. (2005): "Special Schemes of UGC for Empowerment of SC/ST", *University News*, Vol. 43, No. 47, November 21-27.

Kaur, Kuldip (2003): "Higher Education in India (1981-2003)", University Grants Commission, New Delhi.

Naik, J.P. (1974): "Crisis in Indian Education: A Search for Alternatives", Monograph.

Sharma, Kavita A. (2003) "50 Years of University Grants Commission", UGC Publication, New Delhi.

Sudha, Rao K. (2002): Educational Policies: Analysis and Review of Promises and Performances", National Institute of Planning and Administration, New Delhi, pp. 1-114.

Thorat, Sukhdeo (2004): "Marginalized Groups and Democratization of Higher Education" in Challenging Indian Universities, Arun Kumar (Edt.), JNU on October 2, Jawahar Lal Nehru University, pp. 44-47.

Rao, Srinivas S. (2002): "Equality in Higher Education: The Impact of Affirmative Action Policies in India", In The Role of Higher Education in Diverse Democracies, Beckhman, Edgar (Edt.); Association of American Universities and Colleges, Washington DC. pp. 41-61.

3

Higher Education and Tribals

K. HARIHARAN

INTRODUCTION

'Adivasis' meaning earliest inhabitants of a land are called autochthon people. Because of their isolated living in groups for a long period, their beliefs, traditions, religious faith remain unaltered and they were able to considerably retain their identity. This isolation itself has put them into great disadvantage and resulted in their living in poverty, unhealthy surroundings, uneducated and sufferings. During the period prior to our Independence, the then Government failed to come to their rescue as they were preoccupied with day-to-day governance and collection of taxes.

The section allotted to Scheduled Tribes in our Constitution points out the communities living occupy 8 per cent of India's population. These tribes numbering about 573 are spread out in our country. It has been identified that they speak about 270 languages which are totally different from those in vogue around the area they inhabit. According to available data, the Schedule Tribes, numbering about 570, different groups speak in languages belonging to major language families-predominantly Austric, The Drandian, Tibeto-Chinese, Indo European, etc.

Normally, a majority of these STs choose to live in locations which are out of reach for others usually forests and hillsides, etc. The figures enumerated offer the following classification: nearly 22 per cent of tribal settlements have a population of 100, 40 per cent have 100 to less than 300 and the rest having less than 500 people.

The tribal population though only 8 per cent, commands a majority in many States of our country like Mizoram (94.75%), Lakshadweep (93.15%), Nagaland (87.70%) and Meghalaya (55.53%).

Whereas tribals constitute nearly 83 per cent of the total tribal population in States like Bihar, Andhra Pradesh, Gujarat, Madhya Pradesh, Orissa and Rajasthan, they are only in the minority. Others account for majority.

Divided in four major categories, the Indian tribes are distinctly different from others like Hindus and Muslims.

(a) North Eastern Aborginals

Belonging to the Mongal race and speaking a language resembling those of Austric family, these tribes reside in the States of Assam, Manipur and Tripura and number around 21 lakhs.

(b) Central Aboriginals

The Rajasthan, Santhals of Chhotanagpur, HO of Singhbhumi and Manbhumi, *Khond and Kharia* of Orissa, Sawara of Ganjam and the *Mundas*. The Santhals account for 25 lakhs and most of them depend on cultivation for their living. While some are involved in small scale industries, the rest are leading a primitive life as they live in very dense forests and high mountain terrains.

(c) Southern Aboriginals

Kerala claims to have the most ancient tribes in our country the majority being *Kadar*. The *Todas* of Nilgiris, *Chenchu* of Hyderabad and the *Kanikar* and *Kurovan* of Travancore Cochin are other important tribes and a matrilineal type of social organization and family is discerniable in these tribes.

Apart from these, other places where tribes are

flourishing are Andaman and Nicobar, Northern Himalayas, the districts of Chamba and Mahasu, Dehra Dun and as for the vast variety of tribes, it is rightly mentioned as: "A Geographical Survey of India reveals distinct cultural and social regions with marked differences in the type of habitations, social institutions and psychological traits of population".

State-wise Population of Tribals

S.No	State/Territory	Total Population	No. of Tribals	Per cent
1	2	3	4	5
1.	Andhra	435.03	16.50	3.81
2.	Assam	149.58	19.20	12.84
3.	Bihar	563.53	49.33	8.76
4.	Gujarat	266.97	37.34	13.99
5.	Haryana	100.37	...	...
6.	Himachal Pradesh	34.60	1.42	4.09
7.	J. & K.	4617	...	...
8.	Kerala	313.47	2.69	1.26
9.	M.P.	416.54	83.87	20.14
10.	Maharashtra	504.12	29.54	5.86
11.	Manipur	10.73	3.34	31.17
12.	Meghalaya	10.12	8.14	80.43
13.	Karnataka	292.99	2.31	0.79
14.	Nagaland	5.16	4.58	88.61
15.	Orissa	319.45	50.72	23.11
16.	Punjab	135.51	...	...
17.	Rajasthan	257.66	31.26	12.13
18.	Tamil Nadu	411.99	3.12	0.76
19.	Tripura	15.66	4.51	28.95
20.	U.P.	883.42	1.99	0.22
21.	West Bengal	443.12	25.33	5.72
	Centrally Administered Territories			
1.	Andaman and Nicobar	1.15	0.18	15.52
2.	Arunachal	4.68	3.69	79.02
3.	Chandigarh	2.57	...	...
4.	Dadra and Nagar Haweli	0.74	0.64	66.89
5.	Delhi	40.66	...	...
6.	Goa, Daman and Diu	8.58	0.08	0.93
7.	Lakshadweep	0.32	0.30	93.75
8.	Pondicherry	4.79	...	...
	Total	54,79,49809	3,80,15162	6.94

Consequent to becoming a free nation, the national Government as also the State Governments have turned its attention towards the upliftment and welfare of tribal communities so that they may be equal partners in the society. Many welfare activities undertaken by the Government have resulted in creating awareness among the tribals. However, these activities have not brought out visible and major worthwhile changes in the Socio-economic and political lives of the tribals.

GOVERNMENT POLICIES AND PROGRAMMES FOR THE DEVELOPMENT OF TRIBAL EDUCATION AFTER INDEPENDENCE

Among the many developmental measures initiated by the Government special mention is to be made of the tribal sub-plan approach as a main strategy of the 5th Five Year Plan. Elementary education was given top priority to build confidence among the tribes. Taking into account both the qualitative and quantitative aspects of education, the tribal sub-plans accorded top priority to elementary education.

As a second major development, the recommendations of the National Policy of Education (NPE) in 1986 specified many measures relating to the education of tribals. Some of them are:

- Priority will be accorded to opening primary schools in tribal areas.
- There is need to develop curricula and devise instructional material in tribal language at the initial stages with arrangements for switchover to regional languages.
- Promising ST youths will be encouraged to take up teaching in tribal areas.
- Ashram schools/residential schools will be established on a large scale in tribal areas.
- Incentive schemes will be formulated for the STs, keeping in view their special needs and lifestyle.

Recognizing the heterogeneity and diversity of tribal areas, this policy proposed structure of primary education with special emphasis on improving access to tribal areas, besides emphasizing production of suitable text books in local languages, incorporating locally relevant curriculum and content. The policy also stressed the importance of conducting the lessons in the mother tongue.

Another major feature was the relexation of the regulations to start primary schools in tribal areas. Andhra Pradesh came forward to open schools in tribal areas where there were even twenty children in the school-going age-group. Madhya Pradesh fell in line and offered to open schools in areas with a minimum of 200 population. Unfortunately, these did not yield the desired results as even the relaxed criteria could not be met.

At the same time, Madhya Pradesh became the first State to introduce the Panchayat Raj System by a law conforming to the 73rd Constitutional Amendment Act, 1992. The Madhya Pradesh Panchayat Raj Adhiniyam 1993 considered reservation of seats for the reform of tribals in all its three tiers. The quota of reserved seats for the scheduled tribe people was to be in proportion to their strength in the population of the tiers of Gram Panchayats, Janpad Panchayats and Zilla Panchayats. But this could not make the tribals their own masters of their socio-political destinies.

The Government of India formed a committee in June 1994, Shri Dileep Singh Bhuria as its Chairman "to discuss and examine the issues relating to extension of the provisions of Part IX of the Constitution of the Scheduled Areas and to make recommendations on the salient features of the laws for extending the provisions of this Part of the Constitution of the Scheduled Areas", leading subsequently to the passing of Panchayat (Extension of the Schedule Areas) Act, 1996.

PROGRESS OF LITERACY AMONG TRIBAL MASSES IN COMPARISON WITH OTHER PEOPLE

The lack of education has by and large affected the development of tribal people. This was again due to the absence of teachers, institutional facilities, non-availability of text books, etc. at primary, secondary and high school levels. Administrative commitment and political will also were not forthcoming to extend such facilities to the tribals.

On the other side, with the 400 major and minor tribes having their own language, dialect and specific cultural heritage in our country, it has always been an enigma to educationists and researchers in the field of education to find out appropriate forms of language, physical and pedagogic infrastructure, equity in education, mode of instruction, contents, syllabi and modules for tribal education. However, multifaceted case studies were undertaken by Anthropologists and Sociologists on the low literacy rates among tribes in Ragasthan, Andhra Pradesh, Orissa, Madhya Pradesh, Bihar, etc. So also did the NCERT and some Universities. JTRC has been working for tribal education in both formal and informal settings for the last two decades. It had also arranged a National workshop on tribal education in India in 1993. These and many other attempts have brought to the fore many vital issues like:

1. Failure of adequate infrastructural facilities for primary education in remote areas.
2. Complete alienation of modern education from traditional tribal cultures and ethnicity.
3. Problems of drop-outs in primary schools including major dropouts of girl children who were required to look after the household and younger siblings in the absence of both the parents who are engaged in economic pursuits.
4. Problems of languages, dialects and tribal customs *vis-à-vis* formal education.
5. Total marginalisation of traditional tribal institutions as primary institutions to impart education in tribal areas.
6. Role of education as a cultural accomplishment *vis-à-vis* national development.

Still the absence of commitment, understanding and involvement of people stood in the way of any Government conceiving such a holistic approach of education. Hence the only alternative left was to engage the NGO's at local, regional and national level, taking into account their interaction with the tribals, gather their reactions, etc. at the grassroot level. These NGOs can also create a better environment for universal literacy as well as education and skill development in the tribal areas keeping in view the ethnicity and cultural heritage, traditional skills, traditional knowledge and resource base as well as the socio-economic structures of the tribal areas. They could offer suitable choice for higher education and both the central and State Governments should offer support and sponsor NGO's for spreading tribal education in the entire country. To achieve this, it is very essential to create necessary facilities in the tribal areas.

Literacy

According to the results of a temporal analysis of literacy among the tribes undertaken in 1961, 1971, 1981 and 1991 an increase of 8 per cent to 30 per cent was noticed. While States in the north-eastern regid have recorded high literacy rate in the country—Mizoram topping the list in 1971, 1981 and 1991. Andhra Pradesh, Madhya Pradesh, Rajasthan, Bihar, Orissa, Tamil Nadu, Nagar Haveli, West Bengal registered a low percentage of literacy as per findings of 1991 Census. Notably women lagged behind.

The ratio of enrolment of children created considerable variation during the period 1992-93 in the States. It was high in Lahshadweep but very low in Goa. As regards girl students, their enrolment in primary classes in many States like Madhya Pradesh, Bihar, Rajasthan, Orissa and U.P. was unsatisfactory.

In Rajasthan, Orissa, Meghalaya, Madhya Pradesh, Goa and Bihar, the ratio of enrolment of scheduled tribes was low. Though it was high in Himachal Pradesh, Mizoram and Tripura in regard to classes VI to VIII, it registered very low for higher education during 1992-93. The position was no better in many other States too. A survey conducted in 1989-91 on the dropouts revealed that scheduled tribe children in large numbers discontinued their education after class V. It was 67 per cent for classes I to V, 81 per cent for I to VIII and 88 per cent for classes I to X.

Process

Statistices reveal that the level of literarcy for STs has increased from 11.30 per cent in 1971 to 21.50 per cent in 1991. Even though in absolute numbers the illiterates have increased over the years, the gap between ST and non-ST population has also increased from 22.50 per cent to 33.05 per cent between 1971 and 1991. Even today tribal literacy falls well below the national average. In fact, data reveal that STs lag behind even SCs in educational progress. According to data available, States in north-eastern region like Andhra Pradesh, Rajasthan, Orissa and Madhya Pradesh have progressed considerably in achieving higher literarcy rate when compared with other States. In 1971 tribal literacy in Madhya Pradesh was at 7.62 per cent, increasing marginally to 10.68 per cent by 1981 and standing at 21.54 per cent as per the 1991 Census figures. The figures are similar for Bihar, Orissa and Andhra Pradesh. In fact, Andhra Pradesh has the lowest tribal literacy rate in the country at 17.16 per cent in 1991.

There was however a steady increase in the literarcy rate between 1981 and 1991 and it was visible even in backward States link Madhya Pradesh and Bihar. At the same time, the literarcy rate was far behind in educationally developed States like Karnataka, Tamil Nadu and Kerala. On the whole, the disparity among various states in terms of tribal literacy rates is pretty high, ranging between 82.27 per cent in Mizoram and 17.16 per cent in Andhra Pradesh.

Factors

Due to internal, external, Socio-economic and psychological reasons, the tribal communities are still trailing behind the general population education. This is mainly due to problems associated with the school system, content, curriculum, medium of study, pedagogy, academic supervision, as also policy, planning and implementation. At the same time, problems relating to social, economic and cultural background of the tribals as also the psychological problems of the first generation learners play a vital role.

External

While the constraints are discussed, it is with noticing that the population and distance norms formed by the Government have not been beneficial to tribal locations because of their sparse population and sporadic residential patterns. Unfortunately both the departments of Tribal Welfare and Education have not properly understood the complex realities of tribal life and also what they expect from such a system.

The dual administrative system for tribal education has its own disadvantages. While the Tribal Welfare Department lacks in expertise in educational planning, administration and supervision, the Education Department takes care of curriculums text books, teacher recruitment, transfer, etc. The school calendar specifies holidays and vacation which are relvant to formal schools and has no such provision for tribal's festivals, etc.

Another step not friendly with tribals is the defective selection of teachers leading to poor attendance and performance in the schools. Under the circumstances, these pitfalls have resulted in the decrease of educational development of tribals.

Internal

The internal problems affecting tribals' education are multifiarious—lack of suitable curriculam and teachers, supervision, and basic infrastrures like sanitation, etc. In most of the residential ashram schools, no provision is made for space to enable the children to sleep. Such lapes lead to the children being affected by contagious diseases.

Content

A common curriculum structure and teaching has put the tribal children at a disadvantage in that the rigid system of formal schooling, routine norms, discipline, teacher-centric instruction, etc. are not worth enforceable.

The inability of the tribal children to establish a friendly communication link with the teacher is another major reason for the dropouts. Though this could be overcome by using the regional languages for instruction, this is not being strictly adhered to on the ground of feasibility.

SOCIO-ECONOMIC AND CULTURAL CONSTRAINTS

The major socio-economic and cultural factors affecting tribal education are poverty and poor economic conditions, social customs, cultural ethos, lack of awareness and understanding of the value of formal education, conflict and gap between the home and school, etc. Studies on educational deprivation of tribals have inevitably linked them to their poor economic condition and poverty. The children are therefore forced to contribute directly or indirectly to the income of the family as they have to cater to the household works like cattle grazing, collecting fuel, fodder, etc.

The incentive schemes formulated by the Government do not reach the actual beneficiaries. Apart from education being free, the tribals may not be able to spend for writing materials, clothing, etc. While survival itself is a big struggle, the education rarely provides any immediate and visible benefits to the tribals. So much so, the participation of the tribal children is limited.

To overcome the problems, the Goverment has introduced many developmental schemes which generally relate to agriculture, horticulture, cattle rearing, etc. These are backed by subsidies, monetary and non-monetary inputs. A critical analysis of development programmes and their effect on tribal households shows that till tribal households reach a threshold level of income and land size, the economic development programmes can come into conflict with other activities like education, etc. In a way, it can be said that these development programmes seem to be adversely affecting the education of tribal children.

Broadly classified, the problems affecting the education of tribal children may be scoio-economic, psychological, academic, administrative and finally parental/teacher indifference.

PERSPECTIVES

The impact of modernity has terribly affected the homogeneity of the tribals. Even the educated and privileged few among the tribals are enjoying the resultant benefits and do not move their little fingers for uplifting their own brotheren. The disgust of the under privledged towards such 'babus' has created a negative attitude towards education. In addition, the modern education has brought in many new values which, according to the uneducated tribals, clash with their age-old traditional values.

These are but a few of the thorns in the flesh of tribals changing them antagonistic towards modern education.

The late Shri Humayum Kabir rightly remarked that even the best system of education is bound to fail without an efficient and resourceful teacher. The cultural rift between the teacher and the tribal student has created an insurmountable barrier between them. The teachers deputed for educating the tribal children have their own reservations too like lodging facility, reasonable compensation, and above all, social distance from the tribal people. No one can expect the best standard of dedicated teaching from such disgruntled and dejected teachers. The many remedial measures brought about by the Government have not yielded the desired results. This may be attributed to the lack of sincerity and devotion on the part of the officials charged with the implementation of such measures. Under the circumstances, a change in the base orientation in tribal education seems to be the only remedy.

The efforts of the Government to provide many welfare measures assaults to the tribals like building hostels to the students, supplying free textbooks, offering scholarships, etc. have in effect widened the rift.

A feeling of isolation has thus been created in the minds of the tribal students. The remedy lies in accommodating them in the general hostels and encouraging them to actively partake in the college and hostel activities. This is sure to bring them into the mainstream and relieve them from their imaginary isolation.

Unlike the general student who starts at school with basic linguistic information and conceptualization, the tribal student feels as a stranger at the initial stage. Therefore, a sound pre-schooling is a vital prerequisite for the tribal student to put him on par with others.

Another proposal is to appoint teachers from among the tribals themselves to add credibility to the efforts. Such properly oriented teachers should be conversant with the tribal languages. Text books in tribal languages will go a long way to encourage roping in most students. Such education should also be of functional importance leading to employment.

The curriculum should be related to socio-economic and cultural life of the tribals. Emphasis must be on imparting skills and modern information on agriculture, poultry, forestry and carpentry, etc. To put the dreams of the makers of our Constitution into reality the Government must inculcate suitable attitudinal changes in the tribal population towards education and offer better communication facilities, basic sanitary needs, teaching materials, etc.

The Government should evolve new strategies to remove the internal and external constraints and ensure imparting an uniformly satisfactory standard of education to the tribals.

A number of measures as enumerated below may be undertaken to ensure faster literary growth among the tribals:

(a) Use of mother tongue.
(b) Co-ordination between planners, administrators, students and teachers cutting short redtapism.
(c) Creating congenial and friendly environment.
(d) Avoidance of clashes of cultural activities.
(e) Freedom to the tribals to retain identity and cultural tradition without affecting their educational pursuits.

CONCLUSION

Recently the Union Cabinet has given its approval for the establishment of Indira Gandhi National Tribal University in Amarkanthak, Mathya Pradesh with Central Government funding. The Cabinet has also approved the Indira Gandhi National Tribal University Bill, 2007 in the Parliament. Hope this would ensure establishment of a teaching and affiliating University for facilitating and promoting avenues of higher education and research facilities for the tribal population of our country. We fervently hope that the University would promote studies and research in tribal art, culture, tradition language, caste, medical systems, forest and agriculture-based economic activities and advancement of technologies relating to natural resources in the tribal areas and pave the way for the development of tribal higher education focussing all the aspects of tribal life and the much needed development of tribal areas. To conclude, it is of utmost important that a Special Committee should be constituted with a knowledgeable tribal leader as its Chairman to identify the various problems pertaining to higher education, in order to arrive at a good decision. The decision so taken could be forwarded to the Government for effective implementation so as to achieve the desired result.

The present occasion gets more important when the global awareness is fully felt by the Leaders of Australia and other nations who stand foremost in their achievements. The Apology rendered by the Prime Minister of Australia formed the aboriginal communities for their misdeeds and discarding them by not providing the equal opportunities to State.

References

The World Bank (2000), Higher Education in Developing Countries: Peril and Promise.

Joshi, K.L. (1977) Problems of Higher Education in India, Popular, Bombay.

Hammadi, Ali (1984) University Administration in Developing Countries, Indian Bibliographies Bureau, Delhi.

Jayaram, N. (1990) Sociology of Education in India, Rawat, Jaipur.

Peer, Mohammed (1994) Higher Education and Employment, Rawat, Jaipur.

Knight, Jane (2002) Trade in Higher Education Services: The Implications of GATS, The Observatory on Borderless Higher Education. London.

Sharma, Vijendar (2002), WTO, GATS and Future of Higher Education in India in People's Democracy, Vol. 26, No. 6, Feb. 10.

Altbach, P. (2006), Higher Education in India; *The Hindu*.

Bernheim, C.T. and Chaui, M. (2003). Challenges of the University in the Knowledge Society, Five Years after the World Conference on Higher Education, UNESCO Forum Occasional Paper Series, Paper No.4, Paris.

Cameron, R. (2004), From old to new learning: global imperatives, exemplary Asian dilemmas and ICT as a key to cultural change in education. Globalization, Socieities and Education Vol. 2, No. 3, pp. 337-53.

Padma, T.V. (2005); Teaching *vs.* Research; *Sc. Edu. News*; 1st July 2005.

UNESCO, 2004. Higher Education in a Globalized Society, Education Position Paper, United Nations Educational, Scientific and Cultural Organization, France.

Weiler, H.N., Rosenblit, S.G. and Sawyerr, A. (2006), Colloquium on Research and Higher Education Policies, UNESCO, Paris.

Goldfired, M.R. and Davidson, G.C (1976). Clinical Behaviour Therapy, New York: Holt, Rinehart and Winston.

Porter, A.C. and Brophy, J. (1998). Synthesis of Research on Good Teaching: Insights from the Work of the Institute of Research on Teaching Educational Leadership, 45(8), p. 75.

Barth, R.S. (1988). Principles, Teachers and School Leadership. Ph. Delta Kappan 69(9), 639-42.

D.C. Sah, Yatindra Singh Sisodia, Tribal Issues in India.

Bose, N.K. (1977), The Hindu Method of Tribal Absorption in Culture and Society in India, Asia Publishing House, Bombay (Reprint).

Dube, S.C. (1998), "Development Design and Tribal People", in Dube, S.C. (ed.), Antiquity to Modernity in Tribal India: Volume I, Continuity and Change among Indian Tribes, Inter-India Publication, New Delhi.

Mishra, S.N. (1998), "Introdcution", in Mishra S.N. (ed.), Antiquity to Modernity in Tribal India: Volume III, Ownership and Control of Resources among Indian Tribes, Inter-India Publication, New Delhi

Russell and Hiralal (1975), Tribes and Castes of Central Province of India, Cosmo Publishing, Delhi (Reprint).

R.N. Sharma, Social Anthropology and Indian Tribes.

Sah, D.C. (1999), "Pressure on Land, Employment and Migration", *Review of Development and Change,* Vol. 4 (2).

Srinivas, M.N. (1952), Religion and Society among the Coorg of South India, Oxford University Press, 1952.

Sarkar, Jayanta (1986), Social Mobility in Tribal Madhya Pradesh, B.R. Publishing Corporation, Delhi.

Present Status of Indian Higher Education

YOGENDRA NATH MANN AND K.N. MANN

Higher education in India is at crossroad as our higher education system is facing greater challenges in the twenty-first century. This scenario has emerged because of certain developments over the past few years. For the first time, India is recognised internationally as a nation which is providing value-added trained human power at a premier level. Indian experts are now persons who generate wealth and also are the backbone in many global science and technology revolutions. Indians have made their presence felt in the field of information technology (both in software and hardware), electronics, biotechnology, pure sciences and economics; in financial management and in fields related to humanities and social sciences. It is interesting to note that the employment opportunity pattern is also undergoing a change. Jobs in government and government supported/ funded organisations are declining. In industry too, the job profile is changing. The manufacturing sector is going through a sea change all over the world: with downsizing of staff strength, outsourcing of jobs and a new approach in managing of industries. This means the workforce in core and allied support industries is declining. This does not mean that such industries would be closed but only that they would be operating under a decentralised and diversified structure, spread across the world. This requires a workforce that can come up with innovative ways of product design, manufacturing, and marketing and organising the entire gamut of industry activities in a different manner. There will no longer be localisation of industry in any particular country but enterprises will be spread across different nations. Indian industry is also facing the challenge. It no longer has a protected market but has to face global competition. In addition, firms have to enter the world market with quality products in order to enhance exports. They will, therefore, have to innovate. Hence their job requirements are changing. Whether it is domestic industry or industry located outside India, both need skilled human power. This means the world will be looking for trained persons in all basic fields with a sound knowledge base in their core discipline and the ability to adapt to new demands.

The world will be looking for trained persons in all basic fields with a sound knowledge base in their core discipline and with the ability to adapt to new demands. The service sector is a fast-expanding sector. It is projected that in twenty years' time at the global level, the sector would account for almost sixty to seventy per cent of jobs. The world is looking for not only persons who are experts and/or innovators at the high end but also for skilled persons who can work in the low-value added segments. Hence, globally, there is increasing demand for education in the pure science and technology sectors, social sciences and humanities, in economics and commerce as well as in utility sectors. It is in these areas that there is a shortage of human power and the gap between demand and supply is going to widen. World demography is also changing. While in twenty years time, many of the advanced nations would have large percentage of senior persons, 45 per cent of Indians would be in their twenties. This means young Indians would be in demand in other nations. They would have more scope for competing in a global market as entrepreneurs compete or as service providers. This would open doors for more opportunities domestically as well. Thus, demographic change gives India an advantage but also poses a challenge. The advantage arises from the fact that those working abroad retain their links with the country and contribute towards its growth by sharing their knowledge and wealth. The creation of jobs within the country also fosters economic growth. The challenge that this poses is the demand for quality in higher education, for, in order to take advantage of this demographic change we need to produce trained persons who are at par with global standards. The universalisation of the job market and the acceptance of Indian skills at a global level have opened up opportunities for the creation of new jobs internally. Moreover, the service sector, which is on the rise, requires trained human power at various levels. Globalisation has thus spurred the demand for quality in education as well as increased the numbers of those wanting such education. In the fifties, sixties and even in seventies, India was worried about what was called "brain drain". There was much concern about the difficulties in establishing institutional infrastructure to create skills, huge government investment and of educational subsidies. It was believed that those going abroad would not give back to India what they had gained from it. But the scenario is changing. Indians abroad have realised their strengths; they are not merely skilled workers providing support services, but are creators of wealth. The frontline innovators who start industries and companies abroad and they have started reaping unique advantages by working in both India and abroad. They do high-end work in the country of the customer but do all the preparatory tasks and linking of the processes in India. In some cases, even the high-end work and the total task is done in India and then delivered to the country of destination. As skills build up, India will have a wide range of opportunities both at the global level and domestically. Thus, the export of value-added trained human power would lead to a return flow to India of investment and jobs, thus ensuring a healthier economy.

The world demography is changing. To take advantage of this change, we need to produce trained persons, on par with global standards. The recognition of Indian graduates at the global level has led to rising aspirations among the masses in the country. The student community in the rural, semi-urban and urban areas is craving to be a part of changing India. Students not only want education in modern subjects but they want quality education which will give them an identity. They do not want to be deprived of opportunities because of their social or economic background. They want to be a part of the new revolution, which has given the pride of place to Indians globally.

The Indian economy is also on the move. It is now linked with global economy. This linkage has direct impact on our education, our science and research and development efforts. The country needs trained human resources for managing its internal affairs, be it in agriculture and related fields or small and heavy industry, telecommunication, power and water or science and technology. Today, more than ever before, thanks to the integration with the world economy, the Indian higher education system is faced with the challenge of providing skilled human-power which is confident, flexible and has the knowledge and technical skills needed to effectively confront the social and economic realities of the twenty-first century. The student community in rural, semi-urban and urban areas wants to be apart of the new economic revolution.

Interestingly, when the world is coming closer due to economic interdependency, nations are simultaneously making efforts to invent, adopt and operate modern technology in all sectors, in isolation. This means India must also remain at the frontline of science and technology. Our research laboratories, whether they belong to the Council for Scientific and Industrial Research (CSIR), Department of Atomic Energy (DAE), Department of Biotechnology (DBT), Indian Space Research Organisation (ISRO), Department of Science and Technology (DST) or Defence Research and Development Organisation (DRDO), are facing a severe shortage of good science undergraduates. This problem will be exacerbated in the coming decade and special efforts must be made to sustain and strengthen undergraduate science education. Science and technology education has to face an increasingly daunting challenge of giving our graduates sound fundamentals with skills.

ACCESS PARAMETER

- Access parameter (formal + non-formal) rose from 5.8 per cent in 1992-93 to 6.9 per cent in 1999-2000.
- Access parameter in the case of women students (formal + non-formal) rose from 4.02 per cent in 1992-93 to 5.34 per cent in 1999-2000.
- Access ratios in the case of developed countries is around 40 per cent.
- There is higher access in the case of developed countries like 59 per cent in US, 54 per cent in Canada, 33 per cent in Israel, 30 per cent in Germany, 29 per cent in Japan, 22 per cent in the UK.
- The Indian access parameter is approximately one-sixth of that of the developed countries.

India represent a major share in the world economy and hence "globalisation" has an internal meaning as well, specific to our nation. There is one more area which is going to be important in these times of globalisation and liberalisation, and that is social and human sciences and it is important to realise that "economic revolution" is too important to be left to be managed as it is at present, because it has the capacity to influence the world economy as many of India's 28 states are equal to medium-size countries in size, population and diversity. It not only involves growing dependence at the global level but states are also dependent on each other. The growing interdependence of people's lives calls for shared values and a shared commitment to the human development of all people. Thus, social sciences, which make systematic efforts to understand human relationships in organised group life by the study of verifiable aspects of human behaviour and human sciences comprising the languages and literature, the fine arts, philosophy, and history, become important. It is here that teaching, learning and research in social and human sciences has to be re-elaborated in terms of conceptualisation, formalisation, and synthesis so as to transcend the frontiers of the new world. In the modern world, it is true that highly specialised education has got its own importance. But the higher education system has to meet many different goals, one of which is to produce young minds that have developed general intellectual capacities in contrast to a professional curriculum. A general education is an excellent form of creating experts for flexible and knowledge-based careers at all tiers of the modern labour force. A general education stream may concentrate, apart from developing cognitive skills, on breadth of knowledge across a number of disciplines. General education should impart a sound and comprehensive educational foundation that contributes to broad-mindedness, critical thinking, and communication skills. These are essential elements of effective participatory democracy for an emerging nation like India. Universities need to reactivate degree programmes at a general level with the objective of developing the intellectual capacities of young minds in order to broaden their perspective.

It is little more than half a century ever since the government initiated a planned development of higher education in the country particularly with the establishment of University Grants Commission in 1953. Thus early 1950's is an important reference points from which we could look back at our progress of higher education.

An Approach to the 11th Five Year Plan is being formulated. Currently the issue of higher education is being discussed at various levels. Several issues have figured in the discussion on the higher education but among those relating to Access, Equity and Quality are the most important which have prominently figured in the discussion at various levels and for this, it is necessary to recognize that the present approach towards higher education is governed by the "National Policy on Education" of 1986 and Program of Action of 1992. The 1986 Policy and Action Plan of 1992 was based on the two land marks report namely the "University Education Commission" of 1948-49 (popularly known as Radhakrishnan Commission), and the "Education

Commission" of 1964-66, (popularly known as Kothari Commission Report). These two landmark reports in fact laid down the basic framework for the National policy for higher education in the country.

The University Education Report had set goals for development of higher education in the country. While articulating these goals Radakrishnan Commission on University Education, 1948-49 put it in following words:

> "The most important and urgent reform needed in education is to transform it, to endeavor to relate it to the life, needs and aspirations of the people and thereby make it the powerful instrument of social, economic and cultural transformation necessary for the realization of the national goals. For this purpose, education should be developed so as to increase productivity, achieve social and national integration, accelerate the process of modernization and cultivate social, moral and spiritual values."

The National Policy on higher education of 1986 translate this vision of Radhakrishnan and Kothari Commission in five principle goals for higher education which include Greater access, Equal access (or equity), Quality and excellence, Relevance and promotion of social values.

The policy directions and actions covered in 1992 "Program of Action" have been developed in a manner such that it translates these goals in to practice.

Since the early 1950's higher education has been diversified and extended its reach and coverage quite significantly. At the time of independence, 1947, the size of higher education system in terms of number of educational institutions, and teachers was meager but since that time there has been an exponential increase in three indicators of higher education, namely the number of educational institutions, teachers and students.

The number of universities has increased from 20 in 1947 to about 357 in 2005 indicating a thirteen-fold increase. There are now 20 Central Universities, 217 State Universities,

106 Deemed to be Universities, and 13 Institutes of National Importance established through Central legislation and 5 Institutions established through State legislation. The number of colleges increased from 500 in 1947 to 17,625 in 2005, indicating twenty-six-fold increase. In the spheres of technical education by 2004 we had about 1265 engineering and technology collages, 320 pharmacies, 107 Architecture, 40 hotel management, making a total about 1749 institutions. In respect of post-graduate educational institutions there are 958 MBA/PGDM and 1034 MCA in 2004. Similarly the number of teachers has increased from 700 in 1950 to 4.72 lakhs in 2005. Thus there has been spectacular increase in the educational institutions and number of teachers. With this progress in the educational infrastructure in terms of institutions and faculty, the improvement in the level of higher education in terms of aggregate access, access to disadvantage groups and the quality of higher education is quite inevitable.

The extent of higher education is generally measured by enrolment ratio in higher education. Three alternative methods are used to estimate the extent of access to higher education namely Gross Enrolment Ratio (GER), Net Enrolment Ratio (NER) and Enrolment of Eligible Ratio (EER). The GER measure the access level by taking the ratio of persons in all age groups enrolled in various programmes to total population in age group of 18 to 23. The NER measures the level of enrolment for age specific groups namely those in age group of 18 to 23. While the EER measure the level of enrolment of those who completed higher secondary level education. These three concepts thus look at the access to higher education from three different angles. There are three alternative sources namely Selected Education Statistics, (SES) National Sample Survey (NSS) and Population Census (PC) which provide data on number of student enrolment.

The undernoted data need a merit to review the past performance:

(a) In 1950-51 the enrolment rate was 0.7 per cent, which increased to 1.4 per cent in 1960-61.

(b) For the early 2000 the GER based on the SES is 8. per cent. The NSS and PC arrived at enrolment ratio of about 10 per cent and 14 per cent respectively. Thus the SES data under reports gross enrolment rate by 4-5 per cent. For 2003/4 the GER work out to 9 per cent, 13.22 per cent and 14.48 per cent respectively.

(c) The SES under estimates enrolment rates because of the under-reporting of enrolment in unrecognized institutions and also due to non-reporting of enrolment data on an annual basis by some of the State governments. Extrapolations are used to fill the gaps arising from non-reporting by some of the States. The problem with the NSS and also Census data is that as it is collected from households, it is likely to over estimate the student enrolment in colleges and universities as it might include those who are doing diploma or training programmes (e.g. computer training) in unrecognized institutions also. A further problem with the population Census data is that it does not distinguish between enrolment in professional degree and diploma programmes. The population in the age group of 18-23 and number of students enrolled in Colleges and Universities (graduate and above) and vocational institutions (Diploma/certificate). In 2003/04 the enrolment in graduate and above (degree) level is 104.9 lakhs from SES and 161.1 lakhs from NSS and 182.3 lakhs from population Census. The higher estimates from the Census may be due to the inclusion of enrolment in vocational and professional courses, which include both degree, diploma and certificate. The vocations and professions include engineering (ITI, Polytechnic), Agriculture, Medicine, Management, Law, Teaching, etc. A wide variation is observed in the estimates of enrolment in diploma/certificate courses from the three sources. The enrolment at the certificate/diploma (vocational, teacher training, etc.) level is 10 lakhs, 25 lakhs and 17 lakhs respectively from SES, NSS and Census sources. The coverage of SES in the case of degree/diploma would have been limited as it excludes enrolment in unrecognized institutions. Both NSS and Census sources include enrolment in unrecognized vocational institutions and hence the estimates turn out to be higher than the SES. As mentioned above, Census data included vocational diploma along with professional degree yielding a figure lower than the NSS.

After having assessed the progress at aggregate level, it is desirable to look at the progress with respect to certain groups and reflect on the situation with respect to inter-group disparities of multiple natures. It will be of use to study the disparities between undernoted groups:

Rural and Urban

There are significant disparities in enrolment ratio between rural and urban area. In 2003/4 the GER for rural and urban area was 7.76 per cent and 27.20 per cent respectively—GER in urban area being four times higher compared with rural area. The population Census came up with the GER of 8.99 per cent for rural area and 24.52 per cent for urban area in 2001—the GER in rural area being all most three time lower compared with urban area. The EER worked out to 51.1 per cent for rural and 66 per cent for urban area-latter being higher by about 15 per cent points.

Inter-State Variation

There are considerable inter-state variation in the level of higher education. While the GER at aggregate level is about 13 per cent, it is more than national average in state like Nagaland (38.6%), Goa (27.3%), Kerala (24.2%), Manipur (24.7%), H.P. (20.0%) and J&K, T.N. and Pondicherry (with 18%).

By national comparison the GER is lower than the national average in state like Tripura (3.2%), Assam (6.6%), Meghalaya (7.2%), Chhattisgarh (7.6%), Orissa (8.2%), Jharkhand (10.3%), West Bengal (9.7%), Bihar (10%), Sikkim

(10.8%), and Rajasthan (11%). The enrolment ratio based on eligible student (ERE) is useful estimate as it indicates the access to education to those who have completed the higher secondary stage. In 2003/4 about 59 per cent of those who completed higher secondary entered in higher education stream. This ratio is higher than the national average by substantial margin in Mizoram (87.1%), Manipur (87.7%), Nagaland (85.6%), J&K (76.6%) and Kerala (70.6%). By national comparison the ratio is much lower, in Tripura (37.8%), Chhattishgarh (49.6%), Orissa (50.2%), Arunachal Pradesh (53.5%). In rest of the major states the ratio was around national average of 59 per cent.

POLICY MEASURES ANNOUNCED IN THE ANNUAL BUDGET FOR THE YEAR 2008-09

1. The total allocation for the education sector (including NER) will be increased by 20 per cent from Rs. 28,674 crore in 2007-08 to Rs. 34,400 crore in 2008-09.
2. Focussed attention on Sarva Shiksha Abhiyan (SSA). The focus will be shifted from access and infrastructure at the primary level to enhancing retention, improving quality of learning and ensuring access to upper primary classes.
3. Strengthening the set-up of Jawahar Navodaya Vidyalayas and Kasturba Gandhi Balika Vidyalayas.
4. Setting up of Institutes of Higher Education. The Finance Minister has stated in his Budget Speech for 2008-09 that knowledge is power. It is knowledge that will drive success in the 21st Century. India has opportunity to become a knowledge society. As per the announcement made by the Prime Minister, an IIM at Shillong; three IISERs at Mohali, Pune and Kolkata; and an IIT at Kanchipuram have started functioning. Government will establish on Central University in each of the hitherto uncovered States. It has been proposed to make a beginning in 2008-09 by

establishing 16 Central Universities. Besides it is also proposed to set-up three IITs in Andhra Pradesh, Bihar and Rajasthan; two IISERs at Bhopal and Tiruvananthapur and two Schools of Planning and Architecture at Bhopal and Vijayawada. More institutes of higher education, as promised by the Prime Minister, will be established during the Eleventh Plan Period.

5. The children are to be encouraged to take careers in Science and Research and Development. Ministry of Science and Technology will introduce a scheme call Innovation In Science Pursuit for Inspired Research (INSPIRE) that will include Scholarships for young learners (10-17 years), Scholarships for continuing Science Education (17-22 years), and opportunities for Research Careers (22-32 years). The Finance Minister has provided Rs. 85 crores in 2008-09 for this inspired contribution to building a knowledge society.
6. A proposal has been made in the Budget Speech for 2008-08 to make a grant of Rs. 5 crore to the Deccan College Post-Graduate and Research Institute, Pune which is one of the oldest institutions of modern learning in India.
7. The recommendations of National Knowledge Commission submitted from time to time have active consideration. Some of them have been incorporated in Eleventh Plan. Government has accepted an important recommendation to interconnect all knowledge institutions through an electronic digital broadband network. This will encourage sharing of resources and collaborative research and an amount of Rs. 100 crore has been provided to the Ministry of Information and Technology for establishing the National Knowledge Network.

CONCLUSION

Education has its own importance in the all round

development of a country and for which, a well knit policy framework is also of utmost importance. India being a vast country and some of its 28 States are bigger in size, demography, cultural variations than some of the countries in the world. In the wake of globalisation, liberalization and financial sector reforms, there are a plethora of challenges as well opportunities in the world for which there is a need for job specific education in the various fields, viz., Humanities; Science and Technology and various areas of Management. The industry specific education should be imparted to the students at higher level for which there need for co-ordination at various levels in various Ministries for curriculum-development.

For funding of educational programmes, though it has become imperative to resort to the participation of Corporates but at the same time, it should be ensured that the education does not become costly so that students from most of the areas and communities may be benefited. It should also be ensured that there is no commodification of education as is happening in most of the educational institutions in the areas of Management and Engineering where there has been mushroom like growth in the recent past.

As regards the assistance to students by Banks and other financial institutions, it has been the experience that the private institutions have drastically increased their fees due to more and more students joining these institutions after taking loans from the Banks, etc. This, therefore, leads to a conclusion that indirectly instead of students, the educational institutions have benefited from these loans.

As regards placement of the pass outs from various institutions, it has been the experience that there is no uniform policy and much depends upon the maneuvering capacity of the institutions. It is not that all the pass outs of a particular institution only may be best as compared to the other institutions. There is, therefore, a need for some policy that representation of almost all the institutions be made in the placement and if there is poor or NIL placement record of any institution, corrective steps should be taken by the University/AICTE, etc. so that these institutions try to come up with required standards to cope up with the universal job market requirements.

References

Higher Education in India: by Sukhdeo Thorat: Nehru Memorial Lecture.

Web sites of the University Grants Commission, AICTE and other various educational institutions.

Website of the World Bank and World Bank Institute.

Annual Budgets of India of various years.

Annual Economic Reviews presented by the Finance Minister.

Indian Higher Education and Tribals

B.N. Ghosh and P.K. Bose

The constitution of India had promised the tribals of India protection against exploitation, respect for their tradition and heritage, assistance for the improvement of their socio-economic and educational status. Ironically, despite constitutional grantee the tribals have been the most adversely effected ethnic group by the so-called big development projects. Development has become synonymous with deprivation, breeding discontent.

The tribals constitute about 8 per cent of the Indian population; there are about 212 scheduled tribes in India. The constitution of India promised several protective measures for the well-being of the tribals. Article 46 assured educational and economic benefits and protection against social injustice and exploitation. Article 335 promised reservation in recruitment.

The last four decades of development in India though dams, factories and mines have made the tribals victims and refugees of development. W. Fernandes has rightly remarked that national development and tribal deprivation have become synonymous.

Recent events like the *Narmada Bachao Andolan* leaders' efforts to create public opinion against a project that will deprive more that a lakh persons, about two-thirds of them tribals, of their livelihood, the Jharkhand movement in Chhotanagpore, the anti-land alienation agitation in the South, the Boroland struggle in the North East and similar conflicts have thus come to symbolize many other struggles elsewhere in India against the type of natural development that impoverishes the tribals and other communities living in the resource-rich regions. Most of the struggles are also a search of a new identity at a time when tribal peoples are feeling alienated from their culture because of the threat to the natural resources around which they had built their cultural, economic and political structures.

For Scheduled Tribes education is an input not only for their economic development, but also for promoting in them-self, confidence and inner strength to face new challenges. In the Indian constitution a great deal of emphases is laid on the spread of education amongst scheduled castes and Schedule Tribes. It is worthwhile to note that education increased at a faster rate amongst Scheduled Tribes than in the general population. For example, while among the general population the percentage of literacy increased from 0.7 in 1931 to 8.54 in 1961 and 11.30 in 1971 to 16.35 in 1981. It is interesting to note that while in the case of the general population the increase in the percentage of literacy in 1971 over that 1961 was 27.30, the same figure for Scheduled Tribes was 32.3. According to 1981 Census, the percentage of literacy rate in the sub-plan area of Bihar was 27.2 (higher than the general literacy of Bihar according to 1981 Census) against the all India rate of 36.17 per cent.

Thus the pace of increase in literacy amongst the Scheduled Tribes during the period 1961-71 had been faster than the growth of literacy among the general population but the fact remains that literacy among these communities has not reached the level of satisfaction.

While British India did not give any reservation to the Scheduled Tribes, the Indian constitution provided them reservation in services and educational institutions. The working of these provisions has benefited much in this regard. While their representation was almost zero in ICS in pre-independence days, a substantial number of them are now in IFS, IAS, IPS and Allied services of our nation. 5.2 per cent Scheduled Tribes were represented in IAS, 3.4 per cent in IPS, 2.5 per cent in IAAS Services as on 1st January, 1980.

Though there is no clear reservation policy in universities, yet during 1975-80 in the 112 Universities, out of 2748 there were 20 Professors belonging to Scheduled Castes/ Scheduled Tribes which is 0.7 per cent. In the case of Readers their representation was 0.6 and in the post-of lecturers their percentage was 0.9 per cent.

Lack of an integrated approach to tribal education has finally proved to be a disaster despite a considerable investment towards this end by the welfare Government of India. It is commonly observed that institutions of various types governed by various bodies with their own teaching curriculum and standards have been allowed to undertake and continue the task of education in tribal pockets. This created utter confusion and may be due to an absence of proper coordination between various ministries responsible for streamlining tribal education in India. This fact becomes clear from the following excerpts of the ST and STC report: That ministry (of Education), while it accepted its responsibility for the education of tribal children explained that it had so far left the matter to the Ministry of Home Affirms which was chiefly concerned with tribal problems. It was stated to us that the Ministry of Home Affairs and the Ministry of Education had not had any occasion to discuss the question of a proper system of education, for tribal children. This is hardly understandable.

Further, a state of confusion and a feeling of subjugation pervade the minds of the tribal children due to the systems of education that they undergo. Right from the pre-primary stage a tribal child is forced to a learn an alien language of the state, about an 'alien' cultural symbols prescribed in the text books and by a teacher from an 'alien' cultural background. A tribal child finds it hard to compromise and hence, prefers to stay away from the school. Those who even complete their schooling, land up in a situation of complete perplexity. Education without a vocational backing creates frustration among the educated unemployed tribal youth, which breeds discontent and promotes developing an attitude of anti-establishment. They become an immediate victim of any radical political ideology and remain a great social challenge. Invariably they reset against the traditional authorities in their own societies and break the tribal solidarity.

Contrary to the expectations of many, tribalism today has become a potential deterrent force in the process of national integration in India, which is virtually reduced to a mere political slogan. The reasons lie at a great historical depth. The isolationistic colonial and post-Independence policies were highly conducive to promote primordial loyalties among the tribals and to make them apprehensive to the rest of India. On the other hand, language planning, educational policy and development effort could not be properly geared so as to integrate them with the national mainstream. Large scale exploitation and perpetual indifference naturally provoked consolidation of tribal socio-cultural identities and prompted tribal separatism.

Education in the post-Independence India has failed to be an agent of social mobility. It has been "the god that failed" because the benefits of educational development, as indeed of other developmental sectors have been usurped by handful of upper strata of the Indian society. Education has almost completely by-passed the lower socio-economic strata touching tangentially only a few of them. Education, embedded, as it is in the capitalistic Indian politico-economic structure, has proved to be the god that failed to emancipate the poverty-stricken Indian masses.

There has been a growing discontent among the tribals: Generally three kinds of explanations have been offered for the tribal discontent. These are: (i) conspiracy-oriented, (ii) exploitation-oriented, and (iii) development-oriented.

The conspiracy-oriented theory has tried to explain tribal discontent in Jharkhand and Bihar similar to the explanations of separatist movements of North-East tribal dominated states, particularly Nagaland and Khalistan Movement in the Punjab. The main contention of this theory is that certain Western powers do not want to be economically and militarily a strong nation mainly because of India's non-aligned foreign policy. The Western nations, particularly America has therefore, consistently taken a pro-Pakistani attitude against India and has supported dictators in Pakistan, against the democratic Indian government. It is true that on sensitive issue of Kashmere, India has never received support from Western capitalistic nations. It is also true that Christian-dominated Nagaland evoked sympathies during its insurgency and the leader of the separist movement, Phizo had received political asylum in England. It is also evident that Pakistan, with the help of America has been giving training to terrorists of the Khalistan movement.

The Christian missionaries, despite their impressive humanitarian work particularly in the areas of education and health, have been contemptuous of Hindu religion and society beginning from Miss Mayo.

The unfriendly foreign countries may have tried to use the Christian missionaries and the Bengal intellectuals to foment the separatist tendencies in the tribals of South Bihar by utilizing the illiteracy and backwardness of the tribal population and their exploitation by the non-tribals. Though there may be an element of truth in the conspiracy theory, the tribal discontent and the support for the social and economic justice for the tribal population by many tribals is also an expression of genuine sympathy for the legitimate rights of the tribal population. The tribal population even after five decades of Independence are the most backward community in the country, the poorest, the most illiterate and unhealthy. The socio-economic backwardness of the tribal community is despite the fact that the constitution of India has offered safeguards for their education, welfare and development.

The tribal discontent as a result of their economic exploitation has been argued by Munda. He has pointed out that the region of Chhotanagpur contributes 70 per cent of the revenue of the State and receives back only 20 per cent. Only 5 per cent of the total land in Chhotanagpur is irrigated as against 50 per cent of the rest of the State Land alienation and job deprivatation are the two other main reasons for the tribal discontent which Munda has emphasized. Land alienation of the tribals around Ranchi has been documented by Sinha Mishra has argued that for the tribals, land is more dear than life.

The development-oriented theory of tribal discontent tries to explain it as a natural social process of political change and educational development. Singh found that education, aspirations, industrial and urban exposure and political participation were positively correlated with social and political discontent in tribal workers. He found that higher the education, the greater the industrial and urban exposure, higher the aspirations and socio-political modernity, greater were political participation and socio-political discontent. This pattern was common to both tribal and non-tribal workers.

The tribals are the most backward ethnic group in India in relation to the main indicators of development: education, health and income. Their status is even worse than that of the scheduled castes, another backward group, with constitutional protection. Because of their extreme backwardness, the tribals become a natural national concern. They constitute 8 per cent of the total Indian population but in certain parts of the country they have a very substantial number and in some parts they constitute the majority of the population. Despite of their extreme backwardness, they have shown a spirit of rebellion against exploitation and injustice from the British Raj to the present Indian Government. The Indian social psychology have not offered any objective data-based explanation of tribal psychologies, protest and dissent. Neither the conspiracy theory, nor the exploitation theory adequately explain the tribal situation in Jharkhand. The development theory attempts to explain tribal discontent in Jharkhand as a result of a combination of several factors: increasing education and mass media exposure, industrialization and urbanization, aspiration and a sense of relative deprivation and political participation.

A UNESCO preamble states that wars originate in the minds of men and therefore the defenses of peace should be built there. Accepting the truism, the attitude of the people of India should change towards the tribal.

References

Singh, A.K., Tribal Development in India.
Singh, K.S., The Scheduled Tribes, Vol. III.
Fernandes, W. (ed.), National Development and tribal deprivation.
Sharma, B.D., Tribal Development: The Concept and the Frame.
United Nations 1987, Indigenous Peoples, ILO Convention, 107.

6

Higher Education in India: An Analysis

R.U. SINGH AND SANGEETA

"I wish to see a revolution in the field of modern education in the next few years. My fervent desire that India becomes a fully educated, modern, progressive nation. From the Red Fort, I would like this massage to go to every corner of India. We will make India a nation of educated people, of skilled people, of creative people." It was the Prime Minister's address to the nation from the Red Fort on Independence Day, 2007.

Education is a pre-requisite for empowering people. Empowerment of people means developing them as individuals who are politically active, economically productive and independent and are able to make informed choices and intelligent decisions in matters that affect them and their nation. Education can serve as a powerful instrument for individuals to achieve upward social and economic mobility and achieve power and status in society. It is a source of mobility, equality and empowerment both at the individual and at the societal level. Education inspires people to advance on all fronts. It helps individuals to be more aware of their constitutional and legal rights and of the opportunities available for them to live better. Education also helps people to evolve as workers, citizens and human beings.

Education shapes the destiny of mankind. The quality of life in-depth can not be achieved unless the human society is empowered with input of knowledge and progress of the mind, spirit through developmental process of science and technology. Education also plays a very important role for character building and developments. This can be achieved better through contacts with universal faces. Education does not teach to accept human as negative tools of hammering upon disastrous conditions of mankind. But a forceful component that inspires human to promote vision to liberate the society from curse of poverty and slavery to the dicatates of ruthless concept of mankind (Varma, P.L.).[1] An illiterate person can hardly be expected to enter into a rational economic transaction on the basis of calculation of cost, price and profit. Literacy and education help to improve the skill of a person.

They have a large and significant impact of growth of productivity. Modern technology is easily adopted by the educated. Spread of technology depends on the earning potential and motivation that are linked to the development of former schooling. Educational attainment and literacy have another important role in the society as the positively affect efficiency in resource allocation, leading to higher income and more equal distribution of such income (Kishore, C. Samal).[2] Actually, economic reforms and educational reforms should go hand in hand. Whether we can provide facilities so that the poor can exercise this right should be the primary responsibility of all economic and educational reforms.

WTO AND HIGHER EDUCATION

Today every aspect of higher education is decided and shaped by the market forces of demand supply and profitability. The concerns are now related to the profitability of a particular course, with an eye on the job market. The teaching-learning process has become mechanical and pragmatic. The entry of the private sector has necessitated marketing of higher education. Export of the education services from India has become an important source of earning foreign exchange. The Australian Government accepts that revenue from education is worth as much as wool and more than wheat, thereby highlighting its importance. In USA educational exports were fifth largest service sector exports in 1998, and were valued at $11.7 billion (NAFSA, 2000). According to an estimate Britain could earn up to £ 13 billion by 2020 from export of educational, which has become an important export industry in the country. Other important countries exporting education are New Zealand, Canada and Germany.

TABLE I

Leading Exporters of Tertiary Education in the World

S. No.	*Host Country*	*Year*	*Total No. of Students*	*% of total export*
1.	U.S.A.	1995-96	453,785	29
2.	U.K.	1996-97	198,839	13
3.	Germany	1996-97	165,977	10
4.	France	1995-96	138,191	9
5.	Australia	1997	102,284	6
6.	Canada	1993-94	35,451	2
	Total		1094527	69

Source: Adapted form UNESCO 1997, 1999.

In the above table we find that these six countries account for almost 70 per cent of total tertiary level educational exports in the world. Asia is the most important market for transnational or cross-border education which account for 76 per cent of students in Australia, 64 per cent in USA, and more than one-third in UK and Germany. The Global Student Mobility 2025 estimates that there are 2 million students who study outside their home country. This is expected to grow more than three times, to 7.2 million in 2025, with Asia dominating total Global demand at 70 per cent. Foreign students from the Asia-Pacific region in tertiary institutions in OECD Countries and USA in 2001 has been shown in the table ahead. The largest source countries are China, Korea, India and Japan. With growing importance of globally mobile labour, business and knowledge, foreign education particularly in the provider nation is considered advantageous. America and Europe to Asia, while the flow of people in the reverse direction. Of the foreign students from Asia-Pacific in higher education in OECD countries, 44.3 per cent went to United States, 12.5 per cent to Australia and 11.3 per cent to UK. Approximately 71.8 per cent were enrolled in English-speaking systems. (IEA, Vol. 2005).[3]

TABLE 2

Foreign Students in Tertiary Education from Asia-Pacific Region in OECD Countries, 2001 and United States, 2000-01

Country origin	*No. of students in*	*Proportion of OECD Nation all foreign students in*	*Students in US degree granting Institutions OECD Nations*
China	124000	8.5	59900
Korea	70523	4.8	45700
India	61179	4.2	54700
Japan	55041	3.8	46500
Malaysia	32709	2.2	8100
Indonesia	26615	1.8	11600
Hong Kong	23261	1.6	7800
Singapore	19514	1.3	
Thailand	18172	1.2	11200
Pakistan	10478	0.7	

Source: OECD, 2003a; Skelton, 2003.

Export of education, and removing barriers to its emphasized in GATS. USA has put proposals before Egypt, India, Mexico, Philippines and Thailand at GATS negotiations in January 2004 regarding removal of prohibitions on joint ventures (in higher education) with local partners. According to survey by Education World (2001) on reasons for study aboard of 1000 undergraduate international students in USA, UK and Australia from ten major Asian sources China, Hong Kong, India, Indonesia, Japan, Malaysia, Singapore, Korea, Chinese Taipei and Thailand, has brought forth the various responses.

In considering the choice of destination, the key choice factors were country (54%) course (18%) institution (17%) and city (10%). Three-quarter of the students had friend or relatives in the country of study, international study was financed by the family in 87 per cent of cases, followed by students self-financing (8%) and government scholarships (4%).

INDIAN HIGHER EDUCATION SYSTEM

The Indian Higher Education System has undergone a tremendous transformation from elite system, nurtured by colonial roots to a mass system attempt to meet the demands of a vibrant democracy. But it is still continued to be considered as a social service rather than a trade service. Learning is considered to be an excellence of wealth that none can destroy and which cannot be attained by chance. The educational system in India passed through three main eras viz. *Gurukul* era, British era and Independence era. In the 'Gurukuls', the main objective was to provide overall personality development of the pupil. This concept of education still prevails in India. During the British era, emphasis was on training a class of people qualified by their intelligence and morality for employment in the civil administration of India. Efforts were made to make natives of the country thoroughly good English Scholars. The promotion of European literature and science amongst the people of India was emphasized during British era. The whole education system was tailored to suit the needs of the British regime, making the system more or less elitist in nature.

The independent India had started its journey on a social philosophical base of education with the Nehruvian approach. The rapid course of globalization has started transforming that to an individualized philosophical base. On account of that the national objective has now shifted from the establishment of an egalitarian social order to the encouragement of technological innovation, increased efficiency and maximization of profits. Public investment in areas like health and education has been drastically cut to hand them over to the private parties. Hence, the state sponsored education is being fetched out and replaced by privatized education. Education under globalization is no more a social product for social consumption rather it is a private product for private consumption (Pathy, M.K.).[4] It is argued that elementary and mass education is the first condition for a healthy global economy and thus, this sector of education warrants larger share of investment than the other two viz., secondary and higher education.

Every Nation around the world provides higher education for human resource development to man about its industry, science and technology and socio-economic development. In this regard, India is no exception the such provision, higher education institutions in the country have rapidly expanded after Independence. Today, there are 254 university level institutions and 7929 colleges. Further, there are 86 lakh students in degree colleges and 36 lakh students in Professional courses. This system is considered for India as one of the largest in the world's higher education.

CHALLENGES FOR HIGHER EDUCATION

GATS and Globalization has thrown new challenges to the Indian educational institutions. The Indian education system needs to adopt the emerging technologies in order to face the challenges. The challenges faced by the Indian educational institutions are multidimensional. Some of them are as follows:

The major risk in the globalised world is country risk, arising out of intrusion and investment characterized by political, financial and economic uncertainties. The already widening global inequality will be further fuelled by educational inequality in appropriating opportunities. Where the role of market becomes paramount and rural development turns out to be the kingpin of development of India. Globalisation of education has a potential danger for developing country like India as inequalities are likely to be accentuated with the developed countries becoming stronger and dominant. Higher education will become commercialized and values of the market place will dominate university campuses.

The globalization of education under GATS is thus posing serious threats before the conventional system of higher education in India.

Social Relevance in higher education should be evaluated in terms of the fitness between what society except from institutions of higher education and what they actually do to the society as a whole. In the Indian scenario relevance has assumed importance because of the high rate of unemployment and unrest amongst educated youths. The need of reconciling the new global emphasis on the market economy with the United Nations pronouncement on promoting sustainable economic and social development and the survival of its human population at an adequate level of the quality of life, demand a whole range of skills from all the disciplines such as social humanities and professionals to their application in the economic development and having adequate field based on experience to enhance knowledge with the skill and develop appropriate attitudes in the context of social Progress and prosperity. Economic development with social justice can be covered by higher education like the problems of distribution of natural resources as income and wealth producing assets, food availability and distribution and underemployment and unemployment problems of rural development, labour intensive as well as well capital demanding technologies, appropriate distribution between small medium and large manufacturing industries. The population problems of infant mortality, morbidity, health care, growing disparities and poverty ratio, gender discrimination, social and communal harmony incidence of child labour, etc. Social relevance of education will have to be evolved by keeping all these socio-economic problems. The crucial role of higher education in fostering development in increasing the knowledge base and specifically in contributing to economic development is well recognised by policy-makers. There is need to support, strengthen and expand the education system, so as to ensure—both quantity and quality for rapid socio-economic transition.

Funding of higher education is another vital issue. As quality of higher education, depends largely on two factors; quality of teaching and avilability of required infrastructure. Both these factors, in turn, depend largely upon the availability of funds with universities. If universities do not find themselves in a position to provide attractive salaries and perks to teachers, the best of the lot could not attract to university jobs. Similarly, development of appropriate infrastucture for quality education also call for massive investment. The state's resources for higher education have become grossly inadequate. Most universities in the State have been starving for funds. It is high time the Government should shun its callous attitude towards higher education. The government must devise ways and means to provide adequate resources for higher learning, to enable them to grow and contribute to the multidimensional growth of the state.

Politicisation of higher education is yet another serious malady. In developed countries, public sources for educational funding in 1991 was 99 per cent in Denmark, 98 per cent in Netherlands, 93 per cent in Ireland, 90 per cent in Canada, and 78.6 per cent in USA. Among low and middle income countries, it was 89 per cent in India, 62.8 per cent in Indonesia and 62.2 per cent in Kenya (World Bank, 1995, p. 54). Thus low and middle income group countries have lower public outlays on education. But, in order to overcome the financial crisis, it is essential to enhance public resources by increasing budgetary and plan allocations on education. Indian higher education public allocations is 1/10 of the American higher education. Although the National Policy on Education, 1986 revised in 1992 had promised to commit 6 per cent of the GDP to spend on education sub-committee of Central Education Advisiory Board (CEAB) has also recommended in 2005 that public expenditure on education should be 6 per cent of GDP in India. Manmohan Government has kept an agenda to increase public expenditure on education 6 per cent of GDP in Common Minimum Programme but yet it is to be implemented. The Tenth Five Year Plan has proposed to increase education budget expendiute over in the Ninth plan by 76 per cent. It is pertinent to mention here as according to very strong recommendation made by Justice Dr. D.K. Punnayya Committee appointed by UGC that the govermment cannot give up its responsibility to the Higher Education sector. The state must continuue to accept the major responsibility for funding the essential maintenance and development requirement of the universities and therefore, the financial crisis must be sorted out by increasing the public resources. Payment from the users can also be increased as a solution to this problem.

Annual Tuition Fees for Undergraduate Courses

(Amount in Dollar)

Country	*Arts*	*Science*
India	2,000-2,600	2,000-5,000
Australia	5,400-8,600	8,000-10,500
U.K.	8,100-16.200	8,100-17,150
USA (public)	7,000-10,000	7,000-10,000
USA (private)	16,000-20,000	16,000-20,000
Canada	2,700-9,400	2,300,9,400
Holland	1,200–onward	–
Singapore	3,900-3,600	
Singapore		10,200

The Committee further said that the universities will increase their earning within period of 10 years by about 25 per cent, it should be 15 to 20 per cent of the cost of education from the students through fees. Another 5 to 10 per cent could be generated by the universites through other internal sources. The Central Education Advisory Board (CEAB) also decided that students' tuition fee collection will be 20 per cent for the total expenditure on education. It is worth mentioning that even in the USA students fee is of 25 per cent, in China it is 10 per cent and in Japan 5 per cent (World Bank, 1994, p. 42) while in India, it is less than 3 per cent, although at the time of independence it was 20 per cent.

Thus it is clear that the students' tuition fee level in India is lower than Australia, U.K., USA. Canada, Holland and Singapore also as indicated in the above table. So there is great scope to increase the tuition fees in the institutions of higher education.

In countries of the OCED (Organisation for Economic Cooperation and Development) public sources of funding was, in 2001, as high as 99 per cent in Denmark, 98 per cent in the Netherlands and 90 per cent in Canada, 78 per cent in USA and 89 per cent in India. Cost sharing between Government and beneficiaries is a relatively new suggestion.

SUGGESTIONS

The institutes of higher education in India, till now, have not set any clear goals in higher education. Now, under the fast globalization of higher education under GATS (General Agreement on Trade Services) there is a need to review the present dimensions of higher education and provide directions with clear goals for achievements. In different areas of higher education, we have strengths as well as weaknesses. How much of our higher education should be committed to GATS depends on our strengths, the level of preparedness of higher education in different branches of higher education. In this connection, following suggestions my be helpful:

(i) Produce a large number of technocrats so that no field of activity should suffer from lack of manpower.

(ii) Develop higher education and human resources in order to pave way for economic development.

(iii) Create a level of excellency in students that should be directly reflected in their achievements so that there is more demand for them in India and abroad.

(iv) Mobilize resources in the universities towards financial self-sufficiency through consultancy, patenting and other contractual services.

(v) The share of expenditure on education must be raised to the recommended level of 6 per cent from the present level of around 3 per cent.

(vi) The quality of higher education is very poor as assessed by the NAAC. So all steps should be taken to improve the quality of education by replacing outmoded methods of teaching and material with modern methods and materials.

(vii) To prevent inequalities from increasing, the government should provide liberal scholarships and loans to deserving poor students.

(viii) With respect to foreign education provided in India, the government should give permission to educational institutions only when they meet certain requirements for maintenance of a minimum standard.

(ix) Creation of global environment on campuses so that our students may have international outlook to deal with issues of their concern.

(x) Our own socio-cultural heritage should be preserved along with the acceptance of international exposure and technological advancement.

CONCLUSION

Higher education in the present context is facing with many challenges. Issues and debates are raised from time to time regarding autonomy of premier institutions and universities, fee hikes, reservations of seats, industry-academy interface, role of regulatory bodies such as UGC/AICTE/ NAAC, declining students' interest in traditional courses, lack of funds for infrastructure, political interference in day-to-day functioning of universities, etc. The situation has become dismal because in the last decade, the government funding of higher education in science, technology, engineering, medicine, etc. requires huge investments in infrastructure, all of which cannot be recovered through student fees. Not only poor funding, government funded colleges and universities are suffering from decades of government neglect, frequent ban on faculty recruitments, and promotions, reduction in library budget, lack of investments in modernization leading to obsolescence of equipments and infrastructure.

Another challenge is the entry of foreign universities. Due to GATS, foreign universities are fast making inroads into the country's educational system. This has undoubtedly enhanced competence but at the same time, these factors have put at stake the fate of many state funded institutions that have been regarded as centres of excellence engaged in promoting quality research and knowledge generation.

The higher education has been converted into merit good from public good. It has given birth to commercialization of education which is another major fallout of privatization that the resulted in mushrooming of private institutions, running self-financed courses, coaching institutes, charging high fees, making a fast back, depriving the vast rural youth to the benefits of higher education. On account of commercialization and marketization, higher educational institutions are fast converting into seats of imparting information rather than producing knowledge and learning. Teachers have been converted into tutors and teaching into coaching. The crucial issues of equity, relevance and governance are still unsolved. Thus Indian higher education is at crossroads.

After focusing upon prospects and challenges of higher education, paper concludes that to make India a knowledge destination, government must give top priority to the higher education and research. The government is responsible to ensure the access, quality and equity in higher education as for the future of the country, these cannot be leff upon market forces. Recently, a committee appointed by the MHRD, has also assigned the responsibility of higher education to state. If the present government stick on its resolution of 6 per cent expenditure of GDP on education and allocate the resources suggested by the Tapas Mazumdar Committee, the problems of funds can easily be solved. It also requires effective and optimum use of the resources. In case of scarcity of resources, the teaching fee can be raised upto a reasonable degree (as suggested by the Punnaiah Committee), Government should redefine the higher education as a public/meritorious desirous and economically backward students at an affordable cost. Excellence in educational standards should be maintained. Equity based educational loans can also be provided to the economically backward students. Private Universities and colleges should be checked and reviewed periodically by the competent authorities, representatives of students, parents, media, etc.

Notes and References

1. Varma, P.L.: "Globalisation and Impact on Human Development with a Focus on Education.
2. Kishor, C. Samal: "Equity and Financing Education in NIEPA (Ed.).
3. Indian Economic Conference Volume 2005.
4. Pathy, M.K.: "Globalisation: The Threat Perceptions to Equality of Educational Opporturnities."
5. Singh, L.P. (2001): Bihar at the Cross Road, *Hindustan Times*, Milestone, August.
6. *Bihar Economic Journal*, Conf. Vol. 2005, Prabhu, K. Seeta (1994), The Budget and Structural Adjustment with Human Face, *Economic and Political Weekly*, 26 April.
7. Singh, J. (2004), Education and Human Resource Development, Deep & Deep Publications Pvt. Ltd., Delhi.

Tribal Women in Higher Education: Problems and Prospects

Baij Nath Singh

Tribal development is one of the prime concerns of our constitution which provides clear goals. Since independence several development strategies and structures have involved for all round development of these people. They are indigenous and real setters of India. They live generally in hill area where scenic forest stretched and rich natural resources are available. In India there are 257 tribal communities according to Census report 1991. They are mainly *Munda, Uraon, Santhali, Toda, Kota, Paniyas, Kurumbas, Irulas, Kattu, Naykkas, sholagas, Malayali's tribals, Van gujjar, Akawe, Chisak, Dual, Machi, Ambeg, Metabeng, Chibok, Ruga, Ganching, Atong and Megam*, etc. Under the Constitution of India certain tribe communities have been specified as scheduled tribes (ST) and they are given special treatment and facilities envisaged under the Constitution. Scheduled Tribes from one of the most backward class of our country. Though there has been gradual increase in their literacy rates since independence, the present position is far from satisfaction. According to our Constitution, every one has fundamental right to be educated. Therefore, all sections of the society whether advantaged or disadvantaged, rich or poor, gifted and handicapped, rural or urban, male or female, tribal or general must be provided with educational opportunities. But even now in our society, the creamy layer of people enjoys all educational facilities. So there is a need to provide special care and educational opportunities to this weaker section. The tribal female literacy is much less than female of general and female of scheduled castes also. If it is compared with rural and urban than education level of urban people are more than rural people. Unfortunately most of the tribal women live in rural area.

India has broad base of higher education with a few, very sporadic peaks. These are few professional institutions and unitary universities that border on centres of excellence. But they are too few for a country of this size. At the time of independence in 1947, the size of higher education system in terms of educational institutions and number of teachers was very small but since that time onwards there has been exponential increase in higher education. The number of universities has increased from 20 in 1947 to about 357 in 2005 indicating a seventeen-fold increase. There are now 20 central universities, 216 state universities, 102 deemed universities, 5 institutions established through state legislation and 113 institutions of national importance established through central legislation. The number of colleges increased from 500 in 1947 to 17,625 in 2005 (including 1700 women colleges) in the country indicating thirty-five-fold increase. But Japan relatively small country has 684 universities, 512 of them private. The United States has 2,364 universities, 1752 of them private. Germany has 330 universities, United Kingdom 104 universities and 231 autonomous institutions that can award degrees.

In the Sphere of technical education by 2004 we had about 1265 engineering and technology colleges, 320 pharmacies, 107 architecture, 40 hotel management, 958 MBA and 1034 MCA Institutions in this country. The number of teachers had increased from 700 in 1950 to 4.72 lakh in 2005. The number of teachers increased by six hundred seventy-four-fold. Thus there has been several-fold increase in the educational infrastructure in terms of institutions and faculty. We expect improvement in the level of higher education in terms of aggregate access, access to disadvantage groups and the quality of higher education. The national policy on higher education of 1986 translate the vision of Radha Krishnan and Kothari Commission in five principal goals of higher education which include greater access, equal access or equity, quality and excellence, relevance and value-based education.

With the introduction of new pattern of education the number of tribal girls enrolled in Secondary classes increased, tribal girls generally got this level education after the Secondary educational they like to enrol in diploma certificate classes. It has increased very fastly in recent years. However, there is substantial decrease in number of tribal girls enrolled in higher education during this era. It may be due to either of two possible reasons: (i) absence of facilities for the higher education in rural area where tribal population is concentrated, (ii) Parents want early earnings by their ward, so they are not ready to enrol their girls for excess time taking courses in colleges and universities education. Although only a negligible number of tribal girls are enrolled in post-graduate degree courses. The enrolment of tribal girls in graduation degree course is not adequate.

However, this change may be due to an increasing awakening among some of the scheduled tribes population about the importance of education and consequent increase in the utilization of special government assistance, especially by the relatively privileged among them but this is also fact that tribal persons do not have adequate incentives and resources to educate their girls. The technical education among tribal girls is nil.

Government Initiatives to Promote tribal Education during the last four decades, the governments both at the state and centre levels have been adopting various special measures for the educational development of tribals.

- Various incentives and special facilities such as setting up college building and hostels are some of the measures taken by government to motive and facilitate their participation in higher education.

- The central government in some tribal states adopted flexible policies and norms for establishing central universities and appointment of teachers from local people who have minimum required qualification.
- Tribal Welfare Department has special provision of assistance to the college going schedule tribe students. It is distributed through college administration among tribal girls also.

With these provisions tribal women are facing some challenges in higher education.

PROBLEMS

To impart education to the make tribal and to successful the different programmes for the development of education which are running out by the government, there are so many impediments which stand on the way such as—

Lower Enrolment Rate

First and foremost, the factor of extreme poverty operates as a check on educational growth in tribals area. Due to this they prefer to send their ward to earn some wages rather than send them to colleges. There is positive relation between poverty and lower college enrolment rate. In India enrolment ratio in higher education is 9.2 per cent but tribal women 3.5 per cent, which is much lower than developed countries. The proportion of relevant age group (18-23) entering in higher education was in 2000 the United States 80 per cent, Canada 88 per cent, Australia 80 per cent, Finland 74 per cent and United Kingdom 52 per cent. In general, the advance countries have more than 50 per cent of the relevant age group in university level education. How a Indian tribal woman can compete in international market of education.

Social Attitudes

In general tribal family, girls give every kind of help to their mothers in work at home. They have to clean the houses, collect the safe drinking water and dry wood for fuel to make the meals and fodder for animals. These works are so tedious due to hilly area. During the agriculture season they work in field with their parents. Even tribal mothers have not interested in higher education their girls. Other members of the family do not want to educate them highly, they will be idle and fashionable. More money will be incurred and increased productivity of girls will go with father in laws house. So this social attitude is one of the reason for lower participation of tribal women in higher education.

Lack of Quality Education

The tribal students are not attracted to the curriculum as it is not life-oriented. Therefore they have no interest in getting formal higher education. Now UGC has provision to evaluate the quality of college and university teaching by NAAC and deliver grading them. It is found in course of survey that only universities and 97 colleges have potential for excellence and only 12 universities have been identified as centre of excellence in certain specialization and only 477 departments have been identified as those with a potential for excellence. It is because university and college education has suffered from lack of adequate academic and physical infrastructure.

Lack of Employment-based Education

After getting higher education today only a part of tribal women get good employment and rest are either unemployed, underemployed. Therefore, the unavailability of adequate employment restricts other women to educate other members of the society. Non-guarantee of Service generates lack of interest for higher education among tribals.

Geographical Problems

The tribal students have to walk a long distance without any conveyance facility due to hilly area. In way of colleges there is fear of wild animals also. Soft hearted tribal women discourage to go colleges.

Teacher's Absenteeism

Most of the tribal colleges are in hilly area but teachers from plane. So they can not mix up with different culture and environment. They do not fully settle here. It is generally found teacher's absenteeism in tribal colleges. Ultimately students suffer from this case.

PROSPECTS

In order to make use of the human resource potential of tribal for national building a systematic action plan is necessary for which the following steps are to be taken with fullest commitment on the part of planners, administrators and political leaders.

Linking with Industrial

First of all higher education general and technical must have links with, all industries and societal endeavors. Towards this end a large number of centres for excellence, to turn out quality manpower in areas relevant to industry and society. It need to be established with triangular partnership of academic industry and government.

Joint Efforts

In the tribal area Voluntary association trade unions, religious organizations, political parties and rich people play a significant role in development of higher education. They may contribute in terms of money may involve mobilizing more resources for higher education, chalking out plans from which this area could get more resources. Efforts should be made to motivate to persons to come forward and make their contribution by taking people into confidence, which will also easier for them to enter into meaningful partnership in the field of higher education.

Quality Improvement

Basic issue of quality importance would be addressed

and brought about through the modernization syllabi, increase researches, networking of departments and increased allocation of funds. Networking would lead to increased academic activities and research. It is expected that the university system would utilize the autonomy, it enjoys and persuing high quality of researches. The emphasis would be on conferring autonomous status to more tribal colleges because they can appoint local teachers.

Multidimensional Approach

It is required to remove the hurdles of higher education. This hilly area contains different religion people like Hindu, Muslims, Sikh, Jain, Buddhist and Christian. Different religion people have different education level like Muslims is on bottom and highest with Christian. Any regulation of education be careful towards any religion. So every educated tribal person make their heartily affords to motivate the people of their society towards higher education, as it is a necessary condition for the development of their tribal society.

CONCLUSION

Special attention should be given and measures have to be taken to increase education among tribal women. There is need to change the perceptions about tribal women. Every agency working in this field should work as mission. Tribal women have equal status with male, there is need of motivation only.

References

Jha, U.S, Mehta, Araty, Menon, Latika (1998): Status of Indian Women Crisis and Conflict in Gender Issue, Vols. 1, 2 and 3, Kanishka Publisher, New Delhi.

Sapru, R.K. (1989): Women and Development, Ashish Publishing House, New Delhi.

Rana, Kranti (1998): Modern Working Women and the Development Debate, Kanshika Publishers, New Delhi.

Basu, Ashok Ranjan (1985): Tribal Development Programmers and Administration in India, National Book Organization, The Mall, Shimla-1.

Thorat, Sukhdeo (2007): Higher Education: Emerging Issues, *Yojana*, Vol. 50, May, New Delhi.

Dashora, Rakesh and Sharma, Anushree (2003): Role of Tribal Women in Higher Education, *Yojana*, Vol. 47, No. 6, New Delhi.

Kunnunkal, Tom (2007): Women and Education: to Create a Gender Just Future Society, *Women Link*, Vol. 13, No. 1, January-March, New Delhi.

8

Education: A Way Out for Tribal

PUSHPA SINHA

A tribe is an Indian group which possesses certain qualities and characteristics that make it a unique cultural, social and political entity. The nature of which constitutes Indian tribes and very nature of tribes have changed considerably over the course of centuries, but certain characteristics have remained.

With effect from 15th November 2000 after the new state Jharkhand was formed, most of the tribal areas mainly in the forest tracks of Chhotanagpur plateau and Santhal Paragana have been separated from the farmer state of Bihar to Jharkhand. The information the tribal population is divided into 30 different tribal groups representatives of Negrito, Proto. A ustraloid, Mongoloid, Mediator a near and Nordic races are found in the population of Bihar, certain Negrito features were noticed by anthropologists among the aborigines of Rajmahal hells the proto. Australiod features are found in the Kharwar Munda, Bhumij and mal Pahariyas. Some admixture of Mongoloid blood may be found among the Jharus of champaran.

Austric speaking groups include Munda, Santhal, to Bihar, Kharea and others. There is a considerable difference between Munda and oraous. The differences between the Santhals and the Sauria, Pahariyas are significant as they are indicative of differences between the Austric speaking and the Dravidian speaking people ever since Indian attained independence so many efforts are being made to meet the challenge of backwardness in Indian society. There are various sections who are deprived of the fruits of growth and development due to there very basic social set they are in accessible to the common population among this group tribes are the prominent section who weeds special consideration. For making them a part of the main gentry the best way outs to educate them.

Education is the key catalyst to the development of the human resources. In the past education was one of the main consideration of hierarchical class faction in Hindu society. Lack of education is the main reason of most of the existing problems of tribals, because for the tribals education is the favor on which their success depends. Education disseminates knowledge, knowledge gives inner strength which is very essential for the tribals for attaining freedom from all sorts of exploitation and most importantly poverty. Due to ignorance arising out of illiteracy, the tribals have not been able to take advantage of new economic opportunities.

Opening of tribal areas in the wake of developmental process have brought in juxtaposition two distinct value system, one based on tradition and ignorance and the other on technology and innovation. Harmonious synchtronisation of the two systems is essential for the development of tribal people. In this process, education has to play a key role. The most important aspect of education in the tribal areas is that of informing the community of the new innovations in science and technology as well as the developments in the economic and political fields. Education must be meaningful to the people.

The tribal areas are rich in natural resources. A number of projects both major and medium like irrigation energy generation and Industrial have been set-up in the tribal areas. The tribals due to lack of education and requisite skill are not able to take advantage of new economic opportunities which have been grabbed by the outsiders who migrated to the tribal areas. It not only deprives them of the opportunities in the new ventures but also alienates them for their resource base i.e land and subjects them to exploitation by the middle men and contractors in forestry operations and also by money-lenders.

Recognising the importance of education the framers of the constitution have made specific provisions in Article 15(4) and 46 for promoting education among the scheduled tribes. Article 15(4) is an exception to the fundamental right of the people of equal treatment irrespective of religion, caste, race, or sex granted under Article 15(1). It empowers the state to make any special provision for advancement of any socially or educationally backward class of citizens for the schedules castes or scheduled Tribes. Article 46 contains as directive to the state government to promote with a special care the educational and economic interests of the weaker sections of the people and in particular of the scheduled castes and scheduled tribes education is a state and central subject and the basic responsibility of promoting education has been cast upon the state governments. The main efforts in the central sector help the schedule tribes pertain to intimation of post-metric scholarships setting up of boys and girls hostels and coaching centre for competitive examinations, special central assistance is provided for this programme by the ministry of welfare, some of the important facilities provided by the ministry of education include 7½ per cent reservation of seats for scheduled tribes and 15 per cent for scheduled castes in all central universities. Indian Institute of Technology, Medical and engineering colleges, and central school.

According to 1991 Census the literacy among the scheduled tribes was 29.6 per cent against the general literacy

	Total persons (%)		*Male%*		*Female%*	
	1981	*1991*	*1981*	*1991*	*1981*	*1991*
General	36.23	52.21	46.89	64.13	24.82	39.29
Schedule Caste	21.38	37.41	31.12	49.91	10.93	23.76
Schedule Tribe	16.35	29.60	24.52	40.65	80.4	18.19

Source: O.S Srivastava.

of 52.21 per cent. A comparative positions of literacy any among the general population.

(in Percentage)

Literacy Rate	*1991*
Schedule Tribe	29.6

States	*Female Literacy Rate*
Rajasthan	4.7
Andhra Pradesh	8.7
Orissa	10.2
M.P	10.7
Bihar	14.8
U.P	18.0

Female Literacy Rate

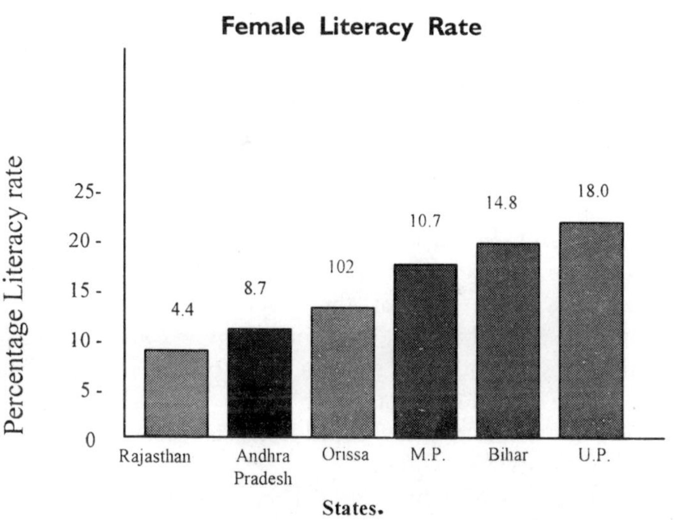

As in their economic organisation, so also in their world view, tradition, orientation and commitment to their past, the tribals differ among themselves. In some cases their levels of socio-cultural integration is low in others it is vigorous and potent. Among some cultural institutions are extremely simple among others they are complex and elaborate.

In the tribal areas of undivided Bihar i.e the present Jharkhand (We will be using 'Bihar' state for Jharkhand previously was the part of it till 15th Nov., 2000). The education system is influenced mostly by the initiatives of Christian Missionaries. The medium of instruction in Chhotanagpur and Santal Paragana at all levels is Hindi. According to Government instructions the medium at the primary level should be the mother tongue but it is not possible to be implemented in all the places either due to poverty of teachers or due to lack of good text books with the result that percentage of literacy among the tribes is only 11.64 percentage which is slightly more than the half of the average for the Bihar state. Primary educations can spread faster in the tribal areas with the mother tongue as the medium of instruction. A section of the tribals donot like the tribal language as medium as they suppose that if they would not take Hindi they would lag behind in the regional and national life. If they are taught everything through Hindi they would be in a better position to compete with others. The locus of powers stands with the Christian missionaries with large number of converter, Missionaries have been working in Chhotanagpur since 1845. The other denominations are the Roman Catholic, the G.E.L Missionaries and the Baptist Mission. All these Missions have put education in the forefront of their welfare programme education has been one of the important factors for the conversion of the tribals but even non-converts are allowed in these schools some of these schools are working in such areas which are even now inaccessible. It is their spirit of dedication that missionaries could establish schools in those areas even eighty years ago.

Two agencies which have been working in this field since 1946 are the Adimjati Seva Mandal and Santal Pharia Seva Mandal both affiliates of Adimjati Sevak Sangh. The former is active in Chhotanagpur and the latter in Santhal Paragan they use to run a network of school and hostels including some residential schools. In the tribal areas with the help of funds received from state government. The organisations were established by some enthusiastic people who want to raise the level of tribal at par with other sections of the population. Now most of the schools run by them have been taken over by the government. In their service for uplifting the tribals both the Missionaries and Seva Mandal denigrated tribal culture and succeeded in alienatining the tribal child from their own home. The educated child did not go back to their village and remains in the town only for getting some job. This type of education created sense of inferiority among the tribals.

After independence most of the schools were started directly by the government. But the atmosphere in the government managed school was not better than that obtaining in the schools managed by Seva of Mandal because most of the teachers in such schools came from the non-tribal background. So they do not have any emotional understanding of tribal culture and they generally consider less intelligent. In mission schools in contrast to the other schools their prevails some sympathises and friendliness.

There are some residential schools also where tribal students live and learns in a better atmosphere. Various scholarships were granted and reservations are given to them in most of the areas. Every tribal society has its own social institution where the youths are provided with moral, social and educational values. They generally use to have 'village Dormitory' like 'Dhumkuria' among Oraon, where their youths are trained. The boys and girls are kept separably under strict vigilance of the leader in case of boys and of an old lady in case of girls. They enter the dormitory usually at the age of 10 to 11 and live there till they attain the age of 20 or 22. It is not essential for every tribe to have such institutions.

CAUSES OF SLOW PROGRESS IN LITERACY

- For the poverty-ridden parents, education of their children is a luxury which they can hardly afford the children assist their parents in earning their livelihood. Grown-up children also look after the younger ones when the parents go out for work either as cultivators or as labourers. Absence of child care centres, creches, Balwadis, etc., in the remote tribal areas, also has to share the blame for depriving the children of the poor parents of the facility of education. The Curriculum of education for the tribals has to be carefully evolved. It has to take into consideration the socio-cultural milieu of the Scheduled Tribes. Presently, the general contents of education have been extended to the tribal areas which in many cases are not relevant, particularly at the primary stage. The tribal areas suffer from inadequacy of education institutions, boarding and lodging facilities. Even where centres have been opened about 40 per cent of them are without buildings. The supporting services, such as the incentives in terms of scholarships, book banks, etc., are very insignificant and generally do not attract the children.

In the tribal areas the problems of absenteeism of the teachers is one of the important factors affecting the education. They generally remain absent for days together due to absence of supervision over them and also due to lack of dedication to the cause of education of the tribals. The children and also the parents, cannot afford to waste their time and generally opt to dropout from the schools.

For the tribals the medium of instruction in the schools is a difficult problem. Even after 40 years of Independence we have not been able to provide the tribals education in their mother tongue. The tribal children are not generally able to follow the lessons given to them in the school in the language which is totally strange to them.

The tribals undoubtedly, form linguistic minority groups and are entitled to facility of instruction in their mother tongue at the primary school stage. Article 350 (A) of the constitution specifically provides for adequate facilities for instruction in mother tongue at the primary stage of education to children belonging to linguistic minority groups. The President has also been vested with the power of issuing directives to any state for this purpose.

So for there is no clear educational policy for the tribal area. In spite of the recommendations and suggestions of various Committees and Commissions, no policy for the tribal areas has been evolved. In some states the schools in tribal areas are under the control of Education Department and in some under the Social Welfare Department. Lack of administrative policy regarding the education institutions in tribal areas adversely affect the education of the tribals.

The Constitution of India that came into effect from 26 January 1950 prohibits any discrimination based on religion, race, caste, sex and place of birth. But while providing equality of opportunity for all citizens, the Constitution also contains special clauses to ensure reservation for the advancement of any socially and educationally backward classes of citizens or for the Scheduled Castes and the Scheduled Tribes.

With a view to provide and safeguards these communities against exploitation and to promote and protect their social, educational, economic and cultural interest, special provisions were also made in the constitution.

For effective implementation of various safeguards provided to them in the Constitution and other protective legislations, a Special Officer, designated as 'Commissioner for SCs/STs was also appointed under Article 338 of the constitution.

Although originally supposed to last only for 10 years, the Indian reservation system has continued till date, and applies to higher education and legislative office, Currently, 22.5 per cent (15 for SCs and 7.5 for STs) in all government jobs and seats in higher education institutions under the central government are reserved for Scheduled Castes and Scheduled Tribes.

Reservation is intended to increase the social diversity in campuses and workplaces by lowering the entry criteria for certain identifiable groups who are grossly under-represented in proportion to their numbers in general population.

Inspite of reservation being implemented as a tool to improve the Scheduled Castes and Scheduled Tribes or the Other Backward Classes, it becomes just a compensation the needs to be in place for the well-being of these peoples since they are not at par with the rest of the country. As long as such improvement is not achieved, reservation will be mandated to keep these underprivileged peoples to be able to compete with the rest of the country.

In August 2006, based on the recommendations of an independent panel, the UPA Government at the centre proposed to implement quota system for Scheduled Castes,

Schedule Tribes, Other Backward Classes (OBC) and other minority communities in IITs and IIMs (for both student and faculty). This led to sharp reactions from the unreserved category students in the institutes concerned especially students from the Medical fraternity.

As far as higher education is concerned the state of Jharkhand has three Universities namely Ranchi University, Vinoba Bhabe University, and Sidhhu Kanu University. But inspite of several reservations and facilities provided to the tribes the number of tribes having higher education is very low. Moreover this education is concentrated in the districts where missionaries are working. There are several districts like Singhbhum where the percentage of higher education is very less.

It has been confronted even tough those who get themselves qualified and placed with good jobs don't want to get back to their own villages. This shows lack of strong bondange which is due to the poor economical and orthodox society of tribes. The social or generations or tribes could provide in their youths only basics of education even though they are not ready to send out their children outside the village irrespective of facilities provided to them, as they fears that they will loose their children because they will not come back to their homeland after they are educated. It has also come out that educated tribals are generally the convert Christians and so the society also fears that they will loose their identity by conversion thereby having a set back the tribal culture itself. In tribal society another hurdle is language, since there is lack of institutions even at the primary level which opt for their mother tongue as mode of instruction, it checks them from going to schools. So their is need of teachers who have the knowledge of the tribal changes so as to promote primary education. Hindi should be taught as a subject to bring them to the main line society only then the students could qualify for higher education.

The tribals leagues are good in skill, they are good learners so non-formal vocational education with the motto, earn while you learn should be incorporated them so that their economic condition should not come in way of their education industrial training centres are one of the example of promoting such knowledge this centers should take into consideration the basic tribal needs. They are inherent sportsmen so they should be trained in sports too.

Thus we came to the conclusion that education plays a key role in the development of tribes and therefore as laid down in the Directive Principle of State Policy they should be promoted with special care. For this first we have to promote basic education because a report shown in India TV reveals a very surprising scene, there is a tribe called Saber belonging to Jharia Goon of East Singhbhum earning their livelihood by selling wood, when asked above that do they know Bhalat? Replied it may come of some village far away. So education is the way out for bringing the tribes to the main land and help them to explore themselves.

Higher Education in India: A Path to Success

YADWENDRA SINGH

Education is the Light of Life. It dispels the darkness of ignorance and removes mental dullness of the people. Virtually education is an integral part of the country's development process and thus has obtained a high priority in our society. Higher Education is the crown section of education system in India from immemorial times. Nalanda University is the classic example of our ancient glory in the field of higher education.

According to statistical information during the post-independence period the number of universities has increased from 36 to 385 and affiliating nearly twenty thousand colleges. About twelve million students are inrolled in higher education in different faculties covering ten per cent of youth. Whereas the percentage was only three at the time of independence.

FUND ALLOCATION

Recently, Central Government of India is actively

planning to sanction and implement different programmes with required fund in this core sector. In this regard on 1st March 2008 in his Budget speech inside Parliament House of our Sovereign Nation, Finance Minister, Sir P. Chidambaram has announced the following in the sector of higher education:

"Knowledge is power. It is knowledge that will drive success in the 21st century. India has the opportunity to become a knowledge society. Following the Prime Minister's announcement, an IIM at Shillong: three IISERs at Mohali, Pune and Kolkata: and an IIT at Kanchipuram have started functioning. Government will establish one central university in each of the hitherto uncovered states. We propose to make a beginning in 2008-09 by establishing 16 central universities. Besides, we propose to setup three IITs in Andhra Pradesh, Bihar and Rajashtan; two IISERs at Bhopal and Tiruvananthapuram; and two schools of planning and Architecture at Bhopal and Bijaywada. More institutes of higher education as promised by the Prime Minister will be established during the Eleventh Plan Period:

In his Budget speech Finance Minister has also proposed to make a grant of Rs. 5 crore to the Deccan College Post-Graduate and Research Institute, Pune which is one of the oldest institutions of Modern Learning in India.

According to Finance Minister, we must encourage our children to take to careers in science and research and development. Ministry of Science and Technology will introduce a scheme called Innovation in Science pursuit for inspired Research (INSPIRE) that will include scholarships for young learners (10-17 years), Scholarships for continuing Science education (17-22 years) and opportunities for research career (22-32 years) government has proposed to provide Rs. 85 crore in 2008-09 for this inspired contribution to building a knowledge society.

The recommendation of the National Knowledge Commission submitted from time to time are under active consideration. Some of them have been incorporated in the Eleventh Plan. Government has accepted an important recommendation to inter-connect all knowledge institutions through an electronic digital broadband network. This will encourage sharing of resources and collaborative research. Government has proposed to provide Rs. 100 crore to the Ministry of Information and Technology for establishing the National knowledge network. These steps can play fruitful role in the development of higher education. Major expansion of higher education from next fiscal. This includes 8 new IITs, 7 new IIMs, 10 new NITS, 3 IISERs, 20 IIITs and 2 new SPAs. Work to start on 16 new central universities, 14 world class universities and 370 new degree colleges. (*Times of India,* 29/02/08)

But for the proper function of the mechanism of higher education there should be done something more. Pune University vice-chancellor Narendra Jadhav feels more could have been done. "Any developing nation should set aside 6 per cent of its GDP for education. Even with the new allocation we will not touch 4 per cent he says.

Another fact is—"The 20 per cent increased out lay in the education sector is a very positive step but we have hoped that Finance Minister would do something about educational loans. The collateral Fee Loan could have been hiked to Rs. 5-6 lakh, said Atul Chauhan, Chancellor, Amity University. (*Times of India,* 01/03/08)

ORGANISATIONS FOR STRUCTURAL DEVELOPMENT IN HIGHER EDUCATION

University Grants Commission: (UGC)

Coordination and determination of higher education is a subject in the union list and a special responsibility of the central government (India, 1994, p. 98). This responsibility is discharged mainly through University Grants Commission (UGC), which has established in 1956 as a result of Universities Regulation Bill presented to the Parliament in the year 1951 (Singh, 2007). However, two main provisions contained in the bill, which are vital for the development of higher education, have been deleted subsequently. They are as follows: (a) No universities to be established unless it has been found acceptable both by the Ministry of Education and UGC; and (b) The UGC would have the power to de-recognise any university degree.

With the deletion of the above two essential provisions, UGC has been established as a mere recommendatory body than an entity which could lay down the law. Therefore, for the smooth development of Higher Education the University Education Commission presided over by S. Radhakrishnan has recommended that education be made a concurrent subject. Now these days UGC is working by achieving its objectives in right manner.

Indira Gandhi National Open University (IGNOU)

Indira Gandhi National Open University (IGNOU) was established by an Act of Parliament in September 1985 for the introduction and promotion of Open University and distant education system in the educational pattern of the country and for the coordination and determination of standards in such systems. (India, 1994, p. 99) The major objectives of the university include widening of excess to higher education by providing opportunities to larger segments of the population particularly the disadvantaged groups, organizing programmes of continuing education and initiating special programmes of higher education for specific targets groups like women, people living in backward regions, hilly areas, etc.

Special Research Organisations

Indian Council of Historical Research, New Delhi, set-up in 1972, enunciates and implements a national policy on historical research and encourages scientific writing of history. It operates research projects, provides financial support of research projects by individual scholars, awards fellowships and undertakes publication and translation work.

Indian Council of Philosophical Research, which started functioning from 1981 with offices in New Delhi and Lucknow, reviews of the progress of research in philosophy from time to time sponsors or assists projects and programmes of research in Philosophy, gives financial assistance to institutions and individuals to conduct research in philosophy and allied disciplines.

Indian Institute of Advanced Study, Shimla set-up in 1965 is residential center for advanced research on humanities, social sciences and natural sciences. It is community of scholars engaged in exploring new frontiers of knowledge aimed at making measures conceptual development and offering interdisciplinary perspectives on question of contemporary relevance.

Indian Council of Social Science Research, New Delhi is an autonomous body for promoting and coordinating social science research. Its main functions are to review the progress of social science research, give advice on research activities in Government or outside, sponsor research programmes and give grants to institutions and individuals for research in social sciences.

Thus different organizations are actively engaged in research and other academic activities. Education should be available to all and equity of knowledge should maintain at regional level also.

Regional Scenario of Higher Education

In Tamil Nadu during post-independence era the state government started a large number of universities and colleges in various disciplines. The Gross enrolment ratio in higher education was estimated as 12.5 per cent in 1999-2000. This is higher than the national average of 10.8 per cent by 1.7 percentage points, all told Tamil Nadu has nearly 1300 higher educational institutions. This state has become front runner in medical, information technology and other sectors also (Srinivasan, 2008).

State of Bihar and Jharkhand are actively trying to achieve their high position in the field of Higher Education. State and Central Governments are jointly accelerating different programmes in the sector of Higher Education. These two states are extremely poor at the level of higher education with only about 6 per cent of the relevant age group of 17 to 23 enrolled. Infrastructure should be provided to all.

References

Budget Speech of Finance Minister P. Chidambaram, published in *The Economic Times*, 1st March 2008.

The Times of India, Patna, National, February 29, 2008, p. 6.

The Times of India, Patna, March 1, 2008, p. 9.

India, 1994, A Reference Annual Compiled and Edited by Research, Reference and Training Division and Published by Publication Division, Ministry of Information and Broadcasting, Government of India, New Delhi, pp. 98-99.

Singh, Amrik (2004), "Challenges in Higher Education", *Economic and Political Weekly*, May 22.

Srinivasan, R. (2008), Full Time Member of the State Planning Commission of Government of Tamil Nadu, *Times of India*, March 10.

10

Height of Higher Education in Developing India

SURENDRA PRASAD GAIN

I. INTRODUCTION:

The crucial role of education in the process of modernization, building up of a democratic and pluralistic society, and development of both the socio-economic resources and the country's human resources, to achieve social justice and equality, was clearly recognised right from the beginning of Indian planning. Hence the role of higher education in contributing to the development of the economy and in changing the social structure, was given a prime place duly recognising the fact that the human resource development would lead to the country's development in its various spheres. Plan allocations reflected this policy as 20 to 25 per cent of the budget of education was given to higher education. By the end of the century, there has been a marked change in the perception of higher education, and issues of quantity/quality, relevance, management, funding and the questioning of the role of higher education, for the coming decades, has emerged.

2. COVERAGE

In the last five decades, the Indian education system has grown into one of the largest systems of the world and the largest in a developing country. The number of universities has increased from 20 at the time of independence to 385 in 2007 and colleges from 500 to 20,000. However, this has not been planned growth. If higher education has to play a more vital role in national development and the global scenario, as it will be required to do in the twenty-first century, an essential task will be to place it either on the Union list or to have a more effective state-centre coordination. Higher education has now reached a stage of development where both policy and planning has to provide for a balanced development in the country as a whole, not only in relation to geographical location, but also in relation to the courses offered in order to avoid duplicaton, and under utilisation of seats or over production of graduates as new areas emerge and catch the fancy of the students and the administrators of the system, as well as to ensure diversity in the system to cater to differing needs of students. This expansion will need to consider the necessary difference in the content and objectives of education depending on the local area needs. Hence, diversity in course structure and design will have to take greater priority over the similarities and rigidities in the present system.

3. ENROLMENT RATE

There has been a considerable improvement in the enrolment from one per cent in early 1950's to about 19 per cent in the 2003. The 13 per cent is title more than average for developing countries which is 11 per cent. But it is too low compared to 23 per cent of world average of 36.5 per cent for countries in transition or 54.6 per cent for developed countries.

There has been huge increase in the demand for the higher education since the independence. However, the increase in demand has not been matched by corresponding increase in the education infrastructure in terms of educational institutions and other facilities. Due to the demand outstripping the capacity, a large number of aspirants are also denied access to higher educations. This has led to a situation where institutions are required to manage more students than they afford leading pressure on the facilities. Therefore, in addition to creating new universities and colleges the strengthening and expansion of existing institutions is equally necessary. If our target is to come closer to world average of 23 per cent we need to expand the intake capacity during the 11th plan quite substantially.

4. GENDER ISSUES

Women constitute 34 per cent of the enrolment. There are 5 women's universities and 1700 women's colleges. The enrolment of women in higher education will have to increase if equity and social justice are to be assured. This is a world trend. However, it is also a matter of more effective utilisation of our human resource. Moreover, the system is yet largely patriarchal. It still persists in having a large number of men in both academic and administrative positions. Women are not very visible as Vice-Chancellors, Principals, Heads of Departments, Rectors and Deans. Often they are in the lower rung of the academic positions or in clerical posts where they serve a male hierarchy. The problem of harassment of women students and women at work is emerging and needs to be addressed. Even before the Supreme Court gave its verdict on the harassment of women in the workplace, the Commission (UGC) had already finalised its recommendations on this issue which included the establishment of a Committee at the university for the purpose. If we want to increase women's participation in higher education, they must do so with dignity and assurance of safety.

5. ISSUES OF EQUITY

This issue relates to multiple disparities. Although the overall enrolment ratio is about 13 per cent, there are disparities across like between states, rural-urban, male-female, inter-caste and inter-religions, poor-non-poor and between occupation groups. And in some of these there is a considerable overlap.

The extent of enrolment is low in rural area compared with urban area low in some states. It is particularly low among the ST, SC, OBC compared with male. Among the religious groups, the enrolment is lower the Muslims and Hindus compared with Jains, Sikhs and Christians.

The enrolment is also low among the poor and particularly low among person engaged in some economic activities such as wage labour household as compared with those engaged in business as self-employed.

Therefore, There is need for comprehensive policy of inclusiveness which will be to reduce disparity among them.

6. VALUE ORIENTATION

Another area which needs attention to make higher education more purposeful is value orientation. The need for launching the programme of value orientation of Education has assumed very great urgency. This is particularly because of the growing divisive force, narrow parochialism, separatist tendencies, considerable fall in moral, social, ethical and national values both in personal and public life. It is recognised that development of human values through education is a tasks of national importance. Value orientation of education, commended by various high powered Commissions and Committees and endorsed in the National Development Plans, during the last five decades, has not been implemented with all seriousness, in terms of concrete educational programmes and activities.

7. ACADEMIC ISSUES

Education must prepare for three life roles: for the work place, family maker and citizen. Therefore, the content of education must be such as to prepare for these roles. Hence, education at higher levels will need to view its content to include courses and curricular activities by which these roles can be fulfilled. The present curricula defined by narrow discipline boundaries. However, the twenty-first century is going to see many changes, whether it be in governance of the country, the structure and functioning of the workplace, or the social structure and function of the family and the community. Hence, many of its present courses will become irrelevant. What is the preparation we need to make to meet major socio-economic and political changes? I am not being futuristic, the signs and portends of such change are already with us.

With the changes that have taken place in the recent past with globalization and liberalisation, India has to maintain her competitive edge. In the last decade of this century, we have witnessed phenomena never envisaged earlier. The breakdown of the Berlin Wall symbolised the breakdown of all national barriers as economic changes swept the globe. The strengthening of market economics and, consequentially, the "mantra" of liberalization, followed by treaties such as WTO and the issue of intellectual property rights, have affected our country as also our universities. Besides the fact that our industries have to wake up a new economic order, there is also an onus on them to maintain their competitive edge both within the nation and globally. The need for R and D has become very evident but not all industries can afford to maintain separate structures and investments, especially the medium and small scale industries. On the other hand, the universities have been involved in research for many decades, and a large number do have considerable investment, both in human resource and in infrastructure through the funding from the UGC, the Department of Science and Technology (DST) and other Government organizations. The problem is that, while industry wants short-term research with quick results, universities have normally been involved in basic research which is essentially of a long-terms nature. Hence, there is a need for both to appreciate the other's requirement and be capable of achieving the goals of developing a strong indigenous base of R and D. In a globalising economy, we cannot overlook this joint university industry enterprise.

The universities will have to break out of their rigid

structure of offering degrees and diploma for young students who continue to acquire qualifications beyond school education. They require to stretch their efforts to provide continuing education to adults and society is marked by rapid technological change and also to serve populations, today, who are experiencing a longer life span. They either need new skills in a changing environment, or to meet their individual needs for self-fulfilment. If we have to nurture the social development of the nation through bringing knowledge to the wider society, the universities will have to extend themselves also to the public through extension education to those who would not ordinarily be enrolled in the universities. It is only then that we will gain public support.

8. FUNDING

The issue of funding of higher education has received considerable attention and led to many debates in the last decade of this century and, therefore, does not need to be repeated here. However, there are a few issues which will continue to concern us in the beginning years of the next century and, if not addressed, will have serious effects on Indian higher education holding its own in the twenty-first century, the repercussions of which will be on all aspects of society and India's competitive edge in the global economic order.

Because of the decline in public funding for education, a phenomenon with which we are grappling in that of privatisation of higher education. Governments have been pleading that, when there are less funds for primary education, privatisation of higher education is a necessity. However, the issue overlooks the question of first generation learners in a country which has large proportions of the disadvantaged. For them to improve their life situation and of their families, the only means is through higher education. We cannot and should not limit the aspirations of our people. Where a majority are outside the formal sector or the propertied landed class, few will afford private education except the elite, resulting in the further polarisation of an already polirized society. It does not mean that those who can afford to pay for their education will also be subsidised. Populism has led to a sorry state of education where fee structures have remained static in higher education which is fully public supported, while school education has a fairly large participation of the private sector with high fees. Both need our attention in India. Higher educations provides the backbone for the human resource for the manufacturing, technical and service sectors, the professions and management (public and private), agriculture, forestry and dairy development, the civil services and others. Hence, funding of higher educations is an investment in human resource infrastructure and not an expenditure.

Today, many foreign universities are vying to woo our students particularly because the pool is large and English speaking, U.K., Canada and Australia, besides USA, have been target in our student community. Not only are they recruiting students for the universities in their own countries, but setting up programmes in India, sometimes by twinning and other times through their representatives. Like industry often claims that our policies do not provide a level playing field, it is similar with the university system. It is an irony that, starved of funds, higher education is required to stand up to global competition. We may have some way to regulate to see that only the quality foreign institutions set-up their programmes in India, so that, our students are protected from "fly by night" institutions. However, in this age of globalisation, it is not posible to fully keep out the best or even appropriate to deny such access to our students, especially as information technology knows no geographical barriers. Instead, we must provide the qualitative infrastructure as also attract the best to the teaching profession. Only then, we will stand the global competition which has already been unleashed as education becomes internationalised.

SYSTEMIC CHANGE

We are well aware of the problems our system faces from within and without. The tensions in the system result from different perceptions of goals by its sub-systems such as the students, the academicians, and the rest of the administrative and support staff and the technical staff. In spite of the fact that the universities have been providing managers to industry, they have done little for their own system. We cannot survive in present century with the way the system works, not its size and span of administrative control, not its scope of work. It will require to develop an efficient and effective managerial system through programmes of human resource development. It will also need a very different decision-making structure from the present bodies of the university. Hence, it will need a radical change in the structure and constitution of its management bodies if decision-making has to be time-bound and professional.

Its span of control will have to be reduced with the decentralisation of the system particularly the affiliating colleges. With decentralisation, autonomy of the colleges, and even departments of universities, will have to be promoted while ensuring accountability. This is the only way in which there will be a significant change in the present out-moded examination system where there is neither continuous evaluation nor the teacher has any role in it. In the present system, examinations become the be all and end all of academic activity resulting in rigid curricula and memory, based learning which results in guide books and teaching shops system can change only if systemic changes are effected.

The political system has been impinging on the higher education system, largely through the organisations of its teachers, students and staff, which are associated with the existing and newly emerging political parties. Democratic structures of governance would obviate their need. However, as long as such democratic structures do not exist, certainly, the right to association has to be exercised on the campuses by students, teachers, or other staff, but these should be based on campus issue, especially related to its academic concerns, and not be governed by political considerations as it has led to disastrous consequences of turmoil on the campus and even some murders at the time of student elections. A person has a right to belong to a political party as a citizen but the university is not the place for its expression, although many of our parliamentarians and ministers were one time student or teacher leaders. Political influence on appointments from Vice-Chancellors to other categories of staff, of the Governing Boards of affiliated colleges, has further exacerbated the problems and led to a lowering of standards of education. Public debate on education is non-existent and it has little or no place in party manifestos, Campuses do not invite the party candidates, at election time, to quiz them on their agenda for higher education. Unless civil society begins to voice its concern and plays also an enabling role, education will remain a poor cousin is the national priorities. There is hope only if the teachers' associations take on a new role for themselves, that is, to focus on the qualitative improvement of the system and its relevance to societal needs.

CONCLUSION

To raise the height to India higher education involves in enabling the system to the emerging challenges to globlisation and changed economic scenario is tams of training men and women of caliber and competence and in terms of providing the needed R & D capability on the one hand to produce highly talented men and women whose vast grasp of knowledge would enable them to respond to the desired innovations in advancing frontiers of knowledge and know-how on the other. The implication of this is that the system should build up excellence and maintain quality and relevance. In this process of making higher and technical education more purposeful, however, it is imperative that suitable environment is created through freeing the system from unnecessary constraints and political interference and thus providing the needed academic, administrative and financial freedom. Finally, it is equally necessary that the system itself should be amenable to accountability.

References

Yojna, Vol. 38, Nos. 1 and 2, January 26, 1994.
Yojna, Vol. 51, May 2007.
Yojna, Vol. 49, September, 2005.
Shaikshik Sanvad, Year 2, No. 2, February 2008.

11

Economics of Education and Reconstruction of Higher Education in India

TARANI PD. SINGH AND PREMLATA KUMARI

Education is considered as an instrument for social and economic change, catalyst in development efforts and facilitator of a better quality of life. Education supplies the economy with human resources, with the requisite knowledge, training and qualification to meet the demand for economic development. Education is both as consumption goods and investment goods. Investment in skill and knowledge increases future earnings, while the satisfaction derived from education is the consumption component. The economic value of education in the process of economic development is broadly assessed by the resources involved in the formulation of human capital and physical capital. The relationship between ratio of educated manpower to physical capital and the increments in per capita net domestic product over a period of time brings out the value of education.

The economists like Kuznets, Schultez, Denison and Bowman have analysed the contribution of education to growth in national income in the U.S. from the 1900 to 1956, and came to conclusion that the resources allocated to education rose about 6.5 times. Schultz analysed that the income elasticity of the demand for education was 3.5 times over a period and alternatively, investment in education contributed 3.5 times more to increase in gross national income than investment in physical capital.

Education generates externalities which induces Social benefits in the long period. Education has both empowering and distributive roles. It allows deprived and disadvantaged groups to protest against injustice, to resist oppression and to organise politically. It helps to reduce other forms of deprivation for example, in Kerala, education has led to lowering of cast barriers and reduced gender bias.

Higher education is one of the driving forces of economic development and its impact has been felt on population control, life expectancy, infant mortality, improving nutritional status and strengthening civil institutions. It is both repository and creator of knowledge. In a world where resources of knowledge will dominate over material resources as factors in development, the importance of higher education and of higher educational institutions can only grow. The crucial role of higher education in fostering development in increasing the knowledge base and specifically in contributing to economic development is well recognized by policy knowledge.

Coming in higher education, only 6-7 per cent of India's youth aged between 18-23 years, have access to it as compared to 34 per cent in Singapore and 50 per cent in the USA. There has been mushrooming of private institutes offering professional courses across the country. Most of them are lacking quality faculty and research facilities. There is a need to revamp higher education in India. A university can fulfil its job if it is allowed the freedom and autonomy to experiment with new ideas and adopt innovative techniques of curriculum formulation.

RESTRUCTURE OF HIGHER EDUCATION

The present structure of higher education is not only

outdated but also weak and unequal in task. All over the world, higher education is in university institutions, there are big campus with a critical mass of students and staff strength can sustain large libraries, modern elaborates and advanced centers. Higher education in India is fragmented, scattered, and takes place in nearly 16,000 institutions called affiliated colleges. Many of which are tiny and a trace better than higher secondary schools. These institutions perform only classroom teaching, preparing students for examinations like tutorial classes. Unfortunately, the entire higher education in India takes places only in the ill-equipped, under staffed, affiliated colleges as 89 per cent of the under-graduate students 66 per cent of post-graduate students, and 85 per cent of faculty are in the affiliated colleges. According to UGC report of 2001-02, India has 213 university and 52 deemed universities. This number is very small for the size of India and for meeting the emerging needs of advanced research. India with nearly 300 universities and 16,000 colleges has only 7 per cent of the relevant age group entering the portals of education. There are following steps for restructuring the higher education:

1. Urgent Reforms

The higher education system in India is characterized by extreme rigidity and total lack of flexibility. As a first step, introduce semester system in all the educational institutions bring major examination reform by adopting continuous interval evaluation and well-defined academic auditing and adopt the credit system.

2. Medium-term Reforms

The out-dated affiliating system is curse on our higher education system. It has converted colleges in to coaching centres and teachers into mere tutors. It should be changed. Autonomy must be granted to many deserving colleges as possible, for each major university, an autonomous board of examinations under the full charge of P.V.C. must be set-up.

3. Long-term Reforms

Higher education must be in universities and the outdated anachronistic affiliating system must vanish from Indian soil. We must pass the pending private universities act, especially to prevent the haphazard development of private university. The Government must setup more universities on a planned basis.

4. General Reforms

Education must move beyond classroom and outside the text books to make learning a joyful exercise.

The Government must draw up a plan and programme of action, allot the necessary funds under mission 'Reconstruction of Higher Education' and implement it in 3 successive five year plans.

References

Bhardwaj, K. (2001), "Unrest in Higher Education: The Broader Issues", *Economic and Poltical Weekly*, Oct. 17-21.

Choudhary, K. (2002), "Dalits in Higher Education", *Journal of Higher Education*, 21 (3), 432-42.

Power, K.B. (2001), "Indian Higher Education: A Conglomerate of Concepts", Facts and Practices, Concept, New Delhi.

Sethi, J.D. (2001), Crisis and Collapse of Higher Education in India, Vikash Publishing, New Delhi.

Singhal, Sushila (1995), "Organisations and Functioning of Universities in India", *Journal of Higher Education*, Autumm, Delhi.

12

Globalization and its Challenges for Higher Education

V. LOGANATHAN

INTRODUCTION

This paper makes an attempt to present the challenges of globalization for higher education in India. After briefly dealing with the concept and process of globalization and its impact on inequality, it considers the challenges of globalization for higher education in general and to India in particular. It describes how commodification, privatisation and commercialisation of higher education make things worse in a system marked by inequities and underlines the need for maintaining and increasing social sector expenditure by the State. It also traces the issue of Five Year Plans and Literacy among Tribals.

GLOBALIZATION AND INEQUALITY

The term 'globalization' is used in a positive sense to describe a process of increasing integration into the world economy. . . . It is used in a normative sense to prescribe a strategy of development based on a rapid integration with the world economy. Some see it as salvation, while others see it as damnation. (Deepak Nayyar, 1995)

There are some who think that globalization is a totally new phenomenon. In fact, we are in the second phase of globalization. In many ways, the world economy in the late 20th century resembled the world economy in the late 19th century. In both phases, globalization coincided with the technological revolution in transport and communications.

Globalization led to uneven development then and without correctives, it is bound to produce uneven development now. That is because on account of inequalities and asymmetries, in a world of unequal partners then and now (Deepak Nayyar, 1995).

In a positive sense and simple terms, globalization refers to expansion of economic activities across political boundaries of nation states. The major policy measures that globalization stands for, such as reduction of subsidies, tax reform, privatization and deregulation directly hurt the poor. These and some more policies of this sort are known as the golden rules of the golden straight jacket and this jacket is 'one size fits all' (Thomas Friedman, 1999). These policies are also collectively known as the "Washington Consensus".

Some commentators regard colonialism and neo-colonialism as the features of globalization. The other major feature of globalization is the dominance of "neo-liberalism". In the Third World, neo-liberalism has been presented under the structural adjustment plans.

There is unanimity among economists that global inequality has increased under globalization. Inequality is no myth (Joe, W. Pitts III, 2002). For example in 1997, 20 per cent of people living in rich countries had 86 per cent of world GDP, while 20 per cent of the people at the bottom had only one per cent. Globazliation has also created *digital divide.*

Globalization has made it very difficult for the poor country governments to provide social insurance. At present, international economic integration is taking place against the background of receding government and diminished social obligations. The welfare state has been under attack for more than two decades.

GLOBALIZATION AND ITS IMPACT ON HIGHER EDUCATION

The policies under globalization have implications for public education. Though globalization does not mean the end of the nation state, downsizing of the government and reduced government expenditures on social sector mean less money for public education. Some of these reductions may be effected by privatization, assuring a higher quality and level of education to those who can afford it, leaving an inferior system for the rest. Some of the reductions can also be achieved by attacking and weakening the unions that represent teachers. The government may impose limitations on the rights of teachers to unionize and of their unions to represent them, and strike work if necessary.

Universities and colleges are not immune to the globalization of production, distribution and consumption. The technological revolution in transport and communications has affected higher education.

Digital broadcasting, the web, e-mail and other fast, cheap and user-friendly communications have produced a global market in teaching and learning. There are some successful *virtual universities* in the United States without campus or faculty, which provide courses on the internet and guidance to learners at study centres, staffed by course assistants who are internet specialists, not traditional academic staff and they are making profits in millions of dollars. As education is a social as well as a cognitive process, students who leave the school, want not only qualification but experience of student life. So there will continue to be a substantial market for student places in colleges and universities. Of course, distance education will cater to some categories.

The first two elements in the transformation of higher education are globalization of markets and C.I.T. The third one is the rapid expansion of demand for higher education and the dominant language of instruction at the global level will be English, whether we like it or not. And some look at it as linguistic imperialism or cultural imperialism.

There is a decline in public funding of higher education

throughout the world. The government's response to the funding crisis varies from country to country. Encouragement of fee-based private sector and increase in fees are some of the measures followed. Brain drain is another problem. Roughly, one lakh Indian professionals used to take visas to the United States before September 11, 2001 and this is an estimated resource loss of $2 billion. Thus, developing country investments in education subsidize industrial country economies. The argument that brain drain is also a brain gain for it often generates a Diaspora that can provide valuable networks of finance, business contacts and skill transfer for the home country, is not a great solace.

Each country needs the capacity to understand and adapt global technologies for local needs. That means more investment in education and working people. Chile is a good example of a country pursuing privatization and regulation simultaneously. In the network age, concentrating on primary education is not enough. The advanced skills developed in secondary schools and colleges are increasingly important.

Two major goals of universities in developed countries (e.g. UK) are:

1. Making the economy globally competitive by training students for employment in knowledge economy . . . and transferring knowledge to private business; and
2. Promoting social inclusion by enhancing opportunities for a wider section of society to obtain higher education in some form whenever they require it. With a focus on science and technology, practically a go-by has been given to the proper balance between sciences and humanities.

In Canada, "the university policies and practices have been harnessed to the process of commodification, commercialization and privatization of higher education". (Sujata Patel, 2004)

There will be change in relation of students to university. The students will regard themselves as customers entitled to the service for which they have paid.

The impact of globalization on academic profession may take the form of erosion of autonomy over curriculum, and assessment and contraction of tenure and permanent jobs. The only functional monopoly that universities possess is the accreditation of degrees, based on assurance of quality and standards.

INDIA

In India, it is generally argued that higher education gets more attention at the expense of primary or secondary education. But we need more and better quality education at all levels and for many more students than at present. The foundations of good quality education can only be laid by sound and widely accessible secondary education. Primary education for every one is the foundation for all education and social reform (I.G. Patel, 1998).

In most of the countries, higher education is heavily subsidized by the state. Blaug and Woodhall found that in Europe, "the direct costs of tuition are subsidized by grants to colleges and universities so as to allow fees to be reduced to minimum levels and the indirect costs of tuition (borne by students in the earnings foregone) are subsidized by grants or loans to individuals (Maureen Woodhall and Mark Blaug). In India too, higher education is heavily subsidized by the State. While the direct costs of tuition are subsidized by grants to colleges in order to keep the fees at minimum levels, indirect costs are subsidized mainly in the form of fee concessions and scholarships. Until recently, loans have played an insignificant role in student aid programmes.

There have been persistent doubts on the egalitarian base of public education. The findings of Hansen and Weisbrod have emphasized that the general effect of subsidies to higher education in California was "to promote rather than to discourage inequalities in income among people of various social and economic backgrounds, by making available subsidies that lower-income families either are not eligible for or cannot make use of because of other conditions and constraints associated with their income position". The essence of their finding is that the present system of financing higher education is regressive.

Almost identical views have been expressed by our economists on the inequitable and regressive nature of financing of higher education in India. Higher education can be advantageously used for preserving if not accentuating the unequal distribution of resources through the regressive effects of public financing of higher education (see Tilak 1989). Bhagwati observed that "higher education forms an excellent vehicle for the government to transfer the resources from the poor to the rich without obvious dissatisfaction, as in principle higher education is open to all classes, and therefore conceals the inegalitarian effect" (See Bhagwati, 1973, p. 24).

State funding to higher education should continue. Raising fees, promoting consultancy with industries thereby raising funds, introducing self-financing courses and promoting student loans will not promote equality of opportunities with reference to access to higher education for the disadvantage sections.

The unchecked and unregulated growth of self-financing universities which charge extremely high fees is a matter of concern and goes against the goal of education for all.

The Ambani-Birla Committee set-up by the Prime Minister's Office wanted to convert education into an industry and encourage the growth of private universities with their own fee structure. Probably, the committee had in mind the private universities in the USA, which is a rich and leading capitalist country, forgetting for a moment that we have to deal with the goal of expansion of higher education opportunities in a poor country like ours where the basic structure of the society is unjust marked by inequalities created by caste and class.

Right now, only about 7-8 per cent of India's population between 17 and 23 age group was enrolled in colleges and universities. Privatization and raising of fees will not promote egalitarianism in higher education.

After globalization, education has become a tradable commodity. And this trade in education is crossing national boundaries. Already foreign institutions are competing with our institutions and some of the foreign governments/

universities are asking for special zones for higher education on the lines of Special Economic Zones (SEZs).

To make higher education equally accessible to all, there is a strong case for public subsides for higher education by the state and the ratio of expenditure on higher education must be increased. For instance, as a consequence or privatization, public expenditure on higher education as a proportion of GNP had declined from nearly one per cent in 1980-81 to 0.55 per cent in 1989-90 and it further declined to 0.39 per cent in 1998-99. And if we look at education as a whole, we find that as a proportion of GNP, it declined from 4 per cent in the late 1980s to 3.6 per cent in late 1990s. And Higher education suffered most in real terms in less than a decade in real prices (JBG Tilak, 2004). It is imperative that the state must take a major responsibility for subsidizing higher education to make it equally accessible to all.

HIGHER EDUCATION IN TAMIL NADU

Tamil Nadu is one of the educationally progressive states in India. The literacy rates for both males and females are more than the national average. According to 2001 Census, the overall literacy rate in Tamil Nadu was 73.47 as against the national average of 65.38 per cent. It is one of the top three states in literacy and it is next only to Kerala and Maharashtra.

The present system of financing collegiate education is generally regarded as inequitable and inefficient. In Tamil Nadu too, public higher education is highly subsidized and majority of the users are from the non-poor category (V. Loganathan, 1981).

Technical education in the state is today dominated by self-financing colleges. In all the government and government-aided engineering colleges including REC, Trichy and IRTT, Erode, the student strength in 1998-99 was 2,462 whereas the figure for self-financing engineering colleges was 20,411. It means more than 89 per cent of the students study in self-financing engineering colleges (Policy Note on Higher Education, 1999-2000).

The self-financing colleges may turn out to be socially

and economically divisive in the future. They do not fulfil either the efficiency criterion or the equity principle, nor do they contribute significantly to education finances in the country. Yet, they grow in number, particularly in cosmopolitan urban areas to satisfy the needs of the "gullible parents" (Government of India, 1985). Not only that, the objective of equal opportunities for all in education would be jeopardized in a big way.

"The State has a very positive, very important role to pay in the promotion of mass education, which cannot and should not be left to private sector alone" (Weiner, 1994).

Social Sector

The term *social sector* is a flexible one that refers to activities which contribute to human capital formation and human development. Some of the important sub-sectors of social sector are education, health and medical care, housing, water supply and rural development. Many countries of the developing world have shown that broad human development is possible, *with or without* economic growth. The focus is on health and education. Governments in these countries have chosen to empower the weaker sections so that, with some support, they could enjoy longevity, knowledge and well-being. The role of the government is central in social sector development.

The experience of countries with social achievements display high degree of equity—social, economic, political and gender equity, sometimes in access to opportunities and sometimes in access to outcomes. These countries enjoy high levels of literacy and health and also gender equity. *While globalization causes inequality, social development promotes equity.* The moral is that economic and social strategies are complementary, not antagonistic or one-sided because the relationship is bi-directional.

Five Year Plans and Literacy among Tribals

One of the Directive Principles of State Policy in the Constitution enjoins that the "State will promote with special care the educational and economic interests of weaker sections of the people, and in particular of the scheduled castes and the scheduled tribes and shall protect them from social injustice and all forms of exploitation". This directive has been reflected in the Five Year Plans. However, nearly six decades of development have not had the desired impact on these socially, economically handicapped groups.

The term "backward classes" is "commonly applied to the following four sections of the population:

(1) Scheduled Tribes,
(2) Scheduled Castes,
(3) Communities formerly described as 'criminal tribes', and
(4) Other socially and educationally backward classes who may be declared as such by the Central Government in the light of recommendations made by the Backward Classes Commission". (Chapter on "Welfare of Backward Classes in Second Five Year Plan").

Article 275 of the Constitution requires that a special financial grant should be provided for programmes for the social and economic welfare of the tribal population living in the scheduled areas.

And article 46 of the Constitution requires that special attention should be given to the education of the children of the scheduled tribes.

State programmes of tribal education include the creation of residential education ashrams, vocational and technical training schools and hostels for tribal students. During the Second Five Year Plan, an important step taken was the training in Hyderabad and elsewhere of an increasing number of tribals as teachers. For the Second Five Year Plan, an amount of about Rs. 47 crores was earmarked for tribal welfare compared to about Rs. 25 crores in the First Five Year Plan.

The outlay for education and culture of tribals during the Second Plan was Rs. 8 cores. Post-matric Scholarships, Stipends, fee concessions, opening schools and hostels were some of the incentives and programmes for the educational development of tribals. The broad policy approach during the early plans was that "the tribal people should be enabled to develop along the lines of their own genius, with genuine respect and support for their own traditional arts and culture and without pressure or imposition from outside" (Third Five Year Plan, Chapter-24). This applied to education as well. The Third Five Year Plan provided an outlay of Rs. 12.26 crore for the education of scheduled tribes.

During the Fourth Plan, in the field of higher education, the scheme of Post-matric scholarships was continued and Rs. 11 crores were provided for the same for SC/ST students. As SC/STs were educationally at a low level, special efforts were made to reduce dropouts and stagnation at the middle and secondary stages.

The Sixth Five Year Plan rightly noted that "the development programmes for the scheduled castes and scheduled tribes in the earlier plans tended to be formulated in an *ad hoc* manner without any perspective and were more in the nature of welfare schemes. The special programmes for these groups were conceived as a supplement to the total development effort under general sectors of development... "

> "The provision of funds for these programmes rose from Rs. 39 crores in the First Plan to Rs.327 crores in the Fifth Plan and a total of Rs. 744 crores was spent till the end of 1978-79. Of this amount, 48 per cent was spent on educational schemes..." (Sixth Plan: Chapter on Development of Backward Classes).

An interesting and welcome feature in the Fifth Plan was that for the first time, a strategy of earmarking funds for the development of scheduled tribes was evolved. For the scheduled tribes, because of their population concentration in specific areas, the instrument of **Tribal Sub-Plan** was developed to ensure flow of benefits from all sectoral programmes and to provide integrated delivery of services in the tribal areas. In addition, pockets with 50 per cent or more tribals in a population of 10,000 in a contiguous area have been included in the Tribal Sub-Plan areas from 1979-80 onwards. The tentative outlay for education during the Sixth Plan was Rs. 506.50 crore.

During the Sixth Plan period, for manpower development, schemes for an increase in the supply of skilled and semi-skilled manpower were continued under the plans of North Eastern Council (NEC) and States/UTs of the region. Some highlights are:

(1) Students of the North Eastern region were sponsored for various undergraduate, post-graduate and doctoral studies in agriculture, allied activities and engineering;
(2) In-service personnel were sponsored for short duration specialised courses including management development;
(3) The existing technical institutions were expanded and strengthened; and
(4) New technical institutions were set-up in the region. In this context, it may be worth noting that the literacy rate in the North Eastern region (Assam, Manipur, Meghalaya, Nagaland and Tripura and two Union Territories of Arunachal Pradesh and Mizoram) was above the all-India average of 36.2 per cent in 1981 except for Arunachal Pradesh (20.1%) and Meghalaya (33.2%).

The Seventh Plan rightly realised that "it is essential that the monitoring system be put on sound footing so that there is adequate feedback from the grassroots to the State and National levels on a regular basis. Correct policy prescriptions can be evolved through monitoring. Evaluation, aggregative and sectoral, as well as concurrent and post-implemental, will provide valuable insights, to arrive at right policy formulations.

The Seventh Plan laid emphasis on the educational development of SCs and STs. While the State Governments provided pre-matric stipends and scholarships, and other incentives such as free supply of uniforms, stationery and text books, the Union Government provided scholarships to students of post-matriculation/post-secondary courses of study in Arts, Science, Commerce as well as professional and technical degree/diploma and certificate courses on the basis of graded means test. The recent decision to insist on 60 per cent aggregate marks to avail post-matric scholarship is a retrograde step. A scheme of Book banks was started in 1978-79 for SC/ST students studying in Medicine and Engineering Colleges and hostels were expanded.

The existing programmes for pre-matric and post-matric education of scheduled tribes were continued during the Eighth Plan. Residential schools were expanded and priority was accorded for opening primary schools in tribal areas.

The Ninth Plan laid emphasis on the empowerment of the socially and educationally disadvantaged groups. So "these groups which have passed through the process of welfare and development during the past four and a half development decades, will now the empowered to act as agents of socio-economic change and development ("Ninth Plan, p. 355).

Literacy Rates among Tribals

According to 2001 Census, the literacy rate of scheduled castes was 54.69 per cent and that of scheduled tribes was 47.10 per cent as against the national average of 64.84 per cent. The educational data of STs reveal that there is very high dropout rate of 86 per cent from classes I-X during 1990-91 (Ninth Plan).

Table 1 reveals that there are wide disparities in the Gross Enrolment Ratios and dropout rates of children of all communities and SC/ST children.

There is also wide gap between female literacy rate of STs and of all communities. It was 21.10 per cent in 1991 (Ninth Plan, Table 39.2, p. 358). Not only that, the variation in literacy rates among different tribes across the states is also fairly pronounced. For instance, according to the 2001 Census, Manipur had a literacy rate of 65.85 per cent, while Andhra Pradesh had 37.04 per cent; the literacy rate for Orissa was 37.37 per cent and Bihar 28.17 per cent. The literacy rate for Jharkhand was 40.67 per cent.

From the foregoing analysis, it is clear that the solution for the problem at the top (development of higher education of tribals) lies at the bottom (Primary education sector).

TABLE 1

Gross Enrolment Ratios of Children of All Communities and SC/STs

Level	*Year*	*Children of all Communities*	*Scheduled Caste Children*	*Scheduled Tribes Children*
Primary	1990-91	100.1	106.4	104.0
	2002-03	95.4	85.8	98.7
Upper Primary	1990-91	62.1	52.7	40.7
	2002-03	61.6	56.3	48.2

TABLE 2

Dropout Rates

Level	*Year*	*Children of all Communities*	*Scheduled Caste Children*	*Scheduled Tribes Children*
Primary	1990-91	42.6	59.4	62.5
	2002-03	34.9	41.5	51.4
Upper Primary	1990-91	60.9	67.8	78.6
	2002-03	52.8	59.9	68.7

Source for Tables 1 and 2: Derived from MHRD, GOI, *Selected Educational Statistics, 2002-03 (as on 30th September, 2002)*, New Delhi, 2004, pp. 84-85 and 89-90.

Tamil Nadu may serve as a model for addressing some of the problems relating to the educational advancement of tribals. Recently, the Government of Tamil Nadu has made education free upto the under-graduate level in all Government and Aided Colleges by abolishing the tuition fees. This decision, it took based on the recommendation of the State Planning Commission, which in turn, was based on the finding that the administrative expenditure relating to the grant of fees and scholarships was more than the amount given towards tuition fee concessions and scholarships.

In Tamil Nadu from the year of the introduction of 10+2+3 pattern of education in the year 1978-79 and with the abolition of the Pre-University Course (PUC) in colleges for subsequent year, i.e., 1970-80, with the object of adding one more year to school education, the growth in the enrolment of students in the age group 16-18 has been remarkable.

The +2 course with vocational stream has been designed as a terminal course. But there are some empirical findings to the effect that the system of higher secondary education has not made significant impact on employment prospects of students who entered labour market after the completion of +2 course (C. Ramamoorthy, 1993).

One of the positive outcomes of the introduction of +2 course in schools is the enormous increase in enrolment of students from rural and semi-urban areas in the course because of locational advantage. Further, as the medium of instruction is Tamil in a majority of schools, students from socially and educationally backward classes managed to find places in professional colleges in very large numbers. This positive outcome may be kept in mind and the earlier it is introduced, the better for the state of Jharkhand.

There is need for starting more Teacher Training Institutions for Tribals.

CONCLUSION

In India, the bulk of the social expenditure is incurred by the State Governments. The lack of "political commitment, not of financial resources, is often considered as the real cause of human neglect (UNDP, 1991, p. 1). Social justice should be the cornerstone of the policy of the State. Tamil Nadu Government since 1967 by maintaining a high level of social expenditure has made great strides in the field of education and health. That is how, it has met the emerging challenges of globalization. So, the State of Jharkhand can follow suit and focus on keeping up the size of its expenditure on social sector in order to promote the education of tribals.

Note

1. The term "Washington Consensus" was coined by Williamson in 1989. He called it so because of the support it enjoyed from the American Government and from the IMF and the World Bank, all based in Washington.

References

Deepak Nayyar, (1995): Globalization: The Past in Our Present, Presidential Address 78th Annual Conference, Indian Economic Association, Chandigarh, 28-30 December.

Jandhyala, B.G. Tilak (2004): Public Subsidies in Education in India, *Economic and Political Weekly*, Jan. 24.

Joe W. Pitts III (2002): 'Inequality is no Myth', Foreign Affairs, July/August.

W. Lee Hansen and Burton A. Weisbrod (1969): The Distribution of the Costs and Direct Benefits of Public Higher Education, *Journal of Human Resources*, Vol. IV, Spring.

Loganathan, V. (1981), State and Higher Education: Financing Collegiate Education with *special reference* to Arts and Science Colleges in Tamil Nadu, unpublished Ph.D. Thesis (Degree awarded) University of Madras.

Loganathan, V. (2002), Education in Tamil Nadu: Trends and Issues in Tamil Nadu Economy: Trends and Prospects, M. Naganathan (e.d.) University of Madras, Chennai-600 005.

Maureen, Woodhall and Mark, Blaug, Patterns of Subsidies to Higher Education in Europe, a research paper sponsored by the United States Education Policy Research Center for Higher Education and Society under HEW Contract No. 300-76-P1.

Pael, I.G. (1998), Economic Reform and Global Change, Macmillan India Limited, New Delhi.

Thomas, Friedman (1999), The Lexus and the Olive Tree, Harper Collins, London, *The Economist* (2001): Special Section, September 29, Volume 360, Issue 8241, p. 2.

13

Indian Higher Education in Globalised Era: Challenges and Opportunities

Maheshwar Goit and Sheela Sharan Singh

INTRODUCTION

In recent years, there is an acceleration in the growth of education in India. The government now convinced that education is one of the most effective means of stimulating economic growth.

There has been a massive quantitative expansion of higher education because of the setting up new universities and affiliated colleges. It has created widespread unemployment among the young educated students in India at one hand and at the same time there became a quantitative expansion of higher education in a developing country like in India. The tragedy lies behind the fact that proper planning has not been initiated in higher education and the maintenance of standards has not been evenly poised because of massive political pressure in the parliamentary system of India. As a result, the recommendations of the Education

Commission could not be properly utilized. Higher education is not a static phenomenon, it has an organic entity.

After Independence of India, consistent efforts have been taken to bring about the desired and meaningful changes in higher education. As a result of which there became a massive expansion in higher education. An estimate of expansion of higher education in India can be gauged from the fact that there were only 500 colleges in 1947 which increased to about 17625 in 2005. There were only 30 universities in 1950-51 when rose upto 357 in 2005. in addition to above there was 3.6 lakh students in 1950-51 in these institution which also increased 99,53506 upto 2001-2002. Hence, we find that there is a quantitative expansion of higher education institutes as well as students.

GROWTH OF EDUCATIONAL INSTITUTIONS AND DECLINING FINANCIAL SUPPORT

The budgetary provisions of government shows a declining financial support for higher education which clearly speaks that government is influenced by reform policy and socio-economic philosophy for disadvantaged groups contained in constitution have been ignored by the government. Tables 1 and 2 displays the clear picture of government intention.

In fact the 1990s had the fastest decadal growth in the literacy rate since independence and the data would suggest an improved spread as well. For instance, there was a narrowing of the gender gap from 25 in 1991 to 22 per cent in 2001, and of the rural-urban gap, from 28.4 to 20.9 over the same period. The number of recognized educational institutions also continued to grow, as may be seen from Table 1.

Table 2 show the trends in per capita expenditure at constant (1993-94) prices on different levels of education, viz. elementary primary education, secondary education and higher education. A comparison of these trends reveals that while budgetary support for elementary education has increased over the last decade that on secondary education has stagnated and the same on higher education has in fact

TABLE I

Growth of Recognised Educational Institutions in India, 1990-91 to 2001-02.

Years	*Primary*	*Upper primary*	*High/ Hr. Sec./ Inter-/ Pre-Jr. College*	*Colleges for general education (Engg. Tech. Arch, Medical Education Colleges)*	*Colleges for profes-sional education*	*Universities Deemed Univ./ Inst. of National Importance*
1990-91	560935	151456	79796	4862	886	184
1991-92	566744	155926	82576	5058	950	196
1992-93	571248	158498	84608	5334	989	207
1993-94	570455	162804	89226	5639	1125	213
1994-95	586810	168772	94946	6089	1230	219
1995-96	593410	174145	99274	6569	1354	226
1996-97	603646	180293	103241	6759	1770	228
1997-98	619222	185961	107140	7199	2075	229
1998-99	626737	190166	112438	7494	2113	237
1999-00	641695	198004	116820	7782	2124	244
2000-01	638738	206269	126047	7929	2223	254
2001-02	664041	219626	133492	8737	2409	272

Source: Website of the Ministry of Human Resource Development (MHRD), Government of India (GOI).

declined drastically over 2000-01 to 2002-03. Thus, we may argue that increased budgetary support from the union government for elementary/primary education has come up at the cost of reduced budgetary support to higher education and secondary education in the country. This is in tune with the policy of the union government in India, in the recent past, of withdrawing support from the secondary and higher education sectors expecting the same to come from the private sector.

TABLE 2

Per Head Expenditure on Different Levels of Education by the Central Government (Constant 1993-94 prices in Rs.)

Year	*Elementary*	*Secondary*	*University and Higher Education*
1994-95	20.5	28.1	34.8
1995-96	52.6	30.8	35.9
1996-97	53.7	28.0	33.6
1997-98	73.0	26.1	41.43
1998-99	82.0	33.9	64.4
1999-00	81.2	34.2	82.5
2000-01	82.2	35.2	90.4
2001-02	88.5	34.4	54.4
2002-03	88.5	32.4	54.6

Concern of Quality Education

Quality is a never-ending journey. It is dynamic concept and process. To map the quality in higher education is not an easy task. The key areas may be identified as curriculum, teachers, staff resources, organizational set-ups, teaching-learning environments, assessment, appraisal and monitoring. In India several bodies exist to ensure quality in higher education. UGC, AICTE, DEC, NCTE, MCI, ICAR, NAC are the important one. In spite of the existence of those bodies, quality higher educations in several parts of the country is still a distant dream. Quality education, as reported by the International Commission on Education for Twenty-first Century will help the students in the following ways:

- To think logically, analytically and critically.
- To provide employability through occupational skills and work experience.
- To realize one's potential for self-development.

- To acquire the capability appreciate and imbibe the emerging values of our times such as concern for ecology, equality, civility, harmony and cultural pluralism.

Apprehensions of GATS under Globalised era:

- GATS will undermine the sovereignty of the country.
- Government will be forced to reduce subsidies in higher education.
- Professional courses alone will find place in the education system.
- The poor in the developing countries will be deprived of the benefits of higher education and benefits will accrue only to the upper middle and rich class.
- Development of unrest among students.
- Threat to long term sustainability of cultural and linguistic diversity especially through dominance of English.
- COM modification of higher education will erode the autonomy of university and academic freedom of the teachers.
- Higher education under GATS may not be in congruence with national policy of education which will lead to larger socio-political turbulence.
- GATS could undermine cooperative internationalization.

CHALLENGES TO BE FACED BY INDIAN HIGHER EDUCATION

Indian higher education is facing several challenges. Although almost all countries in the world are facing more or less the same challenges the intensity differs from one country to the other based on its local situation. The points mentioned here mainly address the Indian situation.

1. The need for increasing access with huge rise in the population.
2. The dire necessity of maintaining equity in tune with the increased access.
3. The requirement of enhancing sustainable quality to meet the global requirements.
4. Maintenance of balance between universal objectives and those which fulfil the changed social needs.
5. Growing impact of ICT, globalization and external forces.
6. Decline in the State support.
7. Market orientation that is strongly emerging in higher education

Opportunities before Indian Higher Education

At the same time these changed times offer great opportunities. India is highly suitable for seizing these advantages provided some wilful effort is made. Some of the promising features are:

1. The country going to be youthful for the next twenty years.
2. The new millennium ushered in a new turn knowledge driven economy in place of 'industry drive economy' of the last century.
3. 'Knowledge driven economy' is more suitable to Indian situation which missed the industrial revolution but has strong knowledge base.
4. The advantage of English language knowledge of Indians.
5. Ability to rise up to the levels of expectation when situations demand.

It has, therefore, become a demanding, exciting and risky time for our universities and colleges. The Challenges are to be converted into opportunities. Considering India's socio-economic compulsions and multiplicity, a comprehensive approach is needed drawing the best of both worlds.

Marketisation of Higher Education

The economic reform policies introduced in almost all developing countries during the last quarter of the century, required (a) a drastic cut in public expenditures across the board, including higher education, and (b) promotion of markets in higher education. In fact, these policies set the tone for drastic reforms in higher education; and on the whole, higher education suffered severely. Public expenditure on higher education declined in many developing countries— in terms of relative priorities (proportion of GNP or of total government expenditure that is allocated to higher education), and/or in public expenditure on higher education in absolute terms in real prices (and sometimes even in nominal prices)— total as well as per student. Noticeable cuts could also be noted in several countries, specifically in public expenditure on quality and equity-related inputs in higher education (e.g. research, and scholarships). Recovery of costs of higher education from the students (in the form of high and even full cost-equivalent fees) has been an important strategy adopted in most countries, along with raising of resources from other non-governmental sources including industry, by forging close university-industry links.

Along with these and the public apathy for higher education, one can note a strong emergence of forces in favour of private higher education. The lack of resources is one oft-cited reason for the growth of private higher education. But an equally important reason is the change in attitudes towards higher education, and towards private higher education, and toward 'for profit' private institutions of higher education, in particular. The public and merit good nature of higher education is being increasingly discounted. Private higher education is projected as an efficient system that can improve access and quality as well as equity!

Governments have either implicitly encouraged higher education institutions to adopt market relevant policies, or explicitly formulated policies that contribute to rapid privatization of higher education. Such policies include withdrawal of government grants and incentives to mobilize financial resources from non-governmental sources, including fees and others, introduction of 'marketable' courses of study that can be 'sold' to the students in place of long-term courses of study, appointment of industrialists as heads and/ or chairpersons of governing bodies of higher education institutions. Management, financial management including cost recovery and profit/surplus-making, have become the traits that are looked for in such appointments. The march towards marketisation of higher education is taking place through a variety of measures: financial privatization of public universities, transfer of ownership of public institutions and establishment of private institutions—private institutions with government support, self-financing private institutions (with no government support), and profit-making private institutions—all focusing on short-term market considerations and immediate market relevance. The emerging private institutions also consist more of institutions without government recognition. Universities also began to transform themselves into 'entrepreneurial universities and autonomy from the government has also become a buzzword'.

The emerging scenario depicts varying degrees of privatization of higher education. First, an 'extreme' version of privatization implies total privatization of higher education colleges and universities being managed and funded by the private sector with little government intervention. Second, there is 'strong' degree of privatization, which means recovery of full costs of public higher education from users—students, their employers or both. Third, there is a moderate form of privatization implying public provision of higher education but with a reasonable level of financing from non-governmental sources. Lastly, there is what can be termed 'pseudo-privatisation', which cannot be really called privatization; institutions offering higher education under this category are privately managed but government-aided. They were originally created by private bodies, but receive nearly the whole of their expenditure from governments. All types and forms of privatistion seem to take place rapidly in many developing countries without any coherent perspective and plan, producing different kinds of problems.

The adoption of the new economic policy in the form of liberalization, privatization and globalization in our economy has given a new shape to higher education in an area of globalization which brought many new challenges and opportunities. Hence, there became a tough competition among the foreign players on the platform of higher education. Academics in India must prepare themselves for international competition in the field of Higher Education. The entry of private enterprise in higher education will bring in new initiatives, more enterprising and innovative experiments and programs.

After the National Policy on Education, 1986, was introduced, quite a few reforms were brought into existence which have had a significant impact on the quality, quantity and equity in higher education and to improve the quality of higher education through different programes like orientation and refresher courses for college teachers on a regular basis, a number of Academic Staff Colleges are established. Besides, some university departments organize Refresher Courses for college teachers. Also, to encourage institutional innovations and experimentation, a number of colleges have been given autonomy under the programme of according autonomous status to such colleges which fulfil the UGC-laid down norms. In addition to above, efforts have also been made to improve access to higher education in villages by opening institutions of higher learning in rural areas, promoting open and distance education and introduction of vocational courses at the college level. Last but not the least, realizing the importance of technology in higher education, information technology has also been introduced through computer application courses and other facilities for modernization and automation.

But the great issue relates to the role of government in higher education in the present phase.

CONCLUSION

The issue of autonomy is closely related to the imperatives of accountability. Autonomy should not be confused with sovereignty and license. It has its limits—Lakshman Rekha. After all, Universities and colleges are the public institutions which must be accountable to the society. Their performance should be accounted for and assessed from time to time. National Assessment and Accreditation Council (NAAC), set-up by the UGC, has an important role to play in this regard. However, we have both—challenges and opportunities. We have to face the challenges cautiously and exploit the opportunities wise fully. If the government is financially weak, private partnership may be adopted in higher education.

There are several reasons why state subsidization of higher education should continue in our country. First, subsidy is favoured on equity grounds as education is considered to be a major source of equality. Many countries where private sector plays a predominant role in higher education, government support continues to be an important source of funding entirely to private sector whose motivation in establishing self-financial college, especially in the medical and engineering field, quality, not quantity, should be the aim of all genuine university work. If the quality is the underlying idea of excellence in higher education the present feverish craze for degree has to be stopped by delinking one from eligibility conditions of securing various types of manual mechanical and other skill-based, occupations and vocations. This will, hopefully, reduce the pressure of increasing student population on most of the universities and colleges. A massive vocational orientation of secondary education is also necessary to stop the maddening rush to universities. We must try to control the flood of numbers is higher education by putting appropriate barriers at the secondary education itself. We will have to diversify and vocationalise higher secondary education so that it becomes a terminal point for majority of students who aimlessly throng universities and colleges.

Distance education and open university education system can reduce the pressure on the universities. In addition, and in spite of all theoretical arguments to the contrary, we will have to regulate the expansion of the system of higher education within manageable proportions and relate one more realistically to the manpower needs of the employment opportunities. Above all, it the government which can provide education on the basis of equality of education barring the barrier of caste and cured. In the present phase the marginalized people like ST, SC and OBC can not afford to take admission in privately managed institutions where there is heavy donations and large fee structures only the government funded institutions can convert the challenges of reform into opportunities and the issues of disadvantaged groups can be protected.

Impact of Globalization

Globalization has multidimensional impact on a highly heterogeneous system like the India education, while it may bring some benefits, unless effective controls are thought of and implemented, it could resulted in more loss than gain.

Benefits of Globalization

- o Improvement in the quality of Higher Education due to competition.
- o Large number of agencies provide higher education opportunities domestically and internationally use of information and communication technologies (ICT) for domestic and cross-border delivery of programs.
- o Students can have greater access to a wider range of education opportunities at home and abroad.
- o Increasing access to education and reducing gap in developing countries.
- o Easier access of Higher Education in developing countries as governments in those countries are finding it difficult to provide additional resources to Higher Education institutions to meet the increasing demand.

References

Reetha Rani, (2004): Economic Reforms and Financing Higher Education in India, NIEPA, New Delhi.

Government of India: *Economic Survey*, 2004-05.

Union Budget, different years.

Krishnakumar, Asha (2004): 'The Decline of Public Education', *Frontline*, Vol. 21, No. 16.

RBI (2004): Handbook of Statistics on State Government Finances (Available at ww.rbi.org.in).

Saxena, N.C. (2004): 'Central Transfers to States and Centrally Sponsored Schemes', Website of the National Advisory Council.

UNESCO (2005): Education for All: Global Monitoring Report, Paris.

Impact of GATS on Indian Higher Education Services: Risks and Benefits

REWATI RAMAN JHA

1. INTRODUCTION

Higher education services play a significant role in bringing desirable human capital development. The development of higher education is correlated with economic development of the nation. Higher education in the 21st century can truly be a borderless world of knowledge and ideas, which will yield reciprocal benefits for all nations. At present, higher education is increasingly seen as a commercial product to be brought and sold like any other commodity in the market. Hence, globalisation and commercialization of higher education has thus become a reality and India being a signatory to the WTO as also to the GATS.

2. SHAPE OF GATS AND HIGHER EDUCATION.

The general agreement on trade in services (GATS) is

being negotiated under the auspices of the World Trade Organisation (WTO). The GATS is also a product of Uruguay Round (1986-94), one of many WTO agreements, in force from January 1, 1995. GATS is a comprehensive legal framework of rules and disciplines covering 161 service activities across 12 classified sectors, which are mentioned as follow:

(a) Business (including professional and computer services)
(b) Communication
(c) Construction and Engineering
(d) Distribution
(e) Education
(f) Environmental
(g) Finance
(h) Health
(i) Tourism and Travel
(j) Recreation
(k) Transport
(l) Other services not included elsewhere

GATS aim is deregulating international market in services including education. Before this agreement, trade agreements used to be in relation to eliminating tariffs and other barriers for the goods produced in one country and sold in other countries. Some services used to be exchanged but there was no mechanism for trade in services, because they were considered to be place specific and thus non-tradable. The objective of GATS is to liberalise trade in services as quickly as possible. It is clear from the preamble of GATS that it is a "multilateral framework of principles and rules for trade in services with view to the expansion of such trade under conditions of transparency and progressive liberalization" and with a desire for the "early achievement of progressively higher levels of liberalization of trade in services through successive Rounds of multilateral negotiations." According to the European Commission, the GATS is "first and foremost an instrument for the benefit of business." GATS has two components: (i) The framework agreement containing 29 Articles, and (ii) a number of annexes, Ministerial decisions, etc. as well as the schedules of commitments by each member government, which bind them to allow market access, and/or remove existing restrictions to market access. This agreement covers all services including education.

Those services which are entirely provided by the government, they do not come under the GATS rule. A service which is out of the purview of the GATS rule it has to be entirely free. However, when the services have been provided either by the government partially or some prices are charged (as happens in education where some fees is charged), or provided by the private providers, they shall fall under the GATS rule. The idea behind this is the creation of an open global market place where services like education can be traded to the highest bidder. GATS covers the educational services of all countries whose educational systems are not eclusively provided by the public sector, or those educational systems that have commercial purposes. Since total public monopolies in education are extremely rare, almost all of the worlds educational system fall under the GATS rule. Indian education can not get exemption from the application of GATS because education at all levels, particularly at higher education level is not entirely free.

According to the UN provisional Central product classification (UN-1991), education services have been grouped under following categories covered by GATS:

(i) Primary education Service including primary education and pre-school education but exceeding child care and adult literacy programme.
(ii) Secondary education service.
(iii) Higher education service cover two elements as (a) teaching and training in post-secondary, Sub-degree, technical and vocational training institutions, (b) teaching to university level education, its affiliated colleges and specialized professional education recognized under university level system.
(iv) Adult and continuing service education.
(v) Other education services.

Under the GATS regulation trade in services including education services are grouped under following categories:

(a) Cross Border Supply

It includes education services beyond the boundary of a nation, distance education through print media or other type of materials, on-line education including internet.

(b) Consumption Abroad

It involves the movement of the consumer of a service from one country to the other.

(c) Commercial Presence

It includes the actual presence of service provider from one country to the service receiver in another country.

(d) Movement of Natural Presence

It includes the presence of one individual from one country to another country in order to render its service.

But governments can make commitments for one area, several, all sectors or more of them.

GATS play a potential critical role for major changes in conditions of higher education around the world. They are firstly, globlisation, secondly, improvements in information technology and communication and thirdly, increased competition in higher education.

Global market for international higher education was estimated $ 27 billion in mid 1990s. USA, France, Germany, UK and Australia were the main exporters and China, India, Japan, Korea and Taiwan were the main importers. Importance of international trade and investment in higher education in recent years has been growing. Globalisation of this sector is evident from the increasing number of students going abroad for study, exchange and linkages among faculties and researchers increased international marketing of curricula and programmes, establishment of branch campuses and the development of international mechanisms for educational cooperation between academic institutions across countries. Incidentally India is both an importer and exporter of higher education services. With it come both opportunities and potential threats for Indian higher education. Though the impact in the short-run may be limited the potential long-term consequences are significant. The rapid worldwide expansion of new information technology, improvements in communications technology, and the reduced cost of much of this technology have spawned a major expansion in its application to education. In many parts of the world information technology holds promise for reaching population that could not be served by traditional education institutions.

Since competition in higher education has increased rapidly in recent years, so India will have to turn to market forces to reform higher education and cut costs, we fear that competition from providers in rich nations will disadvantage our still developing higher education systems. If outside providers succeed in recruiting the better prepared and more affluent tuition-paying students away from public institutions, they will deprive government supported higher education of revenue needed to support public education for poor and less prepared students. Developing nations like us should be concerned that GATS demands for unrestricted across in the higher education sector will open the door for foreign diploma mills and providers of questionable quality. India have to develop a sophisticated monetary system which will have the capacity to monitor or police. Thus GATS is seen as hindering their commitments to the "public good" the development of national higher education system essential to national development, efforts to faster national cultural values, promote democracy and provide educational opportunities for all citizens not just those who can pay for them.

Eduation in GATS is the least committed sector in the Uruguay Round only 44 countries (including India) of 144 WTO members have made commitments to education and only 21 of these have included commitments to higher education. It is worth-noting that Congo, Lesotho, Jamaica and Sierra Leo have made full unconditional commitments in higher education. Australia's commitment for higher education covers provision of private tertiary education services including university level. The European Union has included higher education in their schedule with clear limitations on all modes of trade except consumption abroad, which generally means foreign tuition paying students. In this context USA, New Zealand and Australia only out of the 21 countries have submitted negotiating proposal for higher education commitments. This reflects the reluctance of member countries for commitments of higher education.

3. GATS AND INDIAN HIGHER EDUCATION

There is a provision in GATS Article 1.3, that government services remain outside the purview of GATS, provided they are not meant for commercial purpose and do not have any competition from private service suppliers. Hence, as per this article, education dose come under the purview of GATS trade liberalization. Since there are already many institutes, colleges, high schools and coaching classes operating in private sector in India. These private service providers are in direct competition with the government institutions. It can not be neglected here, that the leading government educational institutions like the IITS, IIMs and Agricultural universities were funded primarily by foreign funds. The shrinking budgetary funds for education is also discouraging knowledge promotions in India. As per UNESCO, 1998, the per capita total government expenditure on education for 1995 was less than $ 10 per year in India as against $1400 in USA. The 1990's was a major turn in the history of higher education in India. The decade was one of the turmoil, with an important development being the sustained efforts towards privatisaiton of higher education in India. The financial privatisation of higher education, through reduction in public expenditures and the introduction of cost recovery measures was accompanied by policy measures towards the direct privatization of higher education. A private universities bill was introduced in the upper house of the parliament in August 1995, with view to providing for the establishment of self-financing universities. Mukesh Ambani and Kumar Mangalam Birla Committee in 2001 strongly suggested the government should leave higher education altogether to the private sector and confine itself to elementary and secondary education. But the committee did not mention any valid reasons. The report also urged for passage of the private university bill.

It is also a considerable facts in Indian context, that share of higher education in total planned resources has decreased continuously from 1.24 per cent in the Fourth Five Year Plan to 0.35 per cent in the Eighth Five Year Plan. As a result the state of affairs in the government educational institution is pathetic. Even if government substantially increases its education expenditure through dificit financing it should be proved as inflationary tax. The scarcity of funds points out the fact that capital is a scarce factor and human capital are abundant factor in India. Those who go to provide educational services on contractual basis contribute to India's Gross National Product. Similarly, foreign educational institutions operating in India will contribute significantly to India's Gross Domestic Product, and even more. So if Indian government stipulates a minimum requirement on hiring of Indian faculty and staff. Hence private sector participation and trade education services seems imperative.

India's import interests as per Article 1.2 of GATS is also evident into the following four modes.

Cross Border supply—Prospects for distance education, online courses through interest, educational testing services and educational materials that are provided overseas. It will also include sale of paper back editions of books and sale of educational CDS.

Consumption Abroad

This refers to import of educational services through movement of the consumers/students to other country for pursuing education. Indian students studying in foreign universities of USA, UK and Australia.

Commercial Presence

Foreign institution entering India through twinning and franchise arrangements. Indian students getting foreign degrees, doing professional courses at local branch campuses of foreign institutions in India.

Movement of Natural Persons

Foreign faculty and scholars teaching in India.

Libral FDI policy in education services but poor enforcement of regulations and weak regulartary capacity affect ability to meet objectives of quality, accreditation, equivalence.

4. BENEFITS OF GATS FOR INDIAN HIGHER EDUCATION

India was along experience of providing education testing services. Quality of testing services is well demonstrated by all India qualifying tests such as the CAT (common Admission Test) of the IIMs, JEE (Joint Entrance Examination) of IITS, NET examination of CSIR-UGC and GATE (Graduate Aptitude Test in Engineering). If the experience of these services is adopted for various fields, and, if such services can be offered on a year round basis will sufficient computerization and use of internet facilities, India stands to gain from liberalization of such services. However, markets for such services will have to be actively sought. Hence, India may commit to liberlize these services but an adjustment period of a few years is necessary to up-gradation and marketing of these services to potential clients. Moreover, willingness of stakeholders to conduct this activity in the private sectors needs to be assessed. Only then India can become competitive both in foreign and domestic markets. About 66000 Indian students had enrolled for courses in US in the year 2001-02 (UNESCO). Currently, however the number must have already exceeded 70000 and there are a few more thousand Indian students studying in Europe. A significant proportion of these students on teaching/research assistantships and fee waivers. Moreover, value must be attached to foreign educational experience while centrally widens the horizons of young minds. As far as export of such service by India is concerned, i.e. foreign students coming to India for study, the current prospects are not to bright. However, getting students from developed countries, even from East European countries, would be very difficult as our standards of campus facilities are very poor in general.

However, there is a scope for developing high value rich market for some of the programmes that India may offer. Marketing of programmes on education in Arts and culture, Sanskrit and other languages and literature and traditional medical sciences like Aurveda could be effectively done by upgrading the campus facilities for some of the specialized institutions in India. A gloring example of this is the programme offered in Aurveda by the Department of Aurveda at university of Pune. It has twinning agreements with universities in Italy, Germany and many other countries to send their students here for part of the study. Moreover, there may be rich market for management education as well. India has one of the best management schools in the Asia-pacific region. Indian Institute of Management, Ahmadabad, although does not have any foreign students enrolled in the two years programme, it has a successful exchange programme for students. More than 45 students go abroad for a term for which they do not have to pay fees. One must also remember that fees in western countries are much expensive than those in India. Promoting such exchange programmes on reciprocal fee-waiver basis will certainly be useful to India both in terms of not losing foreign exchange, and providing Indian students an opportunity to broaden their worldview. In doing so Indian institutions will move towards up-gradation of their facilities and infrastructure in the near future. And with that the institution can also attract foreign students for their regulars post-graduate programme in the long-run. Further, it must be remembered that many of the Indian (Post) graduate students who go abroad for higher studies receive teaching and/or research assistantships and tuition waivers. This is a form of export of educational services in the form of movement of natural persons. The fact that western countries need foreign post-graduate students to teach independent courses in their universities shows the need for qualified university level teachers abroad.

5. RISKS OF GATS FOR INDIAN HIGHER EDUCATION

Moreover, it can not be ignored the negative aspects of GATS in India. Because, the quality of education and the perceived value an overseas degree appear to be the most significant factor influencing students decisions to outside India. It is also noteworthy that for majority of students, a major motivation was their desire to broaden their experience by living and working in another country. While the in-country availability of desired courses at the under-graduate level may not be a major factor in the student mobility, the limited capacity of India's institutions to meet the demand for post-graduate education in particular fields may be a more serious problem. It is also well union that the demand for 'Seats' at India's apex institutions for Indian students in highly competitive fields such as engineering, medical and management vastly exceed the supply. Reservation policies, designed to ensure educational opportunities for disadvantaged groups within Indian society, further limit the in-country seats available for students from forward caste back grounds. To a certain extent then, foreign universities provide a safety valve for talented well-off Indian students who can not find seats in their chosen fields within Indian institutions and universities. A final factor worthnoting is the active and growing competition for the best Indian students among foreign universities. While the UK and the USA are well established destination for Indian students. Australia and Canada are rapidly gaining in-market share. Hence balance of trade in education is definitely not in our favour. While all these factors help explain the large number of Indian students studying outside their home country, what accounts for the small number of foreign students studying in India. The answer lies in some of same factors motivating Indian students to study overseas, i.e. the lower perceived quality and marketability of qualification from Indian institutions. But other more easily controlled factors also play a role. Significant among these is the relative paucity of structural and accreditated college study abroad programmes for foreign students in India.

The GATS initiatives pose a severe threat to the traditional ideas of the university as well as to the national and even institutional control of education. The greatest negative impact of GATS on higher education would occur in the developing countries like India. These countries have the greatest need for academic institutions that can contribute to national development, produce research relevant to the local needs and participate in strengthening of civil society. Increasing interest of parents to get their children admitted to foreign educational institutions will cost the Indian economy foreign exchange loss. Sometimes there is also the possibility of substandard courses being offered to the students, which may lead to cheating the Indian students. Owing to commitment of GATS, globalisation and privatization of higher education in India will lead to the creation of three different classes of educated students—those educated in foreign universities, those from costly private domestic institutions and those from economically weaker sections studying in government funded institutions. This will only lead to social tensions. In view of the nature of the globalised higher education, the commoditification of Indian higher education is bound to have an adverse effect on our culture, the ethics of social welfare and even the quality of Indian higher education system. In addition to these, the most threatening for the inertia ridden Indian higher education establishment is the likelihood of foreign colleges and universities setting up shops in India. With a large English-speaking and affluent middle class, the country is perhaps the most attractive destination in the developing world for overseas education providers. Transnational education shops will become a major threat to our higher education system.

6. A FEW SUGGESTIONS

After the above discussion of impact of GATS some proposal for improvement of our higher education system is needed because internationalization would lead to an improvement in the quality of education, promote Indian culture abroad, inculcate the cult of international understanding, generate good will and social interaction and yield rich financial harvests. Partnership and networking are essential for the enrichment of the teaching-learning process for improved quality in research. An urgent action should be taken in the matter of finalization of government policies relating to the promotion of Indian education abroad. One committee for the promotion of Indian education abroad is constituted at an early date and its functioning activated. The UGC Act, 1956, and the Acts of other Statutory Councils need to be amended to include a specific provision allowing universities to open off-shore campuses and export Indian education through the distance mode. There is also need to enact legislation that would regulate the operation of foreign institutions and thereby prevent the gross commercialization of education. It is also necessary to frame legislation that would regulate the operation of Indian partners of foreign institutions and allow only genuine academic institutions to participate in twining activities. There is a need to simplify, within the existing legal framework, procedures relating to registration, entry test requirement issue of "No objection certificate" as also the issue and extention of Visa. The government should advise Indian embassies and High Commissions abroad to play a proactive role in providing information regarding the facilities for higher education available in India and assist in the conduct of fair entrance examinations and student recruitment. For this purpose the Embassies and High Commissions could establish education counseling and assistance units. There is a need to adopt an open door policy for self-financing students. This would require the raising of the limit of percentage of international students to be admitted to Indian professional institutions and also the creation of supernumerary seats. Urgent steps should be taken to strengthen the date and information base so that prospective international students can obtain information relating to academic programmes available at different universities, eligibility criteria, admission procedures and tuition fees. Apex badies may be asked to create websites for this purpose and these could be linked to a central education website. The government statuary and the UGC should grant greater autonomy and flexibility to universities in dealing with the process of admission of foreign students and in entering into collaborative arrangements with foreign institutions, especially in the establishment of off-shore campuses and centers. The government should set-up a single window clearance mechanism in the form of Task force including representatives of different bodies like the UGC, All

India Council for Technical Education (AICTE) and the Medical Council of India (MCI) for admitting students to different professional programmes. Universities could get their foreign student applicants cleared through this Task force. The government should consider establishing a financing mechanism for International Education, such as a possible International Education Development Bank. This institution should provide soft loans to Indian students going aboard, to foreign students coming to India for higher studies and to educational institutions wishing to develop infrastructure for international education. The government should set-up a mechanism for monitoring the standard of education that is imparted by foreign universities. There is also a need to a National quality Framework that would provide for lateral transfer as well as vertical progression, both nationally and internationally. This would facilitate the coming in of the students for short duration.

Universities and other academic institutions which decide to enrol a large number of international students need to have a good infrastructure in the form of lecture halls, well quipped laboratories, adequate library resources, facilities for sports, recreation facilities and above all special living facilities in the form of international houses/hostels. For institutions planning to offer special short-term courses for groups students on a regular basis it would be desirable to develop a separate complex with classrooms, sectional library and computer unit so that the international student can study in an environment comparable to what he/she has at home. The academic institution must evaluate their strengths in different disciplines of education and identify areas that would attract international students in different level. These areas could be developed further in accordance with the requirements of the foreign students. The procedure for granting admission to international students must be simplified. As indicated elsewhere it is necessary to reserve a certain number of seats for international students or provide for supernumerary seats. If an admission or entry test is necessary then arrangements for it should be made in the home country (or at least the region) of the prospective student. On arrival on the university campus he should be able to complete formalities through a single window operation. The social infrastructure should be strengthen so as to place international students at ease. Programmes such as "home stay" cultural festivals, celebration of national days of different countries should be organized regularily so as to promote cultural exchange and mutual understanding. Each institution must has an Office of International Education (OIE) and an International Student Advisor, International Education is a two-way process and it is essential that Indian academic institutions, and especially the universities should establish partnerships and develop networks with foreign universities in both the developed and the developing countries. The development international education programmes should be given priority, and the faculty must be encouraged to participate in the enrichment of their academic content. International contracts should be nurtured and hopefully these will lead to "twinning" arrangements. Linkages can be "firmed up" through memorandum of understanding (MOU). However, it is noted that many of MOU signed in recent years have failed to "take-off". It will, therefore, be prudent to sign MOU only after the viability of a programme is ensured. Internationalization of higher education can be facilitated if the academic structure of the universities is similar to that available in the universities abroad. Academic restructuring may be necessary for many universities and this could mean a ganut of reforms including permitting the students to chose freely the courses to be studied, introduction semester system (with continuous internal evaluation and credit system) allowing transfer of credits, etc. These changes have been advocated for over two decades now and need to be implemented even if there is to be no internationalization.

The highest priority needs to be given by academic institutions to the updating and internationalization of the curriculum. This implies not only the incorporation of the latest in terms of knowledge but also the diversification of the contents to give an international dimension to the programme on offer. It is necessary that, at least at the Master's level, the curricula incorporate information of different regions of the world, especially, Europe, United

States, Africa and South East and East Asia. Students coming from the Arab World, the CIS countries and countries of south east and East China more often than not have an adequate knowledge of the English language. It is necessary that for students from these countries special English classes be conducted for the first few months of their stay in India. This can be done in a systematic manner if an English language cell is created as a part of the International center. Indian universities should develop special "study India" programmes that could be covered in one semester for the benefit of students from developed countries who would like to visit India to learn more about its culture and heritage, natural resources, diversity, language or indigenous technologies and systems. The doubts about good faculty leaving Indian institutions for the foreign institutions should be alleviated by improving the present working conditions of the teachers like salary, consulting practices, etc. Liberalization of education sector under GATS can be used to promote private investment but limited to such foreign institutions they will offer superior quality services rather than below par services. There should be sufficient and though protection to ensure the good and established universities and institutions in India offering good quality education are not threatened by entry of foreign institutions.

7. CONCLUSIONS

To sum up the impact of GATS on higher education, opinions on the risks and benefits are divided is not polarized. They differ within our states and between countries. Each country must undertake the very serious challenge of balancing opportunities and commitments to liberalise trade for exporting higher education services, with the possible impact, related to the same commitments, of the import of education services. This is not an easy task, one can tend to be liberal while considering exporting opportunities and more protectionists when analysing the implications of importing. GATS can be used to enhance export opportunities, several domestic measures and regulatory reforms required to take advantage of increased markets access overseas. Hence India needs a more effective registration and certification systems, which prevent unapproved institutions from partnering, which protect and inform consumers, enable good quality foreign institutions to enter the Indian markets and which create a level playing field between domestic and foreign institutions so that the former can compete effectively in a liberalised environment. Once such a conducive regulatory framework is in place, India needs not fear scheduling education services under the GATS. So, globalisation of higher education services should also be seen as an opportunity, and the GATS as a framework to exploit this opportunity. So, libralisation of higher education services is required defensive approach, both unilaterally and multilaterally on the import as well as export fronts.

References

Nigavekar, Arun (2004), "GATS and Higher Education—What is Stake for India", Background Paper, National Conference of Internationalization of Indian Higher Education, Quality Dimensions; 24 April 2004, Bangalore.

GATS (1999), General Agreement on Trade in Services", WTO Document, Annex-I-B. http://www.wto.org/e/legal e/final/-e. html.# services.

B.N. Pandabe Niladri Pradhan, Internationalisation of Quality Higher Education in India: Challenge and Future Prospects, *University News*, Vol. 45, No. 34.

Piar Chand, Yogesh Gupta, Meenakshi Sooden and Sanjeev Kumar, Impact of Globlisation on the Higher Education in India, *University News*, Vol. 45, No. 46.

Chandrasekhar, Raja and Chanda, Rupa, Impact of International Conventions and Treaties on WTO and GATS: Reaching out to India's Tactics, Specific Measures and Actionable Initiations, *University News*, Vol. 45, No. 26.

D.G. Mannivannam, The Implications of GATS Trade in Higher Education Services: The Indian Prespective of Private Participation, *University News*, Vol. 42, No. 7

Deodhar, Satish Y. (2001), GATS and Educational Services: Issues for India's Response in WTO Negotiations, October 2001, Indian Institute of Management, Ahmedabad.

15

Educational Inequality and its Impact on Accessibility to Better Quality of Employment to Socially Marginalised Class

Ashwini Kant Jha and Bhavna Jha

The Education Commission of 1966 visualised higher education as an instrument of national development. Higher education ought to be an instrument of promotion of (a) universal values such as Humanism, Tolerance and Universal reason; (b) National ethos and culture which are also compatible with modern constitutional values; (c) expected changes in social, economic political and civic life in a metamorphic and transitional, contemporary (Indian) society; (d) excellence in all works of national life; (e) social mobility of large cross-sections of deprived populations; (f) manpower requirements of a society on the road to modernization and industrialisation; and finally; and (g) promotion of a culture of 'good' life and a 'good society' as well as 'good governance.'

Blaug (1974) explains the importance and value of

higher education from the economical, sociological and psychological angle and points out in his monologue that highly educated people are more productive. Further, he asdds that employers pay highly educated people more, because they are more achievement-motivated, more self-reliant, act with greater initiative in problem-solving situations, adapt themselves more easily to changing circumstances and assume supervisory responsibilities more quickly. Besides, he has also listed some of the widely held shibbolets about the role of education in the context of the employment problem of the country also. As money incurred in higher education is a social investment, it renders people more productive and increases the volume of employment. In the long-run, education works to eliminate poverty directly via controlling the growth rate of population and indirectly via an increase in the period for which children are dependent on their parents. And the lower the rate of population growth, the higher the level of income per head.

Development strategy focusing on adequate and equitable distribution of education, as a human capital, among different sections of the society plays a vital role in ensuring sustained economic growth with equity and social justice in an economy like India. The spread of qualitative education, especially among the socially marginalised and economically disadvantaged sections of the society (SCs, STs and women), *ipso facto,* has enormously beneficial impact on their socio-economic well-being. It has been argued that the workers belonging to SCs/STs with better education are more likely to secure high-end, better-paid jobs and thereby contributing to a greater decline in poverty among them (Thorat, 2005; Biradar, 2005; Biradar and Jayasheela, 2006). It also increases self-esteem, honour and social dignity in the society. More educational attainments are also found to be positively and significantly associated with better health, long and healthy life. Improvement in education, especially in respect of women, is closely associated with low fertility and illness prevalence rates and thus better health attainments. More importantly, an increase in educational status of women is more likely to reduce gender discrimination, isolation, powerlessness and social exclusion and bring out revolution in socio-economic transformation of the society.

Unequal access to education, which creates "information asymmetries", provides unequal access to job opportunities, perpetuates incidence of poverty, causes health hazardous and results in powerlessness and human deprivation. Equitable distribution of quality education can, therefore, convert the "vicious circle of poverty" into the "virtuous cycle of prosperity" especially among the weaker sections of the society. Against this background, the present study attempts to examine the educational inequality among social groups and also its impact on accessibility to good quality of employment including non-agriculture, poverty reduction among social groups in India and also to provide vigorous policy prescriptions to address the long-standing problems of the weaker sections of the society and thereby accelerating their socio-economic well-being cycle.

II. DATABASE AND LIMITATIONS

The study is based on secondary data collected from National Sample Survey Organisation (NSSO), Population Census of India and Planning Commission, Government of India. The data on educational attainments among social groups (SCs, STs and others) were collected at the all India level, including rural as well as urban areas. Similarly, the data on the proportion of workers in different statuses of employment (self-employment: regular salaried/wage employment and casual wage employment), non-agricultural employment and poverty incidence among social groups were also collected, were considered to explore the linkages between educational attainments and poverty among social groups.

III. EDUCATIONAL STATUS OF PERSONS AMONG SOCIAL GROUPS

Since the inception of planning era in 1950-51, the provision of education to the citizens of India, especially the socially marginalised and economically disadvantaged sections of the society, has been accorded top priority in the development paradigm. Since then India started witnessing a rapid improvement in educational stock with varying degrees across gender and social groups both in rural and urban areas. It has been found that at the all-India level, according to the Population Census of India, the rate of literacy increased from 18.30 per cent in 1951 to 65.38 per cent in 2001; it increased from 12.10 per cent to 59.40 per cent in rural areas, whereas in urban areas, it increased from 34.59 per cent to 80.30 per cent during the same period. Although the rate of literacy continues to be lower in rural as compared to urban areas, a greater increase took place in the former than in the latter. A striking trend is that the rural-urban gap in educational status has been on the gradual decline. A considerable gender inequality in educational attainment has also been existed both in rural and urban areas, but it is declining faster in the latter than in the former.

The level of educational status among SCs/STs on par with others is found to be highly unsatisfactory in India, even after more than five decades of developmental struggle. In spite of several programmes implemented towards provision of compulsory education, especially for SCs/STs, the share of illiterates continues to be quite significant among them. The data presented in Table 1 clearly show that at the all India level, the status of education is quite lower in respect of STs followed by SCs as compared to others. Going by gender, the educational status of women is significantly lower than that of male counterpart in all the social groups and more so in respect of STs. The data also indicate that at the all India level the rate of literacy for SCs increased from 37.42 per cent in 1991 to 54.69 per cent in 2001 and in respect of STs, it increased from 29.6 per cent to 47.1 per cent; whereas in the case of others, it increased from 57.69 per cent to 68.81 per cent during the same period. It is evident that although the rate of literacy has increased rapidly in respect of SCs/STs, as compared others in recent years, it is found to be significantly lower in the former than in the latter.

Going by gender among social groups, it has been found that in the case of SCs, the rate of literacy for males increased from 49.90 per cent to 66.60 per cent, in respect of females, it increased from 23.76 per cent to 41.90 per cent

TABLE I

Rate of Literacy among Social Groups in India, 1991 to 2001

(per cent)

	Males		*Females*		*Persons*	
Social Groups	*1991*	*2001*	*1991*	*2001*	*1991*	*2001*
SC	49.9	66.6	23.76	41.9	37.41	54.69
ST	40.65	59.17	18.19	34.76	29.6	47.1
Others	69.53	78.7	44.81	58.17	57.69	68.81
All	64.13	75.85	39.29	54.16	52.21	65.38

Source: GoI (2005).

during the same period; a greater increase occurred for females. Similarly, in the case of STs, the rate of literacy for males increased from 40.65 per cent to 59.17 per cent, in respect of females, it increased from 18.19 per cent to 43.76 per cent during the same period. As regards others, it has been found that the rate of literacy for males rose from 69.53 per cent to 78.70 per cent, whereas in the case of females, it increased from 39.29 per cent to 54.16 per cent during the same period. It can be noted that although the educational status of women is lower than that of men, a greater increase took place in respect of women as compared to men in all the social groups and more so in respect of SCs/STs. A greater male-female gap in educational attainments has existed in respect of SCs/STs as compared to others.

In order to understand the historical perspective of changes in educational attainments among different social groups in India, the data on crude rate of literacy (defined as the proportion of literates to total population) are employed as the comparable time series data on effective rate of literacy (defined as the proportion of literates to total population aged 7 years and above) are not available. The data on crude rate of literacy clearly show that at the all India level, as mentioned earlier, the educational attainment by STs/SCs continues to be significantly lower and started to pick up since 1991. Though educational gap between STs/SCs and others continues to exist, it started to come down in recent times. But, between SCs and STs, it appears to be gradually widening over time.

As far as the rural-urban gap is concerned, the data (Please see Table 2) indicate that the rate of literacy of persons aged 15 and above, is significantly lower in rural areas as compared to urban areas. Further, the rate of literacy among SCs/STs is awfully lower in rural than that of urban areas. Across gender among social groups, it has been found that the SC/ST males have a greater educational status than that of SC/ST females, but lower than that of non-SC/ST males. The educational status of SC/ST females is found to be significantly lower as compared to any other person both in rural and urban areas in India. The data also indicate that a greater increase in the rate of literacy of persons aged 15 and above, occured in rural areas as compared to urban areas during 1993-94 to 1999-2000. Going by social groups, the persons of STs in rural areas and SCs in urban areas showed a greater rise in the rate of literacy as compared to others during the same period. Across gender, it has been observed that the rural females *vis-a-vis* the urban males showed a greater increase in the rate of literacy during the same period. But, the trends are not similar among social groups both in rural and urban areas.

The data presented in Table 3 further reveal that the share of literate persons tends to fall with increasing levels of education. The fall is much faster in respect of STs followed by SCs in rural areas and SCs followed by STs in urban areas as compared to others. There has been a vast majority of illiterate and literate persons at lower levels of education in all the social groups and more so in respect of ST/SC households. The educational status of STs followed by SCs at relatively higher levels of education is, thus, far from satisfactory as compared to others. Comparing between rural and urban areas, the educational background of the persons in urban areas is much better than that of rural areas. It has also been found that a greater decline took place at not literate category in respect of STs/SCs and a corresponding rise occurred at relatively higher levels of education (middle and secondary) as compared to others in rural areas. In the case of urban areas, on the other hand, a greater decline occurred at not literate and literate at lower levels of education (primary) and a corresponding rise took place at relatively higher levels of education (graduate and above).

TABLE 2

Literacy Rates of Persons Aged 15 and Above (UPS) among Social Groups in India, 1993-93 to 1999-2000

(%)

Social groups	*Males*		*Females*		*Persons*		*Per cent point change in 1999-00 over 1993-94*		
	1993-94	*1999-00*	*1993-94*	*1999-00*	*1993-94*	*1999-00*	*Male*	*Female*	*Persons*
Rural									
SC	45.8	52.5	17.6	24.5	32	38.8	6.7	6.9	6.8
ST	41.2	47.7	15.7	22.9	28.5	35.4	6.5	7.2	6.9
Others	65.1	68.3	34.5	39.7	50	54	3.2	5.2	4
All	58.9	62.8	29.2	34.8	44.2	48.9	3.9	5.6	4.7
Urban									
SC	68.1	73.7	38	47.9	53.8	61.5	5.6	9.9	7.7
ST	75	76.7	49.5	54.5	62.8	65.8	1.7	5	3
Others	86.3	88	67.8	72.1	77.5	80.4	1.7	4.3	2.9
All	83.8	85.6	63.7	68.2	74.2	7.3	1.8	4.5	3.1
All Indian									
SC	49.8	56.7	21.1	28.9	35.8	43.2	6.9	7.8	7.4
ST	44.3	51.1	18.6	26.5	31.6	38.9	6.8	7.9	7.3
Others	71.6	74.6	44.2	49.4	58.2	62.2	3	5.2	4
All	65.5	69.2	38	43.6	52	56.6	3.7	5.6	4.6

Source: NSSO (1997-2000).

A striking trend is that the pace of human capital formation in terms of educational stock is found to be quite higher among the weaker sections of the society (SCs, STs and women) both in rural and urban areas. One of the important reasons why the literacy rates are awfully lower among STs/SCs is due to the chronic income poverty experienced by them (Thorat, 2004; Biradar and Jayasheela, 2006). Owing to higher incidence of poverty, the incidence of child labour is also quite significant among STs/SCs as compared to others (Biradar, 2004, 2005). A greater illiteracy, as an index of the world of "darkness", in turn, acts as a major barrier/constraint to obtain good quality of employment and thereby resulting in a perpetuation of income poverty among those who do not have education and being excluded from the world of "knowledge". The Achilles' heel of the Indian labour market, especially in rural areas, is

TABLE 3

Educational Background of Persons Aged 15 and Above (UPS) among Social Groups in India, 1993-94 to 1999-00

(%)

Level of education	*SC*		*ST*		*Others*		*All*	
	1993-94	*1999-00*	*1993-94*	*1999-00*	*1993-94*	*1999-00*	*1993-94*	*1999-00*
Rural								
Non-Literature	68.0	61.2	71.5	64.6	50.0	46.0	55.8	51.1
Primary	18.4	19.4	17.3	18.6	24.0	23.0	22.2	21.8
Middle	7.8	10.9	6.6	9.2	13.1	15.3	11.4	13.7
Secondary	3.6	5.1	2.9	4.2	7.5	9.2	6.3	7.8
Hr. Secondary	1.5	2.1	1.2	2.4	3.3	4.0	2.7	3.4
Gr. and Above	0.6	1.2	0.5	0.9	2.1	2.5	1.6	2.1
All	100.0	100.0	100.0	100.0	100.0	100.0	100.0	100.0
Urban								
Non-Literature	46.2	38.5	37.2	34.2	22.5	19.6	25.8	22.7
Primary	23.7	22.2	23.5	18.2	22.3	19.4	22.5	19.7
Middle	14.2	17.8	15.3	17.7	16.8	17.6	16.5	17.6
Secondary	8.1	11.0	1.3	13.4	16.4	17.7	15.2	16.6
Hr. Secondary	4.7	5.8	6.5	7.5	9.9	11.1	9.2	10.2
Gr. and Above	3.1	4.6	5.9	8.9	12.0	14.5	10.8	13.0
All	100.0	100.0	100.0	100.0	100.0	100.0	100.0	100.0

Source: NSSO (1997, 2001).

that there has been a vast illiteracy among STs/SCs as compared to others. This has emerged one of the important constraints in ensuring sustained economic growth with equity and social justice in the market-driven economy.

The unequal distribution of education among different social groups, between males and females, and rural and urban areas has adverse impact on the degree of accessibility to good quality of employment, poverty reduction and health status among them. In view of the above analysis, it can be hypothesised that the persons with more educational attainments are more likely to secure good quality of employment; lack of educational stock tends to have insignificant poverty reduction-effect, and lack of education is also closely associated with lower health attainments.

ACCESSIBILITY TO QUALITATIVE EMPLOYMENT

Accessibility to good quality of employment, *inter alia,* depends on the level and quality of education or skill/ knowledge embodied in a person. Generally speaking, employment can be classified into three categories, namely, self-employment, regular salaried/wage employment and casual wage employment. The quality of employment in the first two categories is relatively more productive, non-exploitative, better paid as compared to that of in the last category in which the employment is casual/contractual, exploitative and lowly paid. The proportion of workers in casual wage employment can be considered as a proxy for the degree of quality of employment. The higher the share of workers in casual wage employment, the lower the quality of employment. The persons with illiterates and literates at lower levels of education are more likely to secure casual contractual, lowly paid, dead-end jobs. The data presented in the following Table reveal that share of workers in casual wage employment is quite significant in respect of SCs/STs as compared to others both in rural and urban areas.

As a matter of fact, due to lack of education, a large chunk of SC/ST persons are largely prevented from accessing good quality of employment as compared to others who have better education, political influence and other factors. Going

TABLE 4

Percentage Distribution of Workers by Status of Emplyment in India, 1993-94 to 1999-2000

Social groups	*SC*		*ST*		*Others*		*All*	
	1993-94	*1999-00*	*1993-94*	*1999-00*	*1993-94*	*1999-00*	*1993-94*	*1999-00*
Rural								
SE	32.7	32.3	49.5	48.5	62.7	60.8	54.9	53.1
RE	6	6.6	4.8	4.8	8.2	8.4	7.3	7.6
CWE	61.3	61.1	46.7	46.7	29.1	30.8	37.8	39.4
All	100	100	100	100	100	100	100	100
Urban								
SE	28.3	31.2	30.4	28.5	42.6	43.1	40.3	40.8
RE	35.4	34.9	38.3	37.3	42.8	42.9	41.7	41.5
CWE	36.3	34	31.4	34.3	14.6	13.9	18	17.7
All	100	100	100	100	100	100	100	100

Note: SE: Self-employment; RE Regular salaried/wage employment; CWE: Casual wage employment.

Source: NSSO (1997, 2001).

by gender among social groups, the data show that an inverse relationship has existed between the rate of literacy and the proportion of workers in casual wage employment. It has also been observed that the growth of casual employment seems to have taken place at the cost of self-employment in rural areas, whereas in urban areas, it seems to have declined and a corresponding rise took place in self-employment during 1993-94 to 1999-2000. The lack of educational stock among STs/SCs has resulted in limited accessibility to good quality of employment (self and regular employment).

NON-AGRICULTURAL EMPLOYMENT

The growth of non-agricultural employment is considered as one of the important factors contributing to a greater decline in poverty. As daily real wage earnings in

TABLE 5

Distribution of Workers in Non-Agricultural Employment among Social Groups in India, 1993-94 to 1999-2000

(per cent)

Social groups	*Males*		*Females*		*Persons*	
	1993-94	*1999-00*	*1993-94*	*1999-00*	*1993-94*	*1999-00*
Rural						
SC	24.6	28.4	13.4	14.8	21.3	24.2
ST	17.3	18.6	9.9	9.4	14.5	15
Others	28.5	30.8	17.1	17.9	25.5	27.3
All	26.5	28.9	15.2	15.8	23.3	25.1
Urban						
SC	87.7	91	71.3	78.8	84.1	88.4
ST	85.1	87	72.1	72.9	81.9	83.3
Others	92.1	94.3	83.1	87.8	90.7	93.3
All	91.4	93.6	80.6	85.3	89.5	92.1

Source: NSSO (1997, 2001).

non-agricultural occupations are quite higher than that of agricultural occupations, the growth of employment in nonagricultural sector has a greater poverty reduction-effect, especially in rural areas. The limited access to non-agricultural employment may result in a greater incidence of poverty. The data presented in *prima facie,* show that the proportion of workers in non-agricultural occupations is quite lower in rural *vis-a-vis* urban areas and in respect of STs/SCs as compared to others both in rural and urban areas.

The workers belonging to STs/SCs have limited accessibility to non-agricultural occupations in which they can get more wages. This may certainly cause a greater incidence of poverty in rural areas as compared to urban areas and among STs/SCs as compared to others, and among STs as compared to SCs. Going by gender, the share of females in non-agricultural occupations is quite lower than of males in all the social groups and more so in the case of STs/SCs in rural areas.

The lower representation of STs/SCs *vis-a-vis* others and females *vis-a-vis* males in non-agricultural employment may be attributed partly to lack of education and partly to human capital discrimination, especially in rural areas. The data also indicate that the share of workers in non-agricultural occupations both in rural and urban areas increased moderately during 1993-94 to 1999-2000; the increase was much faster in respect of STs/SCs as compared to others and in respect of SCs as against STs, and also in urban as compared to rural areas during the same period. The share of workers belonging to STs followed by SCs in non-agricultural occupation, therefore, is lower and vast majority of them involved in low-end, lowly paid casual jobs. Consequently, the income levels of STs followed by SCs will be lower than that of others. The rate of literacy tends to move positively with non-agricultural employment and negatively with the incidence of poverty, especially in rural areas.

CONCLUSION

The foregoing analysis reveals that a considerable social and gender inequality in educational attainments has existed in India, especially in rural areas. It is evident that the STs/SCs have significantly lower educational status as compared to others both in rural and urban areas. Going by gender, it has been found that the rate of female literacy is quite lower than that of male literacy in almost all the social groups and more so in respect of STs/SCs. The rate of female literacy *vis-a-vis* male literacy has been on the rapid rise over time. Nevertheless, there has been a vast illiteracy in respect of ST/SC females as compared to non-ST/SC females. Unequal distribution of education among social groups and between males and females has adverse impact on accessibility to good quality of employment, poverty reduction and health status. It has been found that in India, especially in rural areas, a greater illiteracy in respect of STs/SCs has prevented them from accessing good quality of employment either in agriculture or non-agriculture. Consequently, the proportion of workers in casual wage employment is quite significant in the case of STs/SCs as compared to others. This seems to have resulted in a greater incidence of poverty among them.

The ignorance, illiteracy and incidence of poverty among STs/SCs appear to have ghastly affected their health status as compared to others. The proportion of women accessing the reproductive health care services such as family planning, antenatal checkups, etc., is found to be lower in the case of STs/SCs as compared to others. The population of women suffering from nutritional deficiency, children undernourished, women and child with anaemia is observed to be quite significant in respect of STs/SCs as compared to others. The fertility rates are quite higher in respect of STs/SCs as against others. The infant and child mortality rates are quite significant in the case of STs/SCs as compared to others. This clearly illustrates that the health status of STs/SCs is far from satisfactory as compared to others. It can thus be concluded that the health status of the weaker sections of the society mainly depends, *inter alia,* on the level of educational attainment and poverty reduction further, the reduction of poverty depends on accessibility to qualitative employment and the level of educational attainment will determine accessibility to qualitative employment. The level of educational attainment, therefore, plays a "linchpin" role in reducing the incidence of poverty as well as improving the health status of the socially marginalised and economically disadvantaged sections of the society. A greater emphasis, therefore, should be accorded to provide qualitative education to the weaker sections of the society for accelerating their socio-economic well-being cycle. Appropriate measures should also be chalked out to bridge the educational gap between males and females and STs/SCs and non-STs/SCs both in rural and urban areas to ensure equal accessibility to good quality of employment and better health attainments.

Policy Package

First, higher education should get a lot more funding from the government, gradually moving up to reach some 5 per cent of GDP, in tune with rapid economic growth. Second, private sector should be encouraged to set-up first class institutions with due provision for access and equity. Third we need regulatory mechanism free from throat-choking stagiest and efficiency destroying rules and regulation. The regulatory bodies must be evolved to be incorruptible and truly so. We should go for the setting up of an educational ombudsman, the agency to redress grievance of institution against the regulator. Fourth, a National commission should be set-up to reassess the compensation package of teacher in the higher education sector and recommend changes in line with the need to attract and retain talent and suggest mechanisms to reward research excellence. Fifth, it is important for that commission also to suggest measures to improve the international reputation of our institutions of higher education. Finally in conclusion, we as a country should announce and commit to a fundamental national goal of having, by 2020, at least 40 million 15 to 24 year olds receiving high quality tertiary education leading to high paying

References

Biradar and Jayasheela (2006), Effects of Inequality in Education among Social Groups in Rural India, a paper accepted for publication in *Journal for Rural Develcpment*, Hyderabad (forthcoming).

Biradar, R.R. (2005), *Dynamics of Employment-Unemployment among Social Groups in India: Emerging Issues,* a paper presented at the National Seminar being organised by Mangalore University, Mangalore during 4-5 September (mimeo).

Biradar, R.R. (2004), Human Capital Base of Labour Force among Social Groups in India: Emerging Issues and Challenges, *The Indian Journal of Labour Economics,* Vol. 47, No. 4., October-December, pp. 731-48.

Government of India (GoI) (2005), *Report of the Task Group on Devlopment of Scheduled Castes and Scheduled Tribes,* Planning Commission, Government of India, New Delhi.

Lanjouw, Peter and Abusaleh Shariff (2004), "Rural Non-Farm Employment in India: Access, Income and Poverty Impact", *Economic and Political Weekly,* Vol. 39, No. 40, October 2-8, pp. 4429-46.

National Sample Survey Organisation (NSSO) (1997), *Employment and Unemployment Situation among Social Groups in India, 1993-94, NSS 50111 Round (July 1993-June 1994),* NSSO Report No. 425, Government of India, New Delhi.

NSSO (2001), *Employment and Unemployment Situation among Social Groups in India, 1999-2000, Part-I, NSSO 55111 Round (July 1999-June 2000),* NSSO Report No. 469, Government of India, New Delhi.

Thorat, Sukhadeo (2005), *Affirmative Actions Policy in India: Dimension, Progress and Issues,* a Paper presented at the Workshop on 'Addressing Inequality: Policies for Inclusive Development' organised by Inter-Regional Inequality Facility held at UNECA, Addis Ababa during 11-12 July.

Thorat, Sukhadeo (2004), *Persistence of Poverty: Why do Scheduled Castes and Scheduled Tribes Stay Chronically Poor?* Working Paper for Centre for Chronic Poverty, London. World Bank (WB) (2001), *Global Economic Prospects and the Developing Countries,* World Bank, Oxford University Press, Washington D.C.

16

Education, Skill Formation, and India's Economic Development

PRAVEEN SHARMA

In post-independent India the discourse around (higher) education hardly includes its organic link with 'development' on the contrary, issue of industrial development employment and education have become so disengaged and compared both in theory and practice that practitioners of one hardly take time-off to reflect on the consequences of their policies and strategies for other fields of activities. This disengagement at all levels (policy, research, practice) has led to a heavy toll. In that sixty years after independence, we are still left with large number of formally illiterate persons, large number of literate but non-employable persons, large number of semi-literate but professionally untrained persons, an economy that has experienced pre-mature tertiarisation, where industrial expansion is limited, employment generation is low, and where hardly any substantive R & D takes place. The paper takes a broad sweep of the theme of the interface between education and industrial development. It begins with a discussion of the nature of discourse that took place on this theme in the Madras presidency before engaging with the post-independent or lack of it, to emphasize the fact of the remarkable level of awareness then (that is in the colonial period) of the consequences of not coordinating our notion of development with that of higher education. This is followed by sections on industrial development in the post-independent period, the higher education scenario nature of employment being generated in the economy.

I. THE CONTEXT

The first decade of the 20th century saw intense activity in the Madars presidency in the form of debate/ discussions/memoranda/conferences/resolutions covering the following issues:

(a) The need to bring the scheme of technical education into relation with the industrial needs and conditions of the country.

(b) The insulation of the artisan closes from any forms of formal instruction in school that could be classified as industrial or technical and, therefore, the inability of the system to tackle the real problem of industrial education.

(c) The extreme illiteracy of the vast majority of the population which meant that fundamental or necessarily preliminary instruction had to be imparted before going on the specialized technical instructions.

The need for government intervention in fostering industrial development and embarking on a series of industrial experiments worked on a comparatively large and commercial scale to make industrial and technical education really take-off.

We reproduce a set of observations from different official records to highlight not just the state of higher (read technical/industrial) education in the early part of the 20th century (which we know was abysmal) more important, our purpose is to stress the point that the level of discussion and the range of issue with which officials attempted to come to terms with, even at that period was simply remarkable. The recurring theme of much of official recording at that time and particularly in reports from the Madras presidency was the need to (a) Forge links between education and caste-based occupations, (b) enhance skills in existing occupations and particularly among artisan classes engaged in these caste-based occupations, and (c) raise the standards of general as well as specialized education to enable modern manufacturing industries to be established and developed.

I will assert myself in stating that, in post-independent India, the discourse around education hardly includes its organic link with development, on the contrary, issues of industrial development, employment and education have become so disengaged and compartmentalized, both in theory and praxis, that practitioners of one hardly take time-off to reflect on the consequences of their policies and strategies for other fields of activities. This disengagement all levels (policy, research, practice) has led to heavy toll, in that 60 years after independence, we are still left with: (a) large number of formally illiterate persons; (b) large numbers of Non-employable but literate persons; (c) large number of semi-literate but professionally untrained persons; and (d) an economy that has experienced premature tertiarisation, where industrial expansion is limited employment generation low and where hardly any substantive R & D takes place. I feel myself very strongly that we must recognize that our craftsman, workmen, artisans and ought to receive some education, and that the first principle to be followed in our scheme for industrial development should be that they must be better equipped in the future for their work than they have been in the past.

The note emphasized the need to provide industrial education on three distinct lines:

(1) For operatives in modern factories, mills and workshops.
(2) For indigenous artisans.
(3) For non-Hindus and these teamed the depressed classes.

In 1911 the superintendent of industrial education in the Madras presidency observed:

The conditions of the problem vary from place to place, but a few broad propositions emerge with force of axioms, namely:

(1) Technical work should be connected with a local industry and have a definite object.
(2) The teacher should be a practical expert and should be given a free hand in the scientific branches he should have been in works.
(3) Money must be spent freely on experimental work and in keeping up to date all apparatus, tools, plant and appliances.

The real problem of industrial educations comes out clearly in the following noting:

The most characteristic feature of the educational method now followed in industrial school is their absolute lack of common definite objectives.

What the present system represent is manual training and if we wish to limit education to this—If in fact, our object is merely to multiply the number of workmen irrespective of quality the present system is satisfactory enough. But in this case we must also clearly recognize what the limitations are and not imagine that it represents industrial education.

If we accept the first alternative, then manufacture does not come within our sphere at all and should be entirely ignored. Most of the existing industrial schools provide a very fair course of manual training, which however, they almost invariably associate with manufacture of a more or less inefficient character.

THE CHANGING DISCOURSE ON EDUCATION

In the past five decades the change in Indian higher education Altbach pointed out, among other things to the sclerosis afflicting the university system of higher education rendering it almost inflexible to reform and innovation. The major efforts to open and reform the organizational structure of India higher education had been successful only at the margin in that some alternative models had been introduced-such as the agricultural universities, the institutes of technology, and most recently, autonomous collegess—but these had not made any perceptible dent in the basic structure of the system itself. On the contrary, as Altbach notes, this great monolith of the India academic system had steadily grown for over half a century and (despite changes at the margin) had become a permanent feature of Indian society.

A long held myth that slowly and surely getting exploded is that this country is among the top four or five countries as far as numbers of scientific and technical personnel in the world is concerned. Increasingly the quality and caliber of this personnel is being called into question; more important, the implications of the growing disjuncture between the products of higher education (particularly technical and engineering graduates) and economic development of the country (particularly industrial development), now more than ever, merits serious discussion. While we still lack a clear understanding of the specific linkages, say between university education and technological capability of a nation, what is increasingly becoming evident is that it is not the sheer number of students or the quantity of their training that is important, but the effectiveness with which that training is integrated into the process of improving the technology of operating firms. It is in this context that we need to address the question of the growing disjuncture between the products of our higher education system and the pattern (and therefore needs) of our economic growth, which in turn, implies that we explore the whole question within a framework wherein social policy (including education) is a built-in component of the theory and praxis of development. Literature documenting the process of development in the countries of East Asia demonstrates, among other things, very strikingly the fact that social policy was systematically used to pursue economic development goals thus making economic development and pro-active social policy mutually supportive.

In the next section we provide a brief overview of three aspects of Indian economy, namely, technological performance of its manufacturing sector, the nature of employment being generated in the economy and the educational level of the Indian population. This is followed by brief discussion of select literature which not only attempts to contextualize the role of higher education in a globalised economy but also seeks to draw out the educational implications of continued technological dependence of developing economies for the better has been minimal.

THE INTERFACE THAT NEVER MATERIALISED

Educational Manifestations

The more important interface that we draw from this brief exercise is the following. One of the major lacunas of India's development strategy is that while it thrives on highly skilled services, it had all throughout neglected mass education and health services. India's elite educational institutions stand like isolated ivory towers amidst encircling poverty, illiteracy and backwardness. Rural India is completely neglected in health, education, nutrition and other elements of human capital. The number of universities and colleges are also very small. For one billion plus population 400 odd universities and 16000 odd colleges are too few. According to the latest count, only about 8 per cent of youth manage to get admitted in colleges and universities. Most children drop-out of school for a variety of reasons ranging from poverty to parents unwillingness to get their children educated due to socio-cultural inhibitions. Girls are particularly deprived of education. But even if the parents are willing to educate their children the shortage of schools and colleges hinders education. According to the Indian Planning Commission half the villages do not have a primary school.

Since India's growth behaviour is quite different from China and other East Asian countries, the impact of education and skill formation has also been different in these economies. In East Asia, including China, education broadened knowledge-base and helped in the use of technology across all sectors. With higher literacy and schooling the average educational and health standard of workers in China is much better than in India. This together with better work culture and discipline has maintained a steady growth of productivity of labour in China. With suppressed wage rate, the cost of labour is kept low in China. China has therefore attained international competitiveness in labour-intensive manufacturing goods. In India the average workers, especially in the informal sector, whether in agriculture manufacturing, or in services, is poorly educated. They also suffer from poor health. The average labour productivity is therefore low, and in spite of low wages, the real cost of labour is quite high. India is therefore not able to utilize vast labour surplus for exports of manufacturing.

In India higher education is almost entirely state funded. There are a few private colleges, mainly in professional courses, such as engineering, medicine, law and computer. There is hardly any research in private universities. The state universities are now suffering from budget cut. The fiscal squeeze has adversely affected health and education during the last two decades. Only in the last two federal budgets the allocation for education has been enhanced through an education cess. In spite of this however, state funding of education as a proportion to GDP is one of the lowest among all emerging economies. The quality of education has gone down drastically in most state universities. Only in a few centrally funded universities and research institutions the quality of education and research is up to international standard. There is a general agreement that unless India rejuvenates its education base and quality, we might loose our international competitiveness in science, technology and professional services to China, Russia, Brazil, Israel and other emerging economies of East Asia and Europe. There is already evidence that China which was earlier lagging behind India in scientific publications and patenting has taken a big lead in these fields. Other emerging countries also spending heavily on education in general and Research and development in particular. China's higher education and R&D budget is now many times that of India.

The spread of English language in higher education in other countries could also neutralize India's edge in education and services. All these have serious implications not only for economic growth but also for international competitiveness of India.

Despite this however, past investments in higher education and the quality of India's professionals should be able to maintain the current growth momentum at least for the next couple of decades. There is also a vast potential for enlarging India's scientific pool by broadening education base. Currently about 1 per cent of adults in India are highly educated with professional qualification. Another about 4 per cent has got general education and semi-skilled expertise. In all with about 5 per cent technically qualified and higher educated manpower we are able to maintain a healthy growth of about 8 per cent plus. They also contribute heavily to exports of goods and services. A recent study shows that remittances by Indian workers working abroad are the highest among emerging nations. Not all of this is however contributed by the high skilled professionals working in developed countries. A great deal of it is contributed by semi-skilled workers working in the Middle-East.

From Economic growth point of view formal education could be of classified into three categories: (a) basic education for general awareness and communication, which could include primary and at least some years of secondary education, (b) secondary and general higher education, and finally (c) professional education and higher education leading to research. While primary education is essential this would not be enough to improve technical skill. In the age of competition and innovation there should be a stress on higher education and research. Investments in these activities yield high return. However, the gestation period is very long. As a result the budget for education in general and for higher education in particular is given low priority, especially during the fiscal crunch. It is now well known that the budget for health and education suffered heavily due to fiscal cuts in the post-liberalization era. During the same period China has increased its education and education, international advantages of India in higher education and R&D budget by many times. With China now changing to English medium higher education, international advantages of India in higher education and knowledge would now come under a great stress. It is now becoming evident in many sectors. Apart from China, other emerging countries like Russia, and other eastern European countries are also gradually shifting to English Medium higher education. These Countries also have very good scientific and technical base. So far they could not compete with India in professional services due to lack of command of English. Thus unless India recognizes this threat and starts remedial actions through widening education base we might lose our international competitiveness.

The broadening of education base is also necessary to have a more egalitarian development. It is now well known that salary of skilled workers are rising much faster than that of semi-skilled workers, which in turn is rising faster than that of unskilled workers. Even for balanced growth and egalitarian distribution of income also there should be wider education base.

REFERENCE:

Bacchus, M.K. (1983), "Towards a Development Strategy for Education and Educational Research in Third World Countries", *International Journal of Education Development,* Vol. 3, No. 2, pp. 193-201.

Carnoy, M. (1998), Higher Education in a Global Innovation Economy, Stanford University, 31st July (mimeo).

GOI (1888), Review of Education in India in 1986, Central Printing Office, Calcutta.

Nagaraj, R. (2000), Indian Economy Since 1980; Virtuous Growth or Polarization? Indira Gandhi Institute of Development Research (mimeo).

Swaminathan, Padmini (1992a), "Technical Education and Industrial Development in the Madras Presidency: Illusions of a Policy in the making", *Economic and Political Weekly,* Vol. 27, No. 30, July 25, pp. 1611-22.

———(1993a), "Decay of Higher Education: Review Article", *Economic and Political Weekly,* vol. 28 No. 13-20, pp. 2517-21.

17

Role of Elementary Education in Human Capital Formation: The Indian Experience

ANIL KUMAR JAIN

Human capital formation is a process of acquiring and increasing the number of persons who possess necessary skills, education and experience which are critical for economic development of a country. Human capital is thus associated with investment in man and his development as a creative and productive resource. According to T.W. Schultz[1] formally organized education at the elementary, secondary and higher levels is one of the important methods of developing human capital which is "the process of increasing knowledge, the skills and the capabilities of all the people of the country."[2] T.W. Schultz has calculated that investment in education contributed 3.5 times more to the increase in gross national income than investment in physical capital.[3] The Ninth Five Year Plan of India has rightly emphasized that "Education is the most crucial investment in human development. Education strongly influences improvement in health, hygiene, demographic profile, productivity and practically all that is connected with the quality of life".[4] The Approach Paper to the 11th Five Year Plan also reiterates that "Education, in its broadest sense of development of youth, including sports, is the most critical input for empowering people with skills and knowledge and for giving them access to productive employment in the future."[5] It further observed that "Indeed, inadequate attention to human resource development limits the growth process itself."[6] Education has also been recognized as the most effective instruments for socio-economic empowerment.

While education at all levels—elementary, secondary, college, university and technical, is important but it is well recognized that elementary education is of crucial importance because the basic training and education which a child acquires at the primary level serves as a base for his/her future development, just as the future development of a man is dependent upon what he/she has learnt as a child in the family.

POLICY ON EDUCATION IN INDIA

Before 1976, States were assigned the exclusive responsibility in respect of education. The Constitutional Amendment of 1976 brought education in the concurrent list. After this amendment, the Union Government accepted a larger responsibility of reinforcing the national and integrated character of education, maintaining quality and standards, although there was no change in the role and responsibility of States. National Policy on Education (NPE) was formulated in 1986, as also the Programme of Action (POA) which was updated in 1992. The modified policy envisages a National System of education to bring uniformity in education, providing universal access, retention and quality in elementary education, special emphasis on education of girls, etc.

During the last decade and a half, the strategy of education development has been influenced by several factors. These include, (i) National goal of providing primary education as a universal basic service, (ii) the Supreme Court judgment declaring education to be a fundamental right for children up to 14 years of age, (iii) the need to operationalize programmes through Panchayati Raj Institutions and urban local bodies, (iv) the legal embargo on child labour, (v) greater awareness of human rights violations in respect of women, children and persons from disadvantaged sections of society,[7], etc. Accordingly, the Ninth Five Year Plan treated education as the most crucial investment in human development. In respect of elementary education, the Ninth Plan observed, "It is equally necessary that the problem of universal elementary education and literacy is tackled through a strong social movement with clearly perceived goals and involving the State and Central Government, Panchayati Raj Institutions, Urban Local Bodies, Voluntary agencies, social action groups, the media and every supportive element in society." (Vol. II, p. 101). The Plan Document further observed that "... high priority will be accorded to improving the educational status of SCs and STs, particularly that of women and girl children" (p. 367). This Policy thrust has continued in the Tenth Five Year Plan and will continue in the Eleventh Five Year also. The Approach Paper to 11th Plan observes, "The 11th Plan should ensure that we move towards raising public spending in education to 6 per cent of GDP, which is an NCMP commitment. It must fulfil the constitutional obligation of providing free an- compulsory elementary education of good quality to all children upto the age of 14. This means we must ensure both access and good quality and standards in respect of curriculum, pedagogy, and infrastructure irrespective of the parents' ability to pay" (p. 57). At the international level, India is committed to the 'Millennium Development Goals' and 'Education for all'.

EXPENDITURE ON EDUCATION AND PRIMARY EDUCATION

In line with the commitment of augmenting resources for education, the allocation for education has, over the years, increased. The total expenditure on education increased from Rs. 151 crores during First Plan to Rs. 1,143 crores during Fifth Plan, to Rs. 21,599 crores during Eighth Plan and more rapidly to Rs. 49,838 crores during Ninth Plan and Rs. 1,01,364 crores during Tenth Five Year Plan. (Table 1). While total expenditure on education has increased with the passage of time, it is unfortunate that expenditure on education as a percentage of total Plan outlay which was 7.7 per cent during First Plan and 6.9 per cent during Third Plan, dropped to as low a level as 2.7 per cent during the Sixth Plan. Subsequently, this share has been increased and as per the latest estimates, this share increased to 6.8 per cent during the Tenth Five Year Plan. During the 11th Five Year Plan, it is proposed to increase the Gross Budgetary Support (GBS) for education from 7.68 per cent in the 10th Plan to 19.36 per cent during the 11th Plan.

TABLE I

Expenditure on Education as a Proportion of Plan Outlay

(Rs. crore)

Plan	*Total expenditure on Education*	*Total Plan Outlay*	*2 as% of 3*
1	2	3	4
First Plan (1951-56)	151*	1960	7.7
Second Plan (1956-61)	273*	4672	5.8
Third Plan (1961-66)	589	8576	6.9
Annual Plans (1966-69)	307	6625	4.6
Fourth Plan (1969-74)	774	15779	4.9
Fifth Plan (1974-79)	1143	39426	2.9
Sixth Plan (1980-85)	2977	109292	2.7
Seventh Plan (1985-90)	7685	218730	3.5
Annual Plans (1990-92)	4915	123120	4.0
Eighth Plan (1992-97)	21599	485377	4.4
Ninth Plan (1997-2002)	49838	813998	6.1
Tenth Plan (2002-07) (Latest Estimates)	101364	1491646	6.8

* Comprises of expenditure on Education and Scientific Research

Table 2 provides an account of total expenditure on education (Centre, States and Unions Territories) and its percentage to GDP at current prices since 1990-91. From

TABLE 2

Expenditure on Education as a Percentage of GDP

(Rs. crore)

Year	*Expenditure on Education*	*GDP (at market prices)*	*2 as% of 3*
1	*2*	*3*	*4*
1990-91	2316	568674	4.1
1991-92	2599	653117	3.9
1992-93	2619	748367	3.5
1993-94	3147	859220	3.6
1994-95	3940	1012770	3.9
1995-96	5356	1188012	4.5
1996-97	6536	1368209	4.7
1997-98	7657	1522547	5.0
1998-99	9684	1740985	5.5
1999-00	10000	1936831	5.2
2000-01	11690	2089500	5.6
2001-02	10808	2271984	4.7
2002-03	11603	2463324	4.7
2003-04	13069	2760025	4.7
2004-05	18528	3105512	5.9
2005-06*	25528	3580344	7.1
2006-07**	32577	4145810	7.8

*Revised Estimates.

**Budget Estimates.

Sources: 1. Government of India, *Economic Survey*, 2006-07.
2. RBI, *Handbook of Statistics on Indian Economy*.
3. RBI, *Annual Report*, 2006-07.

Table 2, it is clear that since 1990, total expenditure on education became 5 time from Rs. 2,316 crores in 1990-91 to Rs. 11,690 crores in 2000-01. Further, during a span of another five years total expenditure became 3 times from Rs.10,808 crores in 2001-02 to Rs. 32,577 crores in 2006-07. As a percentage of GDP, total expenditure on education has shown fluctuating trend between 3.5 per cent to 7.8 per cent during the period 1990-91 to 2006-07. It was lowest at 3.5 per cent during 1992-93 and highest at 7.8 per cent during 2006-

07. This trend points that there has been no consistent trend for as proportion of GDP on education is concerned.

Within the education sector, elementary education has been assigned highest priority in sub-sectoral allocations, as shown in Table 3. Total expenditure on primary education in absolute terms increased from Rs. 87 crores on the First Plan to Rs. 374.3 crores in Fourth Plan, to Rs. 10,394 crores during Eighth Plan. During the Ninth Plan, expenditure on elementary education was Rs. 14,523.3 crores and during Tenth Plan it was placed at Rs. 28,750 crores in the Central Sector. However, like the expenditure on education as a percentage of GDP, expenditure on primary education as a proportion of total expenditure on education has shown a fluctuating trend. It was as high as 57.5 per cent in First Plan

TABLE 3

Expenditure on Elementary Education in Different Plans

(Rs. Crore)

Plan	*Expenditure on Elementary Education*	*Total Expenditure on Education*	*2 as% of 3*
1	*2*	*3*	*4*
First Plan (1951-56)	87.0	151.2	57.5
Second Plan (1956-61)	95.0	273.0	34.8
Third Plan (1961-66)	201.0	588.7	34.1
Annual Plans (1966-69)	75.0	306.8	24.4
Fourth Plan (1969-74)	374.3	774.3	48.3
Fifth Plan (1974-79)	591.3	1143.5	51.7
Sixth Plan (1980-85)	841.4	2976.6	28.3
Seventh Plan (1985-90)	2849.4	7685.5	37.1
Annual Plan (1990-92)	1729.0	4915.5	35.2
Eight Plan (1992-97)	10394.0	21598.7	48.1
Ninth Plan (1997-2002)	14523.3	22096.0	65.7
Tenth Plan Outlay (2002-07) Central Sector	28750.0	43825.0	65.6

Sources: 1. Government of India, *INDIA,* 2007, p. 235.
2. Government of India, *Economic Survey,* 2006-07.

and as low as 28.3 per cent in the Sixth Plan. In subsequent Plans, this share improved to 48.1 per cent in Eighth Plan and constituted 65.6 per cent of the central sector outlay in the Tenth Plan.

With the passage of time, with increase in populatio and increasing emphasis on education, total enrolment both at primary and middle levels has increased. At the primary level, total enrolment increased from 161 lakh persons in 1950-51 to 715 lakh person in 1999-2000 and to 796 lakh person in 2003-04. At the middle level, total enrolment increased from 31 lakh persons in 1950-51 to 342 lakh persons in 2000-01 and to 487 lakh persons in 2003-04.

TABLE 4

Progress of Enrolment in Primary Education in India

(Lakh Persons)

Year	*Enrolment*	*Class VI-VIII age 11-14*
1950-51	161	31
1960-61	283	67
1968-69	419	125
1979-80	523	193
1989-90	651	322
1999-00	715	421
2000-01	584	342
2001-02	672	426
2002-03	727	457
2003-04*	796	487

* Provisional as on 30th September, 2003.

Sources: Government of India, *INDIA*, 2007, p. 221.

PROGRAMMES FOR ELEMENTARY EDUCATION

In order to achieve the objectives of elementary education in the country, several programmes are being implemented by the Government. Some of the important programmes are as under:

(a) Sarva Shiksha Abhiyan (SSA)

The scheme of SSA was launched in 2001 with the objectives of (i) bringing all children in the age group of 6-14 years in school, (ii) bridging all gender and social category gap at primary stage by 2007 and at elementary education level by 2010, and (iii) focusing on elementary education of satisfactory quality with emphasis on education for life. This program covers the entire country with sharing arrangements with States (85:15 during Ninth Plan, 75:25 during Tenth Plan and 50:50 thereafter). Under this Programme, special focus has been placed on educational needs of girls, SC/ST and other children in difficult circumstances. Under this programme, new schools are opened in those places which do not have schooling facilities. Existing schools are strengthened through provision of additional class rooms, toilets, drinking water, etc. Education Guarantee Scheme (EGS) and Alternative and Innovative Education (AIE) are important components of SSA to bring out of school children in the fold of elementary education. Till September 30, 2007, under SSA, 1,70,320 school buildings were constructed, 7,13,170 additional classrooms 1,72,381 drinking water facilities, 2,18,075 toilets were constructed, along with supply of free text books to 6.64 crore children and appointment of 8.10 lakh teachers.[8] The allocation under SSA was increased by 41 per cent from Rs. 7,800 crores during 2005-06 to Rs. 11,000 crores during 2006-07 and is proposed to be increased to Rs. 13,100 crores during 2008-09.

(b) Mid-Day Meal (MDM) Scheme

National Programme of Nutritional Support to Primary Education, popularly known on MDM scheme, was launched on August 15, 1995. This programme has emerged as the world's largest school feeding programme and covers today nearly 114 million children.[9] This programme was revised in September, 2004 and again in June, 2006 to improve the quality of meal. Under the scheme, cooked mid-day meal, with a nutritional content of 450 calories and 12 grams protein is served to children studying at primary level in government, government-aided and local body schools. This programme is being implemented in a decentralized manner, with the involvement of local level agencies such as village panchayats, village education committees, school management committees, parent-teacher associations, etc. Steering-*cum*-monitoring committees at different levels have been appointed for effective monitoring of the programme. Funds allocation for MDM programme have been increasing with the passage of time. MDM scheme was allocated Rs. 5,348 crores during 2006-07 and Rs. 7,324 crores during 2007-08 which is proposed to be increased to Rs. 8,000 crores during 2008-09.[10]

(c) District Primary Education Programme (DPEP)

DPEP was launched in 1994 to revitalize the primary education system so as to achieve universalisaiton of primary education. DPEP adopted a holyistic approach and was based on the principle of 'additionality'. It was structured to fill the existing gaps by providing inputs over and above the provisions made under the Central and State Sector Schemes for primary education. Important objectives of the DPEP have been to universalize access, retention and improve learning achievement and to reduce disparities among social groups. At one time, DPEP was operational in 273 districts in 18 States. However, with the progressive closure of the programme, it is now existing only in 123 districts."[11]

(d) Mahila Samakhya Programme (MSP)

MSP was launched in 1989 for the education and empowerment of women in rural areas, particularly those from socially and economically marginalized groups. An important objective of this Programme among other, is to enhance the self-image and self-confidence of women and lay the foundation for women's empowerment or the grass root level. This programme is being implemented in more than 15,800 villages spread over 63 districts of nine States. States of Madhya Pradesh and Chhattisgarh have been brought under MSP during 2006-07.

(e) National Programme for Education of Girls at Elementary Education (NPEGEL)

This programme was launched in July, 2003 with the

objective of enhancing girls' education by developing a 'model school' in every cluster. Gender sensitization of teachers, development of gender-sensitive materials, etc. are some of the objectives of NPEGEL. Under this programme, 35,252 model schools have been developed, 1.85 lakh teachers have been gender-sensitized, remedial teaching has been provided to 96.7 million girls, 184 million girls have benefited till October 31, 2007.[12] For the year 2007-08 an outlay of Rs. 708.44 crores was provided for this programme.

(f) Kasturba Gandhi Balika Vidyalaya (KGBV) Scheme

KGBV Scheme was started in July, 2006 to set-up residential schools to address the issue of equity in the education of girls belonging to SC, ST, OBC and minority communities. The Scheme is being implemented in educationally backward blocks of the country where female rural literacy is below the national average and gender gap in literacy is above the national average. The scheme also provides for a minimum reservation of 75 per cent of the development for girls from SC, ST and OBC or minority communities. So far, 2,180 vidyalayas have been started and the Finance Minister has proposed to allocate funds to set-up additional 410 vidyalayas in educationally backward block. However, KGBV Scheme has been merged with SSA w.e.f. April 1, 2007.

THE PRESENT SCENARIO

While it is true that the Government has been spending increasing sums of money towards elementary education, launching newer and more diversified programmes to bring children to schools, the real situation is far from satisfactory. Mere numbers do not tell the correct story. One has to take note of certain disturbing elements in this regard. ***Firstly,*** the gross enrolment ratio in India during 2004-05 for classes I-VIII (6-14 years) was 94.23 while it was 108.56 for classes I to V, it was only 70.51 for classes VI to VIII. By and large (except in the state of Punjab) the enrolment ratio was higher for boys than for girls and it varied largely across States.[13] ***Secondly,*** the problem has been accentuated by high drop-out rates. During 1992-93, the drop-out rate was 45 per cent at lower primary level and 61.10 per cent at he upper primary stage. No doubt, these drop-out rates have declined in later years but these rates were still 39.58 per cent and 54.14 per cent in 1997-98 which, by any standards, are very high. The problem of drop-out rates has been more serious in educationally backward states like Andhra Pradesh, Arunachal, Assam, Bihar, J&K, Madhya Pradesh, U.P., Orissa, etc. Poverty is probably the major cause of dropping out of schools.[14] These drop-out rates have been highest for STs, followed by SCs. ***Thirdly,*** there are regional disparities. Some States like Kerala, Maharashtra, Gujarat, Tamil Nadu, etc. have done well in providing access to schooling facilities as well as in improving quality of education. However, States like Uttar Pradesh, Bihar, Madhya Pradesh, Orissa and Rajasthan have still a long way to go. ***Fourthly,*** while it is true that literacy rates of SCs and STs have increased with the passage of time, the gap between the literacy rates of SCs/STs and those of the general population still persists. Further, the gap between the literacy rates of general population and STs, has been found to be widening decade after decade. According to 1971 Census, this gap was 18.15 which increased to 22.61 in 1991 Census. Even for SCs, it has at least not declined. Adding to this are the problems of intra and inter-state and intra and inter-community variations in the literacy rates among SCs and STs. ***Fifthly,*** the quality of food supplied under MDM Scheme has been found to be below the prescribed standards and there are frequent complaints reported about the same. ***Sixthly,*** although educational facilities are made available to the weaker sections, the quality of those facilities remain dismal and the content of education is neither found relevant nor meaningful to their socio-economic set-up and needs.[15] Tribal hostels and residential schools in remote interiors are poorly managed and there are delays in payments to students and purchases. Adding fuel to the fine, the stated tribal policy of 'integration' and 'enabling tribal communities to develop according to their own genius' appears to have been entirely forgotten and mainstream school curricula are imposed wholesale on tribal schools.[16] ***Seventhly,*** the education content at the primary level has generally been weak. A recent study[17] has found that 38 per cent of the children who have completed four years of schooling cannot read a small paragraph with short sentences meant to be read by a student of class II. About 55 per cent of such children cannot divide a three digit number by a one digit number. ***Eighthly,*** an important cause of poor quality of teaching is the shortage of teachers reflected in a large number of vacancies. The quality, accountability and motivation of existing teachers are low. In many areas, teacher absenteeism is a major problem. Teacher training is both inadequate and of poor quality.[18]

SUGGESTIONS

It would be evident from the foregoing discussion that education, more so the elementary education, is the most critical input for human capital formation in India. Therefore, there is need to lay increased emphasis on elementary education. Towards this end, the following steps may be undertaken:

1. There is need to address the critical issues and achieve the desired objectives based on ground realities. This will be possible only when such a multi-pronged strategy is adopted which has attributes of decentralization, improvement of quality, cost effectiveness, result-orientation and time-bound commitment.
2. The problem of universal elementary education and literacy should be tackled through a strong social movement with clear cut goals and involvement of all the supportive elements/ agencies in the society.
3. To supplement the efforts towards school effectiveness, an institutional mechanism should be provided for on-the-spot counseling and guidance to teachers located in rural areas.
4. High priority should be accorded to improve the educational Status of SCs, STs and OBC sections,

particularly that of women and girl children. Reservation in admissions at school stage should be strictly adhered to and it should be ensured that reserved seats meant for them are filled. Further, such students should be supplied free standard text books and other necessary materials to improve their knowledge so that they are able to join the mainstream at later stages. Moreover, they may be provided free boarding and lodging in the hostels, instead of cash incentives, to check misuse of funds, as is done in several schools run by communities and different religious groups. Such a step will bring forth not only their social empowerment but also economic empowerment.

5. Schools are meant not only to impart education but are also expected to mould children's attitudes. "Egalitarian values, compassion, tolerance, concern towards others, respect for cultural diversity, gender sensitivity and health education must therefore be integrated in the curriculum at the elementary stage itself to develop healthy attitudes".[19]
6. All efforts in respect of elementary education shall be successful only if we have strong administration to administer different programmes and implement policies, with examples to be set from the top.

Notes and References

1. Schultz, T.W. (1961), "Investment in Human Capital", *American Economic Review,* March.
2. Harbinson, F.H. and C.A. Meyers (1964), *Education, Manpower and Economic Growth.*
3. Schultz, T.W. (1960), "Capital Formation by Education", *Journal of Political Economy,* December.
4. Government of India, Planning Commission, *Ninth Five Year Plan,* 1997-2002, Vol. II, 1999, p. 101.
5. Government of India, Planning Commission, *Towards Faster and More Inclusive Growth,* An Approach paper to the *11th Five Year Plan,* December, 2006, p. 57.

6. *Ibid.*, p. 56.
7. Government of India, Planning Commission, *Ninth Five Year Plan,* 1997-02, Vol. II, 1999, p. 101.
8. Government of India, *Economic Survey,* 2007-08, p. 250.
9. *Finance Minister's Budget Speech,* 2008-09.
10. *Finance Minister's Budget Speech,* 2008-09.
11. Government of India, *INDIA,* 2007, p. 226.
12. Government of India, *Economic Survey,* 2007-08, p. 250.
13. Government of India, *Economic Survey,* 2006-07, p. S-112.
14. *Ninth Five Year Plan,* 1997-2002, Vol. II, p. 115.
15. Government of India, Planning Commission, *Mid Term Appraisal of Ninth Five Year Plan,* October, 2000, p. 229.
16. *Ibid.*
17. Reported in the *Approach Paper to 11th Five Year Plan,* p. 58.
18. *Ibid.*
19. *Ibid.*

18

Tribals Access to Higher Education in the New Millennium: Issues and Alternatives

SHARMISHTHA PRITI AND TARASHANKAR PRASAD SINGH

No discussion on higher education in general and tribals access in particular can begin in right direction without quoting the lofty ideals of a vision unfolded by Pt. Nehru—the first Prime Minister and architect of modern India that " a university stands for Humanism, for Tolerance, for Reason, for the Adventure of Ideas and for the Search for Truth."[1]

The materialisation of such a vision required a vast expansion of higher education, many times more than what the British had established. It calls for equipping the young generation (15-25 year old) about 19 per cent of population with new skills, knowledge and new ideas in the new millennium. Particularly in the present context of glabalisation, we are facing imprecedented demand for higher education: general as well as professional. Commitments that leaders of freedom movement made to the masses and objectives of free India enshrined in the Preamble and

Chapter III and IV of Constitution of India and also on account of rising expectations[2] of comman masses including STs and SCs; there is an increased awareness amang the people, particularly the students passing out of secondary schools; of the vital importance of higher education for socio-cultural development and building the future of the society and Indian polity. It is higher education that provides the techonological base so essential for economic development and that creates the compentencies required in all spheres of human activity.[3] As such access to higher education opportunaties particularly to tribal sections of population and to the backward regions of the country like Jharkhand state is the important paradigm in forming policies and programmes for higher education in the new millennium.

The genesis of the present trend of changes in the pattern, structure, contents, objectives and programmes in higher education quite distinet from Nehruvian Model starts from the National Policy of Education-1986 (NPE-1986) in general and announcement of New Economic Policy (NEP) by the then Finance Minister and present Prime Minister of India, Dr. Manmohan Singh in 1991 in particular. NEP-86 recognised education essential for all and proposed for the consolidation of and expansion of facilities in the existing institutions to protect the system from degradation.[4] It also proposed spending of 6 per cent of GDP on education which was never fulfilled, not even in the current budget of 1908-09. NPE-86 was drafted and adopted when the World Bank had been advocating withdrawal of subsidies on higher education in World Bank's Roport on Financing Higher Education in Developing Countries[5]. The World Bank suggested cost recovery from students; educational loans to students, growth of pure private educational institutions which would charge fees sufficient to meet costs and make profits.

Prior to implementation of economic reform measures (1991); the trend of withdrawing state from the responsibility of higher education was slow and the government was still committed to access to higher education to socially weaker section of society specially to STs and SCs.[6] But the announcement of NEP-1991: Which was another name of Structural Adjustment Programme (SAP) of World Bank;

accelerated the pace of the liberalisation privatisation and globalisation of Indian polity; economy, policy, culture, education and society.

The World Bank in its document "Higher Education: The Lessons of Experiments (1994)[7] and an economist of the World Bank, D.P. Winkler in his study "Documents of Discussion of the World Bank"[8] suggested:

(a) Controlling access to state funded institutions of higher education.
(b) Creating of favourable enviornment for private institutions.
(c) Recovery cost of education from students, i.e. several-fold increase in fees to be paid by the students.
(d) Establishment of loans to students who want to continue higher education.
(e) Giving institutions enough autonomy.
(f) Establishment of monitoring accreditation and evaluation mehanisms to verify their performance.

Tunnerman of UNESCO[9] has observed that World Bank has a powerful influence on the political will a government of these countries which want international loans; putting at stake the future of socially weaker section including in the sphere of higher education. It is true for India where policy planners have been surrendering to the World Bank prescription in the area of higher education. The Department of Economic Affairs, Ministry of Finance put higher education under non-merit goods[10] from which subsidy should be withdrawn as it is appropriated by middle to higher income groups and the poorer sections of society are easily competed out at the stage of stiff Entrance Test Examination itself. So, education beyond primary level is non-merit goods and subsidy should be withdrawn from it to reduce fiscal deficits. This thinking of Finance Ministery is clearly influenced by the approach of the World Bank which believes that developing countries should concentrate their efforts on primary education. Higher education should take care of itself or be taken care by the developed countries.

Consistent with this approach in the report "A Policy Framework for Reforms in Education in 2000 popularly called Birla-Amhans Report considering education as a very profitable market made a case for full cost recovery from students and privatisation of entire education except those areas of education involving liberal arts and performing evidently if this policy is followed it will make higher education inaccessible to weaker sections in general and tribals in particular from higher education.

The deprivation of tribals from higher education is aggravated on account of there factors: (i) budget acts, (ii) shifts in policies, and (iii) other global and national trends resulting into increasing in accessibility to weaker sections in general and scheduled tribes in particular.[11]

TABLE I

Government Expenditure on Education

Year	*Education*	*Higher Education*
1989-90	3.8	0.43
1990-91	3.6	0.39
1991-92	3.4	0.37
1992-93	4.1	0.43
1993-94	4.1	0.42
1994-95	3.9	0.39

Source: Ministry of Human Resource Development (MHRD) and Research and Development (R & D), Department of Science and Techonology (DST).

There has been consistent decline in budget allocations to education in general and higher education in particular in the name of controlling fiscal dificit. It is clear from table that budget allocation on education and specially on higher education has declining trend. With expenditure on education 3.9 per cent of G.N.P. and on higher education 0.39 per cent comes on the bottom line of the Government Policy agenda. These trends are consistent with experiences of other countries that is countries going for SAP[12] (NOSS, 1991, UNESCO, 1993).[13] Even during the five year plans the share of higher education in total expenditure has declined from 18 per cent during Sixth Plan to 7 per cent in the Eighth Plan, the reality is that expenditure in higher education is increasing is absotute terms at current prices but falling in constant prices for example at current price expenditure. On higher education increased from 22097 crores in 1989-90 to Rs. 3253.6 crore in 1994-95 but at constant price of 1980-81, it declined from Rs. 1089.4 crore in 1989-90 to Rs. 951.9 crore in 1994-95. This implies that with the given expenditure, the educational institutions will be buying less infrastructural commodities, although government may be claiming that it is spending more on higher education. All this reflects that higher education is losing its importance for the government of India and this is happening due to policy constraints imposed on it by the forces of globalization. The budget allocation to the research and development is also being curtailed as it fell from 0.93 per cent in 1989-90 to 83 per cent in 1992-93. If we consider the increase in enrolment in higher education, it imlies a sharper decline in per student expenditurer on higher education.

The declining budget expenditure on higher education implies that the government is withdrawing from higher education in order to create space for private institutions especially the corporate houses both Indian and foreign. This leads towards privatisation and commercialization of higher education. These trends will the further intesified in the new millennium one account of loan compulsions for which India is bound to be in line with World Bank. It is very government which is determined to promate FDI in higher education. This has serious implications for the issues of social justice and equity threatening the deprivation of weaker sections specially SCs and STs from availing the benefits of higher quality education with increasing pace of globalisation.

The quality of higher education under public sector will further deteriorate on account of cut in budget allocations with less infrastructural facilities. Thus internal efficiency of education system declines contray to claims of improved efficiency because of budget restructuring and other adjustments.

The basic education is protected as the World Bank seeks to promote basic education at the cost of higher education. The higher education is unprotected with the adeption of the policy of reduction in subsidies and increasing role of private sector as a response to the forces of globalization, Marketisation, Privatization thrust on reduced government subsidy, fee hikes and pressure on the universities to generate resources on their own are some main features of higher education during post-reform period. An importants outcome of the adjustment policies is introduction of increased measures of cost recovery effecting equity by cutting direct and indirect subsidies in higher education. Access to higher education among weaker sections may be seriously restricted and inequalities may increase in terms of lower enrolment rates of women and other socio-economic weaker sections.

Fee revenue is higher education in India constitutes about 15 per cent of the recurring cost of higher education a proportion favourably comparable with other developing and developied countries including USA. It would be neither desirable nor feasible to aim at increasing this proportion unless equity and access considerations were sacrificed. Already in several institutions admission fees, entrance examination fee and miscellanceous service chargers have been hiked. All these regressive policies will have a deferent effect on social demand for higher education and providing opportunity for access to higher education to weaker sections of society. There is no provision for sufficient scholarships to protect the poor and socially deprived section of society. Thus, the process of exclusion of students belonging to weaker sections from higher education initiated by the privatization and fee high competed with the withdrawal for the state protection to them with diminishing scholarships. All this will drastically affect the demand for higher education at a time when the demand for higher educated labour force is likely to increases significantly in the wake of globalisation of labour market and more importantly the composition of students in universities will change in the favour of rich.

Provision of student loans is not so useful to students

of weaker section on account of high interest rate and security in job market. Moreover, the social composition of bank staff in India is such that socially deprived section students have every possibility to be discriminated in getting loans from bank. All this leads to the logical conclusion that upper caste and intermediate caste rich people have access to technical and professional higher education whereas poor SC and ST students will stick to basic and at best secondary education in third grade government schools. Thus in all probability the forces of globalisation have provided and reinforced the already existing caste-based inequalities in terms of educational attainment and access to education.

Now the question as to what does this inequality in terms of educational achievement mean for social mobility of weaker sections through education ? Education has been the most powerful weapon for the upward mobility of the weaker section with linkages with the job market. However, a restructuring of job market has taken place in India in wake of globalisation. In the light of this restructuring of job market the educational qualifications to get a job have dramatically changed and those will get a job who possers required qualifications. Whether weaker sections will be able to compete in the job market and move up the ladder of social strata remains a moot point. It is too obvious that mainly the rich upper and intermediate. caste students in India have the capacity to enter the present globalised job market which has increased the demand for "Symbolic analysists." It seems improbable that the students from weaker section mainly SCs and STs stand any chance of becoming "symbolic analysists" and reaping the benefits of globalisation. They will stick to low paid jobs and remain poor. Majorities of the poor are SCs and STs. So, globalisation process in higher education will re-inforce the caste-based inequality.

The pious dream of the Indian Government and the World Bank along with the economists Amartya Sen to empower the weaker sections in India through universal primary and secondary education may remain a pipe dream in the absence of provision for a strong complementary higher education system for the weaker section. "Universal primary and secondary education is a worthy goal in its own right but alone it does not provide the wherewithal to compete in the international market. What kind of job the students from so poorly equipped third grade government schools will get in a globalised labour market in India is anybody's guess. Thus it seems very illogical to expect that the weaker sections will be empowered through an expansion of basic and secondary education while depriving them of higher (technical and professional) education. It also means more privatization of education and further deprivation of weaker sections.

Again at the school level, dualisation of education occurs where elite schools (in private sector) serve the rich people and poorly equipped third grade government schools serve the students from weaker section. Those schools are so substandard that the doors of higher education get automatically closed for anyone studying in such schools. This is how the restructuring of education system on the basis of principles under globalisation, restricts the access to education to the children belonging to weaker sections. Education has long been recognized an important means of upward social mobility for the weaker sections across the globe. A limited access to higher education will reduce the chances of upward social mobility of such people. Thus globalisation may result in reinforcement of existing inequality and creation of new forms of inequalities. Restructuring of job market reinforces the inequality caused by unequal access to education in the wake of globalisation. A vicious circle of poverty is created which can be shown from the follwing diagram:

Poverty	
Low income	Low educational attainment or Lower access to education Low child skills, low paid jobs

So, what we have argued is that the globalisation is fundamentally market driven process in which education is a commodity and a field of earning profit. It is a highly differentiated process and finds expression in all the domains of social activity. It pulls and pushes societies in opposite to directions: Despite some positive aspects, the globalization of higher education is ultimately based on the market driven fundamentals of globalization. Thus it creates more challenges than opportunities in a developing backward economy like Jharkhand. The most important challenges include quality control, information management, its fitness for local societies, costs and benefits and providing education to all. When all these aspects accompany each other it brings the dangers of total lack of the genuine educational values; total control and regulation. A university turns into training centre and not educational centre. It brings the dangers of total lack of the genuine educational values, quality control and regulation. It is a bad idea to permit caveat emptor to dominate in higher education. Higher education in new millennium needs to be viewed from the perspective of global context of devolution and Marketisation under which national governments cease direct control of the educational system, and move to more of a steering role and education comes to be characterized increasingly as a commodity.

We need to manipulate forces of globalisation according to our own needs so that the vast poor population of India can be protected from the vagaries of the market. This is the central message of our analysis and an humble attempt has been made for some alternative measurments by the state to bring higher education with the access of weaker sections of society. However, these suggestions are subject to further research and empirical investigations:

1. The government expenditure on education, especially higher education should increase at least to 8 per cent. •
2. The primary and secondary education should be made complementary instead of substitutes. There is no meaning of only primary education to the weaker sections, as it will not provide them with necessary skills to compete in globalised labour make.
3. There should be provision of reservation for SCs

and STs at all levels of education and in all types of educational institutions—whether private or public, domestic or foreign. The diversity principle as applied in USA may work as a model for this purpose.

4. SC/ST students should be provided interest free loans from banks with a job guarantee from the government. These loans will be repaid only when the borrowers get job.
5. Weaker section students should be widely protected by adequate provision of scholarships.
6. Globalisation is all about competition and efficiency. Thus SC/ST students should be provided with necessary skills right from childhood to enable them to compete in the global labour market. This would instill self-respect among them, as they will be competing with the general category students.
7. Providing free coaching to SC/ST students in the entrance examination to various institutions of higher technical and professional education like IIT, IIM, JNU, etc.
8. A flexible career structure for SC and ST students should be promoted as shown in the diagram below:

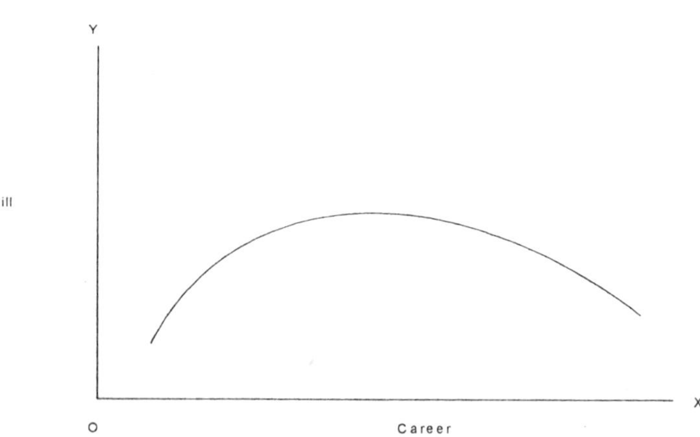

Such career structure means low skill in the early years of career. Such skill can be provide to the school level itself. Further skills can be upgraded at the college level and during the job also through on the job-training programme. The highest skill can be taught at the middle of the career and the person can be brought back to the low level skills again as he approaches the end of his career. This ensures that a weaker section student sticks to training programme because normally they avoid high skills training programme due to long duration and cost involved with it. Here duration is shot and they can bear the cost as training is imparted while they are still earning.

9. Special emphasis should be on improving the English of SC, ST students as it have become global language and prime requisite to get and stay in global labour market.

Again while it is true that under the influence of globalisation, the future of the University as a place where society can examine itself critically is a stake, all hope is not lost. The impact of globalisation is at least partly determined by people's response, which always mirrors local conditions and contexts. The reflexive aspect of the relationship between the individual and the global must be a crucial interest in contemporary debate over educational reform. The individual reproduces the global in day to day life but does actively, not passively and in a context of local cultural influences. Globalisation theory is itself an active indicator of the response that theory must make in new conditions. The globalisation process, then encounters a response that reflects each culture's unique forms of adaptation to change. Alternative responses to the globalisation of higher education must be built up on the educational character of universities. Such responses are an essential part of the globalisation of Indian higher education in the new millennium and required more empirical studies and researches which objective of access of weaker sections to higher education.

Notes and References

1. J.L. Nehru: quoted by Sita Ramyechury in the Intoduction of crisis of Higher Education in India by Vijendra Sharma, ACPI(M) Publication.
2. Dr. M.N. Sri Nivas: India's Village (ed.), Asre Publishing House Bombay.
3. Rinpoche, S. (1998): 'From the President's Desk', *University News*, Vol. 36, No. 24, p. l, June 15.
4. GOI, National Policy on Education-1986, Ministry of Human Resource Development, New Delhi, May 1986.
5. World Bank, 1986: Financing of Higher Education in Developing Countries, The World Bank, Washington, D.C.
6. NPE-86, 1, Part VII, p. 20.
7. World Bank (1994): Higher Education: The Lessons of Experience, The World Bank, Washington, D.C.
8. Winkler Donald R.,: Documents for Discussion of the World Bank, quoted in Tunnerman, Carlus, 'A New Vision of Higher Education, *Higher Education Policy*, Vol. 9, No. 1, pp. 11-27, 1996.
9. Tunnermann, Carles, 1996: A New Vision of Higher Education, *Higher Education Policy*, Vol. 9, No. 1, pp. 11-27.
10. GOI, May 1997: Government Subsidies in India: Discussion Paper; Department of Economic Affairs. Ministry of Finance, New Delhi.
11. GOI, April 2000: A Policy Framework for Reforms in Education, New Delhi. A report submitted by special group with Mukesh Ambani as Chairman and Kumar Manglam as member (Downloaded from the internet).
12. Noss, Andrew (1991): Education and Adjustment: A Review of Literature, working paper No. WPS 70; World Bank, Washington DC.
13. UNESCO (1993): Education, Adjustment and Reconstruction. Option for Change, A UNESCO Policy Discussion Paper, Paris, UNESCO.

19

Tribal Higher Education through e-Learning in India: A Challenging Task

Sandhya Rani and Abhay Shankar

INTRODUCTION

Acquisition of knowledge in the early phase of life and continuing access to it later on are crucial for an individual's advancement in life. In fact, higher education has vital role for the weaker sections of the community in general and tribals in particular. During the transformation of a traditional society into a modern one the traditional institutions are gradually replaced by formal institutions. The centre of authority passes over from the known informal traditional systems, albeit inquisitions, to distant known formal systems which are based on principles of equity and justice. Yet, the people may be seriously handicapped became of lack of understanding about their functioning and the class character of the people who may be occupying commanding position in the new system. In this context ignorance about the system is the biggest weakness of the tribals and therefore, higher education assumes a crucial role as a key to the understanding of these institutions and claiming of rights as member of a democratic society. Higher education is essential for liberation of the poor in the modern world.

Higher Education is expected to develop full potential of every youngman in the country so that an equitable place could be claimed by every one according to merit. That is why, tribal higher education has been accepted as a goal in all formal forums including the successive five year plans. Nevertheless, the pace of tribal higher education has been extremely slow compared to the critical role of education in social equity and justice and the objectives set in the constitution itself.

Higher education is not only a means for betterment of one's position in life but is also indicative of the socio-economic status of an individual group or a community. Educational advancement can be taken to be the best indication of the development of a tribal community.

In the present phase of new economy the higher education is fastly moving towards e-education and in the year to come e-education will prove to be the hub of Indian higher education in general and tribal education in particular. Since the tribals are poor and they do not afford to get higher education at their own cost so the e-education through university education may prove a milestone for the tribals in India.

PRESENT POSITION OF E-LEARNING

With a "global academic campus" in the making, the internet-based e-learning revolution is poised to change the way people will learn, and the way

The education and training business will be transacted. After e-commerce, can e-schools be far behind? "Virtual universities" are already making their presence felt. Some experts are of the opinion that electronic classrooms are ready to storm chalk and blackboard bastions. However, it is too premature to affirm or negate this viewpoint. Though, it is a foregone conclusion that online education will most certainly change learning patterns in the 21st century.

The new education methodology is ready to break free

of the 'Industrial Age' learning models and is priming itself through the application of 'Information Age' learning tools. Instead of recycling the same old classroom techniques riding piggyback on new technology, educators are putting their minds to developing approaches specifically for the e-learning, viz. multidimensional components which integrate features such as books, websites, pocket computers, and audio equipment. In short, they are paving they way for 'virtual classroom' experience.

The emergence of the "virtual classrooms" will result in greater mobility in the delivery and sourcing of coursework. On the content side, higher education providers with considerable international brand equity like, Stanford and Harvard, may exploit online distribution channels to penetrate overseas markets. Opportunities also exist for regional players to create the relationships and infrastructure necessary to deliver bandwidth-intensive services to the Asian markets.

The Computer-Based Tutorials (CBTs), which in the recent past has been growing at a phenomental rate, is being transformed into Web-Based Tutorials (WBTs). A wide range of courses are available on the web which can be taken by learners sitting at home in any part of the world. Since the Internet is emerging as the largest meeting point for researchers, academics in laboratories, students in schools and colleges and professionals at workplaces, educators are using it increasingly to enhance the scope of teaching and training.

The Internet, not only offers inquiry-based learning where queries are answered by experts in the field, it also provides a platform for discussions and exchange of views, resulting in a multidimensional approach to the subject. If, on the one hand, teachers and students come together, study and collaborate, it also gives the teaching community the opportunity to share learning technologies and strategies across the world that can be integrated across curricula.

Teaching and learning have become self-paced and the Internet has dramatically increased the speed of knowledge-gathering. Internet-based pedagogy is different from the traditional classroom approach. The combination and convergence of text, sound, and images produce much better results than education through monologic communication technologies. This, in turn, has spawned a new breed of educators who call themselves "Instructional Technologists"—a community whose focus is on how to deliver education effectively through the confluence of multimedia technologies on the web.

PROCESS OF E-LEARNING

The study on the process of e-learning has revealed that for getting optimal results e-learning needs to be used by combining e-communication, training and e-assessment tools within a networked environment.

e-Communication

This incorporates the use of a variety of learning portals including a live and on-demand video, audio content, knowledge management tools, just in-time information tools, we-sites, e-mail, electronic libraries and archive, electronic conferencing, any time–any place access tools.

e-Training

This is often formal and self-paced, and it often provides modular learning opportunities a learning management system, relevant content, and a structured approach.

e-Assessment

Participants should be able to test their knowledge through online examination and proctored exams, and get acquired skills, validated through certification.

IMPORTANT MERITS OF E-LEARNING METHODS

(i) Availability of Necessary Feedback

Immediate feedback allows both instructors and trainees to monitor progress and adjust instruction accordingly. This feature allows a student to decide how much time he or she needs to spend on a particular area, assuring that the student spends enough time on areas of weakness and not to much time on areas of proficiency.

(ii) Combination of Text, Graphics and Sound

e-learning is an effective option because it appeals to multiple senses—seeing, hearing and doing. According to the Royer Center article, people remember 10 per cent of what they read, 20 per cent of what they hear, 30 per cent of what they see and 50 per cent of what they hear and see is effective for people with various learning styles, and receiving information through more than one sense increases the likelihood that the student will be able to recall the information in the future.

(iii) Affordable Cost

After initial costs, you have a 24 hour per day trainer. A trainer is able to teach any number of trainees at the same time using e-learning. Also, having an on-hand e-learning programme eliminates the cost of hiring professional instructors, renting teaching facilities and travel expenses that may come when training employees with traditional training methods.

(iv) Effective Training for the Adult People

In some cases, adults who are required to attain additional training for employment purposes may feel threatened by the atmosphere of traditional classroom training. With e-learning, the student feels in control because the computer provides a non-threatening and non-judgmental learning environment. It actively involves the student in the training process, providing for increased student satisfaction.

(v) Self-paced, Flexible and Individualised

A student can work at his or her own pace using an e-learning programme. Plus, it can sequence training to match the needs of the student, and provides immediate feedback so a student can keep up with his or her own progress.

(vi) Tireless Education

It is superior training option because it never needs a break, is always available, can train greater number of students in a given time frame than other training methods and meets the need in today's workforce for continuous training. It provides consistency of training in terms of the quality of information presented.

(vii) More Job Opportunity

An e-learning program can help companies successfully train people in specific skills for specific performance while providing increased access to information tools for decision-making and general skills that effect overall employee performance. In its short history, e-learning has come a long way, offering increasing benefits with each interaction. E-learning can be used to reduce cost, improve quality, and accurate time to market-business benefits that directly contribute to top and bottom line of organizations. Substantial as these gains are, they will soon be eclipsed, as organizations capitalize on formal and informal learning through the convergence of e-learning and knowledge management.

STEPS TAKEN BY GOVERNMENT

The Department of Information Technology (DIT) of the Government of India has taken series of initiatives in the development of technology to expand the scope and coverage of e-learning process—

- For competing successfully in the global IT market, it is necessary that the IT workforce of the country is of highest quality and assured competency required to successfully innovate process, systems and processes. While the Government of India, Ministry of HRD and All India Council of Technical Education (AICTE) have already taken steps by permitting opening of new courses in technical institutions and providing concession to IT industry, there is acute need to enhance the competency and improve the quality of training for engineering teachers and working professionals from IT industry especially in advanced areas of mobile computing, embedded systems, etc. perceiving these needs, the

Department of IT has engaged itself actively in the development and promotion of information technology and electronics in the country.

- The main thrust of the e-learning programme is to effectively integrate e-learning methodology and approach with the conventional classroom system to maximize the benefits flowing from the traditional education system, increase its reach to more and more learners and spread e-learning from teaching of IT-related subjects to other subjects.
- In line with the recommendations of National Task Force on IT and 10th Plan Working Group, DIT had initiated development projects involving leading academic and R & D institutions in the area of e-learning.

SELECTED INSTITUTIONS PROMOTING E-LEARNING

1. National Resource Centre for On-Line Learning C-DAC, Mumbai

Under the project a comprehensive portal for on-line learning has been set-up by Centre for Development of Advanced Computing (C-DAC) and is accessible at http:www.ncst.ernet.in/vidyaksh. The portal covers institutions, standards, on-line content, resource material (articles, papers, tutorials, etc.), tools and development environment. The portal contains over 400 links. An international conference on on-line learning—vidyakash, 2002 was also organized. This project is yet to be completed with additional other activities.

2. IGNOU, New Delhi and E-Learning

The PG Diploma course is already running under this project at Indira Gandhi National Open University (IGNOU), New Delhi and about 2000 students have been benefited.

3. Developing Web-based Digitised Collection for Distance and Continuing Education in Information Technology (IT)—A Demonstrative Project on the

Internet-based Online Interactive Courseware: IIT, Delhi.

4. Design and Development of Internet Enabled Multimedia Courseware for a Virtual University: BITS, Pilani.
5. Development of Interactive Multimedia Information Services over a Hybrid Internet and Broadcast Digital TV Netwroks: IIT, Kanpur.
6. Developing Web-based Intelligent Interactive Tutoring (Web IIT): IIT, Delhi.
7. Design and Development of Component-based Funtionality toe-learning tools: C-DAC, Hyderabad.
8. Multimedia Digital Distance Education for IT and Other Critical Technologies: School of Education Technology, Jadavpur University.

FUTURE OF E-LEARNING MARKET

From an outsourcing perspective, the market is fairly large and growing at a healthy rate. International clients are outsourcing work to India, a lot of work, namely, content conversion from one medium to another. Close to 80 per cent of work done by Indian companies is basically content conversion, i.e. turning an academic course to an e-learning one, etc.

The whole market is driven by corporate and government sector keen to bring about uniformity in the internal training and save costs. There is a lot of scope for innovative and R & D projects. Several Indian firms are in to R & D and not be mere programmers. Tapping the intellectual power of the Indian mind is going to be the next big wave.

Standing against a projected global revenue of $23 billion by 2005, e-learning market in India stood at a meager $5 million in 2002, primarily due to poor demand, according to Nasscom, "the e-learning market in India is still in an infant stage and with an expected four year annual growth rate of 20-25 per cent", a Nasscom study said, adding that the demand in Indian market is still low and mainly from MNCs.

Companies such as McGraw-Hill, Digital Think, Skills Soft, Mentergy are setting up operation in India which is a positive sign for the e-learning segment.

North America represents the largest opportunity for corporate e-learning and is expected to account for two-thirds of global revenue through 2010. Western Europe, however, will be the fastest growing market.

In Asia pacific, the softening economy is said to have had a sustained impact on e-learning growth as price-sensitive corporations cut back on their training investments. The countries that will lead in e-learning in the region are Australia, Korea, China and Singapore.

Globally e-learning trend is towards consolidation as clients are increasingly looking at end-to-end solutions and system integrators like IBM e-learning, Cap Gemini are also moving into this space in India. NIIT is one of the top e-learning players in the country.

But growth of e-learning is steadily picking up due to key business needs of cost, access, timeliness, relevance and accountability. Some key driving factors are availability of adequate infrastructure, language barriers being addressed with localized courseware, government incentive to promote e-learning, and shift to knowledge-based economy.

PRESENT PROBLEMS OF E-LEARNING IN INDIA

Some of the major constraints identified by the working group appointed by the Planning Commission on Electronic Industry are listed below:

1. Lack of Teachers.
2. Lack of components.
3. Inadequate availability of access to library books and journals.
4. Lack of adequate access to laboratory facilities to students (which is related sometimes to shortage/ non-availability of technical/supporting staff).
5. Lack of facilities and/or inadequately trained/ motivated support staff for properly maintaining electronic/computer equipment. Or alternately

lack of adequate funds for third party maintenance of the lab equipment.

6. Inadequate exposure of faculty and students to requirements of industry in terms of skill development needed in students.
7. Infrequent revisions in the curriculum. Especially in the areas of computer/IT where the changes are very rapid. There is need to revise curriculum more frequently.

TRIBALS AND E-LEARNING EDUCATION

Since the e-learning is emerging with bright future which will provide ample opportunity for employment. But recently it has been started by the private players which are costly and tribal can not afford to be admitted in such a private institution. Though now-a-days, the tribals are taking much interest in higher education but their economic conditions do not allow them to get such kind of higher education and at this juncture only the government sponsored institutions or the university should show the teaching of e-learing to cater the needs of more finalized people in general and tribals in particular. The e-learning education will ensure the economic empowerment of tribals because the corporate sectors as other sectors will put a huge demand for e-learners in the coming time. Hence, the government is required to make special provisions for tribals e-learning education.

But the fast changing technologies have put some special demands on the education and training sector. The conventional formal educational system was successful in meeting the stable or slowly changing needs of the industry of the earlier times. Technological changes force the pace of development and educational institutions have to respond to those changes with relevant educational programmes, both in content and in delivery. The rapidly changing technology needs new and frequent updating of the courses. The conventional model fails to respond to the needs of the fast changing technologies and situations requiring quick response, which could not respond to the large retraining needs emanating from fast changing technologies. The conventional formal system of education with all its advantages and strength today is under strain to cater to the huge demand for IT professionals.

Although in India leading educational institutions have been developing and experimenting with the curriculum for use in virtual classrooms. To some extent, the experiments have been successful, but since virtual classrooms require an expensive infrastructure and broadband communications for video conferencing, in the near future it will only be practical in a limited number of locations. Nevertheless, with time, this will become a very effective e-learning tool, providing high quality interactive learning to groups of students—wherever they may be.

CONCLUSION

The successful implementation of e-learning will depend upon the availability of the appropriate infrastructure, special software, content, and broadband Internet access. Equally important is the need for a change in the mindsets of both students and teachers regarding the new educational system. Traditional learning systems provided the opportunity to learn from peers; e-learning replaces this experience with a series of new technologies. E-learning is also making its mark in a big way on India incorporates. And it's not just a multinational or the Info Tech businesses that are jumping abroad. Our good old Indian companies, including several traditionally run and family managed corporations, are shifting gears to move into a whole new learning mode...... technologically driven, flexible, self-driven and self-paced. So far the issue of tribals access to e-learning is concerned, it can be possible only if government takes initiative to set-up the institutions for tribals.

REFERENCES

Management Tools and Techniques, pp. 320-28, *Elsevier*, London.htt://www.steatlanta,org/currents04/proceedings/massa.pdf >

Nagy, Attila (2004), 'E-learning reports', ACTeN (Anticipatong Content Technology Needs). http://www.actennet.

Shepherd, Clive, 'Content builders tools for e-learning authors'. http:/ www.adlnet.orgTurner, Laura, '20 technology skills every educator should have'. The journal Jun 2005.

http://ww.thejournal.com/magazine/vault/A5387.cfm

Wagner, Ellen D., 'eemerging technology trends in elearning.Line zine, Fall 2000. http://www.linezinecom/2.1 features/ewette.htm.

E-learnspace: learning, networks, knowledge, technology, community, ten technologies that are going to change the way we learn, Nov. 22, 2004 http://www.elearnspace.org./blog/archives/0011849.html.

Davis, Shirley M. (2001) 'What e-learning can learn from history, USDLA, Vol. 15, nov 100http://www. ala. org/ala/acerl/acrlstandards/ guidelinesdistancelearning.htm

Thakur, Devendra and D.N. Thakur, Tribal Education, Deep & Deep Publications, New Delhi.

Sharma, K.R., Educational Lifestyle of Tribal Student, Classical Publishing Company, New Delhi-15.

20

Quality Improvement in Higher Education in India: Voice and Vision for Hours

ANIRUDDH KUMAR

INTRODUCTION

Education is the transmissions of civilization. Everyone in our society has responsibility towards raising a generation that can continually learn, unlearn and relearn. Our colonial rulers may have introduced higher education as we know it today to ensure they did not have to pay through that nose getting unwilling scholars and workaday factotums to came and carry the so-called white man's burden but they took their job seriously. So much so, in fact, the ended up widening a colonized people's intellectual horizon beyond a mere living. Independent India's rulers took a little time to show their true colour but once they got going education itself began getting the jitter

In the country today there are about twelve million students enrolled in post-secondary level Institutions of all categories including the distance mode. About 85 per cent them are enrolled in general liberal arts and science Institutions and the rest in professional and vocational programs. Though the number of students enrolled appears to be huge, it still works out to just about of the relevant age group between 18 and 22 years of age. This is very low compared to corresponding figure of about 70 per cent for countries like the USA, Finland and Japan. In most of the Western European countries it rages from 20-30 per cent In order to be competitive in the emerging new global economy, suitable measures have to be adopted for which India has a long way to go.

Though the higher education system has produced a few outstanding academic people equipped with scientific and technological capability, by and large, higher education is neither quite relevant nor effective to meet the challenges of 21st century. Thus, it is obvious that increased assess to higher education will not be sufficient unless we also ensure that the higher education system is able and made capable to providing quality education and achieve excellence in the arena of creation and dissemination of knowledge.

OBJECTIVES

1. To describe the current scenario of higher education in India.
2. To explain why there should be a needed concern for quality improvement in higher education in India.

MEANING OF QUALITY IMPROVEMENT

Before explaining what is meant by 'quality improvement' let us first out what does quality mean? Quality has had many interpretations over the years. It is every body's concern. If it is not so realized, it is a kind of policing.

When a product is manufactured, or a service is given according to the specifications of the buyer or customer, we say it is of good quality. But there are cases where the product or customer services will meat the customer specifications, and yet it may not have the quality desired of that product or service. In the post-dead, quality was defined as fulfilment of the purpose for which a product of service was made. But the present definition is that the product will not only satisfy the purpose for which it was made but also be delivered in the time it is required.

According to Oxford English Dictionary (1970) quality has been defined as "the nature, kind or character (of something); now restricted to cases in which there is comparison with other things of some kind; hence the degree of grade of excellence', etc. poses by a thing". The British standard Institution (1991) defines quality as the totality of features and characteristics of a product or service that bear open its ability to satisfy the stated or implied needs.

Navaratnam (1997) describes—'it is characterized by a customer focused approach to continuous improvement of processes, products and services through an interdependent system of planning, implementing; evaluating and decision making'. Whereas Okland (1989) says—

It is the degree of fitness for purpose and function.

From the various descriptions and discussions of quality, according to Dr. Mamer Mukhopadhyay (2001) the concept of quality and its meaning may be explained on the following bases:

(i) In term of the perception of the consumer or the clients.
(ii) In term of manifest quality, i.e. the intrinsic support.
(iii) In operational term quality implies something special.
(iv) In term of an identified specification to be met absolutely.
(v) In term of meeting specific intentions.
(vi) In term of value for money.
(vii) In term of a qualitative change or continuous improvement.

From this summary of point it is obvious that quality improvement means measuring up to the specification and satisfying customer needs. The process of quality improvement depends on a number of quality concepts such as inspection, quality control, quality assurance and total quality management

SCENARIO OF HIGHER EDUCATION IN INDIA

The scenario of higher education in India is marked by a rapid expansion especially during the post-independence period. This has been necessitated by the programs for economic development undertaken over the various plan periods. By and large, this expansion, as observed by the Kothari Commission (1964-65) which holds well even now has outstripped the facilities available in real terms and has had an adverse effect on quality and standard.

The number of universities in the county has increased from 20 in 1947 to 378 whereas number of colleges, which were no more than 500 at the eve of independence, has gone up to 1964. No less significance has been increase in the number of teaching staff which has gone up from a meager 15,000 it nearly 4.80 lakhs during the same period. The number of students enrolled in higher education has to gone up from 1 lakh in 1950 to over 112 lakhs in 2005. Obviously, the institutional capacity of higher education has increased by several folds. This has, in turn, enhanced access to higher education as we find that the enrolment ratio has increased from less than 1 per cent in 1950 to about 10 per cent in 2007. These development notwithstanding, the Gross Enrolment Ratio (GER) in relative term compared quite poorly with 60 per cent in USA and Canada over 40 per cent in several European countries and more than 20 per cent in many developed and developing countries. International experience shows that no country has been able to become an economically advanced country, if its enrolment ratio is higher.

In addition to above, the National Assessment and Accreditation Council (NAAC) is mandate to assess and accredit all institutions of higher education, particularly those that are publicly funded, and grade them on the bases of their academics, governance, physical facilities and infrastructure. Quality status of institutions of higher education as revealed by the NAAC assessment is given below:

- The NAAC have so far accredited 140 universities and 3492 colleges by March 2007. A glance at the status of the accredited institutions reveals that: 68 per cent of colleges are rated as 'B' grade while another 23 per cent colleges are rated as 'C' grade. Similarly, 45 universities are rated as 'B' grade; while another 23 per cent size 'C' grade and the remaining 31 per cent is 'A' grade.
- The NAAC assessment of colleges and universities indicate that inadequacy of funds, resource crunch, inefficiency of faculties and creation of faculty positions are the major reasons for inter-institutions variations in quality.

RECOMMENDATION

1. National Eligibility Test (NET) should be minimum eligibility requirements for appointment as teacher and exemption from the NET should be given in case of reserved from categories, where NET qualifies candidates are usually not available.
2. Similarly, as NET qualified candidates are not available in professional and technical subjects, exemption from NET may be granted to such discipline.
3. Faculty development and preparedness of faculty to introduce academic reforms is of crucial importance. The Academic staff colleges' set-up by the UGC, therefore, will have to play most initial role in academic staff development through continuous upgrading of knowledge and skills to teaching staff in universities and colleges.
4. Offer performance-based incentives to teachers in higher education.
5. The promotion of publication in peer-reviewed journals.

6. Assessment and accreditation should be made mandatory for all institutions of higher education.
7. Universities that are rated high by NAAC assessment should be given incentive grants for their performance.
8. Universities that are rated low by the NAAC assessment due to the deficiencies in physical facilities, infrastructure and teaching staff should be given additional grants for upgrading their facilities.
9. Scientists in Indian Universities and research laboratories should strive to create new knowledge and must work in tandem ensure that the research findings are quickly translated into application and technology.
10. In order to prepare and produce quality scientific manpower universities and research laboratories must collaborate in order to integrate teaching and research and to provide application-oriented teaching to students.
11. Universities should become power house of research and development and industry must come forward to fund universities in their drive to take up researches.
12. A knowledge Grid should be made. It consists of connectivity between constituent colleges, knowledge dissemination and knowledge reuse.

Thus promoting excellence in the education·system will need creation of world class education institutions. This will involve formulation of innovative methods by which information and knowledge are quickly for meeting national challenges.

References

Abdul Kalam, A.P.J. (2006), How to Create More Jobs, *Universal Education*, Vol. 1, Issue 1 (December), pp. 19-24.

Bhadauria, M. and Gore, R. (2004), Innovative Communication Techniques in Higher Education, *University News*, 42(29), July, pp. 5-8.

Mukhopadhyay, M. (2001), Total Quality Management in Education, NIEPA.

Pandey, K.P. (2004), Factors of Quality Improvement in Higher and Professional Education, in UGC, ASC reading material, LVIII Orientation Course, ASC, DDU, Gorakhpur, pp. 1-18.

Singh, Amrik (2004), Challenges in Higher Education, *Economic and Political Weekly*, pp. 2155-58.

Sreenivasan, R. (2006), TQM in Colleges, *Universal Education*, Vol. 1, Issue 1, pp. 32-33. (Feb. 28, 2008) Equitable Access to Quality Higher Education, *The Hindu*.

21

Higher Education—A Paradigm Shift in Multicultural Society

A.K. Singh and R.K. Singh

CONTOUR

Higher education in a repository as well as, arriving force of economic values. It is a prime device to transmit the accumulated knowledged, experiences, and culture from are generation to the another generation. Equitable access to quality higher education only can dispel the improvement of knowledge bring for the beam of hopes in Tribal land "JHARKHAND". It is the only tool to meet the need of the age particularly in the era of globalization the new age is caught in the webs of GOLIT where globalization, open market economy, liberalisation and information technology are directing the future course of the world Aristotle had rightly observed that quality is a habit, an attitude. But the demand of time is to implement, institutionalize and internalize it.

Whether higher education in India finds itself fit to meet the need of society is simply an euphoria is a blazing question before in the reality is, it still stands at the crossroads, in the process of transition. Higher education in India is intricated into the multidecisive bodies of different facets and multidirections.

HIGHER EDUCATION IN MULTICULTURAL SOCIETY

However education is an effective agency of value dissemination particularly in the context of globalized words. With the rapid transformation of the values, the society is experiencing a great threat to preserve and protect cultural heritage. The search for the creation of new values in education has fairly a long history reaching back to the period of early colorial rule. The Indian intelligentsia class was strong from very begining to evolve a system which moght be qualitatively different from the colorial as well as tradition pattern. They also tried to evolve an alternative that was neither colonial nor traditional, although it borrowed from the both. But the search was still born remaining mainly at the level of ideas without much of an impact an practice.

Right from 1948 to 1992, different commissions were constituted to focus on the goal and direction of the higher education and must of them underline a tendency to adopt secular values. Unfortunately it was politically and religious onslaughted. Communal forces forced to insert religious values, on the contract left forces tried to establish socialistic pattern amidst the tug of war scientific and realistic approach were kept a side and the goal of higher education distracted.

In the UNESCO report three pillars of secularism emanated, they are religious universatism, humanism and nationality. In a multi-religious society universalism is one of the ideological bases of secularism. It may only enable to create harmony among different religious groups by emphasizing commonly shared religious truth faith in religious univeralism which is central point to secularism. Actually there is no difference in ideas, they are co-centric, the difference is only in action or in their external manifestations which are done according to the cultivation of values in multi-religious society. Substitution of values in education prominently figures in the India society which only have been remaining the subject of discord. Tolerance philanthropic ideas are only way to way out the problem.

GROWTH OF INSTITUTION INORGANISED SECTOR

There is tremendous growth of informal institution. Numerous educational institutions of 5 star qualities have sprung up and mushrooming rapidly. Most of the informal institutes impart part time and full time technical education specially in engineering, management, commerce, etc. to enhance employable skills and their certificates are recognised by the private sector. Their growth is phenomenal. There are organizations that certify professionals who are found successful in the exam conducted by them. The professionals are authorized to verify and certify documents. These organizations conduct exam in different disciplines like auditing, cost and work accounts, company secretaryship, insurance, engineering, aviation, shipping for the aspirants who have atleast higher secondary qualification. They are given coaching in informal institutional set-up, often at a huge cost. The certified professionals have specialized knowledge and earn more than what the highest degree holder gets from universities.

India has the third largest higher education system in the world comprising of about 330 university level institutions, about 16,000 colleges (including 4500 professional institutions), over 9-5 million students and approximately 350,000 teachers.

However private sectors have been contributing a massive share to the higher education for a long time. The BITS pilane, Rajasthan which is funded and managed by Birla Group Trust became an officially recognized university as far back in 1964 other institutions like Manipal, Karnataka have been running private colleges since 1953, Manipal Academy of Higher Education became a deemed university in 1993. Many other self-financing institutions were set-up early 1990s and a few of them have became deemed universities. And they are imparting education at a very high cost which is far away from the touch of the poor rural population. Hence in public sector government has to set-up special fund for equitable access to quality higher education. Hordes of students are taking admission for obtaining degree. But the question is/are our pass out students getting actually that they should be getting? Students and their families are rightfully questioning the quality of curriculum, institutional delivery, the learning environment, accessibility for the lifelong learning and improvement of knowledge. The manner in which education is being imparted needs to be diagnosed keeping in view all the players in the field.

LIMITED RESOURCE (FUND)

There is limited source of funds for higher education, they are respectively three different sources, viz. Government grants, tution fee, other sources of income from philanthropy industry, sale of publications, etc. Government and allies have almost doubled its resources, on the contract other fees (documents charge etc,) are laid there or have been enhanced a very little due to political sought of the students belonging to member of some parties.

Need of Finance W.R. to G.E.R

The union planning commission's working group on higher education for the eleventh plan proposed the objective of raising the Gross Enrolment Ratio (GER) from 10.5 to 15.5 in 2011-12, the working Group's report estimated that financial resources required to achieve GER 15.5 by 2012 would be in the range of Rs. 54,000 crore Rs. to 88,000 crore. Prof. Sukhadeo Thorat, hon'ble Chairman, University Grants Commission requested the Government to provide 57000 crore for the UGC to carry out activities in general higher education during 11th Plan period. There are separate demand for funds to finance technical higher education

Several NAAC reports point to the inadequacy of infrastructure, lack of funds to meet recurring expenditure like on laboratories, libraries, recruitment of teachers which are major issue responsible for low quality higher education. Hence in order to increase the efficacy of the existing institutions, we may need some hundred crores. Apart from these pay scales of teaching and non-teaching staff likely to be increased after the Sixth Pay Commission award, the total allocation needed for higher education, during the 11th Plan period to achieve GER 15.5 would be much more than 57,000 crore.

Expansion of access to higher education would involve larger recurring expenditure which can't be redeemed through the extra budgetary provision as the Fiscal Responsibility Acts may constrain the union and state Governments to balance their revenue.

Academic Freedom

We stepped up into the new era of 21st century poised with many challenges to the higher education, the inherent question is how to keep academic freedom of the Indian Universities safe with equally important ensuring the value of transparency and accountability in organized or unorganized sector. But it is critical in the context of growing commercialization of education. It will also impact in determining the different aspects of education including curriculum development, programme administration, recruitment of faculty members, teaching pedagogy, assessment regimes and professional engagement of educational institutions. There are certain aspects of political culture, religious intolerance and cultural dogmatism which have perilous to the academic freedom.

Effort of International Institution

The world community felt the need of academic freedom very earlier consequently convened a conference under the auspices of UNESCO in 1950 where universities of the world erected three principles for which universities were expected to stand. First the right to persue knowledge for its own sake and to follow whereever the search for truth may lead, second, the tolerance of divergent opinion and freedom for political interference, and third, the obligation as social institutions to promote through teaching and research, the principles of freedom and justice of human dignity and solidarity and to develop mutually material and moral aid on international level.

More recently on the request of secretary general of UNO in January, the first global colloquim of university presidents met at Columbia University in New York, in which 40 university leaders and professors participated. The main theme of discussion was academic freedom.

Report of the colloquim reveals, "Academic freedom benefits society in two fundamental ways. It benefits society directly and usually immediately, through the impacts and benefits of applied knowledge, the training of skilled professionals and the education of future leaders and citizens. It benefits society indirectly usually over longer periods of time, through the creations, preservation and transmission of knowledge and understanding for its own sake, irrespective of immediate applications."

CONCLUSION

The story of education in India is one of the huge gaps between words and deeds, intentions and actions, input and outcomes. Education is not only a matter of social justice but also crucial to the economic growth and wealther creation. A paradigm shift is being experienced over the last decades, that need of education which always existed has now been turned into a demand for education. In this process education has been commoditized. So far as higher education concerns it is being shrunk to a handfull wealthy class. In an unequal society marginalised sections should be given a preferential treatment interms of reservation besides financial assistance. It should act as an important tool in bridging the gap between rich and poor, rural and urban, agrarian and elite. All new universities and colleges should be opened in backward districts to ameliorate the life and living of the dwellers who are far from the civilized world particularly SC/ST and women.

The extreme dispartics to quality of education is also against the principles of equity and justice. Appointment of V.C. should not be made on political or any type of discerete so that the person chaired on the top may not be prejudiced or having any type of biases, otherwise meaning of academic freedom would be destroyed.

Today's economy is propelled and driven by market forces which inevitably has excluded the poor and uneducated section of the society. Their participation in the economic action is negligible. Unless the neglected and isolated section of society is brought into the mainstream so as to take benefits of economic growth, the aims and objectives of the higher education will remain incomplete and no substainable developments be achieved.

Delinking of degrees from jobs had been subject of talk for years but yet it is not done. The market has to play such role and is doing so. The BPO's especially of the customer care kind hardly look at educational qualifications as long as the person communicate in Engligh. In manufacturing, a trainable person is more desirable than a person with meaningless educational certification. Specific skills are more important than all round knowledge of a subject. Hence degrees and jobs should not be linked together.

References

Yojna, Aug. 2007.

Yojna, Nov. 2006.

Hindu, 28 Feb. 2006.

Hindu, 13 Nov. 2007.

Hindu, 20-21 Jan. 2007.

Hindu, 17 Feb. 2007.

Census of India (2001).

Economic Survey, 2003-04.

Sharma, G.D. (1998), Contribution of Higher Education, in National Development, *Journal of Higher Education,* Vol. 21, No. 2, Summer.

22

Tribals Accessibility to Higher Education: A Case Study of Santhal Parganas Division, Jharkhand

NAGESHWAR SHARMA

I. INTRODUCTION

Knowledge is light. Ignorance is darkness. Knowledge is considered to be the third eye of man. In Sanskrit it has been said, 'Gyanam Tritiyam Manujasya Netram', 'Tamsoma Jyotir Gamaya' and 'Gyan Vigyanam Vimukatye'. All these shlokas show the importance of knowledge. Education, if not the single source of knowledge is a main source of knowledge. Since the Vedic period education has been supposed to such a light which illuminates every sphere of life. This is why education has been called the third eye. Education leads man from darkness to light. (Tamsoma Jyotir Gamaya). It emancipates man's soul from sins. In the present era it is true that education is the first and basic factor of social empowering.

Indian education system is presently divided into three parts: 10+2+3. Higher education starts in all streams after +2 and it includes degree level education which comes under the preview of the UGC.

We are living in such a fast growing world where improved technology and knowledge-based power have been dominating. To face the challenges of modern and the most competitive world education alone is not sufficient but specific and high level education is must. All developed countries are highly developed in respect of higher education. The percentage of highly educated people in developed countries is far higher than that of developing countries. Hence, higher education is presumed to be the most important means of empowering all classes of the society.

II. TRIBALS IN INDIA

The Constitution of India had promised the tribals of India a protection against exploitation, respect for their tradition and heritage, assistance for the improvement of their socio-economic and educational status. But still promises are unfulfilled and they are betrayed despite the guarantees enshrined in the Constitution of India (Article 46).

According to one estimate there are 427 Scheduled Tribe communities in India and Constitute about eight per cent of the Indian population. They occupy a very special position in the Indian society because of the following reasons:

(a) The tribals are the oldest settlers, if not the first settlers in India. The Hindi word 'Adivasi' ('Adi' means oldest and 'Vasi' means inhabitant) is commonly used to designate them. The International Labour Organisation Convention 107 held at Geneva on 5th June 1957 classified these people as indigenous.

(b) The tribals in India (Census 2001) far outnumber the tribal population in any other country. In fact, India has almost as many tribals as all the tribals taken together in nineteen countries with substantial tribals population (Table 1). Myanmar has the second largest tribal population of 14 million tribals. The tribal population in India is more than the total population of France or the United Kingdom. Though the triabals constitute eight per cent of the total Indian population they constitute a majority in several States and Union

TABLE 1

Estimated Population of Indigenous Peoples, Selected Countries, 1992

Country	*Population (Million)*	*Share of National Population (Percentage)*
Papua New Guinea	3.0	77
Bolivia	5.6	70
Guatemala	4.6	47
Peru	9.0	40
Ecuador	3.8	38
Myanmar	14.0	33
Laps	1.3	30
Mexico	10.9	12
New Zealand	0.4	12
Chile	1.2	9
Philippines	6.0	9
India	63.0	7
Malaysia	0.8	4
Canada	0.9	4
Australia	0.4	2
Brazil	1.5	1
Bangladesh	1.2	1
Thailand	0.5	1
United States	2.0	1
Former Soviet Union	1.4	<1

Source: During, A.T. (1993). Supporting Indigenous Peoples in L.R. Brown (Ed.) State of the World, 1993. A Worldwatch Institute Report on Progress Towards a Sustainable Society, New York: W.W. Norton, p. 83.

Territories and substantial numbers in others (Table 2).

TABLE 2

Share of ST Population to Total Population and General Population, 1991

State/UT	*% of ST Population to Total ST Population*	*% of ST Population to General Population*
States with 25 per cent and more Tribal Population		
Meghalaya	2.24	8S.S3
Nagaland	1.57	87.70
Tripura	1.26	30.95
Mizoram	0.96	94.75
Manipur	0.93	34.41
Arunachal Pradesh	0.81	63.66
Dadra and Nagar Haveli	0.16	78.99
Lakshadweep	0.07	93.15
States with 5-25 per cent Tribal Population		
Madhya Pradesh	2.73	23.77
Maharashtra	10.80	9.27
Orissa	10.38	22.21
Bihar	9.77	7.66
Gujarat	9.09	14.92
Rajasthan	8.08	12.44
Andhra Pradesh	6.20	6.31
West Bengal	5.62	5.59
Assam	4.24	24.66
Sikkim	0.13	22.36
Andaman and Niccobar	0.04	9.54
Daman and Diu	0.02	11.54
States with less than 5 per cent Tribal Population		
Karnataka	2.83	4.26
Tamil Nadu	0.85	1.03
Kerala	0.47	1.10
Uttar Pradesh	0.42	0.21
Himachal Pradesh	0.32	4.22
Goa	0.00	0.03

Based on Sensus of India, 1991.

(c) The Constitution of India promised several protective measures for the well-being of the tribals Article 46 assured educational and economic benefits and protection against Social injustice and exploitation. Article 355 promised reservation in recruitment.

The world 'tribe' has not been defined anywere in the Constitution of India. But it states in Articles 342 that the Scheduled Tribes are 'tribes' on the tribal communities or part of groups within tribes or tribal communities which the President may specify from time to time by public notification. The ILO convention held at Geneva on 27 June 1989 recognized the 'aspirations' of these peoples to exercise control over their own institutions, ways of life and economic development and religions within the frame work of the states in which they live . . . Notwithstanding the policy of the Indigenous and tribal peoples' convention, 1989, India, a Secular, Democratic and Socialist Republic has been pursuing a policy of cultural pluralism ever since it became independent. Pandit Jawaharlal Nehru, the first Prime Minister of India had declared that: "We should help the tribals to develop along the lines of their own tradition and genius, teaching them not to despise their pasts but to build upon (quoted in Elwin, 1963:5)

III. A HISTORICAL VIEW

The year of 1857 has been marked as a milestone in the history of higher education. A historical overview of post-higher secondary education in India shows that the first three universities were established in 1857. Though the first college came up in Bombay in the year 1934, the number grew steadily till 1947.

At the time of independence the number of universities and colleges has risen to 18 and 591 respectively. Thereafter, these institutions grew by leaps and bounds across the length and breadth of this country.

During the past 50 years Indian education system has expanded vastly and there has been a tremendous increase in the number of Universities, Colleges, Students and Teachers e.g. number of Universities has increased from 25 to about 350, colleges from 700 to over 16,000, students from 1 million to 10 million and teachers from 15 thousand to about 4.75 lakhs. But, still the access ratio is just 7 per cent as compared 30-60 per cent in developed countries. During 10th Five Year Plan UGC has a target to achieve the access ratio of 10 per cent. In view of "Sarva Shiksha Abhiyan" of the Government of India the UGC has to prepare itself to cater to the increasing demand in view of the several million students entering into the higher education system.

IV. SECOND VISION FOR THE NATION

We all have heard about the first vision of the Nation which commenced in the year 1857. During that period there were few universities in the country. Many of our freedom fighters were educated abroad. Besides, common mass lawyers, educators, poets academicians, industrialists participated in the freedom movement. After a long drawn struggle we got the freedom and our country became independent on 15th August 1947. There has been substantial growth in higher education and today nearly 10 million students are studying in our colleges thereby in our universities. We have designed our own higher education system and educated over Eighty million students during this period who are engaged in a variety of national and international assignments. After five decades of growth our country has to face new challenges. It has a second vision to become a developed India by the year 2020. We have a population of over 3 billion people of which 260 million are still living below the poverty line. They need education, they need habitat, they need health care and creation of employment potential. To meet their needs we need the second vision for the nation. Our GDP is growing at an average rate of nearly 6 P.A.. whereas the economists suggest that to remove the poverty of 260 million people we have to grow at the rate of 10 per cent P.A. consistently for over a decade. Our Prime Minister is of the firm view that we have to build-up new India and it is only possible with infrastructural development. The quality and capacity of infrastructure are the greatest cause of concern and we will have to remove these weaknesses and only then the dream of 'Bharat Mahan' from 'Bharat Nirman' will be achieved.

In order to meet these complex requirements it has to be recognized that the university should also be a place of research. 10 per cent of the university facilities should be allocated exclusively for research. Creation of national institute of science will also help in identifying areas where research and developments are co-located and flow from one another.

V. PRESENT STATUS OF HIGHER EDUCATION SYSTEM

A good number of schemes have been launched by UGC for the development of the universities and colleges, provide access of education to all the sections of the society equitably, especially for the underprivileged and differently able persons. UGC has also launched career advancement courses at the academic staff colleges. To meet the challenges in education and in global society, UGC has evolved a scheme of granting potential for excellence status to selected universities. It is good that UGC is creating four National Institutes of Science at Chennai, Pune, Allahabad and Bhubaneshwar for promotion excellence in science education and Department of Oceanography. Generating the sustained interest in the scientific discipline will need continuity in provision of employment.

There has been substantial growth in our higher educational system during the last decade of 20th century and the first decade of the new millennium and we are generating over 3 million graduates every year. However, our employment generation system is not in a position to absorb the graduates passing out from the universities leading to increase in educated unemployed year after year. So we need higher education backed by employment opportunities.

VI. EDUCATIONAL EXPENDITURE IN INDIA

By the year 1981, educational expenditure had risen to

a level of 3.0 per cent of GDP as against 0.68 per cent in 1951 and 2.41 per cent in 1971.

During 1981 to 1991, a gradual increase in educational expenditure was witnessed and it reached a peak level of 4.39 per cent of GDP in 1990. Thereafter, this percentage has shown a gradual decline from 4.39 per cent in 1990 to 3.76 per cent in 1994 and further to 3.62 per cent in 1997 improved marginally to 4 per cent in 2001-02. This indicates a lower priority given to education in the post-reform period (1991-97) as compared with the pre-reform (1981-90), despite the fact that the government has been proclaiming that it intends to increase it to 6 per cent of GDP. (Ruddar Dutt and K.P.M. Sundharam, 2004)

Dr. P.R. Panchamukhi has calculated the average annual growth rate of per pupil expenditure in education in the pre-reform and post-reform period.

TABLE 3

Average Annual Growth Rate of Per Pupil Expenditure in Education

	Pre-reform Period (1985-90)	*Reform Period (1990-96)*
Elementary Education	6.9	1.2
Secondary Education	5.0	0.0
University Education	0.2	-4.4

Source: Economic and Political Weekly, March 4-10, 2000, p. 839.

The table indicates that there has been a serious deterioration in per pupil expenditure in education in all sectors of education. In the sphere of elementary education, the annual average growth rate of expenditure slumped from 6.9 per cent during 1985-90 to merely 1.2 per cent during 1990-96. In secondary education, there was zero growth rate of per pupil expenditure and in university education this growth rate became negative to the extent of 4.4 per cent in the post-reform period.

VII. HIGHER EDUCTION IN JHARKHAND

After being carved out of Bihar, the state of Jharkhand came into being on November 15, 2006. The creation of this state is the culmination of the half century aspirations of the indigenous tribal people, who had witnessed the ingress of outsiders in their land, their economy and their social system.

The prosperity of any state depends upon its institution and the opportunities provided by these institutions to the people of the state. The ability of the people to make the best use of such opportunities is undoubtedly high, but they can be improved considerably if the large masses are well educated and healthy. Currently none of these conditions are as desired in Jharkhand, but that need not be so far long.

Though Jharkhand is rich in minerals, it is economically as well as educationally poor. Its educational poverty, particularly in the field of higher education can be revealed from the following facts.

There are four universities in Jharkhand. They are Ranchi University, Ranchi, Birsa Agriculture University (BAU), Ranchi, Sido-Kanhu Murmu University, Dumka and Vinoba Bhawe University, Hazaribag. In addition to these three universities, there is a Deemed University-Birla Institute of Technology (BIT), Mesra. Two more universities—Nilamber-Pitamber and Kalhan are yet be started. Among the Universities of Jharkhand, Ranchi University, Ranchi is the oldest University established in the year 1960. BAU, Ranchi, SKMU, Dumka and V.B. University, Hazaribag have been established in the year 1981, 1992 and 1992 respectively Vinoba Bhave University, Hazaribag has got UGC affiliation very recently. S.K.M. University, Dumka, the most backward among the Universities of Jharkhand located in the most backward division of S.P. Twelve Post-graduates departments are running. This University has 13 constituent and 12 affiliated colleges.

VIII. TRIBAL'S ACCESSIBILITY TO HIGHER EDUCATION IN S.P. DIVISION

Jharkhand which has been carved out of Bihar in the

year 2000 has four Divisions. Santhal Parganas Division is one of them. The other Divisions are North Chhotanagpur, South Chhotanagpur and Palamau with their Headquarter in Hazaribag, Ranchi and Palamau respectively. The Headquarter of S.P. Division is in Dumka. This Division has six district segments—Deoghar, Dumka, Godda, Sahibganj, Pakur and Jamtara.

It seems that this Division has been named Santhal Parganas because of the dominance of Santhal Adivase. As per the 1991 Census, the population of Santhals is 20,60,730 in Jharkhand. Out of which 1,463,937 Santhals are living in S.P. Division constituting 31.88 per cent of the total Scheduled Tribe population (Census 1991). But Santhals' population in Jharkhand makes up 35.51 per cent. When we put a cursory look into the higher education system of S.P. Division, we find that there was not a Degree College before independence. The colleges were established only after independence on the land of Sido-Kanhu who fought bravely against the British empire in the year 1853 and were killed.

Even after independence the growth of higher educational institutions remained limited to general colleges. No higher technical institutions have been established till date either by the government or by the private investors. There is only one university, Sido-Kanhu University, Dumka. There are 11 constituent colleges (old) and two newly converted constituent colleges. There are nine degree colleges affiliated to S.K.M. University, Dumka. Three colleges are striving for degree affiliation. Teaching in B.Ed. course is beirtg imparted with 100 intake in five constituent colleges. There is one government Teacher's Training College at Deoghar. There are 13 Post-Graduate departments. The University as well as the P.G. departments have been recognized by the UGC recently in 2007. This is the scene of general higher education institutions in Santhal Paraganas.

So far as the question of tribal's accessibility to higher education is concerned it is abysmally low. It is also a fact that the accessibility of tribal Christians is higher than the tribal non-Christians in Jharkhand as well as in S.P. Division. The majority of tribals in Jharkhand practise their own religion called 'Sarna dharma' which is a primitive version of

Hinduism. The Christian Missionaries have been operating among the tribals of Jharkhand since the year 1850 onwards. R.N. Sahay (1986) has discussed the Christian activities in Jharkhand. Despite dedicated and determined efforts during the last 139 years, only about 14.3 per cent of the tribals have been converted into Christianity in Jharkhand out of which 80 live in Ranchi district (Weiner, 1978). The tribal Christians have been benefited by access to better health, and educational and employment facilities. Though debatable, Christianity has served as an agent of modernization among the tribal Christians. Consequently the literacy rate among tribal Christians is higher than tribal non-Christians in Santhal Praganas.

The percentage literacy rate among male and female tribal Christians is 26.40 and 6.7 respectively and the literacy rate among male and female tribal non-Christians is merely 14.43 and 2.5 per cent which shows the less accessibility of tribal non-Christians to education. It is startling that in the last ten years only 50 Pahadias have passed their matriculation while government expends Rs. 78 lakh per annum on the education of Pahadias children. This is the stark truth that only 4-5 Pahadias are simple graduate in Santhal Paraganas (*Dainik Jagran*, 6 December, 2007) like Pahadias, Bedia, Baske, Besra, Chode/Chonne Genduvar, Poriya have very poor accessibility even less than one per cent to higher education. These scheduled tribe castes be on to Santhal Parganas and it is astonishing that even simple graduates are rarely available. The survey of three villages revealed that there were not graduates in these castes.

It is evident from the Admission Register and Tabulation Register of A.S. College, Deoghar that tribal's accessibility to general higher education is far and far below one per cent. In the year 2003 the total number of students admitted in B.A., B.Sc. and B.Com. Part III was 400, 200 and 300 respectively but the number of Scheduled Tribe Students in this year was Five, Zero and Two in B.A, B.Sc, and B.Com. respectively. Out of which three and one tribal Christian passed the examination. No female took admission in any streams in this year at this college. The figures collected from the college record for the year 2005 show that the total number of students admitted in Part III, B.A., B.Sc. and B.Com. was 450, 225 and 340 respectively but the admission of tribals remained more or less the same as it was in the year 2004. It was four, three and two in B.A., B.Sc. and B.Com. respectively. No tribal students passed B.Sc. Part III examinations, 2005. Only three students passed out these examinations. No students passed the B.Com. examinations 2005. There are 150 seats in P.G. Graduate Department of Commerce. But no tribal students took admission in the year 2003. In the years 2004 and 2005 only one student took admission and passed the examination in the second class. The position in B.Ed. course is certainly better than general courses. It is because that students belonging to tribal Christian from Ranchi come and take admission. However, the quota in Science stream remains vacant. Thus, it is quite obvious that tribal's accessibility to higher education in Santhal Parganas is far below than one per cent. Since there is no higher technical institutions (Medical, Engineering, Pharmacy) so the question of their accessibility to these courses does not arise.

As I feel that the causes behind the low accessibility are the abject poverty among Sarna tribals, lack of awareness and their alienation from others. The indifferent attitude of the officials, teachers and other employees posted for them is very much responsible for this. No matters, whatever amount is spent on educational programmes of the tribal, matters only the honest implementation. It is possible only when the educational institutions will be established particularly for them, among them and run by them. The government should initiate honest efforts in this regard. Unless and until their share in higher education goes up, the concept of inclusive growth will remain meaningless.

References

Elwin, V. (1997), A Philosophy for NEFA, Shillong North-East Frontier Agency.

Sahay, R.N. (1986), Christianity and Culture Change in India, New Delhi: Inter-India Publications.

Weiner, M. (1978), Sons of the Soil: Migration and Ethnic Conflict in India. Princeton: Princeton Uniersity Press.

Dainik Jagran, 6 December 2007.

Editorial, *Journal of Higher Education*, Vol. 20, No. 3, monsoon 1997.

U.G.C. News, Vol. 11, Issue I, January 2004, p. 13.

Prime Minister's Essay, Bharat Nirman Se Banega Bharat Mahan, *Hindustan* (Hindi), 22 Oct., 2006.

U.G.C. News, Vol. 11, Issue 1, January 2004, p. 5.

Bhandari, Laveesh (2006), Jharkhand and Governance, Published in Jharkhand Development Report, 2006.

23

Higher Education of Tribals in India: With Special Reference to Jharkhand

DALIP KUMAR

Considering the importance of higher education in the socio-economic transformation especially in the fast globalising world and in the age of knowledge revolution, the present paper highlights the present state of affairs in higher education, the growth and trends in the expansion of higher education in the framework of preferential treatment and supportive measures for the benefits of scheduled tribes. Pointing out the various shortcomings in the educational policies and programmes, and the inability of the higher education system to encompass the complex social reality, the paper has made sincere efforts to analyse various facts and figures related to the present status of higher education in India, in States and particularly in the State of Jharkhand. The paper highlights various parameters of status of higher education like demographic trends and present educational status of STs in India, literacy rate in STs, gross enrolment ratio, enrolment of Indian students in USA, pupil-teacher ratio in educational institutions imparting higher education, ST students in higher-education, state-wise universities and number of Ph.D. recipients, expenditure on higher education, etc. The paper discusses the strengths and weaknesses of higher education in India, government initiatives to promote higher education among STs and the recommendations made by the "Knowledge Commission". Last but not the least, the paper presents some data-based findings and suggestions also. I have tried to give special focus on various aspects of higher education in the newly carved ST dominated state of Jharkhand.

I. INTRODUCTION

Education is the engine of economic growth and social change. It creates motivation for progress and brings resolution in the ideas necessary for the progress of the country. It teaches honesty, inspires patriotism, enhances social prestige and promotes economic developments. When people are educated, we not only get teaches, professionals and executives but more importantly citizens who are aware, sensitive and responsible. It makes people place social good above personal gain. Not only this, it transforms a human being into a noble soul and an asset to the universe (Kalam, APJ Abdul, 2004).

Economics of Education was born as a formal area of study only four and a half decades ago with the Presidential Address by Theodore W. Schultz (1961) to the America in 1960 on "Investment in Human Capital" (Tilak, 2008). A key role in popularizing economics of Education with famous text book of Mark Blang, 'Readings' and several edited volumes in Economics of Education, was wrong, when he observed that "the Economics of Education now lies dead in the mind of both professional economist and professional educators (Blang, 1987).

The literature produced in the 1960s in Economics of Education by V.K.R.B. Rao (1964, 1970), Baljit Singh (1967), Kothari (1966), H.N. Pandit (1969) and other still stand as the best textbooks references to the students in Economics of Indian Education. The economic analysis of Indian Education by Blang, Layard and Maureen Woodhall (1969) helped in understanding the problems of educated unemploy.

Higher Education

Higher education includes teaching, research and social services activities of universities, and within the realm of teaching, it includes both the undergraduate level (sometimes referred to as tertiary education) and the graduate (or post-graduate) level (sometimes referred to as graduate school). Higher education specifically refers to post-secondary institutions that offer associate degrees, bachelor degrees, master's degrees or Ph.D. degrees or equivalents. Higher general education might be contrasted with higher vocational education, which concentrates on both practice and theory. A university is an institution of higher education and research, which grants academic degrees; including Bachelor's degrees, Master's degrees and Doctorate in a variety of subjects. However, most professional education is included within higher education, and many post-graduate qualifications are strongly vocationally or professionally-oriented, for example, in disciplines such as social work, law and medicine. India has the second largest system of higher education, next only to the U.S (*The Hindu,* Feb. 19, 2002). India's main competitors—especially China but also Singapore, Taiwan and South Korea—are investing much more in large differentiated higher education systems. They are providing access to large number of students at the bottom of the academic system while at the same time building some research-based universities that are able to compete with world's best institutions (Altbach, 2005).

Main Sources of Higher Education System in the Country

All India Council for Technical Education (AICTE),
Distance Education Council (DEC),
Indian Council for Agriculture Research (ICAR),
Bar Council of India (BCI),
National Council for Teacher Education (NCTE),
Rehabilitation Council of India (RCI),
Medical Council of India (MCI),

Pharmacy Council of India (PCI),
Indian Nursing Council (INC),
Dentist Council of India (DCI),
Central Council of Homeopathy (CCH), and
Central Council of Indian Medicine (CCIM).

Who are Scheduled Tribes?

As per our Constitution of India Article 366 (25) refers to Scheduled Tribes as those communities who are scheduled in accordance with Article 342 of the Constitution. This Article says that only those communities who have been declared as such by the President through an initial public notification or through a subsequent amending Act of Parliament will be considered as Scheduled Tribes. Infact scheduled tribes are those people who are socially, educationally and economically backward, who have been living in hills, mountains and forests and who are using primitive technology of production. Gandhiji called them Girijan, i.e. "Children of Mountains".

II DEMOGRAPHIC TRENDS AND PRESENT EDUCATIONAL STATUS OF STS IN INDIA

(i) State-wise Population of STs in India

The tribal population of the country, as per the 2001 Census, is 8.43 crore, constituting 8.2 per cent of the total population. The population of tribes has grown at the rate of 24.45 per cent during the period 1991-2001. The growth of ST population during the Census 1981, 1991 and 2001 was 7.83 per cent of total population, 8.08 per cent in 1991 and 8.2 per cent of total population in Census 2001. More than half the Scheduled Tribe population is concentrated in the States of Madhya Pradesh, Chhattisgarh, Maharashtra, Orissa, Jharkhand and Gujarat. The total population of STs in newly created state of Jharkhand was 26.3 per cent of total population. Tribal communities live in about 15 per cent of the country's areas, in various ecological and geo-climatic conditions ranging from plains and forests to hills and inaccessible areas. The States with predominantly ST Population are Lakshadeep (94.5%), Mizoram (94.5%),

Nagaland (89.1%), Meghalaya (85.9%), etc. The State wise distribution of tribal population has been shown in Table 1 and Figure 1.

FIGURE I

State-wise Distribution of ST Population to Total Population in India, 2001

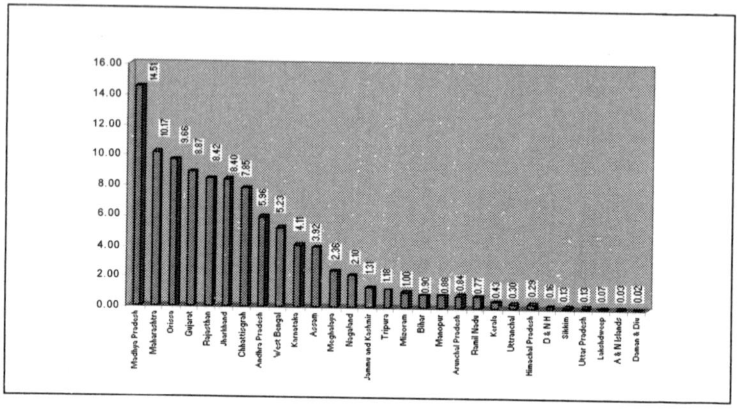

The decadal population growth between the Census years 1981 to 1991 in respect of tribal population has been higher (31.64%) than that of the overall general population (23.51%). Similarly during Census Year 1991 to 2001 it has been 24.45 per cent against the growth rate of 22.66 per cent for the entire population. The ST population in the State of Karnataka has witnessed higher growth rate of 80.82 per cent followed by Nagaland (67.23%) during the decade 1991-2001. The lowest growth rate in respect of ST population as per 2001 Census was recorded in Andaman and Nicobar (10.08%) followed by Himachal Pradesh (12.02%).

(ii) Scheduled Tribes Literacy in India

No nation can progress if half of its population is deprived of equal rights and equal opportunities for development. Women in India have suffered from time immemorial due to high levels of discrimination both at the society and at the household levels. The Constitution of India and other legal provisions provide for positive discrimination in favour of women. However, the progress has been slow. This is amply clear, when 50 per cent of the households in rural areas of India do not have a single literate woman. (Mungekar, 2007)

Increasing literacy rate lays the foundation of higher education. The literacy rate for the total population in India has increased from 52.2 per cent to 68.38 per cent during the period from 1991 to 2001 where as the literacy rate among the STs has increased from 29.62 per cent to 47.10 per cent. Among STs, male literacy increased from 40.65 per cent to 59.20 per cent and ST female literacy increased from 18.20 per cent to 34.80 per cent during the same period. The ST female literacy is lower by approximately 20 per cent as compared to the overall female literacy of the general population. The trends of STs Literacy rates can be seen in Figure 2

FIGURE 2

Male-Female STs Literacy Rate in India

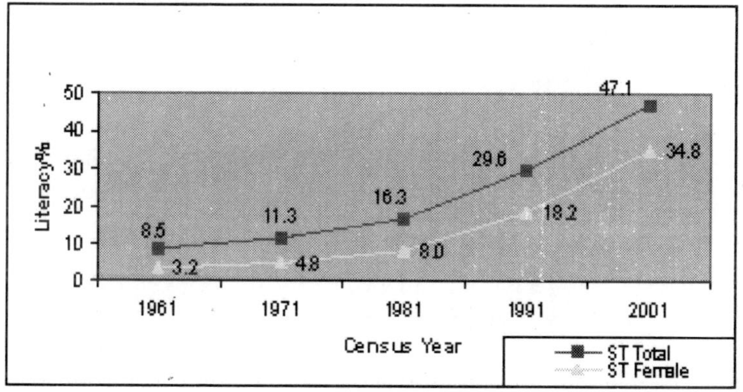

It is heartening to notice that there has been steady growth in the literacy rate in the state of Jharkhand. Literacy among STs in Jharkhand stood at a meager figure of 15.4 per cent in year 1981 and it rose to 27.5 in 1991 and lastly reached at 40.5 per cent in 2001. It is the result of pro-active state interventions through several central government programmes like Sarva Siksha Abhiyan, All India Literacy Mission, Mid-day Meal and efforts of some social organisations and NGOs. A little lesson than 3 times rise in literacy in Jharkhand is a welcome trend but still a lot has to be done to catch up with National average. It is worth-mentioning here that some states with predominant tribal population like Mizoram and Lakshadweep are far ahead on literacy front even from the all India. 89.3 and 86.1 per cent tribals are literate in these two states. These two states are at first and second in ranking, where as Jharkhand is placed at the lower ladder of 26th rank. It can not be denied that the state faces several constraints due to its terrain, under developed infrastructure, economic backwardness and traditional mindset of the tribal society. State wise Literacy rates of STs as whole and STs female literacy from Census 2001 can be seen in Figures 3 and 4 respectively.

FIGURE 3

State-wise Total Literacy of STs in 2001

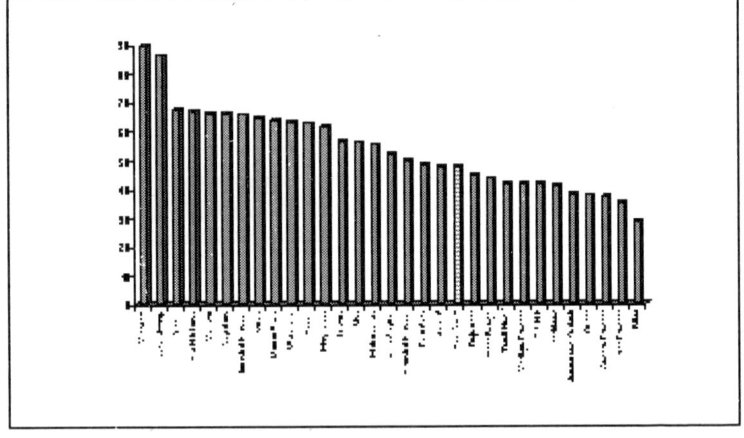

State-wise STs Female literacy rates can be explained in Figure 4. The ST literacy rate in the State of Mizoram has witnessed higher figure of 86.9 per cent followed by Lakshadweep (80.2%) in Census year-2001. The lowest literacy rate of ST as per 2001 Census was recorded in Bihar (15.5%) followed by UP (20.7%).

FIGURE 4

State-wise STs Female Literacy Rates in 2001

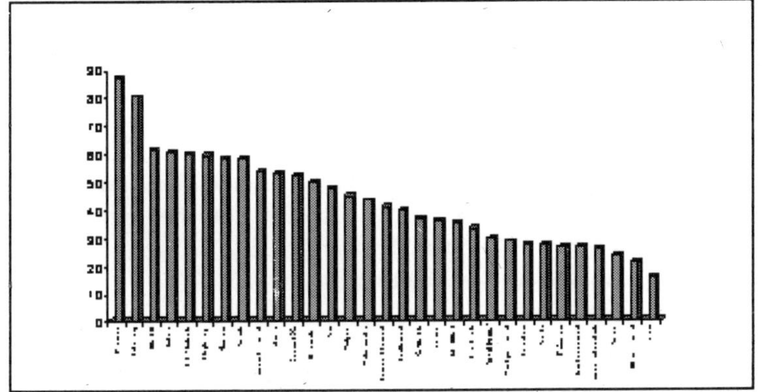

(iii) Gross Enrolment Ratio

Gross enrolment ratio (GER), as defined by UNESCO, designates a nation's total enrolment "in a specific level of education, regardless of age, expressed as a percentage of the population in the official age group corresponding to this level of education". In the country as a whole, gross enrolment ratio in urban areas is four times higher than that in rural areas; the gross enrolment ratio is much lower for SCs, STs, OBCs and for Muslims as compared to the general population; the ratio is 11 per cent for females as compared to over 15 per cent for males; the poor also have a low gross enrolment ratio, that is one fifth of that of the non-poor. Enrolment rates have increased from 0.2 per cent in 1947-48 to 2.0 per cent in year 1970-71, 4.4 per cent in year 1990-91 to 10 per cent in 2005-06. According to the NSS and Population Census, if diploma and certificate courses are also included, then the ratio has increased to about 13-14 per cent.

With an aim to increase the Gross Enrolment Ratio in higher education institutions from the current 10 per cent to 15 per cent by the end of 11th Five Year Plan (2011-12) and to bring more equity in the education system, the University Grants Commission will increase the number of universities and colleges across the country to add to the present intake capacity.

Chinese higher education has expanded rapidly over the past decade—with gross enrolment rates increasing from 3.4 per cent in 1990, to 7.2 per cent in 1995, and to 11 per cent in 2000. Quantitative growth continued till date and reached at 22 per cent in year 2006. China started to control excessive enrolment in 2006, and to invest its effort on improving the quality of higher education. In 2006, 7.24 million Chinese entered colleges. By the end of 2006, there were 25 million college students in China, The number of postgraduate students reached 1,100,000 for the first time in 2006, a 12.88 per cent growth from 2005. The trends of GER in China can be seen in Figure 5.

FIGURE 5

Trends of GER in China's Higher Education

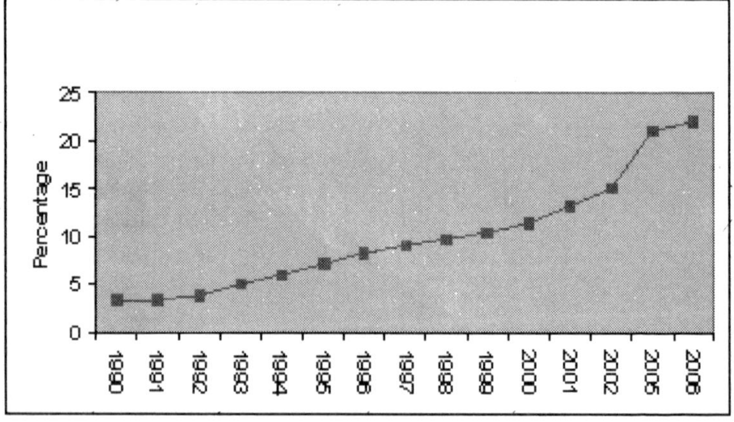

In developed countries population growth is very low and the growth in infrastructures is higher than developing countries. So the gross enrolment of developed countries is much higher than that in developing countries. GER at Tertiary level of Developed countries like Korea, United States, and Australia are more than seven-eight times than the developing country like India. Gross enrolment ratio at higher education of some developed and developing country can be seen in Figure 6.

The gross enrolment ratio in higher education for the education for the developed countries is around 58 per cent,

FIGURE 6

Gross Enrolment Ratio at Higher Education/Tertiary Level, 2005 (in Percentage)

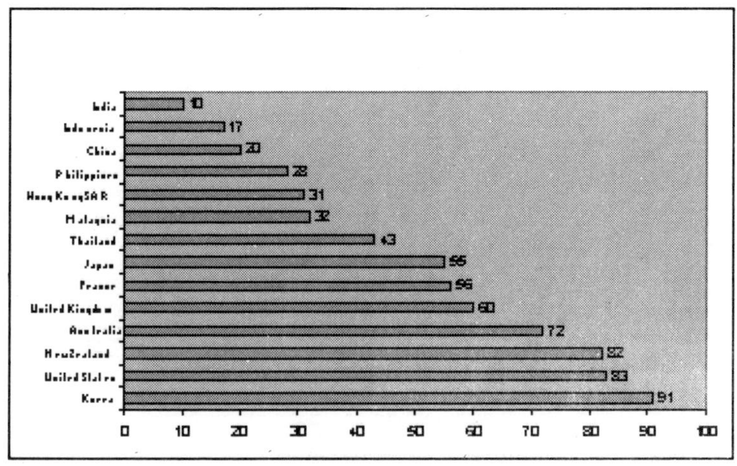

for the countries in transition 38 per cent, for sub- Saharan Africa only 2.5 per cent, as against the world's average of 27 per cent. In the case of India, this ratio is only 10.50 per cent. In other words, about 90 per cent of the school going children in India does not cross three-fold of higher education. The rural GER is 6.7 per cent, while for urban areas it is around 20 per cent; for male, it is 12.4 per cent, while for female it is 9.1 per cent. For the SCs, STs and OBCs, there are 6.57 per cent, 6.52 per cent and 8.77 per cent respectively, as against for others 17.22 per cent (Mungekar, 2007)

The trends of girl enrolment to total enrolment in higher education are gradually rising. Thus Girl enrolment to total enrolment has been increasing from 10 per cent in 1950-51, to 40 per cent in 2001-02, and now 39 per cent in 2004-05. This staggering disparity is the out -come of various factors like low per capita income, non-availability of neighbourhood institutions, social stigma; unattractiveness of higher education due to its weak linkage with the employment, etc. Early marriage and early motherhood also contribute to the lower enrolment of girls in higher education. The Increasing percentage trends of Girls enrolment to total enrolment in higher education can be seen on Figure 7.

FIGURE 7

Percentage of Girls' Enrolment to Total Enrolment in Higher Education (Degree and above level)

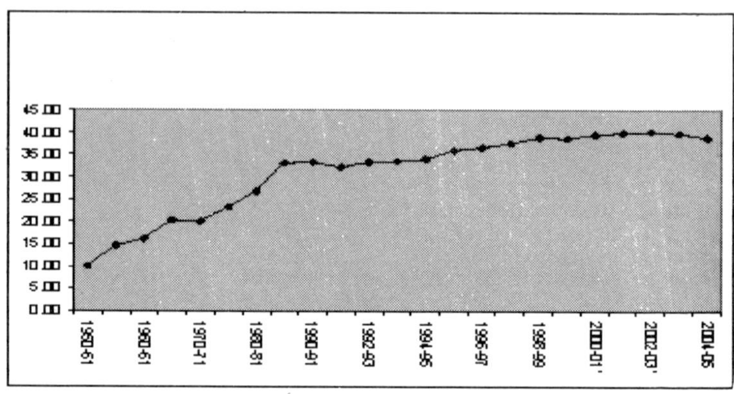

All India figure of gross enrolment ratio in higher education for general categories is 9.97 per cent which includes 11.58 pr cent for boys and 8.17 per cent for girls in the age group 18-24 year. At the beginning of the academic year 2006-07, the total number of students enrolled in the universities and colleges was reported to be 110.28 lakhs, which included 14.27 lakhs (12.94%) in University Department and 96.01 lakhs (87.06%) in affiliated colleges On this front a few tribal dominating states like Manipur, Meghalaya and Mizoram are ahead of all India. Overwhelmingly tribal populated state of Nagaland has only 4.70 against all India figures of 9.97.

Gross enrolment ratio in this aspect of gender gap is also reflected except in the state of Kerala where in number of girls enrolled in higher education is much higher than that of boys. The enrolment of women at the beginning of the academic year 2006-07 was 44.66 lakhs, constituting 40.40 per cent of total enrolment. Of the total enrolment of women, 12.35 per cent were enrolled in professional courses. Enrolment of women as a percentage of total enrolment in a state is the highest in Kerala (66.00%) and lowest in Bihar (24.52%). (GOI, 2006-07)

For tribal population the story of its gross enrolment ratio in higher education is gloomier. All India figures of STs is just 4.86 per cent at against 6.72 pr cent for SCs and 9.97 per cent for general categories in year 2004-05. Girls enrolment ratio in higher education for STs is only 3.45 per cent at all India level as against 5.2 per cent of SCs and 8.17 per cent for general categories. The boys enrolment ratio in higher education of STs is only 6.31 per cent in steed of 8.1 per cent of SCs boys and 11.58 per cent for general categories. Details can be seen in Figure 8.

FIGURE 8

Gross Enrolment Ratio at Higher Education, 2004-05 in India

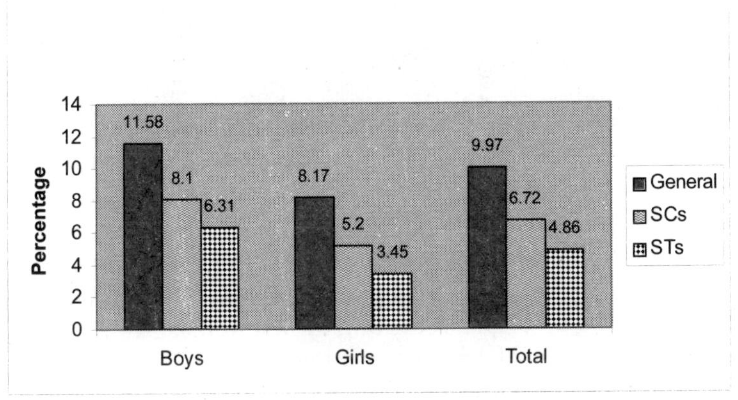

In the state of Jharkhand the enrolment ratio in higher education for total STs is 3.03 per cent as against 3.16 per cent for SCs and 7.05 per cent for general categories in year 2004-05.

Girls enrolment ratio in higher education for STs is only 2.33 per cent in Jharkhand as against 1.95 per cent of SCs and 5.32 per cent for general categories. Girl Enrolment ratio of STs in Higher education is higher than SCs Girl enrolment. The boys enrolment ratio in higher education of STs is only 3.76 per cent in stead of 4.32 per cent of SCs boys and 11.58 per cent for general categories in the state of Jharkhand. There are only 5 Universities and 3 deemed

Universities in Jharkhand imparting higher education. The weak infrastructure, lesser number of teachers in colleges at many places is the major roadblocks in attracting students in the higher education. Details can be seen in Figure 9.

FIGURE 9

GER in Higher Education of Jharkhand, 2004-05

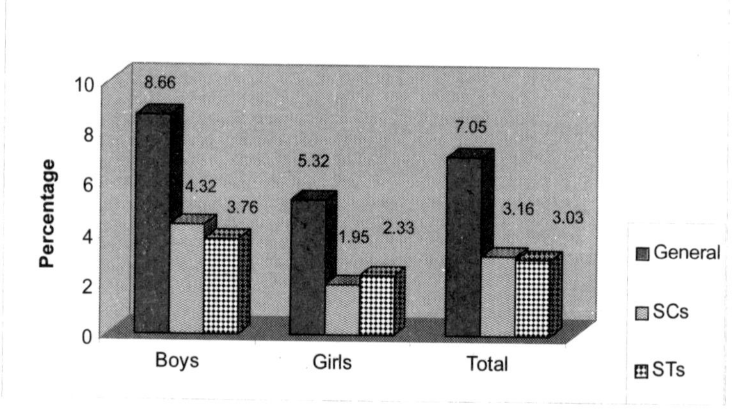

Gross enrolment ratio in higher education among ST students is higher in UP. This is 25 per cent of total ST population in UP. Boys enrolment is about 33 per cent and girls are around 16 per cent. But we know that STs residence only 0.1 per cent of total population in UP. STs only resides in southeastern part of UP. Uttaranchal, Manipur and Himanchal Pradesh are the only three states, where STs Enrolment is higher than 10 per cent. Inter – state disparities can be seen in Figure 10.

(iv) Enrolment of Indian Students in USA

According to Open Door 2004 annual report on international academic mobility published by the Institute of International Education (IIE), the number of international students enrolled in U.S. higher education institutions decreased by 2.4 per cent in 2003-04 to a total of 572,509, from 586,323 in 2002-03. The following data has been obtained from the India country Fact Sheet in the Open Doors 2004 report.

FIGURE 10

State-wise Total GER in Higher Education of STs Students

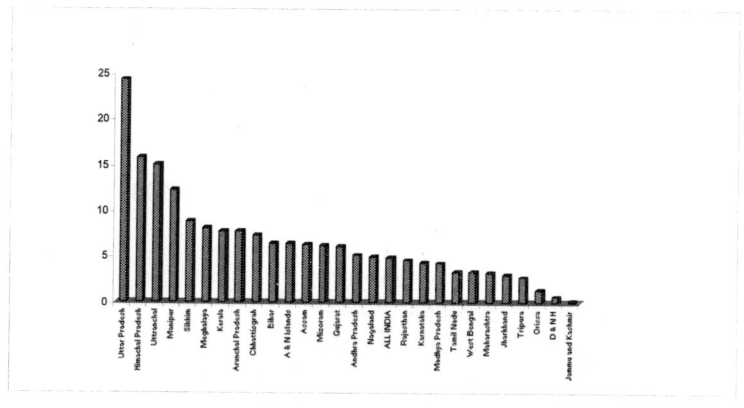

Year	*No. of Students from India in USA*	*Indian Students as a % of Total Foreign Students in USA*
2003-04	79736	13.9
2002-03	74603	12.7
2001-02	66836	11.5
2000-01	54664	9.9
1999-00	42337	8.2
1998-99	37482	7.6
1997-98	33188	7
1996-97	30641	6.7
1995-96	31743	7
1994-95	33537	7.4
1993-94	34796	7.7

Source: India Country Fact Sheet in Open Doors Report, Institute of International Educational, 2004

But, India continues to remain the largest sending country of origin for the 3rd year, and the number of Indian students in USA climbed by 7 per cent over the previous year, to a total of 79,736 in 2003-04, offsetting decreases from a number of other countries which experienced sharp declines. However, India's rate of increase in 2003-04 has slowed from the previous year's dramatic 12 per cent growth.

Total enrolments fell by 5 per cent for students from China (still the second largest sending country with 61,765) of the 74,603 students from India, 79.0 per cent were graduate students, 17.0 per cent undergraduate and 4.0 per cent others. Beginning in 1997-98, number of students from India has been increasing dramatically. Three years ago, there was an increase by 29.1 per cent, followed an increase 22.3 per cent and last year's increase of 11.6 per cent. Two years ago (2001/02), India surpassed China as the leading sending nation of foreign students to the United States. This year's increase of 6.9 per cent kept India in the leading spot, and students from India now make up 14 per cent of all foreign students in the United States.

The Indian University student population is projected to grow from 9.3 million students now to 11 million by 2008, according to the University Grants Commission, which funds and supports central government universities in India. Combining this magnitude of student demand and the value Indian students place on U.S. higher education, there is bound to be a steady increase in the number of students in the U.S. once students are able to finance the education. In India, student loans are more readily available than ever before. Students find that the investment they make in U.S. education is well worth it in terms of career opportunities.

(v) ST Students Studying Different Courses of Higher Education Institutions in India

ST students studying at different courses s of higher education institutions in India can be seen through the Figure 11 and Table 7.

The All India figure related to ST students studying different courses of higher education, reveal that now both boys and girls are opting professional cources like polytechnic, teacher training, management, but in this field also gender disparity is visible. This gender gap is the highest in B.Sc. (Engg. and B. Arch.) Cources whereas it is less in general courses like B.A., MA, M.Sc, etc.

(vi) Pupil-Teacher Ratio in Higher Education Institutions

In India higher education pattern is copied from the

FIGURE 11

STs Students Studying at Different Level of Higher Education, 2004-05 in India

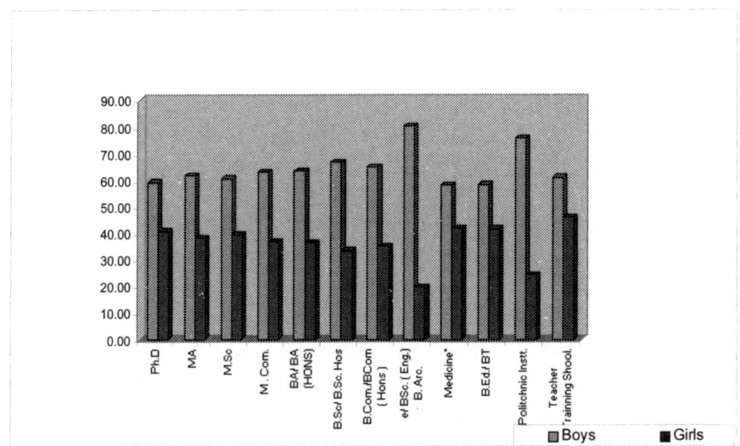

organisation of London University. In India, the average size of the student body of a college consists of over 1500 students and the students–teacher ratio is rarely less than 25:1. (In British Universities this ratio is 9:1). Not unusually, about 150-200 students jointly attend a class (Gore, 1994).

Pupil-teacher ratio is an important indicator of educational standard. At all India level there is one teacher for 25 students enrolled in higher education. Some better states are Manipur, Meghalaya, A&N Island and Chandigrah wherein this ratio is 1:9, Goa (13), Karnataka (14), Karala (15), Assam (15). Above states are better than the national average.. In Jharkhand, a total of 2019176 students were enrolled in higher education institutions and that included 132617 boys and 76559 girls in year 2004-05. Therefore, one teacher was available for 24 students in tribal dominated state. Some states like Chhattisgarh (32), Gujarat (40), HP (29), MP (45) Rajasthan (29), Sikkim (43), UP (48), Uttaranchal (38), WB (30) and Delhi (61) are far away from the national average. Haryana and Maharashtra (26), Mizoram, Punjab, Tripura (24) are around the national average.

(vii) Trends of Recognised Higher Educational Institutions

Higher education in India has largely been the preserve of the Government till recently in terms of both funding and provision of education. But for this to continue, the Government should be in a position to pour in large sums of money to fund higher education. the demand for higher education is continuing to increase with more and more students aspiring for a higher education today than ever before. How can we bridge the gap between increasing demand and decreasing government funding for higher education? The only option is to tap the private sector to participate in the funding and provision of higher education. The process of increasing private participation in higher education has already begun with a few states like Chhattisgarh and Uttaranchal having passed legislation to permit the setting up of private universities in their states

Increasing trends in higher educational institutions in India and Growth of Universities, Deemed Universities and National Level Institutions can be seen in last 60 years in Figures 12 and 13. Number of Colleges for higher education has increased from 370 in 1950 to 10377 in year 2004-05; numbers of professional colleges from 208 to 3201 during the same period. Number of University and deemed universities from 27 in 1950-51 to 407. during the same period. There are 369 Universities at present comprising of 222 State

FIGURE 12

Growth of Recognised Higher Educational Institutions from 1950-51

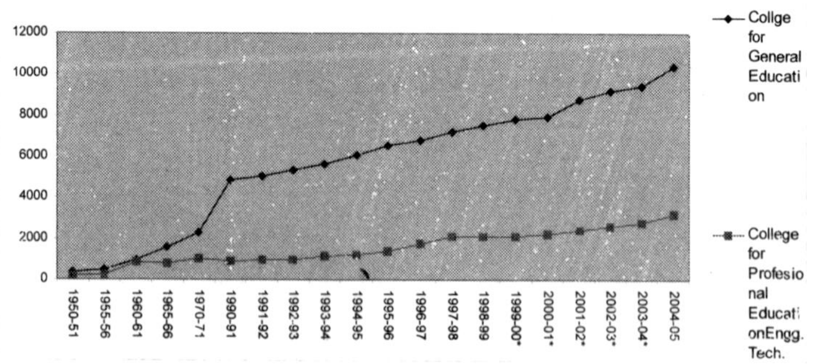

FIGURE 13

Growth of Universities/Deemed Universities/Institutions of National Level

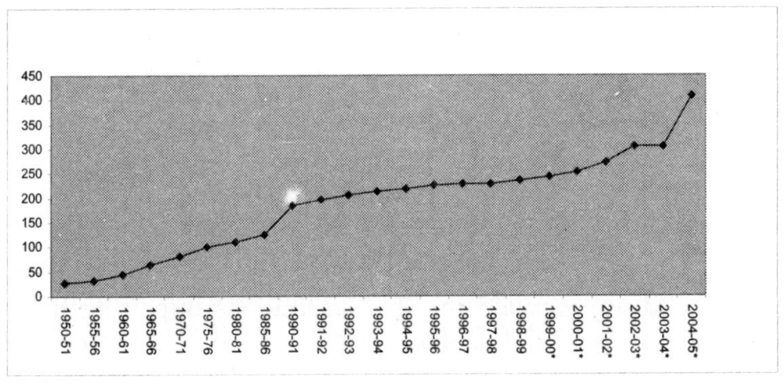

Universities, 20 Central Universities,109 deemed Universities, 5 Institutions established under State legislation and 13 Institutes of national importance functioning in the country in year 2006-07. Number of Universities and deemed universities increased rapidly in 2003-04. Trends can be seen in the Figure 12. There are 18064 colleges including around 1902 women's colleges in year 2006-07. No doubt, the number of higher education institutions has increased but that is not adequate to cater to the needs in the wake of literacy expansion, socio-economic transformation and increasing demands of educational institutions especially those imparting professional and technological courses Whatever is the quantitative expansion, on qualitative improvement front, a lot needs to be done.

There has been significant growth in higher education during the academic year 2005-06. According to University Grants Commission (UGC), enrolment in various courses at all levels of Universities/Colleges and other institutions of higher education in 2005-06 were 11.34 million as compared to 10.50 million in year 2004-05. Out of this, the number of women students was 4.58 million constituting 40.39 per cent. There has also been a significant expansion of central institutions of higher education in recent years. With increased demand for higher quality education, training of teachers has become even more important. (*Economic Survey*, 2007-08).

(viii) ST Students Studying in Higher Education Institutions

State-wise ST students studying in higher education institutions are given in Table 6. A total of 434215 ST students studying in higher education in year 2004-05 included 276731 boys and 157484 girls in the country. The gender disparities can be seen here. The corresponding figure for the state of Jharkhand is 21834, which included 13253 boys and 8561 girls. It is very pathetic to see that only 3.03 per cent STs of the total STs population in Jharkhand are enrolled in the institutions imparting higher education whereas all India figure stands at 4.86 per cent. So far as the percentage of STs in higher education is concerned, some states like HP (15.84%), Uttaranchal (15.02%), and Manipur (12.27%), are better placed. In UP this percentage is the highest (24.36%) but it is worth-mentioning here that the population of STs in this state is only 0.1 per cent and most of STs in the state are not originally from UP. They are employees of central government or may be migrated from other parts of te country.

(ix) State-wise Universities and No. of Ph.D. Degrees Awarded in Year 2004-05

We can see the figures pertaining to the number of Institutions, which awarded Ph.D. degree to researchers in year 2005. At all India level, out of 298 Universities and 96 deemed Universities only 202 Universities could award Ph.D. degree to 8789 researchers in the year 2004-05. The state of UP stood at the top where 1333 scholars got Ph.D. Degree from 13 Universities out of 39 (31 Universities and 8 Deemed Universities). It was followed by Maharashtra (1189) and Rajasthan (627). In Chandigrah there is the only one University which had awarded 160 Ph.D. scholars in the year 2004-05. This is the highest productive Ph.D. scholars in India. The number of doctoral degrees awarded by various universities was 17898 in year 2005. Out of this, the faculties of Arts had the highest number of 7532 degrees, followed by the faculties of Sciences with 5549 degrees. (GOI, 2007)

In the State of Jharkhand, there are 8 Universities including 5 Universities and 3 Deemed Universities. Only three Universities could award Ph.D. degrees to only 78 research scholars in year 2005. It reflects the lukewarm attitude of students and Universities towards research activities. It also speaks about lack of incentives due to shortage of technical equipments, laboratories and libraries and other research facilities. The declining interest towards research activities is not conducive to the expansion of quality education at higher level. There is an earnest need of due attention from universities, research students, state government and UGC.

III. JHARKHAND PROFILE

The State of Jharkhand was carved out of the southern part of Bihar on 15 November 2000. Jharkhand shares its border with the states of Bihar to the north, Uttar Pradesh and Chhattisgarh to the west, Orissa to the south, and West Bengal to the east. Jharkhand has a population of 26.90 million, consisting of 13.86 million males and 13.04 million females. The sex ratio is 941 females to 1000 males. The population consists of 28 per cent tribals, 12 per cent Scheduled Castes and 60 per cent others. There are 274 persons for each square kilometer of land. However, the population density varies considerably from as low as 148 per square kilometer in Gumla district to as high as 1167 per square kilometer in Dhanbad district. Around 10 per cent of the population is Bengali-speaking and 7 per cent Urdu-speaking. Hinduism is the major religion in the state, with 81.6 per cent of the population practicing this faith. Islam stands at the second position with 13.8 per cent of the population, followed by Christianity with 4.1 per cent of the population. Jainism and Buddhism are religions present in the state as well, all with numbers less than 0.5 per cent. Sikhism is also practiced in the state with 0.3 per cent of the population

(i) Types of Tribal in Jharkhand

There are over 700 Scheduled Tribes notified under Article 342 of the Constitution of India. The main concentration of STs population is in Central and North-eastern States. Tribes are presently in eleven states and UTs except Haryana, Punjab, Delhi, Pondicherry and Chandhigrah. List of notified Scheduled Tribes in State Jharkhand are as under:

Asur, Agaria, Baiga, Banjara, Bathudi, Bedia, Binjhia, Birhor, Birjia, Chero, Chik Baraik, Gond, Gorait, Ho, Karmali, Kharia, Dhelki Kharia, Dudh Kharia, Hill Kharia, Kharwar, Khond, Kishan, Nagesia, Kora, Mudi-Kora, Korwa, Lohra, Mahli, Mal, Pahariya, Kumarbhag Paharia Munda, Patar, Oraon, Dhangar (Oraon), Parhaiya Santhal,Sauria Paharia Savar Bhumij, Kawar, Kol. Total 32 types of STs belongs to the state of Jharkhand.

The Jharkhand situation is self-explanatory, about the poor infrastructure and meagre availability of educational institutions in tribal dominated remote areas in Jharkhand. Most of Institutions are located in urban centres like Ranchi, Jamshedpur, Dhanbad, Hazaribag, Dumka, etc. It is a worth-mentioning here that majority of students attending in the higher educational Institutions in urban centres belong to non-tribal population like dikoos or those who or whose fore-fathers have settled there as government employees, traders or industrial workers. Despite reservations given in education, the institutions imparting technological, medical and professional education, greater number of seats are occupied by non-tribal students. This is due to non-availability, non-affordability, and non-accessibility of education for tribals due to socio-economic constraint.

(ii) ST Population and Literacy in Jharkhand

The total population of newly created State of Jharkhand was 2699428 which comprised of 244587 STs. It means STs constitute 26.34 per cent of total population of the State, while the share of STs population in India's population is only 8.2 per cent. In India's STs Population only 8.40 per cent of STs belongs to the State of Jharkhand. District-wise total literacy rates of STs in Jharkhand can be seen in Figure 14. Average literacy rate of STs in Jharkhand as a whole is 40.70 per cent in which male literacy rate is 54.00 per cent as against the female literacy rate of 27.20 per cent.

FIGURE 14

District-wise Total Kiteracy Rate of STs in State of Jharkhand, 2001

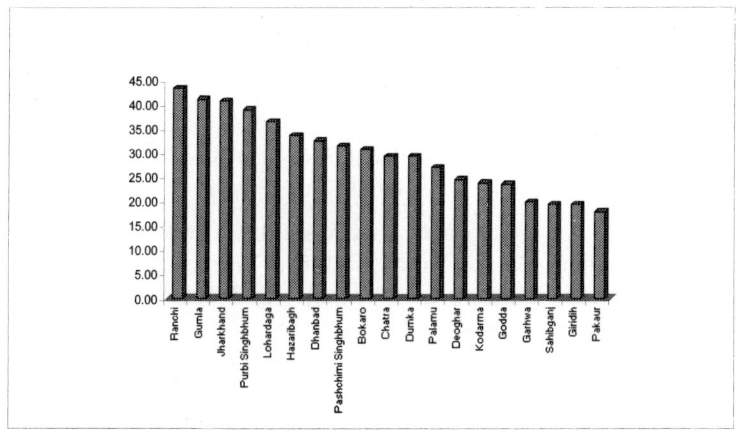

India's total population is comprised of 8.2 per cent of STs. 8.40 pr cent population of STs lives in Jharkhand but the total Jharkhand population consists of 26.34 per cent STs. The literacy rate among STs in Jharkhand is 40.70 per cent including 54 per cent male and 27.20 per cent female literacy. There is a gender disparity as well as regional disparity on literacy front. Ranchi district has 45 per cent literacy whereas the literacy rate in Pakur district is just 20 per cent. Literacy rate in those districts are comparatively higher which emerged as urban centres due to mining and industrial trading activities.

On the front of male-female literacy also, wide gap can be seen in the Figure 15. This gap persists both in the rural as well as urban areas. It reflects among other things, the social stigma and mindset of the people.

District-wise rural female STs literacy in Jharkhand is much lower than the urban female literacy. STs Female rural literacy is as high as 32 per cent in district like Ranchi but

FIGURE 15

District-wise Male-Female Literacy of STs in Jharkhand, 2001

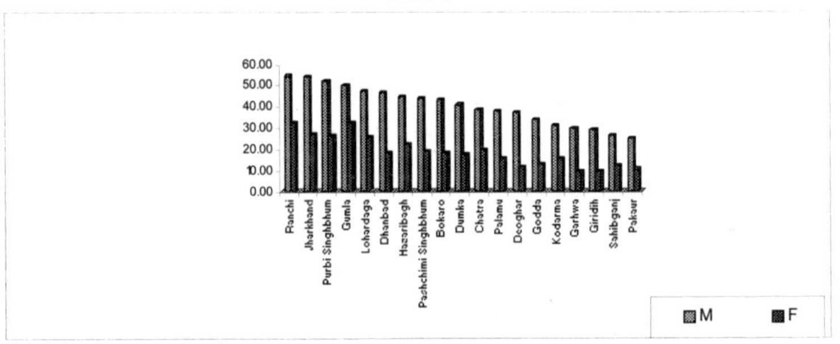

the figure for backward districts like Giridih, Garhwa, Pakur, Deoghar, Bokaro and Kodarma are around 12 per cent. The main reasons are poverty and unavailability of appropriate educational infrastructures. District-wise rural female literacy of STs can be seen in Figure 16.

FIGURE 16

District-wise Rural Female Literacy of STs in Jharkhand, 2001

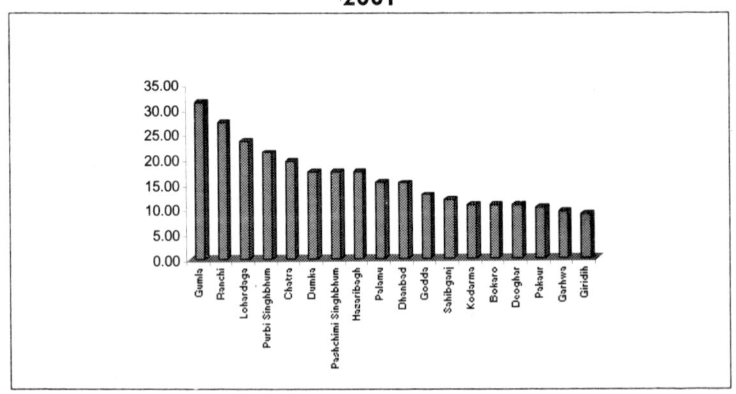

(iii) ST Students Studying at Different Courses of Higher Education in Jharkhand

The highest number of ST boys is studying in Polytechnic institutions followed by B.Sc. and Engineering courses. In all disciplines of higher education boys outnumber the girls. One noticeable fact regarding the higher education in Jharkhand is that number of ST girls opting for B.Ed./BT, Medical, Teachers Training and M.Sc. Courses is more than the boys. Details can be seen in Figure 17.

FIGURE 17

ST Students Studying at Different Level of Higher Education, 2004-05 in Jharkhand

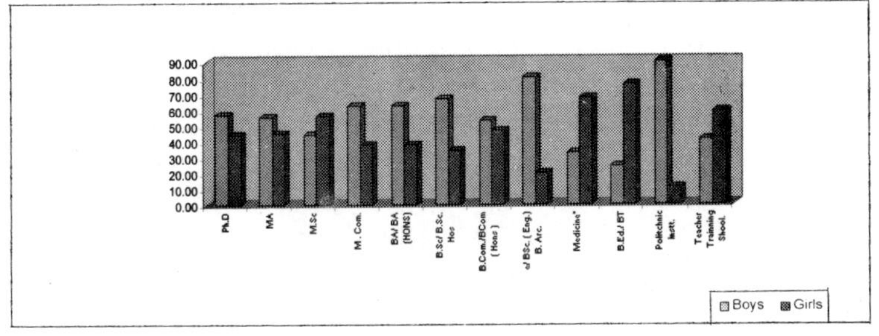

IV. EXPENDITURE IN HIGHER EDUCATION

Expenditure on education is a valuable investment. Education matters, economically for economic growth, reduction in poverty and inequalities, improvement in income distribution, besides contributing to other social, political and cultural dimensions of development and human development. Public expenditure on education is critically important to improve the educational levels of population. Strong and vibrant education system with national values cannot be built by a heavy reliance on private finance. (Tilak, 2006).

In India, over the last several years there has been a phenomenal increase in enrolment. The number of universities and colleges increased. The student population increased faster than the number of teachers but the total expenditure on education and the share of higher education spending declined from 12.2 per cent during 1982-92 to 11.4 per cent for the states, and more dramatically, from 36.2 to 23.3 per cent for the centre. (Kapoor and Mehta, 2007). When we look at university finances around the country, we see a familiar landscape. Bulk of the funds received by both Central and State universities are from public sources. Investment in higher education is far too inadequate. Cost recovery from students has not kept pace with the requirements. Most of the expenditure is on salaries, especially on the non-teaching staff, which in some universities number five times the teaching staff. Salaries and perquisites have grown precipitously with no corresponding reduction in numbers. (*The Hindu*, Feb. 19, 2002) Notwithstanding the high growth rate after economic reforms, the real rate of growth of public expenditure on higher education declined from about 5.5 per cent during 1982-92 to 5.3 per cent during 1993-2004, largely because of deceleration in spending by the states. The average real expenditure on higher education per enrolled students declined at 2.4 per cent annually during this period from Rs. 8322 in the period 1981-82 to 1991-92, to Rs 6790 in the period 1992-93 to 2003-04 (at 1993-94 prices).

According to NSS data, the government's share in overall education has been declining steadily from 80 per cent in 1983 to 67 per cent in 1999. For state like Kerala, the decline is steep, from 75 to 48 per cent, while for MP it is from 84 per cent to 68 per cent. Indeed, while private expenditure on education rose 10.8 times between 1988 and 2004, that for the poor rose even faster, by 12.4 times.

Year	*Expenditure on Education as per cent of GDP*	*Expenditure on Higher Education as per cent of Expenditure on Education*	*Expenditure on Higher Education as per cent of GDP*
1981-1990	3.59	15.6	0.34
1991-2000	3.77	19.3	0.72
2001-2002	3.82	17.9	0.69
2002-2003	3.80	18.5	0.70
2003-2004	3.50	17.8	0.62
2004-2005	3.68	18.0	0.66

Source: Selected Educational Statistic, 2004-05, Ministry of Human Resource Development, GOI.

(Kapoor and Mehta, 2007). The Trends of expenditure on higher education can be seen through by the above tables and also in Figure 18.

FIGURE 18

Percentage GDP Expenditure on University and Higher Education

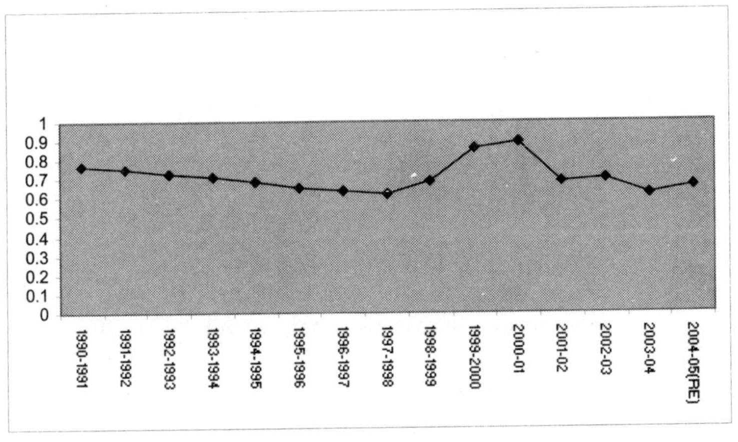

V. STRENGTHS AND WEAKNESSES OF INDIAN HIGHER EDUCATION

(a) Strengths

- One of the second largest education systems in world, next to USA.
- We export the Skilled Manpower and contribute immensely to the "Knowledge Economy".
- We have options for diversification in various sectors.
- Indian students have excelled in every field of knowledge by adopting new technology and curriculum according to the changing needs.
- Distance education provides less expensive education in poor country.

(b) Weaknesses

Prof. Amartya K. Sen (1970) and K.N. Raj (1970) identified and outlined the crisis in Indian Education. Research on educational production function, internal efficiency in education, wastage in education (Dandekar, 1956; AERC, 1971);, etc.; occupied the attention of the educational planner from the beginning. Indian education suffers from a severe degree of wastage. The rural-urban gap in the quality of education has increased over the years, and this puts those educated in rural areas at a disadvantage while competing for good jobs or higher studies in sought after disciplines. Disadvantage is mainly because of poor infrastructure and poor resources available in rural colleges (Hashim, 2008). Important weaknesses are as under:

- Lack of quality education.
- Inequalities and non-uniformity in Higher education among regional, social caste and class and economic groups.
- Facing global and International challenges.
- Less enrolment in Higher education because of in adequate educational facilities in rural and backward areas.
- Lack of equitable system of education.
- Grouping among students may affect the teacher-students relationship.
- Lack of proper social attitude in the rural areas for the education of girls.
- Courses of universities and colleges are unrelated to the realities of the world of work.

VI. GOVERNMENT INITIATIVES FOR PROMOTION OF EDUCATION AMONG SCHEDULED TRIBES

These initiatives can be explained in following heads:

(i) Educational Development of STs.
(ii) Economic Development of STs.
(iii) Social Development of STs.

(i) Educational Development of STs

1. Post-matric Scholarship, Book Banks and up-gradation of merit.
2. Ashram Schools in Tribal Sub-Plan (TSP) areas.
3. Coaching and Allied Assistance—Grant of NGOs.
4. Construction of Hostels for ST boys and girls.
5. Rajiv Gandhi National Fellowship since 2005-06 for STs.
6. Educational complex in low literacy pockets for girls.

Physical and Financial Performance of the Schemes

- 30.02 lakh students availed Post-matric Scholarship for pursuing higher education beyond matriculation (Rs. 400.59) for the first four years of Tenth Plan.
- Released Rs. 44.65 crore to State governments and UTs for construction of 260 hostels for boys providing facilities to 17381 beneficiaries for the first three years of Tenth Plan.
- About Rs. 22.77 crore has been released benefiting 221 Ashram Schools during the first four years of the Tenth Plan.
- 76 Educational complexes in low literacy areas and 193 vocational training centres were supported in tribal areas.
- Important Central Sector and Centrally Sponsored Schemes of Government of India for STs.

(ii) Economic Development of STs

1. Special Central Assistance (SCA) to Tribal Sub Plan (TSP).
2. Grants under Article 275 (1) of the constitution.
3. National Scheduled Tribe Finance and Development Corporation (NSFDC).
4. G.I.A. to State Scheduled Tribes Finance Development Corporation (STDs).

5. Investment and Price Support to Tribal Cooperative Marketing Development Federation Ltd. (TRIFED).
6. Grant-in-aid to STDCs for MFP.
7. Development of Primitive Tribal Groups (PTGs)

Physical and Financial Performance of Schemes

- Rs. 2133.39 crore was released for the first four years of Tenth Plan under SCA to TSP benefiting various income generating and was allocated for development of forest villages.
- Rs. 1244.43 crore has been released (4 years) under Article 275(1) of the constitution benefiting various schemes including 100 Eklavya Model Schools. Rs. 100 crore has been allocated for development of minor irrigation schemes to tribal farmers.
- Rs. 17.95 crore has been released for supporting TRIFED operations in tribal areas involving price support and marketing operations.
- Rs. 51.04 crore has been released (3 years) for the development of 75 PTGs need based projects.
- Rs. 10.74 crore was released (3 years) for the scheme of State Scheduled Tribe Development Corporation BPL ST families.

(iii) Social Development of STs

1. Grant-in-aid to NGOs to provide benefits to STs.
2. Vocational Training Centres in Tribal areas.
3. Research, information and Mass Education, Tribal festivals and others.

Physical and Financial Performance

- Rs. 104.22 crore was released during the last three years of the Tenth Plan.
- Rs. 67.12 crore (Rs. 33.5 crore for States/UTs and the same amount for NGOs) was allocated and 193 vocational training centres were supported for

conducting various training programmes during the first four years of the Tenth Plan.

- There are 16 Tribal Research Institutes (TRIs) and one in A&N Islands is yet to start functioning. Grants for various research schemes, seminars and exchange of tribals, etc. are being supported under the Research, Information and Mass Education, Tribal Festivals and others.

(VI) NATIONAL OVERSEAS SCHOLARSHIP (NOS) AND PASSAGE GRANTS FOR ST STUDENTS FOR PURSUING HIGHER STUDIES ABROAD

Scholarships are provided under the scheme to meritorious SCs, STs denotified, nomadic and semi-nomadic tribes, SC converts to other religions, children of Agriçultural Labourers/Traditional Artisans for post-graduate, Ph.D. and Post-Doctoral Studies in specified fields of science, technology, and engineering. Selected candidates are allowed three years after the year of selection to obtain admission in foreign institutions. The scholarships are provided to the students by the Indian Missions during their stay abroad and cover the payment of tuition fees, maintenance and contingency allowance and travel expenses. The upper income limit for eligibility is Rs. 12,000 per month. Passage grant is provided to students who are in receipt of a merit scholarship from a foreign government or institution, in case such scholarship does not include the cost of passage. The fund allocation of the year 2006-07 is Rs. 40.00 lakh.

(i) Rajiv Gandhi National Fellowship for STs

Rajiv Gandhi National Fellowship, a new scheme to provide attractive fellowships to tribal students pursuing M. Phil. and Ph.D. studies was implemented through the University Grant Commission (UGC). A total of 667 fellowships were awarded during the year 2006-07.

Post-matric Scholarships

Post-matric Scholarship (PMS) continued to be an important centrally sponsored scheme to promote higher education among STs. Under the scheme of PMS, an amount of Rs. 198.92 crore was spent up to 31 March, 2006 to benefit more than 8.40 lakh students.

Construction of Hostels for ST Boys and Girls

The Scheme of 'Hostels for ST Boys and Girls', aim to reduce the present drop-out rates among the STs, by providing a major support service to ST boys and girls. An expenditure of Rs. 11.04 crore was incurred up to 31 March, 2006 in constructing 23 hostels in Karnataka, Manipur, Nagaland, Rajasthan, North Eastern Hill University, Meghalaya, Nagaland University, IIT Delhi and Delhi University.

Ashram Schools

The scheme of Ashram Schools is yet another scheme which aims at extending educational facilities to ST boys and girls through dedicated residential schools with conducive environment for their learning. An amount of Rs. 4.27 crore has been released for construction of Ashram Schools to the State Governments of Gujarat, Maharashtra and Karnataka. The Ministry has funded 57 Educational Complexes under the scheme of Educational Complex in Low Literacy Pockets for development of Female literacy in Tribal areas covering more than 7,528 Scheduled Tribe girl students, by extending grant of Rs. 3.78 crore to voluntary organisations.

(ii) Recommendations of National Knowledge Commission (NKC)

The National Knowledge Commission (NKC), set-up under the chairmanship of Mr. Sam Pitroda, came out with the first set of recommendations by October 2005. Speaking to newspersons after a meeting with the Prime Minister, Dr Manmohan Singh, Mr Pitroda said, "The Commission will look at knowledge from five different perspectives — access to knowledge; knowledge concepts related to education; knowledge creation relating to increase in science and technology labs, patents etc; knowledge application in agriculture, industry and so on; and knowledge services (*The Hindu, Business Line*, 2005).

The National Knowledge Commission (NKC) recommendations on higher education were submitted to the Prime Minister on 29th November 2006. The report focused on the need for excellence in the system, expansion of the higher education sector in the country, and providing access to higher education for larger number of students. In his address to launch the NKC's Report to the Nation on January 12th, the Prime Minister remarked, "The Commission's reports have many useful ideas for reforming higher education. These are all ideas that merit serious discussion. I would urge the Commission to take these ideas across the country and build consensus."

The Knowledge Commission Report has said that India would need 1,500 new universities in the next seven years. It also says that only eight per cent of Indian students' finishing school goes for higher education. In China, the figure is 20 per cent while in developed countries, as many as 70 per cent students leaving school go to college. NKC has also recommended to establish 50 National Universities that can provide education of the highest standard.

There is no denying the fact that higher education has contributed very significantly in the human capital formation, economic development, social change and strengthening of political democracy after independence. But it is matter of regret that still there is a mismatch between the demand and necessary infrastructure for higher education. Only 7 per cent population in the relevant age group enters the campus imparting higher education. Large proportion of population do not have access to higher education. Furthermore, the quality of education is also not to the expectation of changing needs of time. There are several constraints in the availability, accessibility and affordability so far as the growth of higher education in India is concerned. It is the high time some drastic policy decisions and action plans are implemented to enable the nation for achieving the goal of super power by 2020.

The Knowledge Commission under the stewardship of Sam Patroda is engaged in emphasizing on expansion and reform in our school system to ensure that every child gets equal opportunity to enter the arena of higher education. Its final recommendations to the government are expected soon.

To address the issue of higher education the NKC is making formal and informal consultations with wide range of people in the field of higher education, parliamentarians industry, bureaucrats and the Civil Society. The Commission finds almost unanimous view that higher education needs a systematic overhauling so that larger number of students can get higher education without compromising with the quality of academic standards. It is essentially and urgently required because the socio-economic transformation in the 21st Century depends on the quantitative and qualitative expansion of education, especially the higher education. It is also true that an inclusive society can provide the foundation for a knowledge society in the age of knowledge revolution. The prime objectives of reform and change in higher education system must be expansion, inclusion and excellence with a long-term perspective. The task is complex and difficult but imperative. Some of the highlights of prescriptions suggested by the NKC on higher education are as under:

1. Increasing Number of Universities

In order to attain a gross enrolment ratio of at least 15 per cent by 2015 there is need of around 1500 universities. For this some new universities should be created and some clusters of affiliated colleges can be upgraded as universities.

2. Restructuring the Regulatory System

The existing Regulatory system puts barriers of entry in higher education and hence is a big hurdle in the path of both the quantitative and qualitative expansion. Due to multiplicity of regulatory agencies, mandates are confusing and overlapping. As a result, the system is over regulated but under-governed.

Hence there is need of an Independent Regulatory Authority for Higher Education (IRAHE) which should be allowed to operate independent of government control.

IRAHE should be established by a Parliamentary Act.

IRAHE should monitor standards and accord degree granting power to higher education Institutions. The role of UGC should be redefined in the matter of disbursement of grants to and maintenance of public institutions whether private or public and domestic or International Institutions.

3. Public Financing and Diversification of Sources of Finance

The expansion of quality higher education needs more finances. It must come from both the public and private sources. Although the government will remain the main source, the sources of private expanding must be explored to supplement the public expenditure. The government allocation on higher education should be increased to 1.5 per cent of GDP out of a total of at least 6 per cent of GDP for Education. Universities should be allowed to restructure their fees but fees should meet at least 20 per cent of total expenditure in universities. Needy students should be provided with a fee-waiver plus scholarships to meet their costs. The tradition of philanthropic contributions should be nurtured by way of incentives through tax laws and trust laws. Universities should tap other sources like alumini contributions and licensing fees. Private investments should be encouraged.

4. National Universities

The Knowledge Commission has recommended for the creation of 50 National Universities to educate and train students in various disciplines including social sciences, humanities, basic sciences, commerce, and professional subjects at both the undergraduate as well as post-graduate levels. Target of 50 is long-term objective but at least 10 National Universities should be set-up in next 3 years. These can be established both by the government and private sponsoring body. The Commission has suggested many things to make the system of admission of students, recruitment of teachers, and university-Industry relationship to make it more flexible and pragmatic.

5. Reform of Existing Universities

The Knowledge Commission has suggested various reforms in the existing universities with regard to restructuring of curricula, internal assessment, retaining of talented faculty members by creating better working condition, etc., there is dire need for reform in the system of governance of universities which do not preserve autonomy and which do not promote accountability. The appointment of vice-chancellor must be freed from government intervention. It should be done through search processes and peer judgement alone.

6. Restructuring Undergraduate Colleges

The system of undergraduate colleges affiliated to Universities should be restructured by providing autonomy to colleges at individual or cluster basis. Some affiliated colleges should be remodeled as community colleges. A control board of undergraduate education should be established to set curricula and to conduct colleges.

7. Promoting Quality

To promote the quality expansion of higher education, the Knowledge Commission has made several recommendations like information disclosure norms for all educational institutions, evaluation of courses and teachers by students and peer teachers, upgrading infrastructure. The higher education system must focus on diversity and pluralism. It should avoid uniform one-size-fits-all approach.

8. Social Inclusion

Educational Institutions should adopt a needs blind admission policy and the financial factor should not be considered in the admission policy. National Scholarship Scheme should target economically unprivileged students and those belonging to historically socially disadvantaged groups.

9. Affirmative Action

Some affirmative actions are required to ensure the higher education accessible to socially and economically disadvantaged students

The Knowledge Commission admits that there is quiet crisis in higher education in India which runs deep. There is urgent need to address this crisis in a systematic and forthright manner. There is an opportunity in the crisis.

Considering the demographic reality of young India,

expansion, inclusion and excellence in higher education can drive economic development and social progress at much faster rate and that can transform Indian Society and Economy.

VII. FINDINGS AND SUGGESTIONS

Some important findings are as under:

- ST literacy rate is 47.10 per cent as against all India figure of 68.38 per cent in year 2001.
- There is wide gender disparity in literacy rate (ST Male 47.1 and Female 34.8%).
- The girl enrolment in higher education for STs is only 3.45 per cent whereas at all India level it is 5.2 per cent for SCs and 8.17 per cent for general category students.
- No. of Universities and deemed universities has increased from 27 in 1950-51 to 407 in 2004-05.
- No. of ST students in higher education in 2004-05 was 434215 whereas the corresponding figure in Jharkhand was just 21834 which included 13253 boys and 8561 girls. The figures reflect the gender disparity also.
- A total of 8789 researchers were awarded Ph.D. degree in 2004-05. It points towards the lukewarm attitude towards research activities.
- The expenditure on higher education in 2001-02 was only 0.69 per cent of GDP.

Following are the important suggestions:

- Improvement in provision of Infrastructure and human resources for Higher Education.
- To increase the enrolment in Higher education and to improve the Literacy rate especially among backward and weaker sections of the society.
- To improve the quality of teaching and modern method.

- To promote maximum scholarship in Higher Education.
- To encourage Teacher Capacity building.
- To establish more universities across the country.
- To change the system of directives for higher education.
- To increase public spending and spread sources of financing.
- To set-up more and more National Universities.
- To transform existing universities.
- To streamline under graduate colleges.
- To encourage improved quality.
- To ensure right of entry for all deserving students.
- To provide access to education for economically and socially underprivileged students.
- Education should be concerned with ideas and experience rather than with only books and printed materials.
- Coaching classes and teaching shops opened by college teacher should be banned.

References

Altbach, Philip G. (2005), Higher Education In India, *The Hindu*, 12 April, 2005.

Blang, Mark (1987), Book Review; Review of Economics of Education: Research and Studies, *Journal of Human Research*, 24 (2), pp-33-35

Business Line (2005), Knowledge Commission to come out with first report by October, Friday, August 5, 2005.

GOI (2007), Annual Report 2006-07, Ministry of Tribal Affairs, Government of India

GOI (2007), Annual Report, 2006-07, Ministry of Human Resource Development, Government of India, Department of Higher Education.

Gore, M.S. (1994), Indian Education and Process, Rawat Publications, pp. 152-53.

Kachhap, A., Suvashi Kachhap (2008), Tribal at a Glance A Statistical Profile, Manak Publication Pvt. Ltd., Delhi.

GOI (2007), Selected Educational Statistics, 2004-05, Ministry of Human Resources Development, Department of Higher Education, Government of India.

IIE (2004), India Country Fact Sheet in Open Doors Report, Institute Of International Education, Foreign student data embargoed for release November 10, 2004.

Kalam, APJ Abdul (2005), President's Address to the Nation on the Eve of Independence Day, 2004, Published in *Yojana*, September, p. 2.

Kapur, D. and P.B. Mehta (2007), Indian Higher Education Reform: From Half Baked Socialism to Half Baked Capitalism, Paper presented at the Brooking NCAER India Policy Forum-2007, July 17-18 at New Delhi.

Kothari, V.N. (1966), (Rapporteur), Investment in Human Resources, Bombay, Popular Prakashan for the Indian Economic Association.

Hashim, S.R. (2008), State of Higher Education in India, India Development Report 2008, edited by R. Radhakrishna, Indira Gandhi Institute of Development Research, Mumbai, pp. 71-85.

Mungekar, B.L. (2007), Inequality and Development: Some Urgent Concerns, Presidential Address on the eve of 31st Indian Social Science Congress at Mumbai on 27-31 December, 2007.

Pandit, H.N. (ed.), (1969), Measurement of Cost Productivity and Efficiency of Education, NCERT, New Delhi.

Raj, K.N. (1970), Crisis in Higher Education in India, Sardar Vallabh Bhai Patel Memorial Lecture, New Delhi

Rao, V.K.R.V. (1964), Education and Economic Development, NCERT, New Delhi.

Schultz, Theodore W. (1961), Investment in Human Capital, *American Economic Review*, 51 (2), March, pp. 1-17.

Sen, Amartya K. (1970), Crisis in Indian Education, Lal Bahadur Shastri Memorial Lecturer, Hyderabad Administrative Staff College of India.

Singh, Baljit, (eds.), (1967), Education as Investment, Meerut, Meenakshi Prakashan.

The Hindu (2002), Financing of Higher Education, Tuesday, Feb 19, 2002.

Tilak, J B G (2006), Economics of Human Capital in India, Keynote address delivered of 89th Annual Conference of Indian Economic Association, Kurukshetra University, Kurukshetra.

———(2008), Economics of Human Capital in India, Economics of Education and Health in India (eds.), edited by Anil Kr. Thakur and Abdus Salam, Deep and Deep Publications Pvt. Ltd., Delhi.

TABLE I

State-wise Population of ST in India 2001

States	Population 1991		Population 2001		State-wise % of ST Population of total state population	% of ST Population in State/ UTs to the total STs Population of the country
	Total	ST Population	Total	ST Population		
Andhra Pradesh	66508008	4199481	75727541	5024104	6.6	5.96
Arunchal Pradesh	8644558	550351	1091117	705158	64.2	0.84
Assam	22414322	2874441	26638407	3308570	12.4	3.92
Bihar	86374465	6616914	82878796	758351	0.9	0.90
Chhattisgrah			20795956	6616596	31.8	7.85
Gujarat	41309582	6161775	50596992	7481160	14.8	8.87
Himachal Pradesh	5170877	218349	6077248	244587	4	0.29
Jharkhand			26909428	7087068	26.3	8.40
J & K			10069917	1105979	10.9	1.31
Karnataka	44977201	1915691	52733958	3463986	6.6	4.11
Kerala	29098518	320967	31838619	364189	1.1	0.43
Madhya Pradesh	66181170	15399034	60385118	12233474	20.3	14.51
Maharashtra	78937187	7318281	96752247	8577276	8.9	10.17

Manipur	1837149	632173	2388634	741141	34.2	0.88
Meghalaya	1774778	1517927	2306069	1992862	85.9	2.36
Mizoram	689756	653565	891058	839310	94.5	1.00
Nagaland	1209546	1060822	1988636	1774026	89.1	2.10
Orissa	31659756	7032214	36706920	8145081	22.1	9.66
Rajasthan	44005990	5474881	56473122	7097706	12.6	8.42
Sikkim	406457	90901	540493	111405	20.6	0.13
Tamil Nadu	55858946	574194	62110839	651321	1.1	0.77
Tripura	2757205	853345	3191168	993426	31.1	1.18
Uttar Pradesh	139112287	287901	166052859	107963	0.1	0.13
Uttaranchal			8479562	256129	3	0.30
West Bengal	68077965	3808760	80221171	4406794	5.5	5.23
A & N Islands	280661	26770	356265	29469	8.3	0.03
D & N H	138477	109380	220451	137225	62.2	0.16
Daman and Diu	101586	11724	158059	13997	8.8	0.02
Lakshadweep	51707	48163	60595	59321	94.5	0.07
ALL INDIA	838583988*	67758380	1027015247	84326240	8.2	100.00

Sources: Census of India, 1991, Part II–B(iii), Primary Census Abstract, Scheduled Tribe Population, Office of the Registrar General and Census Commissioner, India, Ministry of Home Affairs, New Delhi, and Census of India, 2001.

TABLE 2

State-wise Literacy Rate of STs as per Census 1991 and 2001

States	*Lit. Rate 2001*		*Lit. Rate 1991*		*STs Females Literacy*	
	General	*STs*	*General*	*STs*	*2001*	*1991*
Andhra Pradesh	63.8	37	48.6	17.2	26.1	8.7
Arunchal Pradesh	62.5	49.6	53.7	34.4	40.6	24.9
Assam	63.1	62.5	53.4	49.2	52.4	39
Bihar	50.6	28.2	41.1	18.9	15.5	7.5
Goa	82.2	55.9	75.9	42.9	47.3	29
Chhattisgrah	71.7	52.1	53.2	26.7	39.3	13.9
Gujarat	72.9	47.7	65.9	36.4	36	24.2
HP	79.2	65.5	68.6	47.1	53.3	31.2
Jharkhand	·61.9	40.7	51.1	27.5	27.2	15.4
J & K	57.5	37.5	0	0	25.5	
Karnataka	71	48.3	60.6	36	36.6	23.6
Kerala	92.1	64.4	91.3	57.2	58.1	51.1
Madhya Pradesh	71.6	41.2	54.8	18.4	28.4	8.8
Maharashtra	79.7	55.2	69.1	36.8	43.1	24
Manipur	73	65.9	63.4	53.6	58.4	44.5
Meghalaya	70	61.3	62.9	46.7	59.2	43.6
Mizoram	80.2	89.3	75.2	82.7	86.9	78.7
Nagaland	71.9	65.9	69	60.6	61.3	54.5
Orissa	73.9	37.4	61.6	22.3	23.4	10.2
Rajasthan	65	44.7	44.8	19.4	26.2	4.4
Sikkim	69.7	67.1	56.8	59	60.2	50.4
Tamil Nadu	76.2	41.5	66.8	27.9	32.8	20.2
Tripura	82.3	56.5	72.8	40.4	44.6	27.3
Uttar Pradesh	58.9	35.1	44.6	20	20.7	5.9
Uttaranchal	73.7	63.2	61.7	41.2	49.4	24.5
West Bengal	73.6	43.4	65	27.8	29.2	15
A & N Islands	82.6	66.8	74.7	56.6	59.6	48.7
D & N H	82.6	41.2	84.6	28.2	27	15.9
Daman and Diu	79.4	63.4	73.3	52.9	51.9	41.5
Lakshadweep	94.8	86.1	96.1	80.6	80.2	71.7
ALL INDIA	68.8	47.1	57.7	29.6	34.8	18.2

Source: Census of India, 2001.

TABLE 3.

Gross Enrolment Ratio among among Higher Education, 2004-05

States/UTs	*General Class*			*STs*		
	Higher Education (18-24 years)			*Higher Education (18-24 years)*		
	Boys	*Girls*	*Total*	*Boys*	*Girls*	*Total*
Andhra Pradesh	14.57	8.55	11.52	8.04	2.74	5.17
Arunachal Pradesh	7.12	4.50	5.85	9.94	5.72	7.75
Assam	8.17	5.70	6.94	7.36	5.42	6.35
Bihar8.44	3.19	6.02	9.22	3.34	6.43	
Chhattisgarh	9.43	5.54	7.51	9.58	5.24	7.35
Goa 11.47	15.71	13.41	-	-	-	
Gujarat	11.88	9.29	10.67	7.31	4.87	6.09
Haryana	11.07	10.06	10.63	-	-	-
Himachal Pradesh	14.59	13.58	14.10	18.31	13.37	15.84
Jammu and Kashmir	6.76	6.29	6.54	0.20	0.06	0.13
Jharkhand	8.66	5.32	7.05	3.76	2.33	3.03
Karnataka	12.72	10.36	11.58	5.46	3.15	4.36
Kerala	8.15	9.96	9.08	7.74	7.80	7.77
Madhya Pradesh	14.15	7.40	11.02	5.59	2.99	4.28
Maharashtra	15.17	10.92	13.24	4.51	1.98	3.25
Manipur	14.81	11.77	13.27	13.79	10.80	12.27
Meghalaya	12.67	10.52	11.58	8.40	7.76	8.07
Mizoram	12.85	7.77	10.39	6.69	5.71	6.20
Nagaland	4.96	4.40	4.70	5.56	4.46	5.03
Orissa	13.62	3.48	8.59	2.52	0.21	1.32
Punjab	9.40	11.23	10.24	-	-	-
Rajasthan	7.55	4.31	6.04	7.17	1.93	4.61
Sikkim	10.88	8.15	9.61	8.37	9.29	8.83
Tamil Nadu	13.03	9.95	11.47	4.37	2.42	3.32
Tripura	7.19	5.14	6.16	3.77	1.79	2.73
Uttar Pradesh	9.21	6.84	8.13	32.92	15.80	24.36
Uttaranchal	13.22	12.70	12.97	17.06	12.85	15.02
West Bengal	10.00	6.09	8.09	4.43	2.30	3.32
A&N Islands	4.97	7.06	5.87	5.40	7.40	6.40
Chandigarh	30.93	46.12	37.01	-	-	-
D&N Haveli	2.80	0.43	1.96	0.86	0.39	0.63
Daman and Diu	1.95	3.55	2.40	-	-	-
Delhi33.15	42.94	37.25	-	-	-	
Lakshadweep	0.00	0.00	0.00	0.00	0.00	0.00
Pondicherry	17.70	16.96	17.33	-	-	-
ALL INDIA	11.58	8.17	9.97	6.31	3.45	4.86

Source: Selected Educational Statistics, 2004-05, Ministry of Human Resources Development, Department of Higher Education, Government of India.

TABLE 4

Higher Education Institutions and Enrolment Ratio: 2004-05

States/UTs	*All Categories of Students*						
	Higher Education (18-24 years)			*Total Population*	*Total Population in Higher Education*	*Total Higher Institutions*	*Per Higher Education Enrolment Ratio*
	Boys	*Girls*	*Total*				
Andhra Pradesh	14.57	8.55	11.52	75727541	8723813	1839	4743.8
Arunachal Pradesh	7.12	4.50	5.85	1091117	63830	15	4255.4
Assam	8.17	5.70	6.94	26638407	1848705	388	4764.7
Bihar	8.44	3.19	6.02	82878796	4989304	851	5862.9
Chhattisgarh	9.43	5.54	7.51	20795956	2788738	250	11155.0
Goa	11.47	15.71	13.41	1343998	100934	43	2347.3
Gujarat	11.88	9.29	10.67	50596992	5398699	900	5998.6
Haryana	11.07	10.06	10.63	21082989	2241122	314	7137.3
Himachal Pradesh	14.59	13.58	14.10	6077248	856892	146	5869.1
Jammu and Kashmir	6.76	6.29	6.54	10069917	658573	221	2980.0
Jharkhand	8.66	5.32	7.05	26909428	709929	147	4829.4
Karnataka	12.72	10.36	11.58	52733958	6106592	1504	4060.2
Kerala	8.15	9.96	9.08	31838619	2890947	395	7318.9
Madhya Pradesh	14.15	7.40	11.02	60385118	6654440	1078	6172.9
Maharashtra	15.17	10.92	13.24	96752247	12809998	1786	7172.5

Manipur	14.81	11.77	13.27	2388634	316972	64	4952.7
Meghalaya	12.67	10.52	11.58	2306069	267043	56	4768.6
Mizoram	12.85	7.77	10.39	891058	92581	29	3192.4
Nagaland	4.96	4.40	4.70	1988636	93466	56	1669.0
Orissa	13.62	3.48	8.59	36706920	3153124	882	3575.0
Punjab	9.40	11.23	10.24	24289296	2487224	363	6851.9
Rajasthan	7.55	4.31	6.04	56473122	3410977	841	4055.9
Sikkim	10.88	8.15	9.61	540493	51941	7	7420.2
Tamil Nadu	13.03	9.95	11.47	62110839	7124113	991	7188.8
Tripura	7.19	5.14	6.16	3191168	196576	22	8935.3
Uttar Pradesh	9.21	6.84	8.13	166052859	13500097	1935	6976.8
Uttaranchal	13.22	12.70	12.97	8479562	1099799	118	9320.3
West Bengal	10.00	6.09	8.09	80221171	6489893	546	11886.3
A&N Islands	4.97	7.06	5.87	356265	20913	5	4182.6
Chandigarh	30.93	46.12	37.01	900914	333428	22	15155.8
D&N Haveli	2.80	0.43	1.96	220451	4321	0	#DIV/0!
Daman and Diu	1.95	3.55	2.40	158059	3793	2	1896.7
Delhi	33.15	42.94	37.25	13782989	5134163	160	32088.5
Lakshadweep	0.00	0.00	0.00	60595	0	0	#DIV/0!
Pondicherry	17.70	16.96	17.33	973829	168765	33	5114.1
ALL INDIA	11.58	8.17	9.97	1027015247	102393420.1	16009	6396.0

Source: Computed from Selected Educational Statistics, 2004-05.

TABLE 5

Higher Education Institutions and Enrolment Ratio: 2004-05

States/UTs	*All Categories of Students*						
	GER Higher Education (18-24 years)			*Total Population*	*Total Population in Higher Education*	*Total Higher Institutions 2004-05*	*Per Higher Education Enrolment Ratio*
	Boys	*Girls*	*Total*				
Andhra Pradesh	14.57	8.55	11.52	75727541	8723813	1839	4743.8
Arunachal Pradesh	7.12	4.50	5.85	1091117	63830	15	4255.4
Assam	8.17	5.70	6.94	26638407	1848705	388	4764.7
Bihar	8.44	3.19	6.02	82878796	4989304	851	5862.9
Chhattisgarh	9.43	5.54	7.51	20795956	2788738	250	11155.0
Goa	11.47	15.71	13.41	1343998	100934	43	2347.3
Gujarat	11.88	9.29	10.67	50596992	5398699	900	5998.6
Haryana	11.07	10.06	10.63	21082989	2241122	314	7137.3
HP	14.59	13.58	14.10	6077248	856892	146	5869.1
J & K	6.76	6.29	6.54	10069917	658573	221	2980.0
Jharkhand	8.66	5.32	7.05	26909428	709929	147	4829.4
Karnataka	12.72	10.36	11.58	52733958	6106592	1504	4060.2
Kerala	8.15	9.96	9.08	31838619	2890947	395	7318.9
MP	14.15	7.40	11.02	60385118	6654440	1078	6172.9
Maharashtra	15.17	10.92	13.24	96752247	12809998	1786	7172.5
Manipur	14.81	11.77	13.27	2388634	316972	64	4952.7
Meghalaya	12.67	10.52	11.58	2306069	267043	56	4768.6

Mizoram	12.85	7.77	10.39	891058	92581	29	3192.4
Nagaland	4.96	4.40	4.70	1988636	93466	56	1669.0
Orissa	13.62	3.48	8.59	36706920	3153124	882	3575.0
Punjab	9.40	11.23	10.24	24289296	2487224	363	6851.9
Rajasthan	7.55	4.31	6.04	56473122	3410977	841	4055.9
Sikkim	10.88	8.15	9.61	540493	51941	7	7420.2
Tamil Nadu	13.03	9.95	11.47	62110839	7124113	991	7188.8
Tripura	7.19	5.14	6.16	3191168	196576	22	8935.3
Uttar Pradesh	9.21	6.84	8.13	166052859	13500097	1935	6976.8
Uttaranchal	13.22	12.70	12.97	8479562	1099799	118	9320.3
WB	10.00	6.09	8.09	80221171	6489893	546	11886.3
A&N Islands	4.97	7.06	5.87	356265	20913	5	4182.6
Chandigarh	30.93	46.12	37.01	900914	333428	22	15155.8
D&N Haveli	2.80	0.43	1.96	220451	4321	0	#DIV/0!
Daman and Diu	1.95	3.55	2.40	158059	3793	2	1896.7
Delhi	33.15	42.94	37.25	13782989	5134163	160	32088.5
Lakshadweep	0.00	0.00	0.00	60595	0	0	#DIV/0!
Pondicherry	17.70	16.96	17.33	973829	168765	33	5114.1
ALL INDIA	11.58	8.17	9.97	1027015247	102393420.1	16009	6396.0

Source: Computed from Selected Educational Statistics, 2004-05.

TABLE 6

State-wise Scheduled Tribe Students Studying at Different Level of Higher Education/Institutions, 2004-05

States	*Number of Students*			*Percentage of Students*		
	Boys	*Girls*	*Total*	*Boys (%)*	*Girls (%)*	*Total*
Andhra Pradesh	19870	7770	27640	71.9	28.1	100.0
Arunachal Pradesh	3464	2152	5616	61.7	38.3	100.0
Assam	14289	11445	25734	55.5	44.5	100.0
Bihar	3824	1256	5080	75.3	24.7	100.0
Chhattisgarh	30091	17504	47595	63.2	36.8	100.0
Goa	282	174	456	61.8	38.2	100.0
Gujarat	26944	19232	46176	58.4	41.6	100.0
HP	2673	1993	4666	57.3	42.7	100.0
J&K	65	16	81	80.2	19.8	100.0
Jharkhand	13253	8581	21834	60.7	39.3	100.0
Karnataka	10619	5824	16443	64.6	35.4	100.0
Kerala	1435	1876	3311	43.3	56.7	100.0
MP	33239	18321	51560	64.5	35.5	100.0
Maharashtra	21166	9241	30407	69.6	30.4	100.0
Manipur	7228	5920	13148	55.0	45.0	100.0
Meghalaya	8993	9025	18018	49.9	50.1	100.0
Mizoram	3574	2993	6567	54.4	45.6	100.0
Nagaland	7440	5691	13131	56.7	43.3	100.0
Orissa	9911	901	10812	91.7	8.3	100.0
Punjab	45	18	63	71.4	28.6	100.0
Rajasthan	27733	7157	34890	79.5	20.5	100.0
Sikkim	554	637	1191	46.5	53.5	100.0
Tamil Nadu	1339	984	2323	57.6	42.4	100.0
Tripura	1880	994	2874	65.4	34.6	100.0
Uttar Pradesh	1947	942	2889	67.4	32.6	100.0
Uttaranchal	2688	1894	4582	58.7	41.3	100.0
West Bengal	10354	5878	16232	63.8	36.2	100.0
A&N Islands	106	143	249	42.6	57.4	100.0
Chandigarh	278	242	520	53.5	46.5	100.0
Delhi	11447	8680	20127	56.9	43.1	100.0
ALL INDIA	276731	157484	434215	63.7	36.3	100.0

Source: Computed from Selected Educational Statistics, 2004-05.

TABLE 7

STs Students Studying at Different Level of Education: 2004-05

Degree	India					Jharkhand				
	Boys	Girls	Total	Boys (%)	Girls (%)	Boys	Girls	Total	Boys (%)	Girls (%)
Ph.D.	793	544	1337	59.31	40.69	75	58	133	56.39	43.61
M.A.	14271	8808	23079	61.84	38.16	434	350	784	55.36	44.64
M.Sc.	3324	2160	5484	60.61	39.39	222	281	503	44.14	55.86
M.Com.	2296	1347	3643	63.02	36.98	305	184	489	62.37	37.63
B.A./B.A. (Hons.)	124645	71533	196178	63.54	36.46	5456	3280	8736	62.45	37.55
B.Sc/B.Sc. (Hons.)	33142	16620	49762	66.60	33.40	3514	1781	5295	66.36	33.64
B.Com./B.Com. (Hons.)	31353	17018	48371	64.82	35.18	2187	1936	4123	53.04	46.96
B.Sc. (Eng.) B.Arc.	17288	4219	21507	80.38	19.62	675	166	841	80.26	19.74
Medicine*	5549	3990	9539	58.17	41.83	32	67	99	32.32	67.68
B.Ed./BT	5316	3800	9116	58.32	41.68	65	207	272	23.90	76.10
Politechnic Instt.	9721	3094	12815	75.86	24.14	62	7	69	89.86	10.14
Teacher Trainning Schools	4349	3267	7116	61.12	45.91	7	10	17	41.18	58.82

*Medicine, Dentistry, Nursing, Pharmacy, Ayurvedic and Unani, Homeopathy, etc.

Source: Computed from Selected Educational Statistics, 2004-05.

TABLE 8

Expenditure on University and Higher Education in India

Years	*Expenditure*	*%age to GDP*	*%age to Total Expenditure on all sectors*
1990-91	3956.09	0.77	2.70
1991-92	4396.78	0.75	2.58
1992-93	4922.9	0.73	2.59
1993-94	5557.20	0.71	2.54
1994-95	6299.53	0.69	2.50
1995-96	6954.07	0.65	2.43
1996-97	7983.11	0.64	2.42
1997-98	8595.67	0.62	2.32
1998-99	11097.42	0.69	2.52
1999-00	15112.89	0.86	2.95
2000-01	16928.21	0.89	2.96
2001-02	14323.32	0.69	2.31
2002-03	15858.83	0.70	2.34
2003-04	15858.34	0.62	2.13
2004-05 (RE)	18813.07	0.66	2.30

TABLE 9

District-wise STs Literacy in Jharkhand (2001)

Districts	*Total*	*Male*	*Female*
Garhwa	19.80	29.48	9.60
Palamu	26.95	37.81	15.73
Chatra	29.37	38.41	19.87
Hazaribagh	33.57	44.61	22.14
Kodarma	23.83	31.26	15.46
Giridih	19.37	29.06	9.29
Deoghar	24.51	37.18	11.32
Godda	23.58	33.91	13.09
Sahibganj	19.49	26.57	12.40
Pakur	17.86	25.05	10.54
Dumka	29.34	40.74	17.85
Dhanbad	32.59	46.47	18.23
Bokaro	30.88	43.13	17.96
Ranchi	43.47	54.15	32.67
Lohardagga	36.55	47.25	25.77
Gumla	41.12	49.79	32.50
Pashchimi Singhbhum	31.50	44.04	19.05
Purbi Singhbhum	39.00	51.67	26.13
Jharkhand	40.70	54.00	27.20

24

Tribal Education of Jharkhand: Concerns and Scrutiny

Basabi Mukhopadhyay and Debes Mukhopadhyay

"Historically, Indigenous peoples have insisted upon the right of access to education. Invariably, the nature, and consequently the outcome of this education has been constructed through and measured by non-Indigenous standards, values and philosophies. Ultimately, the purpose of this education has been able to assimilate societies. Volumes of studies, research and reports dealing with Indigenous peoples in non-Indigenous educational systems paint a familiar picture of failure and despair. When measured in non-Indigenous terms, the educational outcomes of Indigenous peoples are still far below that of non-Indigenous peoples. This fact exists not because Indigenous peoples are less intelligent, but because educational theories and practices are developed and controlled by non-Indigenous peoples."[1]

Education is firmly intertwined into the core of economic life of any society at any time of history. It is vital to economic development in fostering economic prosperity. A learning society demands more and more of education.

Education is a vehicle of social change. Citing Kerala's experience, V.K. Ramchandran brings out a dialectical relationship between educational progress and social change: 'the spread of education helps to overcome the traditional inequalities of caste, class, and gender, just as the removal of these inequalities contributes to the spread of education'.[2] Thus entitlement to education must be the key element in the process of development of any society. Amartya Sen says that economic development needs to be measured in terms of freedom. To him, development requires the removal of major sources of unfreedom. Barring its intrinsic importance, education, he argues, can be seen to be valuable to the freedom of a person in various distinct ways. It has not only both instrumental: (i) personal, (ii) social, and (iii) process roles but also its (iv) empowerment and distributive roles are of great strategic importance in the process of economic development.[3]

Development policies that are being pursued in India largely circumvent the needs of poor, disadvantaged, low-caste people, and thus delinked from mainstream development process. In fact, the 'assetlessness', 'powerlessness' and 'voicelessness' of a 'small-number' people eludes policy-makers to adopt less broad, and less sensitive approach towards development. Through education, such underdevelopment of the lower-caste people can be removed. Thus, the value of basic education as a tool to facilitate social upward mobility for this category of people is undeniable. John Rawls in his book *A Theory of Justice* articulated: "In a society divided by caste, religion, and ethnicity, equal opportunities of access to "primary goods" such as health, nutrition, and education can create the basis for social mobility and social cohesion." Social inclusiveness calls for fostering the basic ingredients of human capital or the "primary goods". In addition, the policy of protective discrimination for political recognition for the untouchables or Dalits promise a chance of social upward mobility of the lower castes. Ambedkar saw 'education as a cornerstone of his strategy for the liberation of oppressed castes'.[4]

The Indian Constitution has defined the term "Scheduled Tribes" under Article 366(25). It refers to indigenous ethnic minority people who live in clusters generally in far-flung areas, which are either remote or near forest or mountainous regions. India can boast of having the largest population of tribal people or 'Adivasis' in the world, possibly excluding Africa. At present, nearly 700 communities are recognized STs, spread over different States and Union Territories. In India, the population of Scheduled Tribes (henceforth, STs) in the country was 8.43 crore or 8.2 per cent of the total population. The concentration of these tribal people can be found largely in Central and Western states like Madhya Pradesh, Gujarat, Maharashtra, Chhattishgarh, Orissa, Jharkhand, etc. However, tribal people constitute more than 50 per cent of the total population in North-Eastern States. Between the Central and Western States, one finds the highest concentration of tribal people in Jharkhand (28% of the total, as per 2001 Census), then comes Orissa (22.1%). It is estimated that India's tribal population account for more than the total population of France and Britain, and four times larger than Australia. The decade of 1991-2001 recorded a 24.45 per cent growth rate of the STs. Article 46 of the Constitution recognizes both 'Scheduled Tribes' and 'Scheduled Castes' as the weaker sections of the society for whom developmental needs need to be addressed with all sincerity and seriousness. Historically, these 'Adivasis' are excluded from the main development process and thus remains disadvantaged and live on the margins of existence.

Historically, as the Indian education system is elitist in character, tribals are the most marginalized sections of our population who receive financial doles from the government, of course, in trickle. Further, India's present higher education system is not only skewed and centralized but also highly political. Politically motivated and class-conscious higher-caste people harvest bulk of the governmental resources in their favour, thereby denying equal access and opportunities to all. And the worst victim of this system is the tribal people who are socially, economically and ecologically vulnerable. Anyway, HDI of India's tribal population is too low even compared to the Scheduled Castes population. Various development programmes launched by different layers of government dodge the tribal population 'for the reasons of inaccessibility and difficult terrain'.[5] Thus development what we experience is 'development through exclusion', of course, in a subtle, diplomatic way.

However, the Government of India (GOI) and many State Governments have taken several measures to improve the conditions of STs. Despite laws preventing the ills of casteism and untouchability practices and the policy of discriminatory reservation in education and jobs for STs and SCs, the role of the government in addressing the issues of the primitive people are subject to serious scrutiny. Even the GOI admits that a lot needs to be done in their favour. Truly speaking, education and awareness generation have received lackluster attention in the Government's agenda. In spite of pious intention, the National Common Minimum Programme of the present UPA Government has also given half-hearted emphasis on the development of the STs. We believe that what is needed is "development with identity" and "social support" to the most defenseless sections of the society who is unable to articulate their cases. "While dalits and Muslims have had some impact in shaping the national discourse on democracy and governance, the tribals are not just marginal but invisible."[6] Amit Bhaduri says that our basic aim is to ensure that all citizens of India live with economic, social and political dignity. This is what he calls "Development with dignity". "Dignity for the poor... gives them an independent voice", says Bhaduri.[7]

Dr. Ambedkar said that expansion of educational opportunities leads to the liberation of oppressed and exploited castes. Illiteracy means educational deprivation and hence unfreedom. Promotion of social justice and removal of unfreedoms can only be achieved through (quality) education. Before we discuss the number of measures taken to provide (quality) education or in a broad sense to correct the "historical deprivations" of tribals, we must say that since the Fifth Plan, the Government had been pursuing 'Welfarist Approach' (i.e. concentrating on poverty reduction, i.e. *'garibi hatao'* and improvement of physical infrastructure in tribal pockets) towards tribal development. As time progressed, this approach was replaced by 'empowerment approach' in very recent decades. For instance, tribal people are now being encouraged to participate in local governance through PRIs with the aim of integrating tribes with the mainstream India, but not at the expense of their cultural distinctiveness.

- *Post-matric Scholarships*—a flagship scheme introduced in 1944 for providing financial assistance pursuing post-matriculation recognized courses including professionals, technical as well as non-professional and non-technical courses. It also includes correspondence courses including distance and continuing education.
- *Hostels for ST Boys and Girls*—The scheme of Girls' Hostels is in operation since the Third Plan, while the Scheme for construction of Boys' Hostels is in operation since 1989-90. Its object is to provide residential facilities to tribal boys and girls studying in middle school and high schools, colleges and universities to reduce dropout rates.
- *Rajiv Gandhi National Fellowship*—This fellowship programmes is implemented through the UGC to the tribals pursuing M.Phil and Ph.D studies since 2005-06.
- *National Overseas Scholarship*—The scheme is meant for higher studies abroad to meritorious ST students in specific fields of Master level courses, Ph.D and Post-Doctoral research programme in the field of engineering, technology and science.
- *Scheme of Top class education*—This scheme for ST students is in operation from 2007-08 with the objective of encouraging meritorious students for pursuing studies at degree and post-degree level in any of the selected list of institutes of excellence.
- *Exchange of visits by STs*—This scheme is meant for providing wide exposure and experience sharing to the tribals by visits to the more developed areas of the country.
- *Upgradation of merit of ST students*—This scheme aims at upgrading the merit of ST students by providing them remedial coaching to remove

deficiencies in subjects they study and special coaching to prepare the students for competitive examinations for seeking entry into professional courses.

All these schemes are in operation in the State of Jharkhand.

In spite of these measures to upgrade ST community of the country educationally as well as financially, marginal sections of India over the years have remained 'not just marginal but invisible' as well as a vanishing tribe. National Policy on Tribes bemoans, "Alienation from the society, lack of adequate infrastructure like schools, hostels and teachers, abject poverty and apathy towards irrelevant curriculum have stood in the way of getting." Vast majority of these communities could not even enter primary school because of massive poverty. Its cascading effect falls on the next higher stages of education. Schemes of higher education or various scholarships for higher studies are in fact simply a luxury to these people and the political parties play to the gallery simply to bamboozle these politically insensitive people.[8] Thus doubt over the empowerment value of education comes under scrutiny. However, benefits of education and the contacts with the people of higher echelons percolate to the traditional societies. The only thing that strikes us is 'modern traditionalism' characterized by the 20th century version of traditional tribal life. The result is cultural interruption that provides the means to new identities and cultures and challenges the conventional outcomes of education. Indian Adivasi communities as compared to SC people are admittedly less educated and less developed as well as less articulated.

Well-known sociologist, T.K. Oommen convincingly argues that various social welfare measures meant for SC people "have produced a Scheduled Caste elite—political, bureaucratic, professional and literary. The prospect of Scheduled Castes occupying top positions in Indian society and polity has become a reality, although the vast majority continue to survive as the wretched of the earth."[9] Thus Indian education, being elitist, is bereft of social change.

Taking all the conventional indicators of socio-economic development (poverty level, literacy rate, dropout rate, constitutional guarantee to provide equal opportunities for social development to all, accessibility to public health care facilities, displacement from roots consequent upon developmental projects undertaken, etc.) into account, one can safely conclude that Advisis are worse-off than the dalits or Harijans. Despite these measures, and policy of reservations in education and jobs, there are no professionals and technical persons from the tribal communities as well as national level political leaders to the stature of late B.R. Ambedkar or Ms. Mayabati championing their cause. These people will have to take a long journey, even after 60 years of independence, to 'catch up' the higher echelons of the society. What is important is that, "our inegalitarian and hierarchical social system just as the inegalitarian educational system arose, in the first instance, from the inegalitarian social system itself."[10] It has remained a distant dream to a movement towards a learning tribal society.

A tribal society at a very first instance needs concerted effort to ensure basic cr elementary education. Tribal education, in fact, is in a mess.

According to 2001 Census, the ST population of Jharkhand State is 28.3 per cent of the total population of the State. The overall literacy rate among the STs has increased from 27.5 per cent in 1991 to 40.7 per cent in 2001—lower than the national average of 47.1 per cent. Male and female literacy rates among the STs account for 54 per cent and 27.2 per cent, respectively and are lower than the national level (59.2% and 34.8%). After Rajasthan, Jharkhand has the second highest gender disparity. What is striking is that the literacy rates of ST population of Jharkhand, though low, are comparatively better placed than the Scheduled Caste population of the state. All these suggest that exclusion from the elementary education is largely concentrated among ST population. The following data reveals the state of education prevailing among the ST people of Jharkhand.

The above data shows that the proportions of the persons educated up to matric/secondary/HS/intermediate are 16.5 per cent. This means that every sixth tribal is a

Levels of Education among the Major STs of Jharkhand

	Names of STs	*Literate without edu-cational level*	*Below Pri-mary*	*Pri-mary*	*Middle*	*Matric/ Secon-dary/ HS/ Inter-mediate etc.*	*Technical and non-techni-cal diploma etc.*	*Gradu-ate and above*
	All STs	3.0	30.6	28.6	17.7%	16.5	0.1	3.5
1.	Santhal	3.5	34.3	30.0	17.0	13.2	0.1	2.0
2.	Oraon	2.4	26.9	25.3	18.5	20.8	0.2	5.9
3.	Munda	2.8	27.9	29.6	18.9	17.1	0.1	3.7
4.	Ho	2.4	26.4	28.4	19.9	19.7	0.1	3.1
5.	Kharwar	5.5	38.2	32.3	11.3	10.8	0.1	1.9
6.	Lohra	3.5	35.5	30.5	16.1	12.5	0.1	1.9
7.	Bhumij	2.9	36.1	32.8	15.7	11.1	0.0	1.4
8.	Kharia	2.0	26.0	26.5	18.3	21.4	0.1	5.6

Source: Census, 2001.

matriculate in this State. Persons having education up to graduate and above constitute just 3.5 per cent and technical and non-technical diploma holder constitutes a miniscule of even less than 1 per cent. The data also reveals that the proportion of tribal literates decline sharply with the level of education. Further, there is a wide literacy rate disparity among the different tribal communities. The two dominant tribal communities of Oraon and Kharia each have the percentage of graduates (just under 6%) while each Bhumij, Lohra and Kharwar communities have the lowest percentage of graduates (under 2%). One also comes across an inter-district divergence in literacy rates both in male and female. According to Census 2001, considering all the 22 districts, district literacy rates for male and female constitute 54 per cent and 27.2 per cent, respectively—just half of the male literacy rate. If we consider district-wise data, we will find considerable spatial disparity in literacy rate across the 22 (at present 24) districts. The district of Pakur has the lowest literacy rate of 30 per cent and East Singhbum district has the highest literacy rate of 69 per cent. However, it may be added that the female literacy rate among ST people is comparatively higher than SCs in the state of Jharkhand, possibly, because the Christian missionaries played an overriding role in educating tribal people of this State.

It is true that literacy rates in the State are rising but not in commensurate with the financial resources spent for them. Lower levels of education always feed into higher education. If lower level of education is in shambles, we are afraid that the attainment of higher education among the ST group and their 'race' to catch with other people of the society will remain a dream, despite larger financial allocation, extension of educational infrastructural facilities so as to increase accessibility, policy of reservation favouring them, etc. In spite of job reservation policies, one often finds 'employment deficit' in some services (like school and college education) mainly because of low levels of education and poor qualifications of the ST population, though this policy of reservation has partly succeeded in raising the representation of these people in various jobs (25 tribal boys had been given training for commercial pilots, air hostess training to 25 tribal and Dalit girls of the State). To achieve the goal of higher employment amongst STs, improvements in education of these people is of great and urgent necessity.

Since promotion of higher education is largely contingent upon the spread of lower level of education, we can point out the reasons behind this sorry state of affairs. It was found in the *SSA Household Census, 2005* in 22 districts of the State of Jharkhand, the most dominant reasons for "out of school" education were: (i) 'household work' (25%), (ii) 'earning compulsion' of the family (23%), (iii) 'lack of interest in studies' (14%), (iv) 'migration' (9%), (v) 'lack of access' (8%). It has been estimated that the average duration of schooling of adult (aged above 14 years) as per the NSS 55th Round stood at 4.25 years. With a very low completion rate, internal efficiency of school seems to be a major concern in this tribal-dominated State.[11]

What is appalling is the endemic problem of absenteeism among teachers, monolingual education in non-indigenous languages and non-acceptance of indigenous languages,[12] school system of education sans indigenous identity. To ensure better attendance in school, the Government has launched the programme of 'mid-day meal'. Unfortunately, very few tribal children of the State of Jharkhand have access to such meals, despite orders from the Supreme Court! The Commissioner of the Supreme Court observed two important problems associated with this scheme in March 2004: (i) this scheme had been sanctioned only in 7 districts only and not all the 22 districts; (ii) erratic supply of food grains. It may also be pointed out that most teachers are non-Adivasis having little or no knowledge of the indigenous languages, cultures and identity.

Further, the pace of construction of hostels for both boys and girls has been not only slow but also the facilities created there are of sub-standard quality. Further, most of the schemes meant for improving the educational attainments of the tribal people often suffer from the absence or delayed release of matching grants from the State Government. The essence of this is that education and constant awareness generation have not been accorded any great importance in the Government's agenda.

Adivasis in the State of Jharkhand and in other States are 'development-induced refugees'. Historically, they have been systematically displaced from land and evicted from the forests and such has gathered momentum under the strong impacts of liberalization, privatization and globalization. "Instead of making tribals' partners in economic development, they marginalize them further. State governments, themselves run and dominated by non-tribals' are signing away tribal land for mining, manufacturing, and energy gestation projects."[13] This is true of old Bihar and present Jharkhand. Even during the early phase of development in the 1960-90s, tribals of this State lost their land and places of habitation due to introduction of many development projects and were uprooted from their cultural setting. To reverse this trend of eviction of tribal communities from land and forests, promises were made by the governments headed by non-tribal people that they would be absorbed in the job market first. Consequently, these "development-induced refugees" are naturally deprived of basic education, leave alone higher education. For these people, higher education is a myth. The political parties often make extravagant promises devoid of rationality and reality as a vote-catching device and most of such promises go into oblivion as soon as they assume power and play a partisan role against the backdrop of low level of education, high level of poverty, and absence of any national level leaders. This means that weak literacy rates of tribal community go *pari passu* with the poor "articulation ratio". A.K. Roy very rightly observes: "Darkness in the midst of light is Jharkhand ... The area contains almost all the steel plants—Bokaro, Rourkella, Jamshedpur, all the power plants of the Damodar Valley project and the Hirakud Dam of Orissa. There is no dearth of development but only at the cost of the people there. Industries displace them, dams down them, afforestation starves them."[14] This is what we may call "fallacy of development". They are exploited by any means and are cut-off from the mainstream economic development of the country.

T.K. Oommen, before the creation of the State of Jharkhand in 2000, predicted that Jharkhand would remain an 'internal colony' dominated by non-Jharkhandis since approximately two-thirds of the population in this tribal dominated State is non-tribals. Though this State was created to protect the interest of the tribal population, historically these people have gained little and lost too much. It is because of the neglect of the Adivasi citizens, the State of Jharkhand has been experiencing the growing incidence of left-wing extremist violence. Fruits of development must reach these people so that they are not marginalized further.

Jharkhand must promote 'social inclusiveness' on a grand scale. There is a great need for civic and political empowerment of these tribal people—crucial for inclusive development. The World Bank says, "Political commitment is needed "to make development happen" in the shortest possible time. There is need to ensure that the *political gains* achieved through years of struggle to create a separate "tribal state" start yielding significant economic benefits. It is time that the voices of the left-out majority of the state are finally heard and their problems acted upon, and that an accelerated and inclusive growth strategy finally ushers in a new development decade for Jharkhand."[15]

A movement towards a 'learning tribal society' needs to be vigorously initiated. And that too can be done by expanding educational facilities among the disadvantaged groups of people, if not all the "necessary architecture of inclusive social growth". However, the education system should not target to 'educate' and 'civilize' tribal children from our point of view. What is urgent is "development with identity", without endangering the cultural heritage of the tribal people. We would be committing grave errors if we ignore the needs of the Adivasis—the first settlers.

Notes and References

1. International Labour Organization (2006), Coolangatta Statement, 1999, (World's Indigenous Peoples' Conference on Education, Convention No. 169) printed in *Guidelines for Combating Child Labour among Indigenous and Tribal Peoples'*.
2. Jean Dreze and A. Sen (1996), *India: Economic Development and Social Opportunity*, p. 109 (Oxford and New Delhi: Oxford University Press)
3. *Ibid.*, pp. 14-15.
4. *Ibid.*, pp. 110.
5. Government of India (2006), *India 2006*, pp. 881, GOI Publication.
6. Ramchandra Guha (2007), 'Adivasis, Naxalites and Indian Democracy'; *Economic and Political Weekly*, 11 August.
7. Amit Bhaduri (2005), *Development with Dignity: A Case for Full Employment*, National Book Trust, India.
8. Financial or monetary aspect involved in different schemes are often made public with great fanfare, but the local people remain largely disconnected. Talking about participatory democracy, Amit Bhaduri highlights an interesting phenomenon that has an important bearing on the 'empowerment of the disadvantaged groups'. "The result is political manipulation. Bus-loads of poor are brought to political rallies of all parties to hear the 'leaders', and give the appearance of democratic participation in politics." See Amit Bhaduri, *Development with Dignity: A Case for full Employment* (p. 76)
9. T.K. Oommen (2002), *Twentieth Century Indian Society in Retrospect* in N.N. Vohra, Sabyasachi Bhattacharya (eds.) *"Looking Back: India in the Twentieth Century"*, p. 171, National Book Trust, India, in association with India International Centre
10. G.S. Shah (1990), *The Bourgeoisie Party and Deprived Communities* in Ghanashyam Shah (eds.) *"Capitalist Development—Critical essays: Felicitation in Honour of Prof. A.R. Desai"*, Popular Prakashan, Bombay
11. World Bank (2007), *Jharkhand: Addressing the Challenge of Inclusive Development: Poverty Reduction and Economic Management*, (Report No.

36437-IN) India Management Unit, South Asia, The World Bank Publication.

12. UNESCO (2001) estimated that all over the world close to half of 6000 languages spoken are likely to die out in the near future.
13. Ramchandra Guha (2007), *Ibid.*, 6.
14. G.S. Shah (1990), *Ibid.*, 10.
15. World Bank (2007), *Ibid.*, 11.

25

Higher Education and Tribals: Problems and Prospects

A Case Study of Jharkhand

N.C. JHA

Study of economics of education is one of the important keys for the alround development of the people of the developing countries like India because it involves a process of learning through which a human being passes from infancy to maturity as in Sanskrit it is observed as *'Tamsoma Jyotir Gamaya'* which aptly describes the purpose if the education—to lead from darkness (ignorance) to light (Knowledge). Although in a broad sense all life is learning but in restricted sense it consists in the transmission of the knowledge and skills in some institutions. In current economic jargon economics of education explains the input-output theory because in education the teachers, the administrators, the buildings and all kinds of physical equipments are inputs whereas the knowledge acquired by the students is the output. In the present dynamic globalised scenario, there is a great demand for highly equipped professionally trained equipped human power so it may be called a consumption goods providing immediate satisfaction but the reality of its nature shows it as an investment good intended to help in the production of additional to help in the production of additional goods at some future date as W. Schultz observes rightly: I propose to treat education as an investment in man and to treat its consequences as a form of capital" That's why knowledge industry being the basis of an overall development of economy has been attracting a large percentage of public expenditure in almost all countries. Since independence, Government of India is making all sincere efforts for lessening the illiteracy as maximum as possible and due to these efforts the rate of literacy which was only 18.33 per cent in 1951 has gone up to 28.30 per cent in 1961, 34.45 per cent in 1971, 4357 per cent in 1981 and 52.21 per cent in 1991 and 65.38 per cent in 2001 Census.

In India during last 60 years the educational development has been phenomenal but still the literacy rate is not at the level of developed countries. The system of education in India is divided into five broad parts primary, secondary, intermediate, graduate and post-graduate. In the higher education, it is the general perception that it begins from intermediate with three faculties—Arts, Science and commerce after that the students move forward to graduation with technical faculties, professional faculties and general faculties upto the graduation level. Since independence, the number of universities is rising at a rapid rate because in 1950-51, the total number of universities is 20 (including deemed universities) which has gone up to 118 in 1973 and 342 in 2006-07. This also includes 18 central university 211 state universities, 95 deemed universities, 5 institution established under university act and 13 Institutes of National importance a part from around 17000 Colleges including 1800 Women Colleges in India of these, 40 Universities/Institutions provide higher education in agriculture (including forestry, dairy, fisheries and veterinary, science), 25 in medicine (including, Ayurveda, Hommeopathhy, Pharmacy, Dental, etc.), 49 engineering and technology, 07 Information and Communication Technology and in Law. The number of Open Universities is 11 and 8 that of Women Universities is 6.

In India University Grant Commission (UGC) which

was established in 1956 under an act of parliament has been given responsibility to take measures for promotion and co-ordination of university education. It has also been made responsible for determination and maintenance of standards in teaching examination and research in universities to fufil its objectives, the commission can acquire among other things into financial needs of universities, allocate and disburse grants to them, establish and maintain common services and facilities, recommend measures for improvement of university education and give advice on allocation of grants and establishment of new universities. It has its regional office at Hyderabad, Pune, Bhopal, Kolkata, Gowahati, and Bangalore.

The role of the state in promoting education has been recognized from the earliest time because the state government's financing and subsidizing education lies in the fact that the social benefits derived from education greater than individual benefits. That's why one of the recommendations of the Radhakrishnan Commission on university education in India was that the state should recognize its responsibility for the financing of higher education. It is, however, essential to make higher education free or compulsory. The beneficiaries should meet some part of the cost in the form of fees. The rest of the cost will have to be met from the public exchequer. Here also the poor and meritorious students should be encouraged to obtain higher education with the help of adequate financial assistance from the state. The state share towards education over the years has a declinig trends. Although the core of government's comman programme and a huge investment is projected as 6 per cent of the G.D.P. on education, half of this on primary and secondary education alone. But if we go through the budgetary provision of the state as well as the centre we find that twenty nine major states together have allocated about 7.2 per centof their aggregate budgetary expenses on education in 2005-06 which was 10.2 per cent in 2000-01. At the individual state level,many states did even worse, for example Punjab—4 per cent, M.P.—4.2 per cent, Gujarat—4.5 per cent, Jharkhand—2.5 per cent, Bihar—5.4 per cent which is substantially lower than the national average, The proportion for higher education may be worse than primary and secondary education expenditure because many a national repute institutions are facing huge financial crunch even paying the salaries to the teaching and non-teaching staff is making more difficult for the administrators.

Jharkhand which is one of the new states, known as the tribal state of Indian union, having geographical areas 79.7 thousand sq. km and 26.9 millions population out of which 27.67 per cent tribal population is predominantly rural in character, where 64.9 per cent population lives below the poverty line against the national average 25 per cent in 2005-06, the state where the largest number of home/people lives under one (dollar) a day. But the main cause of concern for this state even more than poverty which is the result, is the illiteracy because in literacy map of India, this state ranks 34th out of 35th states and union territories having a literacy rate 54.13 per cent against the national average 65 per cent. If we take the division wise literacy rate in Jharkhand, according to 2001 Census, there is a great divergence between the rural and urban areas which we may explain with the help of following Table 1.

TABLE I

Showing Division-wise Literacy Rate of Jharkhand, 2001

(in %)

Name of division	*Rural*	*Urban*
Santhal parganas	33.05	71.13
North Chhotanagpur	34.32	66.32
South Chhotanagpur	34.82	33.12
Palamue	29.03	65.31
Jharkhand	54.31	53.96

Source: Census of India, 2001.

From the above table, the fact is evident that there is a great disparity so far as the percentage literacy in urban and rural areas is concerned. The massive poverty is also due to this massive illiteracy in rural areas where the family is not capable to bear the subsistence cost of the children's education. It is certainly believed that this largest illiteracy is also because of the occupational pattern of tribals of Jharkhand, where 90 per cent tribal labour force is either engaged in cultivation in the form of cultivators or agricultural labourers or household activties. This certainly shows that seasonal, disguised as well as involuntary unemployment is rampant among the rurals tribals because the service sector contribution to the tribal's employment scenario varies between 3.39 per centto 19.54 per centwhich is indeed a great cause of concerns of the massive illiteracy and its correlation with the higher education. The income earned by the majority of tribals is insufficient to maintain even food wants education, even primary, neither secondary or higher education is a distant dream.

TABLE 2

Showing District-wise Population and Number of Higher Secondary or +2 Schools and Number of Degree Collage

Name of district	*Total tribal population (0000)*	*Number of higher +2 schools*	*Number of colleges*
Dumka Jamtara	62.15	10	08
Godda	21.60	02	04
Deoghar	11.91	07	07
Sahibgang/Pakur	50.73	09	03
Hazaribagh	25.06	11	13+2
Dhanbad	31.2	'4	16
Giridih	27.19	05	02
Ranchi	96.4	29	25
Lohardagga	16.3	02	02
Gumla	81.7	06	08
East Singhbhum	46.7	19	13
West Singhbhum	97.8	10	08
Palamu	31.8	18	04
Garhwa	NA	02	01
Jharkhand	46.66	13.8	123

Source: Jharkhand, 2002, S.K. Singh, Reader Corner is, Patna.

The above table shows the number of secondary schools/intermediate colleges/+2 high schools and degree colleges of Jharkhand. so far the distribution of the intermediate college/plus two school, the highest concentration is in Ranchi district followed by Dhanbad and the lowest number is associated with Garhwa. In Santhal Parganna, the highest concentration is associated with Dumka followed by Deoghar, Godda and Sahibganj. With the above distribution, it is itself explained that the divergence in the facilities of educational institutions in case of Degree Colleges in Jharkhand has more skewness than other educational institutions. More over all the degree colleges are almost established in the district or the Subdivisional towns. In recent years, the Government of Jharkhand begins financial aid to the few recognized Inter-Colleges which are fulfilling the desired conditions. But the economic condition of these Non-full-aided colleges is rather unsatisfactory.

In case of Higher Education and the Tribals of Jhakhand, it is indeed not as satisfactory as in case other general Non-tribals because of the family background, access to the higher educational institutions, residential areas, family's economic status, willingness of the parents for investing money into the higher educations, student's mind-set and the current economic problems associated with the particular families, the Government approach towards the tribal students, the teacher's point of view and co-operation to the tribal students. The major hurdle in the correct analysis of tribal's approach towards higher education is the non-availability of data published by the Government of Jharkhand, whatever, information is being collected, that is totally from other sources. The information regarding the exact number of admitted tribal students, those who completed their graduation, their post--graduation are not properly maintained as well as published by the Government of Jharkhand. Again the number of the students enrolled in three years degree course and to maintain their entire data revealing all features are not available.

The educational component and the course to which the tribal students are more interested should be explored positively for their advancement in higher education. Teaching and learning process is seen from two angles, namely, quality of tribal student input which constitutes the human material that stands to benefit from the process and the teacher student ratio which is normally taken an indicator of effectiveness of the teaching process. In Jharkhand, especially in degree college the tribal students fail to make the contact hours within scheduled time table with the teachers.

In Jharkhand, there are four universities namely Ranchi University, Ranchi, Vinobabhave University, Hazaribagh, Sido-Kanu Murmu University, Dumka, Birsa Agricultural University, Ranchi, under which there are constituent units, affliliated units of degree colleges.where honours and pass course level of science, arts, commerce faculties are run and taught. The post-graduate general teaching is being provided at the P.G. Department of different faculties at the headquarters of the university of Jharkhand. In few cases the P.G. teaching was also being started at some premier colleges where there were well equipped teaching as well as other sufficient facilities observed. But due to some reasons or other, it is going to be scrapped. This question arises, whether the tribals are efficient enough to en roll at the P.G. level, whether the family background or economic condition of the families of tribal students is strong enough to bear the cost of investment at post-graduate studies. In many cases, even if the tribal passes the graduation level, they are at present not very interested in doing the post-graduation because they are more interested in searching job. Due to the implementation of reservation policy in different service sector for tribals both at the central level and the state level, many of them get jobs of the fourth grade or peon category or the clerks category. They have higher no desire for studies or post-graduate studies because the economic condition of the families is not storng enough to bear the burden of cost of higher studies. The tribal students are also not mentally strong to go the highest level of objectives.In recent years, the tribals who are in service and become economically sound, are of the opinion to educate the children at the better institutions, better environment and better place.

So far as the technical education in Jharkhand is concerned, there are 12 Engineering Colleges, 3 Medical Colleges, one Agricultural College, 6 (Six) Master of Business

Management Institutes, one Pharmacy College, two Ayurveda College, 2 Law Colleges. In these colleges admission, there is the reservation policy for tribal students. In all over India, there are 670 tribal students who were either doing the M.Phil or fellowship after completing the post-graduate studies. The Government of Jharkhand is providing scholarship for all categories of tribal students for getting higher studies, the tuition fees is totally subsidised by the state government besides this, even the expenditure partly is born by the governmentIn 2006-07, the central government has started Rajiv Gandhi National Fellowship Award for the scheduled tribe student under which Rs. 7.95 crores is being provided. Besides these, in Jharkhand there are many research institute, laboratories, invention centers and training institutes where there is reserved seats for the tribal students. But due to lack of dynamic attitude, high thinking and progressive and globalized approach, the tribal students fail to register their presence in such national repute centers. But the future of the higher education of the tribals in Jharkhand is necessarily bright and hope that the second wave of tribal revolution would make them at par with other general students of the country. There is only one thing which they should resolve is to step forward and to make their approach dynamic and globally suited.

The system in Jharkhand on the one hand is assumed a responsible academic community and on the other hand a responsible trible student community which is reasonably mature. It is supposed that the tribal students on their own would strive to learn as much as possible either from teachers or from books those are kept in libraries, the amount of freedom that is made available to tribal students in institutions of higher education is based on the hypothesis is that they would strive to learn on their own. In the current system, the role of institution is only to provide necessary infrastructure and human inputs and leave the rest of the things to happen their own. But in Jharkhand it is also found that the students especially the tribal students fail to utilize the freedom aspects and their approach towards the study at the higher institution are somehow diluted. The background of the tribal students in the modern days is that today a good number come to the higher institution from the middle and poor or very-poor families who have very poor economic background. The environment in their homes do not provide necessary academic support. Invariably they do not get such guidance. The problems for tribal students in Jharkhand are such that they do not have quality to mix-up with general student's for taking help in teaching and extra-curricullum activities or they try to higher institutions. They are undoubtedly laborious but they are more interested in getting some sorts of jobs whether it is even fourth grade. Learning is the part and parcel but after doing matriculation or Intermediate, they are worry for jobs than doing the higher studies. Due to the different type of central as well as state Government vacancies, advertised in different newpapers, for the fourth grade or clerk or police or guard, etc. teachers in primary or servashiksha Kendra or other private companies, due to the implementation of reservation policy they get the service with the three years degree course or just after completing the graduation. That's why in the post-graduate studies, the number of tribal students or in the researh or fellowship or other competitive examination is found very thin. In this case the tribal students need career counselling the very beginning and the meritorious and dynamic students ought to be provided every type of help for continuing their higher studies. In this context the role of institutions as well as the teachers especially in the modern type of education and industrial dynamic technology invariable should be very helpful and the co-operative—both morally and economically. Therefore, the institutions should assume a positive role, the programme should be planned carefully and effectively implemented, problems of tribal students ranging from personal to accedemic have to be lacked students should be helped to assume a role of responsible, yet free learners this change in the role of institution in Jharkhand would improve, the quality of students in general, but tribal students in particular. Because wastage in education is not only a loss to the institution or to the receivers of education or the subsidizing agencies or government but to the society as a whole and the loss to the institution or to the receivers education or the subsidizing agencies or government but to the society as a whole and the loss of development opportunities of the tribal students of Jharkhand. Let us come forward—all community from school to post-graduate level and give them all possible positive helps so that the tribals reflection of Jharkhand would be the emblems to other tribal dominated states.

References

Baljit Singh, *Economics of Indian Education.*

G.D. Sharma and Mridula, *Economics of College Education.*

Chronicle, Year Book, 2207.

Bihar Econonomic Journal, Conference Volume, 2005.

S.K. Singh, *Readers Corner,* 2002, Jharkhand.

Kurukshetra, Different Volumes.

Yojana, Different Volumes.

Prabhat Khabar, *Special Santhal Hul, Alex Ekka,* 30 June, 2005.

Ghanshyam, Jharkhand.

26

Higher Education System in Jharkhand: Challenges and Opportunities

S.K.L. Das

INTRODUCTION

From time immemorial, India has been a centre for learning. Thousands years ago, great scholars used to teach through the scriptures. A variety of subjects such as Philosophy, Religion, Medicine, Literature, Arts, Astrology, Mathematics and Sociology were taught in our country. We all know that when the rest of the world wore tree leaves, we Indians were busy inventing steel. When the rest of the world had not awakened to the light of learning, Indians were studying science. We had invented the zero much before the others saw the dawn of civilization. Nalanda, Takshashila, Vikramshila were the symbols of our educational capabilities. In higher education system Nalanda University was the centre of attraction of the students of different countries from 5th to 13th century.

Hence, we have a glorious past in respect of our

capabilities in all fields. Science and technology in ancient and medieval India covered all major branches of human knowledge and activities. Mohanjodaro and Harappa are the portraits of India's technologies on design and planning; water management of Vijayanagar Empire, rust free steel was an India's invention. Ayurveda as a science of medicine was well known to all. Ancient scholars of India had dealt with the principles of Ayurveda as long back as 800 BC. Vedic mathematics was the root of mathematical development in the world. Aryabhatta of 5th century, Brahmagupta of 12th, Bhaskracharya of 6th century have made remarkable contributions in the development of mathematical analysis. Everybody knows Ramanujam's contribution. In Astronomy India's contribution cannot be ignored. In Rig Veda astronomical treatises have found. Today we are talking about atomic energy, but the root of this concept of atom is derived from the classification of material world in five basic elements namely earth, water fire air and space. Such was our scientific and cultural heritage.

But today the educational scene has completely changed. The whole process of higher education has become warped, disoriented and dysfunctional, producing a large number of unemployable young men and women. The system of higher education, which had been adopted in British era, is still prevalent in the country. With the arrival of British, English education came into being with the help of European missionaries. In 1817 Hindu College was established in Calcutta (now Kolkata). The Elphistone Institute was set-up in 1834 in Bombay (now Mumbai). Later in 1857 three Universities were established in three important towns of India, i.e. at Calcutta, Madras and Bombay. At the time of Independence, there were 20 Universities and altogether 437 colleges and five institutions offering post-graduate courses in Engineering and 22 in Medicine. Today, there are 342 universities including 18 Central Universities, 211 State Universities, 95 deemed universities, 5 institutes established under state Legislation and 13 institutes of National importance. There are 17973 colleges of which 5386 have been recognized by the UGC.

Perhaps with the exception of China, no other country

in the world has got such a massive structure for higher education as our country has. And the demand for education here in India is expanding at an exponential rate because of the rapidly increasing population and the huge plans for socio-economic development launched by successive governments based on the principles of equality and social justice. Keeping in view growing number of students, India needs at least a thousand universities and hundred thousand colleges. The student population in higher education sector in rural as well as semi-urban areas is greater than the total population of Sweden or Switzerland and other European countries. However, the number of Universities in India is quite low in respect of aspiring students for enrolment.

The question of quantity versus quality assumes national importance in contemporary India because of goals of education in pre-Independence India were different. The British rulers did not finance higher education in any big manner. The objectives of higher education during the British period were very limited and they mostly served the Macaulayan vision of creating a class of people Indian in blood and colour but English in tastes and manners. The economic aspect of life in India, the political imperatives that led to suppression of democratic aspirations of the people and the large-scale drain of wealth from the country did not receive any attention in the syllabi. This resulted in the creation of a very huge number of educated young people who lost touch with the reality of rural as well as backward regions. In the early period of Independent India education in backward regions were completely ignored. This resulted in mass illiteracy, ignorance, and cultural backwardness in the rural India, where the heart of the country lives.

GANDHIAN APPROACH TO HIGHER EDUCATION

At this juncture nobody except Mahatma Gandhi advocated the education of masses in a manner conducive to national development. He was the first in modern India to think of enormity of the problem in a holistic manner and offer national solutions for the removal of ignorance and illiteracy. He was of the view thal it would be better to revolutionize college education and relate it to national necessities. Higher education was to be left to private enterprise and it ought to meet national requirements. Education should lead to the highest development of mind. His thrust was on vocationalization of education at school and college levels. True education would be, according to him, which served the poorest of the poor of the country. But the political decision-makers responsible for educational matters abandoned Gandhiji ideas of education. The old system of liberal arts education got all encouragement. No emphasis was given to vocationalization at higher levels. We have thus created a huge army of unemployed, under-employed and unemployable graduates. And the acquisition of a degree has come to mean a passport to a clerical or other jobs unrelated to the education obtained in colleges. But in rural India such degree is a daydream for youths as there is no facility to pursue study.

INTERNATIONAL TREND OF HIGHER EDUCATION

In all the advanced countries universities and university level institutions constitute the strong centers of research. It is a universal phenomenon because universities alone have a continuous flow of young and fresh minds and an atmosphere highly conducive to talent and creative efforts. Higher education in these countries has acquired the status of a marketable commodity. The market forces of demand, supply and profitability are determining the quantity and quality of higher education in advanced countries. With an eye on the job market, courses are being designed. Export of education services has become an important source of earning of foreign exchange. A British Council study estimates that Britain could earn up to 13 billion pound by 2020 from export of education. In USA educational exports were fifth largest service sector exports in 2002. The following table shows data on leading exporters of education in the world.

The most important market for cross-border education is Asia, which accounts for 76 per cent of total level of tertiary educational exports in the world. OECD has also conducted a study on foreign students from the Asia-Pacific

S. No.	*Country*	*Year*	*Total No. of Students*	*% of total exports*
1.	U.K	2002	254978	14
2.	Australia	2003	155374	6
3.	USA	2002	564958	30
4.	Canada	2000	39556	2
5.	France	2001	175235	10
6.	Germany	2002	213665	12
	Total		1403766	74

Source: World Bank Report, 2003.

region in tertiary institutions in OECD countries and in United States in 2001 as shown in the following table. The largest source countries are China, Korea, India and Japan. With growing importance of globally mobile labour, business and knowledge, foreign education particularly in the provider nation is considered in a profitable condition.

Foreign Students in Tertiary Education from Asia-Pacific Region in OECD Countries—2001 and USA—2001

Country of origin	*No. of students in OECD Nations*	*Proportion of all Foreign Students in OECD Nations*	*Students in US Degree Granting Institutions*
China	124000	8.5	59900
Korea	70523	4.8	45700
India	61179	4.2	54700
Japan	55041	3.8	46500
Malaysia	320709	2.2	8100
Indonesia	26615	1.8	11600
Hong Kong	23261	1.6	7800
Singapore	19514	1.3	—
Thailand	18172	1.2	11200
Pakistan	10478	0.7	—

Source: OECD, 2003.

A study of IDP Education in Australia, the global student mobility estimates that at present there are 2 million students who study outside their home country. This is expected to grow more than three to seven million in 2025, with Asia dominating total demand at 70 per cent. Today on line graduate and post-graduate programmes of international system is available. But it is for those who have capability to cough up the required fee for the different courses. The students of downtrodden area never think of such education both due to lack of finance and poor infrastructure available to them.

HIGHER EDUCATION SCENARIO IN INDIA

Higher education is looked upon as the only way to insure vertical mobility of people in the job market. However, the economic reform based on a strategy of liberalization, privatization and globalization altered the scenario of higher education. While before reforms higher education was heavily subsidized keeping in view its role in national and social development, in the post-reform period government began to promote the idea that higher education

Grants in IXth to Xth Plan under Plan and Non-Plan

(in Crores)

Year	*Plan*	*Non-Plan*
1997-98	352.10	545.00
1998-99	360.35	1009.00
1999-00	376.00	975.00
2000-01	435.00	1000.00
2001-02	467.78	1020.68
2002-03	559.76	1100.00
2003-04	516.75	1132.00
2004-05	719.75	1182.85
2005-06	748.34	1218.22
2006-07	919.75	1582.85
2007-08	1125.34	1918.22

Source:: IXth, Xth and XIth Plan Document.

was a non-merit good and sought a drastic reduction in state funding of it. It was proposed to reduce the subsidy from 90 per cent to less than 25 per cent. Government financing of higher education has drastically reduced from 28 per cent in 1990-91 to 12 per cent in 2004-05. The plan outlay on education has fallen from 7 per cent in First Plan to 2.9 per cent in Tenth plan.

In India, except for a couple of private universities, the nation or state government finances all universities. The Government largely funds the colleges. Hence every institution is being faced severe financial crunch. Backward states like Bihar and Jharkhand major grants of higher education are being diverted to disburse the salaries of the teachers and non-teaching staff. Investments on the overall development of the infrastructures of the colleges are almost dismal. Colleges in this region are tiny and trace better than higher secondary schools. They do not have libraries worth the name. These institutions performs only class room teaching, preparing students for examination like tutorial colleges. Unfortunately, the entire higher education in backward regions takes place only in the ill-equipped, understaffed, affiliated colleges as can be seen from the fact that 89 per cent of under-graduate students are in affiliated colleges. The affiliated system does not exist anywhere in the world but in India it dominates.

Lately these issues, such as declining quality, inadequate facilities, and a mismatch between education and human power requirements have become crucial theme in this millennium. However, it is nothing new, since Independence a number of education commissions and committee appointed to identify the maladies and made several recommendations to revamp the system. Education introduced in the colonial period is still continuing in free India despite all the educational commissions and their recommendations. The Radhakrishnan Commission, the Kothari Commission, the Adiseshiah Commission, the Punnayya Commission and host of UGC Committees and special task forces have made many recommendations, which, if implemented, would have raised the level of higher education. Unfortunately, these recommendations were not implemented, although newer commission and committees came into being. No structural changes were introduced and therefore the old systems continue even today with almost no basic change in almost all regions of the country.

What is worse in this region the major universities are burdened with academic administration of affiliated colleges. Bihar has 243 affiliated colleges, while Jharkhand has about 170 affiliated colleges. This condition prevails almost all major universities in the country. While advanced countries are moving towards mass education but in India the situation is quite alarming.

It is very unfortunate that despite the tremendous growth in the number of colleges and universities in our country, education that should conscientize the educated about their national socio-economic and political condition and help liberate the nation from the shackles of old systems and ways of thinking is still a dream.

There has been over the last decade a proliferation of institutions of higher education in the private sector, especially in the fields of information technology, business management, engineering, hotel management, biotechnology as well as medicines. Today online graduate schools offering post-graduate programmes of International Business Management through a joint venture between universities of 19 leading universities including British Columbia, Glasgow, Hong Kong, Melbourne, New South Wales, etc. These institutions are keenly wooing the Indian students to its fold. However, none of the top ranking foreign universities is operating in India. Many of them do not have a strong base in their own country. They charge exorbitant fees and the degree awarded by them do not have international recognitions.

As per the Commerce Ministry's recent finding total enrolment in higher education institution is 10.5 million, which is just 11 per cent of the total relevant age group of 17-23 in the population. India fares poorly compared to most South West Asian countries like Philippines 31 per cent, Thailand 19 per cent, Malaysia 27 per cent and China 13 per cent. In compares to advanced countries India is lagging behind in case of enrolment in higher education.

Country	Percentage of enrolment	Country	Percentage of enrolment
Canada	88%	Philippines	27%
US	80%	Thailand	20%
Australia	80%	Mexico	14%
Finland	74%	Brazil	11%
U.K.	52%	India	8%

Source: Commerce Ministry, Government of India.

There is a significant slide in the growth of higher education enrolments during 2000-05 compared to the last two decades. While student enrolments had grown by some 20 per cent between 2000-05, between 1990-2000 it grew about 100 per cent and during 1980-90 it was 57 per cent. Similarly the growth of new higher education instates had touched 57 per cent between 2000-05 against 92 per cent in 1990-2000 and 22 per cent between 1980-90. India has the third largest number of higher education enrolments after China and USA. In terms of the number of higher education institutions, India tops global charts with 17973 institutions on September 2006.

This means the average number of students per educational institution here is also lower than in the US and China.

Regarding public expenditure on higher education, India is among the lowest in the world with public expenditure per student at $ 406 compared to China $ 2728, Brazil $ 3986, Indonesia $ 666 and even Malaysia it is $ 625, which is more than India.

While colleges are in dire financial straits, the government of India is almost ready to raise the seats in institutions of higher learning by almost 50 per cent would make the situation worse. Although for improving the fate of downtrodden people of the country present Government is planning to reserve the seats in higher educational institutes.

RESERVATION IN HIGHER EDUCATION

For providing better opportunity to the students of

backward-class, Government of India has making an Act to provide reservation in higher education to the OBC. Although it is not new in India, reservation in educational institutions for other backward classes was started much before Independence. In 1880 the Public Instruction Department of the British Government observed, "The small number of children of lowest castes reading in schools is deplorable. The classes who are taking advantage of schools, public and private, throughout the country are the well-to-do and not the masses of the labouring population." Hence the then British Crown had initiated providing benefits to those population. After Independence under the Chairmanship of Kaka Kalelkar a commission was constituted in 1953, which had recommended a 70 per cent reservation of seats in all technical and professional institutions apart from substantial reservations for government jobs. However, the then Government of Jawaharlal Nehru refused to accept it. In 1979 another commission headed by B.P. Mandal was constituted and the committee had recommended a reservation of 27 per cent for OBC to all educational institutions. Although this recommendation was gathering dust till 1990 when V.P. Singh had announced to implement this report. Now the government to enhance the seats in the higher educational institutions is evolving a new formula. However, the task is stupendous not just for the infrastructure and faculty that need to be enhanced but in this era of globalization quality of education can't be ignored. There were 11 million students enrolled in colleges last year with an average intake of three million. If the 27 per cent reservation norms were imposed without impacting the general quota, then infrastructure and faculty would have to be created to accommodate the students. As per the rough estimate it would cost the exchequer Rs. 40,000 crores, more than the outlay for education since Independence.

Apart from this a pertinent question arises about the beneficiaries of such system. It is being viewed by a large number of rural youths (a survey has been done in rural and tribal dominated area of Jharkhand-Dumka, Palamu, Giridih and Sahibganj districts) reservation would be benefited only rich community of the OBC or SC/ST people. About 55 per cent of OBC in rural area are not literate; the number of illiterate in ST and SC community in this region is about 73 and 70 per cent respectively despite the prevalence of reservation to the SC/ST. In OBC about 1.2 per cent is graduate and above, while in ST and SC community percentage of graduate and above is 0.3 and 0.4 respectively in rural area of Jharkhand and Bihar. On the other hand, in urban area of Jharkhand and Bihar about 12 per cent of OBCs are graduate and above, while per cent of graduates in ST and SC are 8 per cent and 4 per cent respectively.

Thus scenario of higher education is rather disconcerting both with respect in access and equity considerations. Only a small percentage of students of backward community can afford the higher education offered either by the state government and the private institutions despite the reservation policy. At this situation government is gradually withdrawing itself from shouldering the responsibility of financing higher education, it would be very difficult for the weaker sections of the society to pursue education and reservation looks for the elite groups of the OBC only rather than the needy people.

CHALLENGES IN HIGHER EDUCATION IN BACKWARD REGION

In India higher education is faced with deteriorating conditions resulting from expansion and worsened by an affiliation system as well as crunching of funds. Declining quality, inadequate facilities and mismatch between education and human resource development, have become a challenge before the planners and the policy-makers. No doubt, the number of colleges and universities have expanded but quality could not be maintained because of irrational planning, inadequate facilities as well as clarity of purpose. For catering the present requirement of education, India needs more viable institutions of higher education.

In India, except couple of private universities, the national or a state government finances all universities. The government also funds the colleges. The student pays a nominal fee that constitutes less than 10 per cent of the total requirement of the college. Faced with the severe resource crunch the government is insisting colleges and universities to generate their own funds. But in backward region it will be a utopian task for the higher educational institutions to generate funds and become self-reliant. For generating funds university-industry interaction is must. In the changed situation, more and more trained human resources are required; it can be fulfilled by interaction of university and industry.

Vocational education is the need of the hour. It is quite evident that in rural India or even semi-urban area there is completely dearth of vocational system of education. In this region colleges impart perfunctory knowledge of a few subjects, with the result that students neither develop skills nor become fit for self-employment. Until now formation of vocational skills has been a neglected

Another challenges before the higher education is the low rate of enrolments. Most of the seats of the faculties of the universities and colleges remained vacant for the several years, as students prefer to offer some job-oriented courses rather than to get a simple university degree. Domestic institutions of higher education will get marginalized in the process. In this condition the private institutions with the collaboration of foreign institutes are making their roads in the country attracting a large number of students in their fold.

Due to lack of job-oriented education in states like Bihar, Jharkhand, Orissa and Madhya Pradesh a large number of students migrated from their respective states to get enrolled in private institutions. In a rough estimate from Bihar and Jharkhand about five thousands of students migrated from the states to get job-oriented education elsewhere. According to Commerce Ministry, Government of India, about 4 billion dollar per year is being flown out of the country on education.

In the era of liberalization when many foreign universities are to set-up shop in India and attracting students, at this juncture higher education will have to face a stiff competition. For coping up this challenge we should take positive steps in this regard keeping in view of the backward regions and their youths. If we are to realize our true potential as an innovative nation, we must face a big challenge.

STEPS IN RESTRUCTURING HIGHER EDUCATION

Change is the law of life and we must change if we want to make important strides in the world of education. Knowledge is always expanding and unless we change our rigid systems introduced long ago, we cannot bring any good to the country. Today higher education system in our country is completely mismatched with the present economic and social scenario. Students prefer to obtain professional degree so that they may compete with the market demands. Higher education in this millennium has acquired the status of a marketable commodity. The concerns are now related to the profitability of courses. Youths prefer to get admission in technical, professional or job-oriented courses like Computer science, MBA, Information technology, etc. that gives them enough opportunity to get jobs in the market.

At this point of time the reconstruction of higher education is considered significant. Courses in the higher education should be redesigned to match with the present day demand in the market. All those who aspire for higher education have access to the college and university level courses. A national network of community colleges is needed to provide knowledge and job-oriented skills to millions of youths residing in rural areas. The traditional classroom type education is no longer viable in this era.

Today's higher education of India is wholly exam-centred, whereas it ought to be divided into assimilable segments, which are to be evaluated on a continuous basis. Instead of the annual system, we should have the semester system. We, teachers are expected to guide the students to new knowledge through constant updating. Students get an opportunity to prove their worth by facing boldly what our first prime minister called the 'adventure of ideas'. With the introduction of semester-*cum*-credit system in all educational institutions students can improve their own capability and face the challenges of life. Hence the most urgent need is to bring major examination reform by adopting continuous internal evaluation and well-defined academic auditing for coping the higher education with the present day requirements.

Another big problem, which the higher educational institutions face, is outdating affiliation system. It is really a curse on our higher education system. It has converted college into coaching institute and teachers into mere tutors. For restructuring the higher education, steps must be taken to liberate these institutions from the emaciating effects of this curse. Autonomy must be granted to the deserving colleges and those institutions have incapable to fulfil the requirements of autonomy, the government should come forward to make them viable. Apart from this keeping in view of increasing population it would be essential to set a target of about 2500 university level institutions fully equipped with infrastructures by 2020 for catering the need of 25 million students. According to the May 2006 Report of the Technical Group on Population Projections constituted by the National Commission on Population, the projected population numbers in the age group 14-24 in 2026 will be 224 million. The policy-makers could work with a projected enrolment of 40 million in higher education, which will be 4 times the present enrolment. The task is gigantic and it is well nigh impossible to achieve this by public spending.

No doubt, there is a phenomenal growth in higher education, but all those who seek higher education which suits them in this millennium, cannot get it. Courses should be flexible catering the need of the hour. There should be more opportunities for technical and vocational courses to the students of rural area, so that they will capable not only to find suitable employment but also to start their own business enterprises. It will be essential to provide sufficient facilities for library, reading rooms, computerized networking facility along with job-oriented courses in all the institutions situated in rural area.

Full development of India's enormous human potential it will be imperative to make a national priorities, to commit a greater portion of the countries financial resources to the educational sectors. Apart from this, for improving financial condition of the higher education a close links should be fostered between education and industry and private sector initiative and investment should also be encouraged. India's enormous manpower base of scientists and engineers is often coveted. Former President Dr. Kalam observed that India's human resource base is one of its greatest core competencies. This is true in absolute terms, but as a percentage of the total population we are at 1/100th of the US levels and 1/50th of the Korean level. Even total investment in Research and Development India's expenditure is 1/60th of that of Korea, 1/250th of that of the USA and 1/340th of that of Japan.

Hence restructuring our educational institutions is very important. We should establish more informal and open system of learning so that the economic burden of establishing new universities and colleges can be reduced to the maximum extent possible. Today's higher educational institutions do not cater the need of the disadvantaged sections of the society; hence a better system should be evolved which will cater their needs.

It will be better to restructure various bodies of the universities so that they will be more compact and there will be higher representation of academics in them rather than politicians or political appointments. Presently the Senate and the Syndicate of the universities of Bihar and Jharkhand are nominated from the yes men of the party in power causing a great harm in maintaining proper system in the campus.

CONCLUSION

Higher Education in Jharkhand stands at cross-roads today. Neither normal linear expansion nor pace and nature of improvement can meet the needs of the present market situation. In this Millennium innovation as well as creativity has an immense economic value. Intellectual property has become far more valuable than immovable property. But our educational system has tended to dampen rather than encourage creativity and innovation. To enable the youths to benefit in the new environment it requires new designs of human resource development. The coming generation should have the ability to create new ideas constantly and creatively.

They have to be imbued with strong commitment to human values and to social justice. All this implies better higher education in backward areas where a large number of youths are being deprived of proper and meaningful education.

In fact there has been a tremendous growth in Indian Higher education. But such growth is not only inadequate but also patently dangerous. It has to be replaced by educational development based on national priorities, national ethos, skill-based and an international outlook. We can achieve this goal only when there is genuine concern for the poor and the disadvantaged in the society. Greater coverage and better quality and job-oriented education at all levels from basic literacy to hi-tech science and technology is the essential prerequisites for all round development of the country. For this restructuring the higher education is must for competing in the market demands. Besides a variety of new challenges and social needs make it imperative for the government to formulate and implement a New Education Policy for the country to meet the present situation.

Our submission before the intellectuals and policy-makers is that higher education should get more funds from the government. Private sector should be encouraged to set-up first institutions in backward regions with due provisions for access and equity. We should go for the setting up of an educational ombudsman, the agency to redress the grievance of students and parents against private and public institutions. Hope is pinning with the present budget (2008-09), in which a central universities have been proposed here in Jharkhand. But without increasing the infrastructures in different institutions of higher education in Jharkhand, we can't improve the present scenario.

References

Gupta, S.P.: India Vision (2020), A Report, (2002) Planning Commission, Governmentof India.

Kulandaiswamy, V.C. Reconstruction of Higher Education in India, published in *The Hindu*, May 18, 2005.

Larsen, K (2002), International Trade in Educational Services.

Power, K.B. (1998), Indian Higher Education in GATS, Higher Education

Policy and Practices, Vols. 1 and 2.

Uberoi, N.K. (1997), Current Development of India's Higher Education, International Higher Education, May 1995.

Vilanilam, J.V. (1997), Higher Education in India, *Yojna*, Vol. 41, No. 1, Jan. 1997.

Department of Secondary and Higher Education-A report-Government of India, 2001.

Government Subsidies in India, National Institute of Public Finance and Policy, New Delhi, 2002.

National Policy on Education, Government of India.

Ninth and Tenth Plan documents.

Economic Survey, 2001-02 to 2005-06.

Reservation in Higher Education—A Report, *India Today*, July 17, 2006.

National Human Development Report, 2001, Planning Commission Government of India.

OECD (2003), Cross Border Education: An Overview0

Literacy Survey in Tribal Area of Jharkhand by NGO, 2003.

Higher Education in Jharkhand—A Report, 2004, Government of Jharkhand.

27

Economic Solvency and Academic Efficiency: A Case Study

Debasis Mukhopadhyay and Dhurjati Prosad Bagchi

INTRODUCTION

Today India is the third largest higher education system in the world after China and the USA in terms of enrolment which was over one crore five lakhs in 2005-06. However, it is the largest higher education system in the world in terms of the number of institutions. (Table 1)

Student enrolment grew at an estimated rate of 7 per cent between 1987 and 1993 but has now declined to 5.5 per cent compound rate of growth. Even after six decades of independence, higher education is not accessible to the poorest groups of the population. Only about 11 per cent of the population in the age group of 17-23 years is enrolled in the institutions of higher education. (Table 2)

After having examined the enrolment rate at the aggregate level we now look at the same on the basis of caste. There are significant disparities across social groups. The gross enrolment ratio (GER) is much lower for SC, ST and OBC as compared with others, being 7.51 per cent, 5 per

TABLE I

Typology and Growth Trends in Higher Education Institutions

Type	*Owner-ship*	*Financ-ing*	*No. of Institu-tions*	*No. of Stu-dents*
Universities under the Government	Public	Public	240	10,00,000
Private universities	Private	Private	7	10,000
Deemed universities (Aided)	Private or Public	Public	38	40,000
Deemed Universities (Unaided)	Private	Private	63	60,000
Colleges under the Government	Public	Public	4,225	27,50,000
Private Colleges (Aided)	Private	Public	5,750	34,50,000
Private Colleges (Unaided)	Private	Private	7,650	31,50,000
Foreign Institutions	Private	Private	150	8,000
Total			18,123	104,68,000

Source: Pawan Agarwal, "Higher Education in India: The Need for Change", ICRIER, Working paper, June 2006.

cent, 11.34 per cent and 24.89 per cent respectively. The estimates based on the population Census for 2001 also revealed disparities across the social groups in GER. For instance, as against the GER of 15.57 per cent for general Hindu population (non-SC/ST), the GER for SC and ST was 8.39 per cent and 7.46 per cent respectively. The GER for general Hindu population being higher by about two times compared with SC and ST.

In the case of eligible enrolment ratio (EER) in 2003-04 it was 54.4 per cent for ST, 57 per cent for SC, 54.8 per cent for OBC and 62.5 per cent for the other Hindu population. This implies that although the OBC managed to have higher enrolment rate, based on GER, compared with SC and ST, never-the-less, of those who managed to complete higher secondary stage, a small proportion of them entered into the higher education stream compared to the higher caste.

There are also significant difference in enrolment rate among the poor and non-poor. In 1999-2000 the GER for the poor was 2.4 per cent as against 12.91 per cent for non-poor.

TABLE 2

Growth of Higher Education Institutions (HEI) and Enrolment in India

Year	*Universities*	*Colleges*	*Total HEIs*	*Enrolment (in million)*
1947-48	20	496	516	0.2
1950-51	28	578	606	0.2
1960-61	45	1,819	1,864	0.6
1970-71	93	3,277	3,370	2.0
1980-81	123	4,738	4,861	2.8
1990-91	184	5,748	5,932	4.4
2000-01	266	11,146	11,412	8.8
2005-06	348	17,625	17973	10.5

Source: UGC.

Similar disparities are evident in rural and urban areas. In the rural and urban areas the GER for poor was 1.30 per cent and 5.51 per cent compared to 7.12 per cent and 27.15 per cent for non-poor respectively.

Within the poor however the GER was the lowest among the poor belonging to ST and SC, followed by OBC and others. The GER for poor belonging to ST, SC, OBC and others is 1.55 per cent, 1.89 per cent, 2.30 per cent and 3.58 per cent respectively.

Similar pattern is observed for poor in rural and urban areas. In rural area the GER is the lowest for ST with only 1.11 per cent followed by 1.35 per cent for SC, 1.13 per cent for OBC and 1.66 per cent for others—the overall GER being 1.30 per cent.

In urban area the GER for the urban poor is 3.86 per cent, 4.78 per cent, 5.16 per cent and 7 per cent respectively for SC, ST, OBC and others—the average being 5.51 per cent.

Even among the non-poor the GER for the ST, SC and OBC is lower as compared with others. For instance the GER is 6.68 per cent, 9.70 per cent, 8.69 per cent and 19.73 per cent for SC, ST, OBC and others respectively—while all India average is 12.81 per cent.

THE BACKGROUND

A recent McKinsey-NASSCOM study quote that "the total addressable global offshoring market is approximately US 300 billion dollars, of which US 110 billion dollars will be offshored by 2010." It asserts that India has the potential to capture about 50 per cent of this market and in the process can generate direct employment for about 2.3 million people and indirect employment for about 6.5 million people. Therefore, reforms in higher education have been advocated for better human resource development.

So what is urgently required is to have more funding for higher education. But the question is how? Whether it will be more public funding or to open up education system to private entrepreneurs and encourage FDI? In the same line we have the case of tribes in higher education. Whether to have more seat reservations for them or to go for the upliftment of their economic conditions so that they also be the forerunners in the modern higher education along with other castes?

PUBLIC FUNDING

Public spending on higher education is justified on the grounds that it generates positive externalities since it is a merit good and equally it should be discouraged since private benefits far outweigh social benefits. Consequently, public subsidization of higher education benefits the rich, particularly in elite higher education system in India (Tilak, 2005). Moreover, though higher education has low price elasticity, cost recovery through higher fees will reduce enrolment (mainly for the SC, ST and OBCs) or not is a matter of debate. Public investment in higher education is just about 0.37 per cent of the GDP. (Table 3)

In the context of reservations in higher education institutions, raising the seats in the institutions of higher learning by about 50 per cent would require about Rs. 20,000-25,000 crore. Since, this huge amount cannot be provided by the public exchequer, it is a clear indication that higher education be converted into a 'private good'. It is also not

TABLE 3

Growth in Enrolment, Enrolment Ratio, GNP Per-capita (Select Countries)

Country	*Increase in enrolment (1990/91 to 2001/02)%*	*GER-2001 %*	*GNP per capita (US$), 2001*
USA	16.2	81	34,280
China	217.7	13	890
Japan	36.8	49	35,610
India	113.6	11	460
UK	78.1	64	25,120
France	19.4	54	22,730
Italy	27.7	53	19,390
Brazil	103.0	18	3,070
Indonesia	99.7	15	690
Philippines	44.3	31	1,030
Australia	79.1	65	19,900
Malaysia	358.9	27	3,330

Source: Pawan Agarwal, "Higher Education in India: The Need for Change". ICRIER Working Paper, June 2006

understandable how a more liberal regime for private and foreign education providers would help solve the reservation problem.

CASE STUDY

With the problem discussed above we have undergone a study in Itachuna village of Khanyan region under Punduah P.S. It is mainly a rural subsistence area with a high mass of SC, ST and OBC population having more or less a standard enrolment in higher education. The SC, ST population along with their literacy rate compared to the district it belongs, that means, Hooghly is shown in Table 4.

We have collected data from two premier institutions, viz. Bejoy Narayan Mahavidyalaya and the coeducation high school Sree Narayan Institution. The period chosen is the financial year 2006-07. There are about 5690 students in these two institutions—about 2700 students in the College and the

TABLE 4

SC and ST Population and their Literacy Rate

Region		*% of SC population*	*% of ST population*	*Literacy rate excluding (0-6) age group (in%)*		
				General	*SC*	*ST*
	T	23.58	4.21	75.11	56.10	45.45
Hooghly	R	29.27	5.92	71.02	52.96	44.74
	U	12.27	0.80	82.95	70.37	55.04
	T	31.32	16.37	67.18	53.31	48.33
Punduah	R	33.55	17.57	66.30	53.17	28.28
	U	10.18	5.02	75.27	57.55	49.91

T = Total, R = Rural, U = Urban

Source: Census, 2001

rest in the high school. 5690 students are classified in four categories according to intelligence, namely excellent, good, mediocre and dull according to their results in the exams of that year. Their economic conditions are also taken into account and they are mainly sub-divided into two categories namely good and not good. Family income of more than Rs. 1,00,000 per annum in that financial year is taken into the former category, while those with Rs. 1,00,000 or less is considered under the latter category. The result is shown in Table 5.

We are to judge whether there is any association between intelligence and economic conditions.

Here the two attributes are X = economic condition and Y = intelligence. There are two classes of X and four classes of Y. On the basis of the given cell frequencies and the total frequency, we want to test whether the two attributes are related or not. The null hypothesis is H0: X and Y are independent, against the alternative H1: X and Y are associated.

Under H0, the appropriate test statistic we use is ?2 with degrees of freedom, df = (k–1)(L–1). Here k = 2 and L = 4. Now on the basis of the sample H0 is rejected at 100 per cent level of significance if ?2 (observed) > ?2 (k–1)(L–1) and

TABLE 5

Economic condition	Intelligence				Total
	Excellent	Good	Mediocre	Dull	
Good	243	1035	955	475	2708
Not Good	432	937	1033	580	3932
Total	675	1972	1988	1055	5690

will be accepted otherwise. We find that at 5 per cent level of significance H0 is rejected implying that X and Y are associated, but at 1 per cent level of significance it is accepted implying that X and Y are independent.

CONCLUSION

In India in recent years the Government is provisioning reservation quotas for SC, ST and OBCs in higher education. But it will be wiser on the part of the Government to give economic benefits to these classes rather than providing seat or quota reservation to them.

We are not at all against any sort of reservations but the process of reservation followed in India should actually be changed for the good of the tribes. They should be provided with adequate economic assistance rather than only seat and quota reservations in higher education and jobs.

The Government follows up:

For 2006-07, Finance Minister P. Chidambaram had enhanced allocations for schemes, benefiting only SC/STs, by 14.5 per cent to Rs 2,902 crore (Rs 29.02 billion).

The finance ministry is expected to announce a new scheme, focused on education of scheduled castes, in the coming Budget. The ministry is expected to provide Rs 325 crore (Rs. 3.25 billion) for setting up 2,000 Navodaya Vidyalayas (schools).

The idea is to significantly enhance the educational facilities that are available to scheduled caste students. The ministry is also to accept the recommendations of a committee, headed by former Karnataka chief minister

Veerappa Moily, and announce a higher education scholarship of Rs. 120 crore (Rs. 1.20 billion) for other backward classes.

The allocation for schemes, which have at least 20 per centreservation for SC/STs, was also raised by 13.9 per cent to Rs. 9,690 crore (Rs. 96.90 billion).

The allocation for the flagship Sarva Shiksha Abhiyan of the UPA government, may be set at Rs. 10,671 crore (Rs. 106.71 billion). However, only Rs. 8,800 crore (Rs. 88 billion) is the budgetary allocation, while the remaining amount is expected to come from cess collections.

Allocation for secondary education was Rs. 1,837 crore for 2006-07 which is to be enhanced to Rs. 3,794 crore in 2007-08. National Means-*cum*-Merit Scholarship Scheme for Classes IX, X, XI, and XII (total 1 lakh) of Rs. 6,000 per year be given and for that fund of Rs. 750 crore be created.

Post-matric Scholarship programme for SC and ST students will lead an enhancement of provision from Rs. 440 crore in 2006-07 to Rs. 611 crore in 2007-08. Proposal for a separate provision of Rs. 91 crore for similar scholarship to be awarded to students belonging to socially and educationally backward classes.

References

Sharma, Vijender (2006), "Higher Education in India and GATS: A Disastrous Proposal", *People's Democracy Weekly*, Organ of the Communist Party of India (Marxist), Vol. X, No. 44.

Agarwal, Pawan (2006), "Higher Education in India: The Need for Change", ICRIER Working Paper.

Thorat, Sukhadeo, "Higher Education in India: Emerging Issues, Related to Access, Inclusiveness and Quality".

Gupta, Diwaker, "Reservation in Higher Education".

Radhakrishnan, P., "The Right Path to Higher Education".

Kapur, Devesh and Mehta, Pratap Bhanu, "Indian Higher Education Reform: From Half-Baked Socialism to Half-Baked Capitalism."

Government of India (2005). Mid-Term Appraisal of Tenth Five Year Plan, Planning Commission.

Aschauer, D.A. (1989), "Is Public Expenditure Productive?", *Journal of Monetary Economics*, Vol. 23(2): 117-200.

28

Higher Education among Tribal People during Eighties of Twentieth Century in India with Special Reference to Orissa

Rajan Kumar Sahoo and Basanti Das

INTRODUCTION

Tribe is a collection of families or groups of families bearing a common name, member of which occupy the same territory speak the same language and observe certain taboos regarding marriage, profession or occupation and have developed a well assessed system of reciprocity and mutuality of obligations being an endogamous unit, the members of which confine their marriage within the tribe". There are altogether 427 tribal communities all over India constituting 8.08 per cent of total population. They appear in different names in different parts of the country, the most importants among them are the *Gonds* of Madhya Pradesh, Maharashtra, the *Bhills* of Rajasthan and Gujarat. The *Santals* of Bihar, Orissa, the *Chenchus* of Andhra Pradesh and the

Lodhas of West Bengal. Similarly in Orissa there are 62 types of tribal communities constituting 22.43 per cent of the total population of the state. Among the primitive tribes *Bhuyan, Gond, Kisan, Munda, Kharia, Oraon, Santal, Kolha, Bhumija and Bathudi* are found almost exclusively in northern and western Orissa, the *Saora, Kandh, Shabar or Lodha, Paraja and Bhottada* are largely confined to southern Orissa. They are docile, simple, honest, hardworking and hospitable. But economically backward and exploited, physically oppressed, socially ostracized, segregated and humiliated, culturally isolated, politically unconscious and little education to understand the issues in right perspective. But no more they will be left alone to lead an isolated life rather can be brought within the ambit of massive development activities. Generally development without education will remain as myth. Pragmatically socio-economic development and educational development should be viewed as interdependent process and therefore should go hand in hand. Education has assumed a significant part of the very foundation of modern society, an avenue for social mobility, political consciousness, and equality of opportunities to all citizens which calls for suitable strategy as urgent and as important as poverty, sickness or unemployment.

OBJECTIVES

Realizing the importance of education especially the higher education for the upliftment of tribal people the study was planned with the following objectives:

- To study the standard of higher education of tribal communities both in India and State of Orissa.
- To find out the existing government programmes for the development of higher education of tribal communities.
- To point out the problems faced by tribal communities in developing their higher education and to suggest suitable remedies.

METHODOLOGY

The paper has been prepared collecting data from various secondary sources. Many books, research reports and magazines have been consulted for the above purpose.

STANDARD OF HIGHER EDUCATION OF TRIBALS IN INDIA AND ORISSA

The Act cell of UGC established in January 1979, collects information regarding course-wise admissions and appointment of SC/ST candidates to teaching and non-teaching posts from 1977-78 onwards. In January 1985 the UGC published on the position of actual admission and employment of SCs and STs in Universities and Colleges during 1978-79 under the caption "Facilities to Schedule Caste and Schedule Tribes in Universities and Colleges" which has been presented in Table 1 for our understanding.

The Table indicates that the per cent of admission of both SC and ST students for different courses, e.g. Arts, Science, Commerce Education, Engineering/Technology, Medicine, Agriculture, Veterinary Law and others both at graduate and post-graduate level is very less. It is very very less in case of ST students. While the per cent of admission of SC students in these courses varies from 4.44 per cent to 9.79 per cent at under graduate level it varies from 0.90 per cent to 10.14 per cent at post-graduate level. In case of STs the admission at under graduate level varies from 0.42 to 2.46 per cent while at post-graduate level it varies from 0.13 to 1.86 per cent. The admission of ST students in Science, Engineering, Medical, Agriculture, Veterinary and Law is far from satisfactory level.

Similarly, the educational level of Scheduled Tribes at the state level during the Census 1981 has been given in Table 2.

The figures in the table indicates that only 8.18 per cent tribals were literate during 1981 whereas 91.82 per cent were illiterates. Out of them 4.93 per cent had education upto middle class level. In every 100 tribal people only 07 had education level above secondary and below graduation. Only

TABLE I

Admission of SC and ST Students for Different Courses at Higher Education Level during 1978-79 in India

Sl. No.	*Course*	*Total*	*SC (%)*	*ST (%)*
A.	Undergraduate Level			
1.	Arts	9,37,028	91,721(9.79)	23,124(2.46)
2.	Science	4,36,000	19,369(4.44)	3,559(0.82)
3.	Commerce	4,58,472	21,398(4-72)	5.722(1.26)
B.	Post-Graduate Level			
4.	Arts	1,36,004	13,797(10.14)	2,526(1.86)
5.	Science	47,359	1,342 (2.83)	365(0.77)
6.	Commerce	32,449	1,676 (5.17)	372(1.15)
C.	Education			
7.	Undergraduate	63,660	3,782(5.94)	789 (1.24)
8.	Post-Graduate	4,139	136(3.29)	27(0.65)
D.	Engineering/Technology			
9.	Under-Graduate	99,569	5,454(5.48)	1061(1.07)
10.	Post-Graduate	5,151	84(1.63)	8 (0.16)
E.	Medicine			
11.	Under Graduate	95,289	7,266(7.63)	1324(1.39)
12.	Post-Graduate	10,305	287(2.73)	39(0.38)
F.	Agriculture			
13.	Under Graduate	27,102	1,903(7.02)	160 (0.59)
14.	Post-Graduate	6,108	201(3.29)	39 (0.64)
G.	Veterinary Science			
15.	Under Graduate	5589	266(4.76)	44 (0.79)
16.	Post-Graduate	1002	9(0.90)	———
H.	Law			
17.	Under Graduate	1,65,317	10,475(6.37)	1,851(1.12)
18.	Post-Graduate	3085	95 (3.08)	4 (0.13)
I.	Others			
19.	Under Graduate	11,361	671(5.91)	48(0.42)
20.	Post-Graduate	3,550	126(3.55)	20 (0.56)
	TOTAL	25,43,449	1,80,058(7.08)	41,082(1.62)

Figures in parentheses indicate the per cent.

TABLE 2

Educational Level of Tribal People of Orissa according to the 1981 Census

Sl. No.	Education	Total	Male	Female
1.	Both Literate and Illiterates	59,15,067 (100)	29,39,863 (100)	29,75,204 (100)
2.	Literate without any educational level	4,83,619 (8.18)	3,92,545 (13.35)	91,074 (3.06)
3.	Primary and Middle	2,91,520 (4.93)	2,44,584 (8.32)	46,936 (1.58)
4.	Matriculation/Secondary	20,239 (0.34)	17,959 (0.61)	2,280 (0.076)
5.	Above Secondary and below Graduation	3,997 (0.07)	3,558 (0.12)	439 (0.015)
6.	Graduation/Post-Graduation	2,869 (0.05)	26.22 (0.09)	247 (0.008)
7.	Non-Technical Diploma	159 (0.002)	129 (0.004)	30 (0.001)
8.	Technical Diploma	2882 (0.05)	2502 (0.085)	380 (0.013)
9.	Technical Degree	185 (0.003)	130 (0.004)	55 (0.002)

(Figures in parentheses indicate per cent).
Source: Census of India, 1981.

5 is every 100 tribals had education at graduation/post-graduation level. In case of non-technical diploma and technical degree this figure was 2 and 3 in every thousand tribal people respectively. The figures indicate that tribals had very low level of higher education especially in case of Technical Degree.

DIFFERENT PROGRAMMES FOR THE DEVELOPMENT OF HIGHER EDUCATION OF TRIBAL PEOPLE

There are many schemes for the development of Higher Education among the tribal people. They are as follows:

(i) Post-Matric scholarships are being disbursed by

the states to students belonging to Scheduled Tribe communities. In 1944-45 the first year of its introduction, there were only 114 Scheduled Caste scholarship holders. The number of tribal scholarship holder was 84 in 1948-49 when it was introduced for them for the first time. The number of awards of post-matric scholarships to SC/ST students during 1986-87 was likely to be of the order of 10.89 lakhs. The total expenditure on this scheme at the end of the Sixth Plan was Rs. 88.53 crore which became committed expenditure during the Seventh Plan period. An outlay of Rs. 10 crore was provided during 1985-86 which is reported to have been utilized in full. The Planning Commission allocated an amount of Rs. 11 crore only for his scheme during 1986-87. However during that year the total requirement of funds under the scheme was reported to be Rs.18-90 crore. Under the scheme the scholarship is paid to eligible students by the State Government/UT Administrations in accordance with the regulations laid down by the Government of India who provide the funds for the plan scheme on 100 per cent basis. During the Sixth Plan the Ministry of Home Affairs has assigned the National Institute of Education Planning and Administration (NIEPA), New Delhi, the task of monitoring the functioning of the post-matric scholarships scheme. There is slight improvement of enrolment in higher education because of the central programme of scholarships.

(ii) Besides the scholarships direct educational incentives like hostel facilities, material aids in shape of stationery, books, uniforms, etc. have contributed to increase enrolment of Scheduled Tribes in various stages of education.

(iii) Exemptions from payment of fees in schools and colleges, provision of vocational training, supply and essential medicines are provided to the tribal students for their educational development.

(iv) According to earlier guidelines issued by the Ministry of Education (now Ministry of Human Resource Development) the State Government and Universities has reserved 20 per cent of the seats with a district reservation of 15 per cent for the scheduled castes and 5 per cent for scheduled tribes. These reservations are interchangeable between these two categories. The Ministry has also suggested that in case of seats reserved for them remaining unfilled a further relaxation in marks could be given to them. In the 27th Report of the Commissioner for Scheduled Castes and Scheduled Tribes it was recommended that in line with the proportion of Scheduled Tribes in the country's population the number of seats reserved for them, in various educational and technical institutions should be raised from 5 per cent to 7.5 per cent. It is gratifying to note that the reservation percentage was raised in August 1982 to 7.5 per cent for the Scheduled Tribes.

(v) The scheme of Book Bank was started in 1978-79 for SC/ST students pursuing Medical/Engineering courses. At present an amount of Rs. 5,000.00 has been fixed as the total cost for purchase of one set of text books. One set of books is allowed to be used by four students. The life period of one set of books has been fixed as three years which means that in every three years funds will be provided for getting new sets of books. This scheme has proved very useful for SC/ST students pursuing Medical and Engineering courses. A provision of Rs. 3 crore was made for this scheme during the Sixth Plan but unfortunately the expenditure during that period was only Rs. 0.96 crore. For the Seventh Five Year Plan an outlay of Rs. 2.25 crore has been provided for this scheme. During 1985-86 an allocation of Rs. 0.55 crore was made against which an expenditure of Rs. 0.31 crore only was incurred. The number of SC/ST beneficiaries during the year was 16,822. During 1986-87 an allocation of Rs. 0.50 crore was made. Proposals to cover other professional courses like Agriculture and Law and to provide a set of text books to each SC/ST students were reported to have been sent to the Planning Commission for approval.

(vi) Centrally sponsored scheme of Girls' Hostel for Scheduled Tribes was started during Third Plan. Under this scheme the Central Assistance is provided to the State Governments on 50:50 basis and to UT Administrations on 100 per cent basis for construction of hostel buildings for ST Girls (upto 100 in number) studying in middle, high schools, higher secondary institutions, colleges and Universities for their educational development.

(vii) Centrally sponsored scheme of Boys' Hostels for scheduled tribes was started during 1989-90 with a token provision of Rs. 17 lakh. Under this scheme the central assistance is provided to the State Government on 50:50 basis and to UT Administration on 100 per cent basis for construction of hostel buildings for ST boys (upto 100 inmates) studying in middle, high school, higher secondary institutions, colleges and universities for their educational development.

(viii) The Government of India initiated a scheme for the award of National Overseas Scholarships to Scheduled Castes, Schedules Tribes, Denotified Tribes, Nomadic/Semi-Nomadic Tribes and other economically backward classes. In 1954-55 for pursuing post-graduate studies and research abroad in subjects for which suitable facilities were not available in India. The total number of scholarships awarded each year is 21. During 1985-86 the Government of India proposed to award 29 scholarships with a backlog of 8 scholarships of the previous years. However in the year 1985-86, 25 scholars were selected.

The allocation and expenditure under various centrally

sponsored schemes in the welfare of Backward classes during the Sixth Plan 1985-86 and 1987 has been presented in Table 3.

TABLE 3

Allocation and Expenditure under Various Centrally Sponsored Scheme in the Welfare of Backward Classes during the Sixth Plan, 1985-86 and 1986-87

(Rs. in Crores)

Sl. No.	Scheme	Sixth Plan		Allo-cation for VIIth Plan	1985-86		1986-87	
		Allo-cation	Expen-diture		Allo-cation	Expen-diture	Allo-cation	Expen-diture
1.	Post-Matric Scholarships to SC/ST Students	130	140-94	114-57	10.00	10.00	11.00	18.90
2.	Book Banks for SC/ST Students of Engineering/ Medical Colleges	3.00	0.96	2.25	0.55	0.31	0.55	0.50
3.	Girls' Hostels for SC/ST	13.00	14.06	32.05	5.00	3.02	4.55	4.55

PROBLEMS FOR THE DEVELOPMENT OF HIGHER EDUCATION OF TRIBAL PEOPLE

Though the Government have undertaken a lot of schemes for the development of Higher Education of Tribal people still there are many grey areas in this sector.

(i) From the analysis of data from the per cent of literacy to per cent of tribal people prosecuting general graduate and post-graduate level studies it is clear that the stagnation and drop-out cancer the progress of education and create wastage in the field of educational attainments. It results increasing a disequilibrium in the input-output ratio and obliterates the benefit-cost situation. The planners, development administrators and evaluators have been equivocal in identifying this black spot and is suggesting from time to time the remedial measures. But the situation has not improved. The principal causes of stagnation and dropout are stated as follows:

A. Economic Causes

(a) A pertinent fact is that dropout is not always of academically weak students but of economically poor ones.
(b) Participation in household economic pursuits and seasonal collection of minor forest produce.

B. Social Causes

(a) Communication gap among students, teachers and parents/guardians.
(b) Indifference of parents/guardians for educating their children, especially girl children.
(c) Early marriage
(d) Home sickness of tribal students.
(e) Regular attendance in youth organization (dormitory)

C. Religious Causes

(a) School holiday pattern not in consonance with the rituals and festivals in tribal areas.
Without any attempt to follow up action for retention coupled with lack of motivation and incentive for both pupil and parents/ guardians is likely to act as subterfuge, rather than explaining the real situation.

(ii) Parents are strongly averse to education of their children due to several causes.
(a) They regard the spread of education with

apprehension, for they feel that their boys and girls will be turned is to 'sahibs' and 'mem-sahibs' with new and expensive habits which they can ill afford and that when they have left school they will leave their homes.

(b) The educated tribal girls do not get a suitable marriage partner and thus discourages the parents to send the girls to the school.

(c) Weakening the native tongue.

(d) Forsaking tradition-based occupation.

(e) Leading to reduce sociability in the community.

(f) Affecting rural/caste leadership norms.

(g) Insecurity of winning government jobs and suitable employment.

(h) Cultural constraints are some of the important factors responsible for developing such an attitude in them.

(i) Ignorance about the utility and value of education can not be ruled out.

(iii) Dormitories attract the tribal boys and girls more. A number of feasts and festivals celebrated round the year direct their attention from educational institutions.

(iv) At present the quantum of the scholarship in college particularly is very inadequate. Sometimes the first instalment may not be received even till the middle of the session and in some cases the student may collect the entire amount at the fog end of the session. On account of the late availability of the first instalment some students have been unable to join the institutions as they have no funds to make advance payment of the initial fees, caution money hostel dues, etc. Only those tribals who have private resources and who do not therefore really need scholarships can afford to go to college.

(v) The Scheduled Tribe students in the hostels are not given boarding grant in some of the states with the result they have to bring ration from their homes.

(vi) Sometimes Girls' hostels are located at for away places from the educational institutions and girl students do not prefer to stay in such institutions.

(vii) Inability on the part of members of scheduled tribe communities to utilize secondary and higher education facilities as well as job opportunities in full can partly be explained by defects in their education at the preceding lower tiers. The tribal boys or girls are not able to join entry into ITI's and other technical institutes due to their weakness in science learning.

(viii) Inadequacy of educational institutions in tribal concentration areas are other causes of low development of their higher education.

(ix) There are instances that the teachers do not devote attention to their primary job, i.e teaching but keep themselves engaged in other activities. The teachers do not stay in institutions of higher learning located in tribal areas due to lack of accommodation facilities. Besides these causes there is no sincere supervision of the work of the teachers. Often there is non-availability of teachers with many qualifications.

(x) The present of system of delivery of basic education is far from satisfactory. Therefore appropriate institutional technology taking the help of audio-visual aids, radio, television and computers should be devised in order to make it more meaningful adaptive and pragmatic.

(xi) The percentage of literacy/education has a direct linkage with the availability of infrastructure. So lack of infrastructural facilities in institutions of higher learning also retards the development of higher education.

(xii) A wide gap is noticed between the objectives and implementation of higher education.

(xiii) The malaise inherent in the system appears to be highly complex and is difficult to uproot completely.

SUGGESTIONS

Considering the various problems seen in the fields of education the following suggestions may be undertaken:

(i) Stagnation and dropout of tribal students may be checked by motivating their parents. It is necessary to create conducive atmosphere for education through various special steps to attract and motivate the tribals towards education. Incentives should be given to the head of the tribal household or to the housewife in kind for sending their children for higher education.

(ii) It is necessary to streamline the administration of the scholarships programme instituted by the Government of India. In this context we make the following recommendations:

   (a) The administration of scholarships and other aids needs to be decentralized a great deal. Heads of Institutions should be authorized to grant scholarships along with admission on their own authority. For this purpose the necessary amount should be placed at their disposal well in advance of the academic year. This could be done on the basis of the previous year's expenditure with a margin for increase.

   (b) The scope of scholarships should cover all courses available to secondary school bearers and special preference should be given to vocational and technical courses including those at industrial training institutes.

(iii) The Central Government is at present providing assistance only for post-matric Scholarships and girls' hostels. The Central Government should work out a scheme of assisting the states to cover the entire education progrmme for tribals including scholarships, boarding grants, etc.

(iv) The locations/sites for girls' hostels should be selected by a committee of senior officers at the distant level.

(v) In order to overcome the weakness of tribal students in science learning, science teaching should be strengthened. Special classes, outside the study hour might be held for which result linked honorarium may be paid to teachers. Watching of progress, planning ahead of carriers and ensuring placement in appropriate institutions or in other words to provide for a personal follow-up. The staff necessary for purpose should be made available.

(vi) Priority shall be given with the establishment of ITI, Polytechnic, ANM Training Centres, Teachers' Training Institute in the tribal areas. Vocational guidance centre should be set-up in these areas so that tribal boys and girls get sound advice regarding their ability and qualification *vis-à-vis* job opportunities. Institutions like Sahitya Academy, Lalit Kala Academy, Sangeet Natak Academy besides Tribal Research Institutes should take up encouragement along with documentation of various aspects of tribal culture in the sphere of art, painting, music and dance under the auspices of the Department of culture.

Basic education should not stop at the primary level. It must go even beyond the secondary stage and have collegiate courses. The system of basic and post-basic education together with rural institutes is an appropriate system to be introduced in the tribal areas. As tribals are fond of vocational courses so special efforts should therefore be made to place them in the industrial training institutes, polytechnics, etc.

(vii) Teachers' absenteeism shall be curbed by providing residential accommodation. Persons having genuine aptitude for service in tribal areas shall be selected for posting as teacher. Incentives to be provided to government employees posted in tribal areas.

There is need in fact to appoint in the State Directorates of Education specific officers in the rank of Joint Director or Deputy Director to Specifically attend to the problems of education among scheduled tribes and to monitor data.

(viii) Our potential educational/instructional technology need reorientation in order to make it more meaningful, adaptable and pragmatic. It is a serious challenge for the scholars, researchers and experts in the National/State Level Institutes of Educational Technology NCERT/SCERT's and various research institutes undertaking studies of society culture, language and the like to develop appropriate instructional technology, especially in the sphere of tribal education, keeping in view the deficiencies, inadequacies and shortcomings.

(ix) When we have laid considerable emphasis on the education of tribals, the main recommendation should be for extending the national pattern of education to them with a provision for bifurcation at the secondary stage. In our opinion, this would help to open up avenues for tribal children for pursuing higher education without necessarily alienating them from their tribal background.

(x) In the United States the Federal Government had to intervene when they found that the intellectuals and people with some creative ability or initiative in them were leaving the villages for the urban areas. They tried to arrest this flow by establishing educational institutions and colleges oriented to cater to the needs of the land-based section of society and at the same time trying to satisfy their requirements. So different Educational Commissions have given emphasis to pick up tribal youths, give them training through specially organized courses and use them as workers for tribal uplift. The commission was of opinion that "no expenditure is too great for the purpose" of tribal education as it is a major programme of equalization, social and national integration.

(xi) It should be the Union Government's responsibility to co-ordinate facilities and determination of standards in respect of higher education, research scientific and technical education.

(xii) Adequate infrastructural facilities, viz. buildings, hostels, electricity, water supply, road communication, etc. should be provided in the tribal areas which would ultimately contribute to the development of education. Suitable teachings aids, playground, orchards and library facilities shall be provided.

(xiii) Incentives like free residential facilities would give a sense of security and motivation to the teachers, who normally avoid postings in difficult areas due to infrastructural weakness.

(xiv) Multiplicity of management shall be avoided and administration shall be rested with one Department preferably Educational Department to look after tribal education interlinking and integrating other educational programmes.

(xv) The norms for supporting facilities like hostels, scholarship, stipends, free text books, etc. have to be formulated properly with a view to achieving the target fixed. These are to be supplied to the tribal students at the time of enrolment and thereafter at every academic session.

(xvi) Data concerning all aspects of education shall be retained so that it would facilitate future planning, policy implementation and recommending remedial measures.

(xvii) While planning for the development of tribal education in our state care should be taken to estimate the requirement of funds keeping in view the increasing trend in the tribal population.

(xviii) Education the basic input for any sustainable socio-economic development of the tribals is to be conducive to the socio-cultural ethos and environmental condition of the tribals with gradual amalgamation with the formal general education at a certain stage.

(xix) At the National Level, Ministry of Education, the

National Council of Education Research and Training (NCERT), The National Institute of Educational Planning and Administration (NIEPA) might set-up a body to evolve broad guidance for imparting the requisite orientation to the conventional system.

(xx) The curriculum should be suitably restructured so as to have elements of agriculture, forestry, animal husbandry, cottage industry and so on.

(xxi) No foreign fund be allowed to flow to the educational institutions in scheduled areas, whether through foreign agencies or through voluntary organizations within the country, unless specific clearance has been obtained.

CONCLUSION

To streamline the educational development intervention and pave its path for goal attainment especially the higher education in tribal societies, we need to sharpen our tools, develop appropriate strategies, renew our commitment with dedicated zeal and enthusiasm, mobilize resources, priorities, actions and improve the quality of life. We further need expanded horizon of intellectual in developing higher education among the students of tribal community who expect delivery of support services at their door steps. Since education is the essential pre-requisite for sustainable development there is need for a participating approach which would involve the vision of planners and policy-makers, the dedication of development practitioners, the active co-operation of community members, the commitment of teachers, the involvement of parents and pupils in the spheres of planning, implementation and evaluation.

REFERENCES

Government of Orissa (1994); Tribal Education in Orissa In the Context of Education for All by 2000 AD, A Status Paper Tribal Welfare Development, Bhubaneswar.

Sahoo, Rajan Kumar (2001-02); The Tribal Land Alienation Problem in

Mayurbhanj District and Legal Provisions, Upendra Prastha, UNS Mahavidyalaya, Khairabad, Mugpal, Jajpur-755009 (Orissa) pp. 31-40.

Sahoo, Rajan Kumar (2005); Tribal Development in India, Mohit Publications, 4675/21, Ansari Road, Darya Ganj, New Delhi-110002.

Sahoo, Rajan Kumar (2008); Education Among the Women of the Tribal Society: Issues and Evidences in Pati, J.C., R.K. Sahoo and H.B. Dash (Ed. 2008); Women Education: Emerging Issues and Rethinking, Mittal Publications, 4594/9, Darya Ganj, New Delhi-110002.

29

Higher Education among Tribals with Special Reference to Andhra Pradesh

B. SATYANARAYAN AND B. APPA RAO

The Total number of tribal communities recognized by the Government as Scheduled Tribes is 572 in number. Scheduled Tribes are those tribal communities who have been listed so by the President of India in keeping with Articles 341 and 342 of the Constitution. These tribal communities mainly live in Scheduled Areas, or those outlying areas, which during the British times did not come under the direct purview of civil, criminal and revenue administration.

The Scheduled Tribes population of the country, as per 2001 Census, is 8.43 crore, constituting about 8.2 per cent of the total population of the country. More than half of the Scheduled Tribes population is concentrated in 6 States viz. Madhya Pradesh, Chhattisgarh, Maharashtra, Orissa, Jharkhand and Gujarat. Tribal communities live in about 15 per cent of the total geographical area of the country. Article 366(25) of the Constitution of India refers to Scheduled Tribes as those communities, who are scheduled in accordance with the Article 342 of the Constitution. The list of Scheduled Tribes or a community declared as a Scheduled Tribe in a particular State need not be so in another State.

The essential characteristics, first laid down by the Lokur Committee, for a community to be identified as Scheduled Tribes are:

(i) primitive traits,
(ii) distinctive culture,
(iii) shyness of contact with the community at large,
(iv) geographical isolation, and
(v) backwardness—social and economic.

Tribal groups, as such are not homogenous and different communities are at different stages of social, economic and educational development. Some communities have adopted mainstream way of life. But at the other end of spectrum, there are certain Scheduled Tribes, 75 in number, known as Primitive Tribal Groups (PTGs), who are characterized by:

1. a pre-agriculture level of technology,
2. a stagnant or declining population,
3. extremely low literacy, and
4. a subsistence level of economy.

Except Punjab, Haryana, Chandigarh, Delhi and Pondicherry, Scheduled Tribes have been scheduled in all States and UTs. In UTs of Lakshadweep and Dadra and Nagar Haveli and States of Mizoram, Nagaland, Meghalaya and Arunachal Pradesh, Scheduled Tribes are in majority. In all there are about 700 Scheduled Tribes notified under Article 342 of the Constitution of India. Many tribes are present in more than one State.. The largest number of tribes, numbering 62, is scheduled in the State of Orissa. The main concentration of tribal population is in Central India and in the North-Eastern States.

In so far as Scheduled Tribes are concerned, in almost all developmental parameters they lag behind. Tribal Areas are characterized by poor infrastructure and poorer services leading to slower growth.

CONSTITUTIONAL SAFEGUARDS

The constitution has devoted more than 20 Articles on the redressal and upliftment of the underprivileged following the policy of positive discrimination and affirmative action, particularly with reference to the Scheduled Tribes. Recognising the special needs of STs, the Constitution of India made certain special safeguards to protect these communities from all the possible exploitation and thus ensure social justice. While Article 14 confers equal rights and opportunities to all, Article 15 prohibits discrimination against any citizen on the grounds of sex, religion, race, caste etc. Article 15(4) enjoins upon the State to make special provisions for the advancement of any socially and educationally backward classes; Article 16(4) empowers the State to make provisions for reservation in appointments or posts in favour of any backward class of citizens, which in the opinion of the State, is not adequately represented in the services under the State; Article 46 enjoins upon the State to promote with special care the educational and economic interests of the weaker sections of the people and, in particular, the STs and promises to protect them from social injustice and all forms of exploitation. Further, while Article 275(1) promises grant-in-aid for promoting the welfare of STs and for raising the level of administration of the Scheduled Areas, Articles 330, 332 and 335 stipulate reservation of seats for STs in the Lok Sabha and in the State Legislative Assemblies and in services. Finally, the Constitution also empowers the State to appoint a Commission to investigate the conditions of the socially and educationally backward classes (Article 340) and to specify those Tribes or Tribal Communities deemed to be as STs (Article 342).

The Fifth Schedule to the Constitution lays down certain prescriptions about the Scheduled Areas as well as the Scheduled Tribes in States other than Assam, Meghalaya, Tripura and Mizoram by ensuring submission of Annual Reports by the Governors to the President of India regarding the Administration of the Scheduled Areas and setting up of Tribal Advisory Councils to advise on matters pertaining to the welfare and advancement of the STs (Article 244(1)).

Likewise, the Sixth Schedule to the Constitution also refers to the administration of Tribal Areas in the states of Assam, Meghalaya, Tripura and Mizoram by designating certain tribal areas as Autonomous Districts and Autonomous Regions and also by constituting District Councils and Regional Councils (Article 244(2)). To ensure effective participation of the tribals in the process of planning and decision-making, the 73rd and 74th Amendments of the Constitution are extended to the Scheduled Areas through the Panchayats (Extension to the Scheduled Areas) Act, 1996.

DEVELOPMENT PLANS

High priority to the welfare and development of STs has been given right from the beginning of the first five-year plan. The First Five Year Plan (1951-56) clearly laid down the principle stating that 'the general development programmes should be so designed to cater adequately to the backward classes and special provisions should be used for securing additional and more intensified development for STs'. Unfortunately, the same could not take place. The Second Plan (1956-61), which laid emphasis on economic development, gave a special focus on reducing economic inequalities in the society. Further, development programmes for STs have been planned for, based on respect and understanding of their culture and traditions and with an appreciation of their social, psychological and economic problems. In fact, the same was planned in tune with 'Panchasheel'—the philosophy of tribal development as enunciated by the first Prime Minister of the Country, Pandit Jawaharlal Nehru. An important landmark during the Second Plan was the opening of 43 Special Multi-purpose Tribal Blocks, later termed as Tribal Development Blocks (TDBs). The Third Plan (1961-66) continued with the very same principle of advocating reduction in inequalities through various policies and programmes to provide equality of opportunity to STs. The Fourth Plan (1969-74) proclaimed that the 'basic goal was to realise a rapid increase in the standard of living of the people through measures which also promote 'equality and social justice'. An important step in this direction was setting up of six pilot projects in Andhra Pradesh, Bihar, Madhya Pradesh and Orissa in 1971-72 with a separate Tribal Development Agency for each project. The Fifth Plan (1974-78) marked a shift in approach as reflected in the launching of the Tribal Sub-Plan (TSP) for the direct benefit of the development of tribals. The Tribal Sub-Plan has a two pronged strategy, namely: (i) promotion of development activities to raise the level of living standards of Scheduled Tribes, and (ii) protection of their interest through legal and administrative support. The TSP stipulated that funds of the centre and the states should be quantified on the population proportion basis with budgetary mechanisms to ensure accountability, non-divertability and utilisation for the welfare and development of STs.

The Sixth Plan (1980-85) sought to ensure a higher degree of devolution of funds so that at least 50 per cent of tribal families could be provided assistance to cross the poverty line. In the Seventh Plan (1985-90), there was substantial increase in the flow of funds for the development of STs resulting in the expansion of infrastructural facilities and enlargement of coverage. Emphasis was laid on the educational development of STs. For the economic development of STs, two national-level institutions were set-up viz. (i) Tribal Cooperative Marketing Development Federation (TRIFED) in 1987 as an apex body for State Tribal Development Cooperative Corporations, and (ii) National Scheduled Castes and Scheduled Tribes Finance and Development Corporation (NSFDC) in 1989. The former was assigned to provide remunerative prices for the forest and agriculture produce of tribal, while the latter was intended to provide credit support for employment generation.

In the Eighth Plan (1992-97), efforts were intensified to bridge the gap between the levels of development of STs and the other sections of the society. The Plan not only emphasized elimination of exploitation, but also paid attention to the special problems of suppression of rights, land alienation, non-payment of minimum wages and restrictions on the right to collect minor forest produce, etc. However, attention on priority basis was continued to be paid on the socio-economic upliftment of STs.

The Ninth Plan (1997-2002) aimed to empower STs by creating an enabling environment conducive for them to exercise their rights freely, enjoy their privileges and lead a life of self-confidence and dignity, on par with the rest of society. This process essentially encompassed three vital components, viz. (i) Social Empowerment; (ii) Economic Empowerment; and (iii) Social justice. To this effect, while ST-related line Ministries/Departments implemented general development policies and programmes, the nodal Ministry of Tribal Affairs implemented certain ST-specific innovative programmes.

The Tenth Plan approach to the tribal development focused on tackling the unresolved issues and problems on a time bound basis, besides providing adequate space and opportunity for the tribals to empower themselves with the strength of their own potentials.

The Eleventh Plan will attempt a paradigm shift with respect to the overall empowerment of the tribals keeping the issues related to the governance at the centre. The operational imperatives of the Vth Schedule, TSP 1976, PESA 1996, RFRA 2006; the desirability of a tribal-centric, tribal participative and tribal-managed development process, and the need for a conscious departure from dependence on a largely under effective official delivery system will be kept in view during this shift.

SCHEDULED TRIBES IN ANDHRA PRADESH

The following Table 1 gives the Tribal Profile of A.P.

The Educational Position of the Tribals in Andhra Pradesh

The population of tribal people in Andhra Pradesh is 50,24,104. The literacy rate for total population of the State as per the 1991 Census was 44 per cent (Male 55% and female 33%) and these figures have gone up to 61 per cent (male 71% and female 51%) in the 2001 Census, apparently due to the intensive literacy drives initiated by the State Government. The corresponding literacy rate among the tribal population was 17 per cent (male 25 per cent and female 9%) as per the 1991 Census and 22 per cent in the 2001 Census.

TABLE I

Tribal Population in Scheduled Areas of Andhra Pradesh

Sl. No.	*Name of the District*	*Scheduled Tribes*	*Scheduled Villages*	*Population (2001 Census in lakhs)*
1.	Srikakulam	Savara, Jatapu, Gadaba, Konda Doora	108	1,51,249
2.	Vijayanagaram	Savara, Jatapu, Gadaba, Konda Doora	298	2,14,839
3.	Visakhapatnam	Bagata, Gadaba, Kammara Kondadora, Kotia, Khond, Mali, Manne Dora, Mukha Dora, Reddi Dora, Porja Valmiki, Goud, Kulia	3368	5,57,572
4.	East Godavari	Koya, Konda Reddi, Kammara, Konda Dora	559	1,91,561
5.	West Godavari	Koya, Konda Reddi, Yerukula, Yanadi	102	96,659
6.	Khammam	Koya, Konda Reddi, Sugali or Lambada	889	6,82,617
7.	Warangal	Koya, Lambada	412	4,57,679
8.	Adilabad	Gond, Kolam, Pardhan, Thoti, Lambada, Naikpod, Andh	23	4,16,511
9.	Mahaboob Nagar	Lambada, Chenchu	177	2,78,702
	Total		5936	30,47,389

Sources: 1. Mohan Rao, K. (1991), Tribal Profile of Andhra Pradesh, Hyderabad: Tribal Cultural and Training Institute: Mimeograph, and

2. Census of India, 2001, Director of Census Operation, A.P.

This reveals the gap between the general population and the tribal communities.

Although the statistics show a vast change in literacy levels, the issue of literacy depends on how it is defined and the extent to which it is enabling in qualitative terms. While there are special programmes initiated for adult education, the implementation process is far from effective. Fifty-four years after independence on November 28, 2001 the Government enacted the 93rd Amendment to the Constitution making the Right to Education a Fundamental

Right. It puts the onus of sending children to school on parents rather than the State. It is not enough to talk of fundamental rights and fundamental duties of the citizens. It is equally necessary to dwell on the fundamental duties of the Government. The extent to which this enactment will be increasingly backed by resource allocation will be the test of the seriousness of purpose of the government to implement the law.

It is pertinent to look at the education scenario of Andhra Pradesh in this context as far as elementary education is concerned. The Government has undertaken several measures to reach out to tribal communities, such as the Girijana Vidya Vikas Kendras. Tribal Education standards I and II in areas where 'primitive tribal communities' reside; mandal (sub-district) level elementary schools; special residential schools called Ashram Schools mainly in tribal areas; the 'Alternative Schools', etc., and monitoring systems such as the School Complex System. There have also been some special programmes such as bridge courses and back to school initiatives for dropouts. For adult literacy, the State has launched a special programme known as 'Akshara Sankranthi' and Chaduvula Panduga which is for 'adults' above 15 years of age.

All these attempts fall far short of the specific educational needs in tribal areas. Apart from access to education is the issue of quality of the education process. Many of the existing schools do not have adequate number of teachers. The quality of teaching leaves much to be desired let alone the content, which does not take into account the tribal reality situation.

The Scheduled Tribe Members of this Country remain the most vulnerable from all human Development indicators and in spite of the efforts made in the various five year plans, the situation is still critical.

It may be seen from the foregoing table that the literacy among STs is low both in Andhra Pradesh and all India (65%). It is still low among the ST females. Other trends could be observed from Table 2.

It may be observed from Table 3 that the dropout ratio among ST students is relatively the higher (66%) when

TABLE 2

Literacy amongst STs and all Social Groups

Year	*STs*			*All Social Groups*		
	Male	*Female*	*Total*	*Male*	*Female*	*Total*
1961	13.83	3.16	8.53	40.40	15.35	28.30
1971	17.63	4.85	11.30	45.96	21.97	34.45
1981	24.52	8.04	16.35	56.38	29.76	43.57
1991	40.65	18.19	29.60	64.13	39.29	52.21
2001	59.17	34.76	47.10	75.26	53.67	64.84

Source: Selected Educational Statistics, M/HRD, 2004-05

TABLE 3

Dropout Ratio among STs in India

Year	*Primary (I-V)*		*Elementary (I-VIII)*		*Secondary (I-X)*	
	STs	*All*	*STs*	*All*	*STs*	*All*
1996-97	56.5	40.2	75.2	56.5	84.2	70.0
1997-98	55.1	39.2	73.0	56.1	75.8	69.3
1998-99	55.7	41.5	72.4	56.3	82.2	66.7
2001-02	52.3	39.0	69.5	54.6	81.2	66.0
2002-03	51.4	34.9	68.7	52.8	80.3	62.6
2003-04	48.9	31.5	70.1	52.3	79.3	62.7
2004-05	42.3	29.0	65.9	50.8	79.0	61.9
Increase in 2004 over 1996-1997	14.2	11.2	9.3	5.7	5.2	8.1

compared to the Country's general level which is (62%) in 2004. The Government has to do something to bring down the dropout ratio among the STs. Other parameters could be observed from the foregoing table.

It could be seen from Table 4 that the Pupil-Teacher Ratio in ST schools is decreasing as you are moving from Primary level (1:46) to Secondary level (1:33) which is on the right path. As a matter of fact, it should be still less to get the optimal result.

TABLE 4

Pupil-Teacher Ratio (PTR) by Type of Schools

Sl. No.	*Level*	*1950-51*	*2004-05*
1.	Primary	1:24	1:46
2.	Upper Primary	1:20	1:35
3.	Secondary/Senior	1:21	1:33

CONCLUSION

Monitoring and Evaluaion are essential to make the various development programmes and schemes more effective in order to achieve results. In respect of sectoral programmes and schemes of tribal development, Policy Planning, Monitoring and Evaluation and Coordination are the responsibility of the concerned Central Government Ministries, State Governments and Union Territory Administrations, who have to put effective mechanism. In addition, to those adopted by the Ministry of Tribal Affairs, Greater attention has also to be directed to concurrent Monitoring and Evaluation through existing field functionaries, on the principle of checks and balances.

REFERENCES

Sharma, A.K. (2005), National Policy on Tribal: The Case of Education, *The Eastern Anthropologist*, 58(1), 135-38.

National Policy of Education, (1986), Government of India Doucument.

Rao, K. Mohan (1999), Tribal Development in Andhra Pradesh, Performance and Prospects: D.K. Fine Arts Press, New Delhi.

Ramaiah, P. (1998), Issues in Tribal Development, Chugh Publications, Allahabad.

Issac, Thomas (2000), Local Democracy and Development: People's campaign for Decentralized Planning in Kerala, Left World Book, New Delhi.

Human Development Report (2000), Oxford University Press, New Delhi.

Sankaran, S.R. (2000), Welfare of Scheduled Castes and Scheduled Tribes in Independent India: An Overview of State Policies and Programmes, *Journal of Rural Development*, 19(4), 507-36.

Satyanarayan, B., *et. al.* (1999), "Essays in Political Economy, Concept Publishing Company, New Delhi-59.

Higher Education and Tribals in India: The Current Scenario and Future Policies

Raj Kumar Sen

I. INTRODUCTION

India has one of the largest higher education systems in the world, topping all countries in terms of number of higher education institutions and only after China and USA in terms of enrolment of students. But the Census 2001 shows that the overall share of graduates in the literate population of India is only 7.6 per cent for males and 5.4 per cent for females. This shows clearly that Indian higher education remains failed in terms of access and equality as the Indian education system has been historically elitist in character and the development strategies that are being pursued in this country bypass on the whole the needs of the poor people belonging to the weaker sections of the society. And this process has been accelerated under the era of economic reforms and especially under the provisions of the GATS of the WTO. But we cannot deny that through education, underdevelopment of the lower caste people can be removed and the basic education can be used as a tool to facilitate their social upward mobility. In fact, education has been viewed by our leaders as a cornerstone of the strategy for the liberation of the oppressed class.

According to Schultz, formally organized education is one of the important methods of developing human capital which is the process of increasing knowledge, skills and capabilities of all people of the country. Investment in education, according to him, contributes 3.5 times more to the increase in gross national income than investment in physical capital. Education is the process by which the society passes the accumulated knowledge and experience of past generations to its next one in a systematic form. Higher education is a repository of knowledge and wisdom as well as driving force of economic values. In this context, India's first prime minister once said that if all is well with the universities then all will be well within the nation. The 9th has pointed out that education strongly influences improvement in health, hygiene. demographic profile, productivity and practically all that is connected with the quality of life. Similarly the 11th Five Year Plan Approach Paper, which by its title preaches inclusive growth, has mentioned that education, in its broadest sense of development of youth, including sports, is the most crucial input for empowering people with skills and knowledge and for giving them access to productive employment in future.

The tribals in India are generally considered under the Scheduled Tribes (ST) population which is 84.3 million as per 2001 Census consisting nearly 8.20 per cent of the population living in about 15 per cent of the total geographical area and constituting the largest number of tribals in the world, a population larger than the total population of France and Britain and four times that of Australia. 91.4 per cent of them live in rural areas against the national average of 74.3 per cent. The traditional tribal habitats are generally forest clad uplands and their area of living is continuously shrinking as India is loosing 1.3 million ha. of forest a year. It may be mentioned that they are the oldest settlers in India and there is no controversy associated with their country of origin. In

1971, the largest tribe, the Bhil had a population of more than five million and the smallest one, the Onge had a population of 112. More than half of the ST population is concentrated in six states only, i.e., MP, Maharashtra, Jharkhand, Chhattisgarh, Orissa and Gujarat, with MP being the habitat of the largest tribal population.

A large number of communities (nearly 600 to 700) are recognised as STs divided into two broad groups, viz., hill tribes (girijan) and forest tribes and in general different from the non-tribals almost in every aspect of life, i.e., dress, diet, dialect, culture, medicine and even values. They are usually characterized by their primitive traits, distinctive culture, geographical isolation, social and economic backwardness and aloofness from the mainstream society. These qualities and characteristics make them a unique cultural, social and political entity. They are also the most marginalized section of the population and both voiceless and powerless in the national development process. In most cases their rights are violated, their knowledge and potential are not recognized and in the name of their so-called development (defined in modern terms which are mostly opposed to their viewpoints) even their traditional roots are severed. In the economic terminology, this type of growth is known as rootless, ruthless and hence hopeless or futureless. Apart from displacement because of environmental degradation and forest depletion, they are also affected by reservation of forests, displacement caused by industrial and hydel projects and urbanization. Though it is estimated that more than 10 million tribal people are already displaced, a national rehabilitation policy is yet to be formulated, consequently leading to very uneven quality of rehabilitation measures being followed in different parts of the country. It is expected that the spread of quality education among them will have enormously beneficial impact on their socio-economic well-being by enhancing their self-esteem, honour and dignity in the society.

The Articles 15(4) and 46 of the Indian constitution deal with the educational provisions and benefits regarding the Scheduled Caste (SC) (consisting of about 170 million people) and ST people and assured protection against social injustice and economic exploitation. It is expected that with better education it is possible to secure better paid jobs and this will contribute to a rapid decline in poverty in general and this is mere likely to take place among the tribals in particular who are lagging behind the general castes in terms of their educational attainment. The UGC also has established SC/ST cells in as many as 113 universities. Under the present knowledge-based economy, where knowledge resources dominate over material resources, improvement in education is positively and significantly associated with better health through improving nutritional status and higher life expectancy. The 93rd Amendment of the Constitution has made right to education a fundamental right. This right, if properly implemented, can bring a revolutionary socio-economic transformation in the society especially through an improvement in the women's education as this will lead to their lower fertility rates and consequently to lower rate of population growth and also to their better health attainments which is a prime necessity for a healthy future generation. Further, in general, a higher educational status of the women is helpful to reduce gender discrimination, infant mortality and social exclusion and at the same time achieve women empowerment and better integration with the society at large by reducing gender bias, lowering caste barriers and strengthening civil institutions. Naturally, all these apply equally, if not more strongly, for the tribals also. In fact, as they are the most deprived and disadvantaged groups in the society, education generates in them positive externalities in the form of enabling them to protest against oppression, resist injustice and organize politically.

II. THE CURRENT SCENARIO ABOUT INDIAN TRIBALS

The tribals usually lag behind the mainstream society in terms of education in general and higher education in particular. A large number of factors are responsible for their sorry state of affairs. These are abject poverty, dependence on primary activities mainly in rural areas, geographical inaccessibility of the areas of tribal concentration, poor educational infrastructure and expensive education including non-availability of education in tribal languages and most important, the high caste-oriented education system irrelevant to the tribal culture, which is the main reason of high dropout rates among the tribal students. Unless the education system is made relevant and appropriate to the culture of the tribal people, it will not be possible to impart higher education in an effective manner to these people. In fact, there are virtually no significant technical and professional persons from the tribal communities. The most important factor in this context to change our approach towards the tribals as through our education system we target to educate and civilize the tribal children from our point of view and by this approach we further alienate the tribal people who are already marginalized. What they need is development with dignity and we should be cautious so that their identity and cultural heritage is not endangered.

Coming to the statistical situation about the tribal areas of India, we note two geographical belts of tribal concentration. One of them stretches along the Himalayas starting from Jammu and Kashmir (10.9%), Himachal Pradesh (4.6%), Uttarakhand (3%) in the north-west to Assam (12.4%), Meghalaya (85.9%), Tripura (31.1%), Arunachal Pradesh (64.2%), Mizoram (94.5%), Manipur (31.1%), and Nagaland (84.1%) in the north-east (figures in parentheses indicate percentage of tribals in the population of the states). The other belt of tribal concentration is observed in the hilly areas of Central and Western India. This covers states and UTs like Maharashtra (8.9%), Gujarat (14.8%), Dadra and Nagar Haveli (62.2%), Rajasthan (12.6%), MP (20.3%), Chhattisgarh (31.8), Jharkhand (26.3%) and Orissa (22.1%). ST people are concentrated in Lakshadeep (94.5%) also. In Orissa, tribals' share of the population shows a marginal decline since 1971 Census. The dropouts of the tribal students are 70 and 75.3 per cents respectively at the primary and secondary levels. The enrolment ratios of such students at these levels are 24 and 11.97 per cents respectively. In Jharkhand, STs have registered a literacy rate of 40.7 per cent in 2001, which however shows a rising trend. In Andhra Pradesh, the literacy rate for the tribals was 22 per cent in 2001 compared with 61 per cent for the general population.

The social ecology of the tribals has also suffered immensely by large scale infiltration of non-tribals into tribal dominated land due to opening up such areas for commercial exploitation of resources and ancillary activities. Change in physical and social ecology has also affected their nutritional status adversely. In 1986, it was observed that 60 per cent of the tribals suffer from gross nutritional deficiency. In the early 1990s, 53 per cent of them were below poverty line, which was much higher than the national average. The occupational pattern of the tribals in 1991 Census shows that of them 54.5 per cent were cultivators, 32.7 per cent were agricultural labour and the rest were other workers. It has been also observed that diversification of occupation among the tribals also suffered setback in this period. Naturally, in this process of regression and repression. the tribals are losing their own identity including their valuable traditional knowledge in every sphere of life.

III. HIGHER EDUCATION AND TRIBALS

The beginning of the western higher education system in India has started with the establishment of three universities in Calcutta, Bombay and Madras in 1957 by the British rulers. Since then, there has been enormous growth in this field and in particular since independence, but following the Indian tradition it did not percolate to the low-caste backward communities just as the benefits of Indian planning did not trickle down to the lower income strata. Only a small fraction of ST students enrolled in schools, manages to go to higher education where the percentage of ST students is only around 2.5 per cent. It is really a sorry state of affairs that only 19 per cent and 0.25 per cent of the undergraduate tribal students go to PG and doctoral studies respectively. The position of the STs is worse than the SCs as only 2.8 per cent literate ST males and 1.6 per cent females are graduates and above compared with corresponding figures of 3.8 and 1.8 per cents for the SC literates. The wide divergence of the ST and SC people becomes evident when we notice the corresponding status of non-ST/SC literate people, which are 8.6 and 6.2 per cent respectively. This shows clearly that our education system in general and higher education system in particular, lacks the ability to attract the ST students and retain them. In fact since the ancient days, only the higher castes were privileged to receive education and the lower castes were not even spared from corporal punishment (remember the case of Sambuk in Ramayana) if they dared to break this monopoly. Apart from the foreign plunder and destruction of Indian store of knowledge, one major factor of stagnancy in the development of Indian knowledge system has been the widespread practice of the hereditary system (gharana) of perpetuating knowledge from one generation to another.

Though the situation is changing, yet it is changing extremely slowly with the result of an widening gap between the tribals and non-tribals in the field of education is increasing. This has been aggravated since the era of economic reforms in 1991 when India officially adopted the policy of globalization and in particular since 1995 when India became the founder member of WTO which contained the provision of GATS dealing with the trade in services including higher education. By opening our higher education sector to the foreign countries and private investors, the Indian higher education scenario is radically changing in favour of the rich elite class by providing an education curricula completely oriented to the western needs and lifestyles thus subverting the national priorities in the field of higher education. Of course, the present globalization is a truncated one as this involves free trade, free movement of capital and technology as dictated by the high income countries to their own advantage. It is not like the ancient days when India was the leader of globalization which was a true globalization involving free movement of goods and labour and India ruled the waves from Rome in the west to Bali in the east through Ceylon in the south including the Silk Route on the land across the deserts and continents.

Under the present globalization, there are both gainers and losers. The gainers are rich countries, rich and urban people, people with skills, large firms, capitalists, educated, powerful, etc. On the other hand, the losers are poor countries, poor, rural and indigenous people, the unskilled, small firms, workers, uneducated, powerless and similar others. It assaults national sovereignty, erodes local culture and tradition and in the social field, the tidal wave of global culture is sweeping the indigenous and tribal cultures all over the world. India is no exception to it. We have already noted that the developmental activities initiated by the authorities since independence have adversely affected the tribals in many cases through their involuntary displacement from their land and inadequate rehabilitation policies. One such instance is the displacement due to large number of irrigation projects which include construction of big dams and large reservoirs and consequent eviction of the inhabitants of whom the tribals constitute the major share.

In India, forests occupy a central position in tribal culture and economy. The tribal way of life is very much influenced by the forest right from birth to death. Though historically the tribals have been pushed to such forest lands as a consequence of the economic aggression of the various dominant non-tribal groups, yet till the advent of the British rule in India. Their humble way of life was left more or less undisturbed and they continued to live with their indigenous knowledge, customs and habits and values. But with technological advancement and increasing power of world capitalism, extraction of natural resources started in a big way from the ecologically fragile territories of the tribal people. Such exploitation of the tribal resources gets accelerated with the onslaught of globalization and the displaced persons inflated the size of development oustees, a new and paradoxical term in the development literature. A few new areas are added under globalization to the existing activities causing distress to the tribal people. These are privatization of public sector enterprises, new mining activities in different states of India and especially in Orissa and Andhra Pradesh, opening of large amount of areas to private sector in the name of SEZ (special economic zone), etc. In all these cases, globalization for the tribals is associated with rising prices, loss of job security, lack of health care and curtailment of tribal development progammes. Under the present corporate-led growth pattern leading to global convergence the tribal and/or indigenous culture has no place for consideration. For this reason many recommend to follow the path of globalization with a human face. But this is an utopia as the profit-maximising market mechanism has no scope to introduce any human face on it. But this can be introduced by the state only, but by the definition the present development paradigm keeps the state away from intervention of the economy in any manner which is not market-friendly. However, after the recent global economic meltdown which exposed the contradictions of globalization as the corporate sector approached the state for their salvation, there appears the opportunity to overhaul the economic strategies in a people-friendly manner.

IV. AN ATTEMPT TO UTILISE THE POTENTIAL OF THE TRIBALS

We have already noted that like the western missionaries attempting to educate native Indians who were savages according to the former, the mainstream society in India today is also viewing the tribals in a similar manner. Unfortunately, it is forgotten that the tribals are no less civilized from their own standpoint. The tribals are gradually loosing their traditional wisdom over time in this present adverse atmosphere and the modern society is unfortunately unaware of the potential of such wisdom and often looks down on them as backward and useless. This is especially evident in various areas like medicine, environmental knowledge and protection of their ecology. It cannot be denied that the tribals living in a particular ecosystem do possess valuable traditional wisdom to handle the natural resources in an effective, optimum and sustainable manner. Such wisdom are acquired over generations transmitted through oral communications as in most cases they are unwritten. The present non-tribal rulers, being ignorant of the potential of such traditional knowledge often formulate policies in different areas including conservation and restoration of ecology by completely ignoring the indigenous people's skills and traditional techniques with a result often unsatisfactory and sometimes even unacceptable. In this situation an integration of the traditional knowledge with the modern one is urgently required for formulating development policies to obtain effective and sustainable results.

Since independence, the STs were provided with special provisions for their development in the form of reservations in jobs and educational institutions, initially for 10 years but later on continued indefinitely due to political pressure (a policy opposed to the principles of economic reforms) and many other welfare measures which were not very effective as they were based on conventional development paradigm and hence actually opposed to their culture, knowledge and habits. The WTO has opened new frontiers for patenting products based on tribal use, which the government must utilize. Otherwise there will be endless attempts on the part of the MNCs to capture indigenous products through patenting and the country cannot be saved from bio-piracy.

V. CONCLUDING REMARKS

In conclusion it can be said that under the current development paradigm followed in India since her independence up to 1991 and then substituted by the current one based on the LPG strategy, are in fact inimical to the interests of the tribals and in the name of their development, such strategies are alienating from their roots and traditional wisdom, skills and culture ultimately leading them to a situation where they are loosing their identity. In this context we need urgently to change our outlook to them not only for their benefits and development but also for the overall development of the whole economy as the tribals are not only an inseparable part of the society but also they can help it with their traditional wisdom and skill towards the holistic management of the fragile forest and hill ecology and protection and management of valuable environmental resources which are getting degraded under the corporate-led growth only economic strategies. In other words, there is urgent need for reforms of the current economic reforms policy for the tribal development in particular and for the sustainable development of the whole economy in general.

Based on the Presidential Address delivered at the National Seminar on Indian Higher Education and Tribals: Problems and Prospects at A.S. College, Deoghar on 29.3.08.

31

Mission of Higher Education in the Society of Tomorrow

Bikrama Singh

Higher education is an instrument for developing socio-economic culture of a country. By Common Consent, that education is called "higher" which is supplied by Universities and specialized Colleges and Schools. A brilliant historical tradition, Centuries of development and intellectual influence for the good of society and human civilization are linked to the development of higher education. The developed nations of the world have proved that if we are to embark on a planned programme for improving the efficiency of human factor, higher education is necessary in the society. Associated in the Mediterranean area and in Europe, with the Islamic and Christian religions, higher education spread throughout the world after Renaissance and assumed a world wide importance. The violent Hurricane in industrial revolution of Great Britain during the 19th Century was the outcome of the development of higher education. In his respect, our late Prime Minister Pt. Jawahar Lal Nehru has aptly remarked that education of any kind is the rudder to propel the boat of an ration to reach the shore of development. Dr. V.K.R.V. Rao has also supported the view with some deviations that for economic development, higher education in relation to the development means scientific and technical education. Thus, through the multiple aspects of today's higher education, emerge the conditions which should be fulfilled if higher education wants to answer the demands of our time of the scientific and technical education. Conditions are actually indispensable not only for the efficiency and the satisfactory working of this institution, but also for the future of Society as a whole.

But the last three or four decades, higher education has undergone far-reaching changes in all its components. Its social function, its place in the educational system led to being it referred to, even in international documents (those of UNESCO in particular) astertiary (or post-secondary) Education. Higher education of today is not confined to Universities but includes numerous and multifunctional trainings after secondary education has taken place. Post-graduate studies (Ph.D. or its equivalent) is also included is higher education. This is why, tertiary education is not merely a question of terminology. With increasing force and success are education has been established which is new as far as its form and its social functions are concerned and which more and more asserts its specific characteristics and its place in society

EVOLUTION IN HIGHER EDUCATION

Now, higher education has undergone a marked evolution. In developed countries especially, the research carried out by academics has become the main priority. Since long research was carried out within the Universities themselves and even is the half of the last century hardly any other research centre existed. A profound separation between research and training is now a marked feature of higher education. The research carried out in the Universities are now over. This induce to increasing specialization in the field of sciences and social sciences, to the exceptionally through knowledge necessary to carryout research successfully, but mainly to the new place occupied by science in social life.

The conjunction of teaching and research, a fundamental characteristic of the Universities has now been blared and totally annihilated.

Becoming a massteaching higher education has undergone a marked change as to the character and the organisation of the educational process. In most Universities, in order to supply a cheap popular education priority has been given to formal lectures and to practical work involving huge number under the supervision of University teacher, which means that training is reduced to kind of "intellectual assembly line" intended to produce young specialists "Cast in one mould". Whatever material condiations make it possible to avoid this impasse, a few privilege elitist institutions are created, disliked by public opinion and giving access to a limited number of students paying high fees ofter having passed competitive examinations that stultify those who pass as well as those who fail. The traditional system of higher education has been discarded due to demand factor of labour market and the students are husting towards achieving efficient professionalism in a concrete job as quickly as possible.

The social prestige attached to higher education has markedly dwindled. This is the effect of a deep reacted courses which have not between thoroughly brought to light but the bases of which are socio-economic and socio-psychological. Two of them are decisive.

1. The number of graduates in general education has enormously increased and as such the number of institutions and Universities has also increased. In India, at the time of independence there were 25 Universities which is now about more than 200. The number of student was 2 lacs which has increased to 52 lacs and out of which 10 per cent are research scholars. There are 8000 Colleges for general education and 2047 institutions are imarting technical education in India at present.
2. Degrees are meant for social status. It enter in the world of elite, students and guardians of the social ladders want to have the degrees of higher

educational system of India. The students coming from high society try to obtain the degree not for social prestige, but for jobs with social prestige.

These decisive factors have forced the society to opt such education which is attacted with job with social prestige and it is why there has been a shift from traditional education to scientific and technical education. In other words, today higher education is taking a town towards Scientific and Technical revelation.

SCIENTIFIC AND TECHNICAL REVOLUTION (STR) IN HIGHER EDUCATION

The Scientific and Technical Revolution (STR), which is taking place throughout the world characterizes also the European and Asiatic Countries. It is most essential aspects and specifications as regards higher education can be summed up as follows:

I. It is a Constant Process affecting the new state of sciences and technologies in society and production and their soaring rate of growth.

II. Through its almost immediate applications science is becoming a material force, the long way from a discovery to its practical applications, the complex meanders of technical and technological sciences have been and will still be dramatically techniques become fundamental sciences with modifications in their structures and other changes.

III. The cultural and educational frame-work of society become a determining factor in the level of technological development the quality of production and of the life, accordingly the function of education and of all the qualities of the human personality educated by it, becomes more and more important.

IV. Productive labour decreases slowly but clearly in favour of non-productive labour, deconstruction of labour takes, while the productive apparatus becomes more concentrated and intergrated in more developed socio-economic organisation the role played by the individvals, his initiatives and responsibilities increase at the expense of the controlled and managed labour force.

V. The importance of basic knowledge, general education, the behaviour of the workers to ensure the normal and harmonious working of society as a productive organism and as the theatre on which individuals correctly display their specific personality.

Owning to the importance of STR in higher education, almost all countries of the world have adopted STR to enter into the global race of the new type of development especially in the field of computer and electronic appliances. The problem of energy and ecology have also necessitated the STR in higher education. It has been realized that STR creates the conditions which, in the long-term may change the ways of life and may make it possible to overcome its negative repercussions. STR is becoming more important for overcoming the evergy, reducing the cost of production and protection the humanity from environmental pollution. This is why, until the end of the Century and of the last decades, STR has been reasonably expected a general development in higher education. The number of students is increasing. By the year 2000 in India 17 per cent students were in such higher education which has been increased to 31.2 per cent in recent year. Like-wise in Europe 32 per cent in north Africa 14.2 per cent and 66 per cent in the socialist countries and USSR, students are enrolled in the STR curriculum of higher education like information technology, Biotechnology and food processing technology, etc.

PROFESSIONALISATION IN HIGHER ECUCATION

The Process of professionalisation in higher education has been increasing and it will go on unabated in future. Professional education is considered as the basis for vocational training. A good number of professional courses have been emerged such as M.B.A., MCA, Hotal Management Rural Development Management, Entrepreneurial Management, Retail Management, Tour and Travel Management, etc. A part from these, a new type of professionalisation will appear—a mixture of vocational training and Fundamental Knowledge. Specialized schools and Universities will come closer and closer until they merge into a single branch, the unity of which will create the conditions for a multifarious Professionalisation. This will not fail to stimulate multidisciplinary and basically humanistic training as the indispensable pre-condition for any profession.

Higher education where to day "assembly line" training prevails will change and on the basis of more supple and more personalized plan of studies will enable a greater diversification of the curriculum and its closer adaptation to the needs of each individual. The short cycles of training will remain relatively more traditional, while the others will become more and more individualized and will tend to fuse into a mixture of studies and directed personal research.

Higher education will become a capital link in a system of further and adult education and retaining the integration of higher education into such a system is not only a question of curriculum. It is a question of Principles and analysis of all its components at all levels and above all of the whole education process and of its aims. Today, its role increases constantly and becomes more and more diversified. In the future, this should lead to a new type of higher education in the various fields, such as:

I. Higher education will be the source of qualities people in all the fields of production.
II. Higher education will act as a centre of multidimensional intellectual influence which, together with the question, the classification and the assimilation of knowledge will become one of its main function.
III. Higher education will be a means of experiences and knowledge for exchange of international sensibility, better understanding of the new possibilities of humanity.

The influence of Universities in these area and in the world will be all the greater as the institutions face the numerous problems be setting the area and each country and nation. The advancement of fundamental and applied research will develop local resources in the international context along with rediscovery and local cultures. The raising of culture and scientific level of the whole people will bring intellectual, cultural and moral standard and human value.

HIGHER EDUCATIONAL AND SOCIAL CHANGE

The link between higher education and society will be the main object of the increase with the increase in the number of teachers and students. The main question that of ensuring the material and social possibilities to enable Universities to carry out the other mission and obtain result in scientific research will be the underlying base of all debates and conflicts in its main lines, this problem has already been solved in socialist counties, where planning also affect the number of students and staff and where academic research is an ordering part in the national plan for fundamental and applied research, there is however room for making the instrument of planning more precise as well as for implementing the plan more satisfactorily in the interest of society. Higher education can bring about the national and international unity in the society. The following notions are soughted in favour of higher education.

- The understood and accepted necessity of peace and mutual understanding against the threat of a nuclear catastrophe, in which the human race would not only undergo terrible suffering but might perish altogether.
- The struggle for a teaching adopted to today's world in the spirit of material and social progress of peace and humanism, the struggle for more material, moral and Political opportunities to enable universities to work freely usefully the struggle for an efficient link between Universities and society.

- Initiatives taken by Unions of higher education and research to extend information and ideas in order to safeguard the rights and opportunities of students and academics.

But the role of higher educaton taken as a whole will be above all to train young people for all the walks of life and to ever increasing numbers, their new aspirations, their new needs, their knowledge, their will to better life in the broad sense of them will promote in association with the progressive strata of society. The calls for all round reform and over all reconstruction of the entire educational edific to transform the present static society into vibrant one with commitment to development and change. But the crying need of the hour in the filed of higher education is to savr the moral value from its total collapse.

References

UGC Publication: Development of Higher Education in India: A Policy Frame.

Dr. Sheetal Sharma: "Education Foundation For Development", *Kurukshetra,* VoL.55No.Nov.2006

Dr. Ashok Kumar: "Educational status of Rural India", *Kurukshetra,* Nov. .2006.

Malcoms Adisestioh: "Education for International Understanding, Vogna Oct. 18, 1970.

Dr. V.K.R.V. Rao: Essays in Economic Development.

Vladimir V. Topencharov: "Place and Mission of Higher Education", *Vishwvidyalay Shikshak Samachar,* March 1987.

B.K. Jha: Growth of Education and Political Development in Aspects of Education and Politics in India, Sarwan Prakashan, Patna.

The Times of India: "National Integration and Higher Education." April, 20, 1996, Patna.

Report of the National Policy on Education, 1986, Government of India. New Delhi.

32

Issues and Policy Options for Internationalisation of Higher Education in India

B.M. JANI

INTRODUCTION

For emerging market economies like India, where population crossed 2.1 billion, internationalization of higher education is going to play a crucial role so as to improve quantity and quality of higher education. Trade in education services under World Trade Organization (WTO) regime, General Agreements on Trade in services (GATS) are given to the members-countries so as to have trade-led growth in overall growth process in general and globalization process in particular. However, there is great debate among economists, educationists, planners and administrators about public *versus* private higher education system including internationalization issues. Education has become trade commodity than that of a good brings externalities in people. In Indian case higher education has remained beyond the reach of the government from budgetary and non-budgetary resources on one hand

and on another hand not remained cost effective considering fees raising issue, which has become political than that of economic one. Higher education has been caught under the trap of bureaucrats, political leaders and academic maphias. Basic fact is: who should be an Education Minister? Who should be a Vice-Chancellor? And who should be a Professor or faculty member of institutions of higher learning so as to run and manage the system. As such, they are involved in decision-making process of quality of higher education. Then, the thought of quality education become relevant. Higher education system needs to undergo changes of system engineering to cope with the situation. On one hand thousands of students are going abroad due to lack of quality of education and lack of seats and institutions looking to demand of higher education.

This paper is divided into three parts: the first one reviews existing studies carried out by eminent scholars and policy-makers so as to sort our issues of discussion, the second one explores present Scenario of practices in higher education in India, whereas, the third one offers policy options to be followed.

I

RETROSPECT

There are several studies carried out by scholars in India so as to analyze problems of higher education and a case of privatization and internationalization of higher education in era of short supply of higher education institutions. These include, Sharma and Rao (2002)[1], Sharma (1998)[2], Taneja (1995),[3] Goel and Goel (2002),[4] Karnik (2006),[5] Knowledge Commission (2006),[6] Ambani and Birla (2000),[7] Deepak Nayyar (2002),[8] I.L.O.(2004),[9] Tilak (1994),[10] (2007),[11] Bashir (2007),[12] (2007),[13] Government of India (2000),[14] (2007),[15] (2007),[16] OECD (2004),[17] World Bank (1990),[18] (1997).[19] All these studies examined pattern and level of higher education, quality and quantity of higher education, ways and means to fund higher education as well as lacuna in the system of higher education in India. However, an attempt is made in this paper to highlight present practices in higher education as well as policy related in era of General Agreements on Trade on Services (GATS) given by the WTO and thousands of students are migrating from India to abroad for higher education.

Emerging Issues

One can safely draw following issues for debate or further discussion on the basis of the review of literature:

1. Can knowledge-driven economy be successful to nurture globalization process in Indian case?
2. What kind of market orientation required in India higher education system in India? What kind of University-industry interactions are required for market-driven higher education in emerging market economy of India?
3. Is it 100 per cent true that WTO and GATS agreements on education and health sector can promote competition for quality in higher education system by external and internal forces?
4. Looking to free entry to foreign and private India players in the system, what kind of role can be played by the state government and the University Grants Commission (UGC) as regulator and monitor of higher education system in India?
5. What kind of changes or reform required in funding of higher education system in India both by the government as well by the corporate sector?
6. What are the ways and means to restructure rate of fees in different faculties of higher learning in India? Why cost-effective structure of fees not found in Indian case? Is it necessary to have 100 per cent indexation in fees structure?
7. Is it affordable to have reservation system in higher education for quality-based public, private and foreign players' in higher education system in

India? What is a scope for Public-Private Partnership (PPP) in higher education system?

8. How far governmental support is desirable and up to what level in the system? Is it possible for government to spend 6 per cent of GDP for higher education in order to bridge gap between quantity and quality of higher education in India?
9. How to manage trade-led higher education and higher education-led trade growth in the case of internationalization of higher education in India? Or 100 per cent Indianization of higher education can solve the problem of the system?
10. Why Indian students cannot justify their degree in Open Market for jobs and proper placement? Why cream of educated youth migrate from India for higher education and jobs?
11. What kinds of interaction are required between teaching and research as per expectation of by the society in general and markets in particular? Is it possible to have corporatization of higher education for better research quality and management of higher education in India?
12. How to manage affordable higher education system keeping in mind parents from different strata of income groups in India?
13. What is economic logic to raise quality of higher education in India and an increase in number of institutions/seats in the system to save foreign exchange about US $ 2.1 billion per annum spent by the parents to send their children for higher education in USA, UK, Australia and other countries?

The present paper tries to answer some of the said issues as the Government of India is going to frame new Higher Education Policy and XIth Five Year Plan is to be executed.

II

PRESENT PRACTICES OF HIGHER EDUCATION

Economics of higher education is highly debated in emerging market economies in general and India in particular as it is not cost effective on one hand and on the another hand state and the centre are reluctant to provide funds for new universities as well to increase seats in the existing institutions. Looking to the present pattern of the education, India has three types of institutions/Universities which are 100 per cent funded by the centre/UGC, partly funded by the UGC and partly by the state government and 100 per cent self-finance institutions/Universities. And free entry of foreign university/accredited private institutions to enter in the market of higher education of India as per WTO and GATS provision. Basic question how they succeed to manage quality of higher education in Indian emerging market economy

National Knowledge Commission chaired by Mr. Sam Pitroda expressed that India requires quantity and quality of higher education. For this, India needs 2000 universities as we have only 348. This is so as students deprived of admission in present higher education system in India and they have to select to go abroad and compel their parents to spent huge amount in foreign exchange. Right to Education Bill would provide the blueprint for states to enact, which may result to face 100 per cent plus increase in the spending of the government on education. It is estimated that the central legislation of the bill may cost the centre about Rs. 5300 crore over and above the current spending by the states and the centre together about Rs. 47000 crore. The scenario leads the states to demand to be shared by the centre with revenue of the states. The XIIIth Finance Commission will have to keep the issue in mind while devolution of resources from the common pool to the states. Basic question is: will the government of India be succeeded in making provision of 6 per cent of GDP amount to be spent for quantity and quality as per market demand of higher education in India.

Financial crunch appears before all institutions in higher education in general and state funded universities in particular. No institution of higher education is ready to raise fees or alternate sources of revenues. According to Planning commission of the Government of India 44 million youth are currently employed, around 55 per cent in service sector, 28 per cent in manufacturing sector and another 15 per cent in agriculture sector. This means that allocation of fund to new institution need to be in order either in private sector or public sector. Then priority to develop new institution of higher education learning posed challenges for optimum allocation of resources from the budget and off-budget resources and hence economists and management experts maintain to have internationalization of higher education so as to increase number of universities and new institutions to meet with growing need of higher education as well as to improve ranking of higher education institutions in global ranking. It appears that inelastic supply of public higher education with declining budgetary provisions, which has created rivalry between subsidized public higher education and cost effective and profit-oriented private higher education.

Looking to outflow of students going foreign universities nearly about 1,60,000 in 2006-07 resulted in net outflow of foreign exchange about US $ 10 billion per year. The amount is sufficient to build 40 IIMs and 20 IITs or alternatively many new Universities can be developed per year. This means that if government of India is not in a position to fund quantity of higher education. Therefore, there is a case of internationalization of Indian higher education with global competitiveness becomes stronger to raise quantity and quality of the education. However, political indulgence and academic maphias became decision-makers to break set rules in the system, which grossly adversely affected quality of higher education in India.

Still, however, the government machinery is busy with the formulation of guidelines for allowing foreign Universities into India and also to make necessary provision for India students going abroad, even though no clear policy decision on committed education under the GATS seems to have been made (Tilak, 2007). Thus quality of higher education is not required for local institutions like IIMs, IITs and some lead universities, which have potential to export quality education. For any institutions of higher learning to come as global quality institutions, it requires huge investment. Many educationists and economists viewed that such export will be at the cost of domestic level development of new institutions as there is limited comparative advantage to generate sufficient revenues. It is reported that during 2004-05 more than 80,000 students joined US Universities, which accounted 14 per cent of total international students. Similarly, 22000 students joined Australian Universities and 15000 UK Universities. It is possible that rising of sufficient number of Universities or an increase in number of seats in the institutions can stop mobility of the students as well as there would be saving of foreign exchange consumed by them. During the fifties and sixties those students were joining foreign Universities, who were getting scholarships/ fellowships or getting teaching assistanceships. Now parents are spending exorbitantly and encourage their children not only for higher studies but for permanent settlement with promising salaried jobs available after completion of the studies.

There is highly skilled workforce available at low cost and hence economists project that India's large young population will propel India to become the third largest economy in the World by 2040, as against this, the another group viewed that the trend is to down-size governments and expand scope of private corporate sector even into provision of public services like education. Still, however, it is feared that corporate philanthropy cannot solve the problem of resources at large scale as they have business motive with profit-making. One can view that it will be greatest innovation if innovative reforms induce private sector to provide public services like higher education by creating win-win solutions. Corporate sector profiteering is largely due to publicly subsidized educated technical and non-technical skilled manpower and this is high time for them to share expenses of higher education. The Finance Minster has provided several fiscal concessions during the reform period and there is a case for education Cess on them than that of the Common Cess on all income tax payers.

III

POLICY OPTIONS TO BE FOLLOWED

Looking to present scenario and prevailing practices of higher education in India, one can safely propose following policy options:

1. Liberalization, Privatization and Globalization (LPG) provided easiest way to the private players in higher education market of India. It is most necessary for the state and the central governments to provide conducive infrastructure for higher education in India largely due to thousands of students deprived of admission in engineering/medical/MBA/MCA, IITs and IIMs courses for Professional higher education. In Indian case, quantity in terms of number of such institutions and universities need to be increased, whereas, quality as per global standard for market driven education, which can justify degree of student in open market.
2. Very scant attention is paid by the government to raise fees of higher education so as to make it cost effective. It is very difficult to survive for public institutions in open market. As against this, private players including foreign players charging higher fees beyond the capacity of middle class family parents. Such higher cost leads them for making profiteering.
3. Percentage of higher education expenditure show declining trend as per budgetary provisions and there is no logic to reduce such expenditure. Economists, management experts and planners viewed that there should be 6 per cent of GDP level of expenditure for higher education in emerging market economy like India to cope with the situation.

4. Due to lack of monitoring, privatization process in higher education has resulted from breakdown of the system. Self-finance institutions are not concerned with quality education except profit-making business. As such, education policy has remained far away from serving the interest of middle class. There should be limit to charge cost effective fees by such private institutions. The Government of Gujarat appointed Shah Committee to examine level of fees charged by them. Many private institutions had to refund fees in Gujarat, those who charged abnormally. It is equally necessary to not to subsidized higher education in public institutions and universities recognized by the UGC/NAAC or AICTE as fees are not linked with rising index. Cost effective higher education is a cry for viable higher education system in India, as the education provide externalities in emerging market economy like India.
5. It is not always true that private or foreign institution will provide quality education. In many cases they do not have national or international level accreditation to them. It is most necessary that such institutions need to be monitor by the UGC as its norms applicable to all institutions in India.
6. Internationalization of higher education as per GATS means mass higher education at global market place for the students, which required internet-based technologies to nurture academic, economic, politic and social dimensions.
7. In order to maintain quality of higher education, National knowledge commission viewed that there should not be reservation system in higher education. All students should be treated equally. Exclusion of creamy layer of backward class should be immediately executed and economic backwardness is feasible than that of caste-based reservation system created by the politicians in higher education system.

8. Agenda for higher education requires separate higher education policy so as to have good match with quantity and quality of higher education and equity in the system.. Quality education depends upon quality of teachers, researchers for quality students' production. Autonomy need to be concerned with accountability for actors of higher education in India in the society far from battlegrounds for rival political parties.
9. NRI students have got equal rights and residential status in all educational Institutions for opportunities and payment of fess. Our trade with European nations plays a vital role to boost WTO conduct of trade for India. There are 20,000 strong Indian communities to support their parents for country's development pogramme including higher education. It is equally necessary for the government of India to associate them for higher education inclusive industrial collaborations.
10. There is a need to have entry level monitoring of students and teachers in Higher Education system. All teachers are not fit to teach quality education and all students are not fit for formal higher education. For this, it is necessary to have community colleges like the USA to absorb the force for skilled professions. There should more politechniques, Training-*cum*-production centers to absorb them. Content of course need to be have global level standard and as per demand of open market.

Notes and References

1. Sharma, G.D. and Rao, D.N. (2002): Trade in Education Services Under WTO Regime, National Institution of Educational Planning and Administration, New Delhi.
2. Sharma, G.D. (1998): "Contribution of Higher Education in National Development", *Journal of Higher Education*, Vol. 21 No. 2, pp. 201-6.
3. Taneja, V.R. (1995): Educational Thoughts and Practices, Sterling Publication Pvt. Ltd., New Delhi.

4. Goel, Chhaya and Goel, D.R. (2002): "Rationalization of Higher Education", *University News*, 40(26), July 1-7.
5. Karnik, Kiran (2006): "Education for Innovation", *The Economic Times*, Ahmedabad,
6. Knowledge Commission (2006): National Knowledge Commission, Government of India, New Delhi.
7. Ambani, Mukesh and A. Birla Kumar Mangalam (2007): "A Policy Framework for Reform in Education Report submitted to the Prime Minster's Council on Trade and Industry, New Delhi.
8. Nayyar, Deepak (2002): Governing Globalization And Institutions, Oxford University Press, New Delhi.
9. ILO (2004): A Fair Globalization: Creating Opportunities for Al,l World Commission or Social Dimension of Globalization, Geneva.
10. Tilak, J.G.B. (1994): Education and Development in Asia, Sage Publications, New Delhi.
11. ————(2007): Internationalization of Higher Education: Illusory Promises and Daunting Problems, R.S. Bhatt Memorial Lecture, Bhavnagar University, Bhavnagar.
12. Bashir Sajitha (2007): Trends in Internationalization in Higher Education: Implications and Options for the Developing Countries. World Bank, Washington, D.C.
13 ————(2007): South-Asia's Free Trade Agreements: Inclusive Growth and Education: An Appraisal of XIth Five Year Plan, *Economic and Political Weekly*, Vol. XLII, No. 38, pp. 3872 to 77.
14. Government of India (2007): The Foreign Educational (Regulation, Entry and Operation Maintenance of Quality, Prevention of Commercialization) Bill, 2007 (Bill No. XXX of 2007), New Delhi.
15. ————(2006): Higher Education in India and GATS: An Opportunity, Department of Commerce, New Delhi.
16. ———— (2007): An Approach Paper to 11th Five Year Plan, Planning Commission, New Delhi.
17. O.E.C.D. (2004): Internationalization of Trade in Higher Education: Opportunities and Challenges, Paris.
18. World Bank (1990): World Development Report, Washington, D.C.
19. ————(1997): World Development Report, Washington, D.C.

33

Higher Education of Scheduled Tribes and Efficacy of Reservation Policy

RATAN LAL BASU

INTRODUCTION

Tribes in India (or the so-called ST) are the poorest among the poor. Since independence the objective of the Government of India has been to adopt measures to uplift this downtrodden section of the population and reservation has been the most mention worthy measure of the Government in this regard. Fixation of quotas for jobs and admission to educational institutions has been the policy of the Government for empowerment of this weakest section of the population.

Among the various categories of the reserved classes, viz. Scheduled Castes (SC), Scheduled Tribes (ST) and Other Backward Classes (OBC), ST is the most deprived class. This would be clear from the following factual information.

From Table 1, it is clear that in rural India ST on the average is the poorest class in terms of standard indicators of

TABLE 1

Poverty Across Social-Groups in Rural Areas of India: 1999-2000

Social Groups	*Head Count Ratios (%)*		*Poverty-Gap (%)*		*Squared Poverty Gap (%)*	
	Rural	*Urban*	*Rural*	*Urban*	*Rural*	*Urban*
ST	48.02	35.15	11.45	8.98	3.84	3.35
SC	38.38	37.84	7.92	8.77	2.41	2.89
OBC	29.04	28.99	5.48	6.25	1.56	1.95
Others	16.29	14.68	2.89	3.01	0.79	0.91

Source: Sundaram, 2006, Table 2, p. 23.

poverty (Head-count ratio, poverty gap and squared poverty gap). In urban India they are the poorest according to poverty gap and squared poverty gap measures. Only in terms of head-count ratio their position is marginally better than the SC category.

On the average the tribal classes are the most deprived among the races residing in India and the professed objective of the government has been to empower this downtrodden class. One essential measure to this end has been to take measures for providing educational facilities to this class at all levels of education. It is true that there have been some achievements in this regard since independence, but they are hardly satisfactory. In this paper we are going to examine the achievements in providing higher education to the ST category. But a student cannot enter into the arena of higher education unless he passes through the secondary stage. So we are to examine also the achievements at secondary stage of education.

HIGHER EDUCATION OF THE SCHEDULED TRIBES

Educational status of ST and SC categories in the age-group 17-25 is given in the following table.

From the Table 2 it is seen that in rural India, people of age group 17-25 belonging to the ST category is 10.4 per cent, but among those in this age group with Higher

Table 2

Percentage Shares of ST in the Rural Population in 17-25 age-group with H.S. and Admission to Graduate Courses during 1999-2000

Social Groups	*Total Population*		*Population with H.S. Certificate*		*Attending Institutions for Studies*			
					Tech. Subjects*		*All Subjects*	
	Rural	*Urban*	*Rural*	*Urban*	*Rural*	*Urban*	*Rural*	*Urban*
ST	10.4	3.7	9.0	2.7	4.6	3.4	11.8	2.7

* Covers agriculture, engineering and medicine.
Source: Sundaram, 2006, Table 5, p. 27.

Secondary Degree, they are only 9.0 per cent. For urban India these figures are 3.7 per cent and 2.7 per cent respectively. In case of students of this age group admitted to graduate level institutions, shares of ST category are 11.8 per cent and 2.7 per cent for rural and urban India respectively. We see that although for urban India the picture is the same as in the case of students with H.S. degree, for rural India the share of the ST category higher than their share in total population for this age group. But if we look into the case of admission to technical subjects we find that the share of the ST category (only 4.6%) in rural India is really dismal, although the share is fairly good for urban India where the average income of this class is relatively higher and the percentage of well to do people belonging to the ST is much higher than in rural India.

Here we are confronted with a serious problem. With quotas and reservations the gap in share of the ST category in terms of their share in total population may be bridged, but the basic problem of real empowerment would remain unresolved unless the political gimmick of reservation and quota policies are supplemented by direct financial assistance to the poor ST students willing to and capable of undertaking technical and job-oriented courses.

Now let us look into the position of the ST at post-graduate level of studies. The picture is depicted in the following table.

TABLE 3

Percentage Shares of ST in 20-30 age-group with Graduate and above Degree and Post-Graduate Studies during 1999-2000

Social Group	*Total Pop. in 20-30 age group*		*Graduate and above*		*Attending Post-Graduate Studies*	
	Rural	*Urban*	*Rural*	*Urban*	*Rural*	*Urban*
ST	11.0	3.7	3.9	2.2	6.9	2.5

Source: Sundaram, 2006, Table 6, p. 28.

The above table shows that the shortcoming as regards educational achievements of the ST category is much higher at graduate and post-graduate levels. For the age group 20-30 the shares in population of the ST in rural and urban India are respectively 11.0 per cent and 3.7 per cent. For admission to post-graduate studies their shares are 6.9 per cent and 2.5 per cent for rural and urban India respectively. If data for technical and job-oriented education is available it is likely to reveal more disparity as in the case of post-H.S. level of education. Now on the basis of the above study let us look into the efficacy of the reservation policy as a means to empowerment of the ST and for that matter all deprived sections of the population.

EFFICACY OF THE RESERVATION POLICY

Since independence the policy regarding providing opportunities for higher education to the ST has been solely reservation and quotas for this class in various academic institutions providing higher education. But this is in essence meaningless. Higher education is costly especially the technical, vocational and job-oriented courses are far beyond the financial capability of the lower strata of the ST. So even if there is reservation they won't be able to continue studies because of lack of finance. Various studies have revealed that in educational institutions for higher studies reserved quotas for ST, SC and OBC remain vacant. Simple remission of tuition fees will not resolve this problem as higher studies require much expenses for books, instruments, etc. beside tuition fees. Simply for financial reasons many intelligent and capable ST candidates are deprived of the opportunity to undertake higher and technical education and compete with others in the job market. So for empowerment of the ST what is most urgently needed is provision of direct financial assistance to ST students opting for higher and technical education. Otherwise the policy of reservation would simply turn into political gimmick to hoodwink the majority of the ST.

References

Deshpande, S. and Yadav, Y. (2006): "Redesigning Affirmative Actions: Castes and Benefits of Higher Education", *EPW*, June 17.

Rana, Hasan and Mehta, Ashish (2006): "Under-representation of Disadvantaged Classes in Colleges: What Do The Data Tell Us", *EPW*, September 2.

Somanathan, Rohini (2006): "Assumptions and Arithmetic of Caste-Based Reservations", *EPW*, June 17.

Sundaram, K. (2006): "On Backwardness and Fair Access to Higher Education in India: Some Results from NSS 55th Round Surveys 1999-2000", Working Paper No. 151

Centre for Development Economics, Department of Economics, Delhi School of Economics.

Indian Higher Education: Equity and Finance

SATYABRATA MISHRA

SECTION I

INTRODUCTION

Both physical and human capitals constitute ingredients of human development. In the present era of liberalization and globalization human capital has greater preponderance *vis-à-vis* to that of physical capital for accelerating the pace of human development. Educational attainment is the major factor in accumulation human capital. No single nation in the world with illiterate and uneducated people is developed Economics disparity among the states in India has been accentuation in post-reform era. Prosperous states have prospered further while poor states have become poorer. Literacy rates of poorer states have been lagging behind that of richer states. The key parameters such as students' enrolment ratio and student budget expenditure at higher education level have been dismal in respect of poorer states. Dropout ratio in case of poorer states has been significantly higher in poorer states. In case of tribal dominated states the percentage of people being covered by higher education has been inextricably lower compared to developed states. Analogously percentage of people being covered by higher education in case of tribal dominated district has been lower compared to developed district. Benefits of higher education has not been percolated to the under privileged and vulnerable section of the society rather it has been concentrated and confined to elite section of the society. Most of the higher education institutions have been concentrated in urban areas for which rural-urban areas for which rural- urban disparity has been accentuated. Further in the liberalization and globalization era the trend is towards privatization of higher education and considering cost escalation of higher education the affluent and elite class people have appropriated the advantages of higher education and lucrative posts.

The present paper makes an ingenious attempt at examining:

(a) The equity aspect of higher education.
(b) Alternative sources of financing higher education.
(c) How far privatization of higher education is justified from the stand point of equity in higher education.
(d) Whether subsidies to higher education is amendable.

The entire paper has been schematized into four sections. Section I deals with introduction, objectives and plan of the study. Section II delineate genesis of the problem. Section III encompasses major challenges of higher education. Section IV enumerates suggestions, recommendations.

Section II

EQUITY AND FINANCE FOR HIGHER EDUCATION

As stated by Hughes and Kejariwal in 1933 in the Era of liberalization and globalization there has been diminution in the state resources on the one hand and increase in enrolment of students and more pressing need for improvement in quality of education on the other hand. There has been greater preponderance on mobilization of private resources because of resources in poorer states like Orissa, Jharkhand and North Eastern hilly region states. In most of the states there has been move towards privatization, conferment of autonomy status to Government and aided colleges, revision of grant in code for private colleges and upward revision of fees in technical colleges.

The perception about the development of higher education has not been entirely in conformity with the educational needs of the masses where majority of the Indian population, i.e. about 75 per cent live in agrarian sector. Most institutions of higher education are located in urban areas and cater to the educational needs of the upper income group. This is a major flaw in the educational policy. The question that arises as to what extent such biased approach to educational development is responsible for aggravating the socio-economic disparities across the regions and various sections of the society poverty stricken population have no access to higher education. Only 9 per cent of the age specific population in India have participation for higher education. If the percentage to 20 per cent by 2020 a great deal of efforts would be required to democratize higher education.

Educational attainment has positive bearing on efficiency in resource allocation, leading to higher income and egalitarian distribution of income. Since education has a strong impact on individual's earnings, the net effect of the expansion of schooling has been a reduction in the dispersion of earnings and hence a more equitable distribution of income a more equitable distribution of income. If higher education is privatized, only those who can afford to pay tuition fees would benefit. Not only there would be under investment on human capital from social point of view but also income inequality would be accentuated from one generation to another since education itself a determinant of life time income.

Income the context of liberalization the polemic issue that whether higher education subsidized, to what extent and how? In poor states like Orissa, Bihar and Jharkhand full subsidization of the cost of primary and secondary education should be assured before thinking of reduction of grants and subsidies to higher education on the plea of privatization of source of educational finance. Before withdrawing grants and subsidies to higher education Government must stop general state subsidies to sectors. The arguments advanced in favour of privatization are untenable for a developing country like India and backward states. Education being merit goods from which the community benefits to a large extent for which it is argued that Government should assume the major responsibility of finacing higher education.

Alternative Sources of Finance and Equity

If at all there is genuine financial constraint on the part of the Government there are various other alternatives to recover the cost of higher education without adversely affecting the equity such as: (i) upward revision of tuition fees along with increase in number of students scholarship covering fees, mass charge, cloth text books, etc. and timely payment of scholarship, (ii) education loan with proper steps for repayment of these loans, (iii) Graduate tax, (iv) pay roll tax, (v) Brain drain tax, and (vi) Education cess.

All these sources would provide only a small fraction of total requirement of financing higher education. Hence the deficits should be filled by grants and subsidies. While giving grants and subsidies to higher education, various criteria may be taken into consideration. Reduction of subsidies for education could be considered after the withdrawal of all types of general subsidies to different sectors. More grants and subsidies must be given to degree colleges in rural areas. No further opening of Government Colleges in urban areas for a certain period particularly in backward states where greater concentration of colleges in urban areas is. Instead of general subsidies to higher education, grant and subsidies should aim at targeting the vulnerable section, as the share in public subsidies in education is not progressive.

Recently privatization of higher education has been a buzzword. The trust is increasing privatization of sources of education of sources of education finance sector hears around

85 per cent of the total expenditure on education. The percentage of expenditure on higher education increased from 11.2 in 1951-52 to 1981-82 but declined to 13.03 in 1991-92in conformity with 1986 NPE India had committed to allocate 6 per cent of GNP to education. The proportion of GNP allocated to education (revenue and capital accounts) has grown from a very low level of 0.6 in 1951-52 all time high of 4.4 per cent in 2000-01. Then it declined sharply to 3.54 per cent in 2004-05. The proportion of GNP allocated to higher education has sharply declined from 0.46 per cent in 1990-91 to 0.34 per cent in 2004-05. The proportion of outlay in higher education to total budgetary outlay declined from 1.54 per cent in 1990-91 to 1.18 per cent in 2004-05.

Section III

CHALLENGES OF HIGHER EDUCATION

1. *Access*: India is still lagging behind developed and several developing countries in terms of access. The access to higher and technical education is abysmally low at 12 per cent in 2003-04. The primary responsibility of increasing access lies with the state which needs to mobilize additional resources to open new institutions besides increasing the intake capacity of the existing institutions priority must be given to the backward areas in opening new institutions.
2. *Equity*: The representation of SC, ST and women in higher education is less than their proportion in the population. Higher education aims at providing avenues for social mobility for the marginalized sections. The recent demand for reservation for OBC reflects the role of HE in social mobility. High academic standards should be maintained with due consideration to special needs of marginalized groups. Students from marginalized groups should be helped through special arrangements for the required academic rigour. Students of marginalized section must have

access to more progressive and hard disciplines so that social equity in higher education assumes greater importance.

3. *Cost Recovery and Privatization*: The recent craze is for privatizing public sector educational institutions. The higher and technical education is being increasingly by privatized in multiple ways. The public institutions had to resort to cost recovery methods to overcome financial crisis. Private institutions are introducing a number of new courses to change the sphere of higher and technical education. Some of these issues are delineated below.
   (a) *Fees*: Fees of public sector educational institutions remain inextricably low compared to private sector institutions. A student of ICSE/CBSER Board paying @ Rs. 250 per month when entering into +2 and +3 stage of college used to pay Rs. 15 even though possessing higher potentiality of payment. As a contrast private sector technical institutions used to charge exorbitant fees from the students including lump-sum amount of donation of donations. Higher education has become expensive compared to the past. Besides increase in fees beyond affordable level might have repressive effect on the level and composition of enrolments.
   (b) *Self-Financing Courses and Seats*: SFCs are being introduced at the university and Autonomous Colleges with the aim of generating additional revenue. The revenue generated through distance modes are seldom used for the benefit of distant learners but utilized to finance mainstream activities of the University. It adversely affects the interests of underprivileged sections. If the trend of SFCs continues a time may come when the higher education system would gradually be restructured to offer only SFCs. This would

not only lead to truncated growth of higher education but also weaken our society.

(c) Privatization: The Private educational institutions are motivated by profit. The mushroom growth of these institutions commercialization of higher education. These institutions never reserve seats for the marginalized group with adverse repercussion on equity. These institutions never hesitate to admit students with poor academic credentials. They attempt to be financially efficient by reducing cost on vital components which adversely affect quality. The regulation of private institution of brought with several legal issues. The courts are approached on all issues ranging from the criteria to admit students with poor academic credentials. They attempt to be financially efficient by reducing cost on vital components which adversely legal issues. The courts are approached on all issues ranging from the criteria to admit students, fees, reservation policy, etc. The judicial response to privatization is characterized by ambivalence.

(d) *International of Higher Education*: Another challenge faced by the higher education is its international in the field of international trade in educational services. Several foreign institutions have already been operating in India. Many of these institutions are exhibiting keen interest in going abroad to establish off-shore campus. This situation makes things very complex and it is imperative a policy on this subject.

(e) *Needs to Raise Public Funding*: Public allocation to higher and technical education in not only inadequate but also declining since the last decade. As the public funding of higher education could not keep pace with the growing enrolment; the real unit cost has declined drastically since 1990s. The financial stringency has led to reduce expenditure on several items of great importance and relevance to higher education. The austerity measures have undermined the quality of education. It is imperative that these trends in funding be reversed and public funding for higher education be raised.

(f) *Need to evolve EMIS*: The data base on higher and technical education system is very weak and limited to a few areas like enrolment by discipline and gender, aggregate public expenditure, faculty strength, etc. realizing the importance of adequate data CABS Committee recommended undertaking a NCERT survey. i.e. All India Educational Survey of Higher Education. There is good case to evolve the Educational Management and information system in Higher Education.

(g) *Subsidies on Higher Education*: The unanimous understanding among economics that investment in human capital yield as much return if not higher than returns on investment in physical capital has been one important reason for the deep interest that researchers have exhibited since 1960s in educational finance. But synchronizing investment should be efficiently utilized. Higher education institutes are expected to possess facilities by way of basic infrastructure such as room, libraries, laboratories, hostels, technical and research inputs which do not yield any instant return. There are other recurring costs which are maintenance cost, e.g. conducting examinations, scholarship to students, games and sports, etc.

There are also direct private costs associated with higher education which is defined as the value of money directly incurred to households for the education of students such as private tuition fees, stationery, hostel, etc. These are determined by socio-economic condition such as income and occupation of the people. Thus pattern of expenditure efficiency of resource allocation and cost effectiveness of educational expenditure are the areas of recent research. Higher education is heavily subsidized by the state in almost all the countries of the world. Financial assistance by the state is provided in the form of block grants, development grants and special development grants. Subsidies in education are advocated on the grounds of providing equality of opportunity. But some argue against subsidies particularly in higher education because a significant portion of subsidies in higher education is appropriated by middle to high income groups while some others do not favour reduction in public subsidies. Subsidies can be implicit in the form of concessions in tariffs and taxes or explicit in the form of transfer payment. There has been a misconception that higher education in India is heavily subsidized by the states unlike other developed countries and that students do not pay any significant amount of fees. But it may be true.

Section IV

MEASURES FOR FINANCING HIGHER EDUCATION

There are various options for financing higher education as stated by Mathew in 1986. These are: (I) Public financing through budget provision and public production, e.g Government colleges. (II) Public financing and private production e.g. Government aided private colleges, (III) Private financing and public production e.g. Xavier Institute of Management, (IV) Private financing and Private Production, e.g SFS, private engineering colleges. Privatization of higher education means increasing reliance on private sources for educational finance in place of Government Grant and subsidies. Of the above alternatives public control is desirable. Various measures to recover the cost of higher education are enumerated below.

(a) *Upward Revision of Tuition Fees, etc.*: On the basis

of the principle of user's charges the tuition fees can be enhanced, though it is not the major cost of education for a student as there are other costs such as hostel rent, mess charge, books, transport, income foregone, etc. Along with this on the principle of cross-subsidisation the number of student's scholarships can be increased to check dropout of meritorious students because of the upward revision can be done in a phased manner. Scholarship amount should cover fees and mess charges in the hostels and some of the cost of books and clothes.

(b) *Education Loans*: Loans can be advanced to students or their parents. But there are problems of insistence on security by lending institutions and the risk to repay because of unemployment. It has been observed that student loan is a disappointing instrument of recovering cost of education. Subsidies, high default rates and high administration cost have eroded the value of repayment. However, in the budget 2008-09 the Finance Minister has made provision study loan within 15 days to one month by the nationalized banks.

(c) *Graduate Tax*: There is an alternative device to education loans for cost recovery such as graduate tax. Graduates can be made liable to pay proportion of their income for a specified period as repayment of cost of their education on the principle of paying for education with future earnings.

(d) *Payroll Tax*: Instead of graduates themselves paying themselves paying the tax, the employer can pay it for the graduates employed as they use educated manpower.

(e) *Brain Drain Tax*: The idea of taxing non-resident or skilled manpower citizens is gaining momentum. The developed countries should agree to share the revenue earned by them from the income of the citizens of developing nations through coordination of the tax administration of the host and home countries.

(f) *Education Cess*: Education Cess is a levy payable by all members irrespective of participation in higher education. At present 3 per cent education cess is imposed on existing personal income tax, excise and VAT.

(g) *Selection of Teachers, Students and Quality of Courses*: Teachers should be selected on such criteria that the institution in which they serve get more grants from funding agencies like UGC as UGC grants are tied to some specific academic standards. UGC norms should be taken into account while selecting teachers by an institution. For instance, grants are available on the basis of major research projects undertaken or publications in leading all India journals. Teaching experience and proficiency should be taken into account at the time of recruitment of University level Readers and professors. Class room teaching efficiency should be the key parameter for selection of teachers instead of emphasizing too much on pseudo research. Plagiarism should be delinked from teaching efficiency at the time of recruitment of teachers. Quality of teaching has been undermined due to wrong selection criteria such as production of Ph.D. candidates for selection of professor. Enrolment of students to higher education should be only on the basis of exceptional merit, others can proceed for distant education or vocational education.

(h) *Suitable Criteria for Grants and Subsidies*: While providing grants and subsidies to higher education in a developing country like India the following criteria should be taken into consideration:

   (a) *General Subsidies*: Reduction of subsidies for education can be considered only after withdrawal of all types general subsidies to different sectors which constitute about 7 per cent of GDP of India and serve the upper segments of the society.

(b) *Rural*: More grants and subsidies to degree colleges in rural areas and no further opening of Government colleges ion urban areas for a certain period particularly in backward states of India where there is greater concentration of Government colleges in urban centers exclusively without a single Government college in rural belt.

(c) *Informal Education and Training*: Since employment in the informal sector is for higher than that of formal sector grants and subsidies for informal education and training should be taken into account while subsidizing higher education.

(d) *Targeting*: Instead of general subsidies higher education grants and subsidies in education is not progressive, i.e. not proportionately higher for students in the lower socio-economic group.

(e) *Differential Price*: Traditional low and uniform price policy for education should be replaced policies that differentiate prices by types of consumers such as higher fees for science, medical, engineering compared to Arts streams. Students from English medium public school to +2, +3 or technical institutes should be liable to pay higher tuition fees over and above paid at Std. X level compared to students from Oriya medium schools, which would ensure equity in higher education.

Privatisation of higher education may be paradoxical as it contradicts the equity aspect as students of elite class people may reap the benefits of higher education at the expense of depriving vulnerable section students.

Privatization being a world-wide phenomenon, India can't escape global influence. The argument advanced in favour of higher education by the World Bank or the Government of India is untenable for India. Of course, education being a merit goods from which community benefits to a large extent and hence Government should assume the major responsibility of financing higher education.

Full subsidization of primary and secondary education is justified before proceeding to subsidy to Higher Education.

Quality of higher education can be assured only through Government intervention in higher education. The relevant issue at present is the extent of grants and subsidies but not complete withdrawal of the state from the responsibility of higher education by surrendering to the profit haunting private sector and so called self-financing colleges which would pose trade-off between finance and equity-*cum*-welfare aspect of higher education. Highly subsidized educational loans with less stringent norms of repayment to improve their availability from public financial institutions can be conducive to equity aspect of higher education. Accountability of both teachers and students through appropriate reforms of higher education can be pursued for introducing a more rational policy of financing higher education in India.

Necessary convergence between conventional and distant modes has to be ensured besides bringing about qualitative improvement in all programmes of higher education. Private sector with philanthropic motives need to be encouraged with the sole aim of promoting higher education, foreign institutions accredited in their home land should be allowed to offer only those programmes which generate employment potentialities but subject to sanctions as applicable to domestic providers. The fees charged for various programmes should be determined within the regulatory framework prescribed for all institutions of higher learning.

References

Albrecht Douglas and Ziderman Adrian (1993), Student Loan: An Effective Instrument for Cost Recovery in Higher Education; *The World Bank Research Observer*, Vol. 8, No 1, January, pp. 71-90.

Best Practices in Higher Education, Report of the National Conference Organized by NAAC (2005), pp. 11-66.

Bhatnagar, Suresh and Saxena, Anamika (2006), Development of Education in India, R. Lall Book Depot, Meerut, pp. 101-07, 242-47, 365-69.

Despande, V.S. (1994), Privatisation of Higher Education: Inevitability. Problems and Remedies, *Journal of Education and Social Charge*, Vol. VII, Nos. 2 and 3, July-September and October-December.

EPW, Aug. 12-16, 2006, p. 3458.

EPW, Aug 4-10, 2007, pp. 3249-58.

Government of India (1995), Deptt. of Education, MHRD DEP Studies-2, Budgetary Resources for Education, 1951-52 to 1993-94, New Delhi, p. 7.

G. Pankajan Education and Development, Gyan Publishing House, New Delhi, pp. 83-108.

J.L. Singh, R.K. Pandey and A.K. Singh, Approaches to Higher Education, Sunrise Publication, New Delhi, pp. 15-59.

Jimenez Emmanuel (1986), the Public subsidization of Education and Health in Developing Countries, A Review of Equity and Efficiency. The World Bank Research Observer, Vol. 1, No. 1, January, pp. 111-29.

Quality Higher Education and Sustainable Development NAAC Decennial Lectures, pp. 19-77.

Mathew ET (1996) Financing Aspects of Privatisation of Higher Education Issues and Option, *EPW*, Vol. XXXI, No. 14, April 6, pp. 866-69.

Psa Charopoulos George (1988), Education and Development, A Review, the World Bank Research Observer, Vol. 3, N0. 1, January, pp. 99-116.

Samal Kishore, C. (1982), Brain Drain Tax Compensating Developing Nations, *The Economics Times*, Bombay, June 26, Editorial Page.

———(1988), Case Against Privatization Mainstream, Vol. XXVI, No. 40, July 6, pp. 25-28.

———(1999), Privatisation of Higher Education, Is it Possible with Alternative Sources of Finance, Man and Development, Vol. 23, No. 50, pp. 155-62

Shatrugana, M. (1988), Privatizing Higher Education, *EPW*, Vol. XXIII, No. 50, Dec. 10, pp. 2624-26.

Tilak, JBG (1994), Education For Development in Asia, Sage, New Delhi.

Index